The Complete Idiot's Reference Card

Internet Sites for Entrepreneurs

www.entrepreneurmag.com

This site includes online versions of *Entrepreneur* magazine, *Business Start-Ups* magazine, and *Entrepreneur International*, as well as tips on finding money, business plans, and so forth.

www.midnet.sc.edu/smbiz/smallbus.htm

The Small Business Homepage offers help with topics such as business ownership, naming your business, choosing a location, signing a lease, insurance, tax issues, licenses, record keeping, and training seminars.

www.toolkit.cch.com

Called the business owner's toolkit, this site offers information about topics that could be useful for the beginning entrepreneur.

www.uschamber.org/index.html

The U.S. Chamber of Commerce Web site offers a variety of resources and information for entrepreneurs.

www.enterprise.org/enet/

EntrepreNet features information and links for entrepreneurs and small business owners, as well as lots of connections to other Internet sites of interest to entrepreneurs. It also has an extensive online reference library with information on a variety of topics.

www.entreworld.org/

EntreWorld is your connection to many resource sites for entrepreneurs—a great place to get started and linked to other Web sites.

www.the-office.com

The Home Office Mall finds, tests, and provides access to innovative, cutting-edge products and services that might be useful to entrepreneurs.

www.irs.ustreas.gov/

The U.S. Internal Revenue Service's Web site is designed to give you broad and immediate access to IRS tax information and services and includes the IRS's latest electronic publications.

www.abii.com

The Lookup USA Web site is sponsored by American Business Information, Inc., and allows you to find any business in the U.S. and order an in-depth business profile online for $3. The outlines include information such as company name, address and phone number, name of the owner or top decision-maker, number of employees, estimated annual sales, credit rating score, and primary and secondary lines of business.

www.smallbizpartners.com

Sponsored by Pacific Bell, Bank of America, and California Small Business Association, this Web site offers resources for entrepreneurs and has links to other useful sites. You can also find articles from its magazine, *Small Business Success*, at this site.

www.SmallBizSearch.com

SmallBizSearch is a search service dedicated to small business. It includes a series of "Web guides" covering money, marketing, management, franchising, start-up resources, and home-based businesses. It also has links to the "best of the Web," as picked by the editors of *Entrepreneur Magazine*.

www.sba.gov/

The U.S. Small Business Administration Web site provides information about and help with topics such as business plans, the Y2K problem, financing, and so forth. This is a great site, which actually provides plans and other resources that you can use when starting your business. Don't miss this one!

alpha
books

Internet Sites for Entrepreneurs (continued)

www.sbfocus.com

Small Business Focus is a search engine that focuses exclusively on Web sites for entrepreneurs.

www.nasire.org/ss

StateSearch is a service of the National Association of State Information Resource Executives, and is designed to serve as a topical U.S. clearinghouse to state government information on the Internet. Of particular interest to entrepreneurs are StateSearch's links to the Economic and Development offices in each state.

www.bizwomen.com/index.html

BizWomen offers the online interactive community for successful women in business: to communicate, network, exchange ideas, and provide support for each other through the Internet.

www.blackbusiness.com

This Web site provides a referral service for African-American–owned businesses. Users can join BlakTrak, an e-mail service and newsletter designed exclusively for African-American business owners.

www.ey.com/entrepreneur/default.htm

Sponsored by Ernst & Young accounting firm, this Web site offers services to help entrepreneurial companies and their investors, including resources for financing, operating strategies, acquisitions and divestitures, international expansion, and wealth building.

www.isbc.com

The International Small Business Consortium Web site allows entrepreneurs to communicate about business needs, expand their markets, and share their resources, knowledge, and experience.

www.onlinewbc.org

The North Texas Business Development Center developed this free, interactive site for beginning and established women business owners with the cooperation of the U.S. Small Business Administration's 60+ Women's Business Centers nationwide. It supplies information on management techniques, market research, mentoring, and individual counseling, and offers an extensive resource guide.

Sortino's Truisms

(In no particular order of importance)

1. Being persistent is key to being a successful entrepreneur.
2. Write a business plan before you start your business.
3. Don't be afraid to copy a successful business; practically nothing is new.
4. Know your strengths.
5. Know your weaknesses.
6. Making money is okay—really.
7. Learn a good personal selling technique.
8. Have fun.
9. Have a good founders team.
10. Set attainable goals often.
11. Recruit good employees who add to the business and are already knowledgeable.
12. Start a business that has a market large enough to allow you to do what you want.
13. Ask for help.
14. Get a good business accountant.
15. Don't be a control freak.
16. Learn to manage through others.
17. Be a good listener.

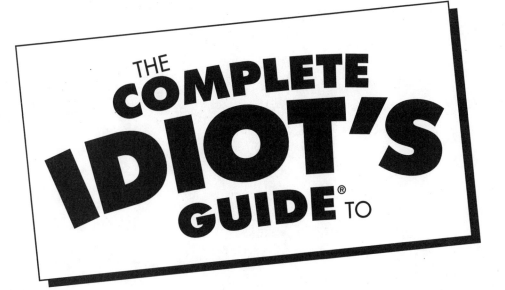

THE **COMPLETE IDIOT'S GUIDE**® TO

Being a Successful Entrepreneur

*by John Sortino
with Susan Shelly*

alpha books

A Division of Macmillan General Reference
A Pearson Education Macmillan Company
1633 Broadway, New York, NY 10019-6785

Lavish Praise for John Sortino and *The Complete Idiot's Guide® to Being a Successful Entrepreneur*

"John Sortino is a living symbol of entrepreneurism. He is passionate about his businesses as well as a tireless worker in making them successful. Best of all he is a dynamic leader that attracts talented people who trust and respect him and his enterprises. John has a working template that should be followed if you are launching a new business ..."

—Larry Winters, Assistant Vice President Business Development and Analysis, Dun & Bradstreet

"The future is limitless, according to the guru who made The Vermont Teddy Bear Company a household word. He had us riding Chicago Bikes to work while our shoes were filled with Lovfeet. Learn from the best ... The man who has taught us all ... John Sortino."

—Joan Hamburg, Broadcast Journalist, WOR

"John Sortino possesses uncommon wit and intelligence. I call him a genius. Wisdom and experience suggest it pays to listen to what he has to say ..."

—Bob Jones, Broadcast Personality

"Learn how one man with a combination of imagination and determination was able to make millions of dollars, while creating millions of smiles!"

—Jim Kerr, Morning Show Personality, WWXY, WWZY, WWVY

"Who knew that when Teddy Roosevelt immortalized the "Teddy Bear" that John Sortino would make it bigger than life. Incredible, that creativity and fun make John "no idiot" but the epitome of an entrepreneur."

—Jane McMichael, Radio Executive, Chancellor Media

"John Sortino ... energetic, witty, childlike, fun, generous, brilliant businessman, and inspiring leader who is always ahead of his time ... a true super role model!"

—Bonnie Pfeifer, Founding Director, DISHES Project, Determined Involved Super role models Helping to End Suffering

This book is dedicated, with all my love, to my three greatest accomplishments: Graham Nicholas, Gabriel John, and Hannah—My kids.

When Graham was a baby, he was my inspiration for the first teddy bear. I've watched with pride and love as he's grown into a man. Gabriel is the best mathematician and super jock I've ever known, and has made me a proud and happy father. And, my Hannah is, without doubt, the love of my life.

Contents at a Glance

Part 1: The Heart and Soul of an Entrepreneur   **1**

1 Having a Dream and Making It Work   3
*It takes persistence, confidence, and hard work, but you
can make your dream come true.*

2 Are You Sure You Want To Do This?   15
*Being an entrepreneur isn't always a walk in the park, but
it's worth it.*

3 Failing at Something Doesn't Make You a Failure   27
A failed business is hardly the end of the world.

4 The Balancing Act   39
*You've got to keep perspective and balance in all areas of
your life.*

5 The Ups and Downs of Entrepreneurship   53
Get ready to ride the roller coaster of owning a business.

6 Being the Best at Whatever You'll Be   67
Whatever you do, give it your best shot.

Part 2: Getting Down to Business   **79**

7 What Kind of Business Makes Sense for You?   81
*There are many factors to consider when choosing a
business.*

8 Identifying Where You Can Be Successful   93
*Some businesses have a better chance at succeeding than
others.*

9 Going It Alone or with a Partner?   105
If you decide on partners, choose them carefully!

10 Basic Things to Consider When Starting a Business   117
Let's talk about structure, taxes, zoning, and so forth.

11 Should You Buy an Existing Business or Start Brand-New?   131
*Learn the advantages and disadvantages of starting fresh,
buying a business already in operation, and franchising.*

12 The All-Important Business Plan   145
*A business plan is an absolute necessity; it helps you run
your business and attract investors to it.*

13 Financing Your Business Venture   157
*There are lots of places to get money, but you've got to
know where to look and how to ask.*

Part 3: Business Basics   171

14 General and Administrative Costs   173
*Knowing how to keep these costs down can save your
business a bundle.*

15 Sales and Marketing   183
Make it a goal to get everyone involved in cost control.

16 Cost of Goods Sold   201
*Marketing and sales are related, but definitely not the
same thing.*

17 Profit   213
*There are lots of things you can do with your profit, but
you've got to make one first.*

Part 4: No Man (or Woman) Is an Island   223

18 Your Founders Team   225
*Choosing the right founders team is crucial to your
business.*

19 Employees   237
*Your employees are much, much more than just people
who work for you.*

20 Board of Directors and Shareholders   249
*Dealing effectively with your board and shareholders can
be a big benefit to your business.*

21 Building a Strong Support System   259
There's lots of help available if you know where to look.

22 Family and Friends   271
*Keeping up with family and friends is essential to a
balanced and healthy life.*

Part 5: Growing and Changing Along with Your Business   281

23 Keeping a Constant Watch over Your Business   283
*You've got to understand everything that's going on in your
business.*

24 Being Ready to Change as Your Business Grows   293
*Understanding how and why growth occurs can help you
prepare for it.*

25 Looking Ahead for Your Business   303
*There are many opportunities to consider for you and your
business.*

26 Going Public   315
    Taking your company public is a great experience, but you
    have to know what you're doing.

Part 6: Entrepreneurial Opportunities   **327**

27 The Whole Entrepreneur Thing   329
    Looking at the whole experience gives you new perspectives.

28 Helping Other Entrepreneurs   339
    There are many ways you can help others who are just
    starting businesses.

29 Becoming an Independent Investor   349
    See what it's like to be on the other side of the fence.

30 Building a Reputation   357
    What you leave behind is way more important than what
    you start.

Appendices

A   Additional Resources   367

B   Glossary   369

    Index   375

Contents

Part 1: The Heart and Soul of an Entrepreneur 1

1 Having a Dream and Making It Work 3

If You Have a Dream, You Can Be an Entrepreneur 4

 Exactly What Is an Entrepreneur? 5

 What's the Motivation? 6

 Deciding To Do It 6

Qualities of an Entrepreneur 7

Persistence: The Most Important Quality 9

Confidence: The Second Most Important Quality 10

 Confidence in Yourself 10

 Confidence in Others 11

 Confidence in Your Environment 12

Finding the Courage to Make the Leap 12

2 Are You Sure You Want To Do This? 15

Take a Good, Hard Look at the Facts 16

Betting Against the Odds 17

 Long Hours, No Guaranteed Salary 18

 This Is Gonna Be Hard Work 20

 Make Sure You Have Fun 22

 And What's All This Talk About Responsibility? 22

Stop Making Excuses 23

Remember Why You Wanted To Be an Entrepreneur in
 the First Place 25

Go for It! 25

3 Failing at Something Doesn't Make You a Failure 27

Winning and Losing 28

Fear of Failing Is a Great Inhibitor 28

Taking Risks Isn't All That Risky 30

 Downsizing: A Corporate Hazard 30

 Life Is a Risky Business 31

 Risk Takers 32

There Are Worse Things in Life Than Failing at a Business 32

Chalk It Up to Life (and Business) Experience 33

Telling Others You've Failed 35
Great Failures 35

4 The Balancing Act   39

It Takes a Good Chunk of Time to Start Up a Business 40
Finding Time for the Important Stuff 41
Work, Work, Work 42
Family and Flextime 42
Tell 'Em 43
Fun and Relaxation 45
How's Your Health? 46
Take a Look at Your Daily Routine 49
Establishing Priorities and Sticking to Them 49
When Work Gets To Be a Problem 50

5 The Ups and Downs of Entrepreneurship   53

Making Money—Lots of Money 54
What's Good About Making Money? 55
What's Bad About Making Money? 56
How Others Might Perceive You 58
Responsibilities of an Entrepreneur 59
Responsibilities to Your Family 60
Responsibility to Your Employees 61
Responsibility to Your Community 62
Being Your Own Boss 63
Some of the Good Stuff 64
Some of the Bad Stuff 64

6 Being the Best at Whatever You'll Be   67

Reaching Inside for the Best Parts of You 68
Give It Your Best 69
Remaining Committed to What's Really Important 72
Keeping the Dream in Sight When the Nightmares Begin 73
Making It Work 75

Part 2: Getting Down to Business   79

7 What Kind of Business Makes Sense for You?   81

Identifying Personal Criteria 82
Finding a Business That Meets Your Criteria 83
   Family Concerns 84
   Financial Needs 86
   Personality and Work Habits 87
Choosing a Venture That Matches Your Interests 88
Putting Your Experience to Work for You...................................89

8 Identifying Where You Can Be Successful   93

Growth Industries 94
   What Is a Growth Industry? 94
   How to Find Growth Industries 95
   Growth Industries for the Next Century 97
Trends and Opportunities 100
   Knowing When to Jump on Board 101
   When Not to Jump on Board 102
   Your Brain, Your Heart, and Your Gut...................................102

9 Going It Alone or with a Partner?   105

Advantages and Disadvantages of Going Solo 106
   The Positives...106
   The Negatives 107
   Popular Forms of a Sole Proprietorship 108
Advantages and Disadvantages of Having a Partner 109
   Partnerships in General 109
   Partnership Limits 110
   A Look at the Positives 110
   A Look at the Negatives 112
Choosing a Partner or Partners 112
   Family Members 113
   Friends 113
   Strictly Business 114
Limited Liability Companies 115

10 Basic Things to Consider When Starting a Business   117

Incorporating Your Business 118
What's It Mean to Incorporate? 118
Should You or Shouldn't You? 118
How to Incorporate 120
Incorporating as a Nonprofit Business 122
Registering Your Business 123
What's All This Talk About Taxes? 124
Put Some Great Players on Your Team 126
Consider Your Local Zoning Laws 127
Other Rules and Regulations 128

**11 Should You Buy an Existing Business or
Start Brand-New?   131**

Buying an Existing Business 131
Pluses of Buying an Existing Business 134
Minuses of Buying an Existing Business 135
Starting from Scratch 136
Pluses of Starting from Scratch 137
Minuses of Starting from Scratch 137
How Do You Find the Business You Want? 138
Negotiating a Business Purchase 139
What About a Franchise? 140
Pros and Cons of Franchising 140
Top-Ranked Franchises 142

12 The All-Important Business Plan   145

What Should Your Business Plan Accomplish? 146
Your Plan as a Working Document 146
Your Plan as a Sales Instrument 147
Your Business Plan Is for Your Business 147
What Your Business Plan Should Include 148
Your Business Description 148
Your Marketing Plan 150
Financial Management Plan 152
Your Management Plan 153
Protecting Your Business Plan 155

13 Financing Your Business Venture **157**

Figuring Out How Much You Need 158
A Long, Hard Look at What You Have 159
   Savings *159*
   Credit Cards and Lines of Credit *160*
   Collateral *161*
Who You Gonna Turn To? 162
   Everyone's Rich Uncle *163*
   Let Somebody Else Do the Work for You *163*
   Family and Friends *164*
   Lending Institutions *164*
   Government Loans *166*
   Other Sources *168*
How to Approach Someone for Money 168
What to Expect When You Ask Somebody for Money 169

Part 3: Business Basics **171**

14 General and Administrative Costs **173**

What Are General and Administrative Costs? 174
   Gotta Pay the Employees: Payroll *174*
   Gotta Have a Roof: Rent *175*
   Gotta Fix It: Maintenance and Repairs *176*
   Gotta Pay It: Taxes and Licenses *176*
   Gotta Have It: Utilities *176*
   Gotta Have Those Professional Services *176*
   Gotta Get Some Insurance *177*
   There Will Always Be Miscellaneous *177*
How to Predict What Your G&A Costs Will Be 177
Keeping G&A Costs Low to Boost Profits 178
   Payroll *178*
   Rent *179*
   Maintenance and Repairs *179*
   Taxes and Licenses *180*
   Utilities *180*
   Professional Services *180*
   Insurance *181*
   Miscellaneous *181*
Keeping Close Tabs on G&A Costs 181
Making It Everybody's Business 182

15 Sales and Marketing   **183**

   Marketing and Sales Are Different Things 184
   How Are You Going to Sell It? 184
   Who Will Work for You? 185
   Eight Very Important Steps 187
   Different Kinds of Salespeople 188
      Attracting Good Salespeople 188
   Determining Your Marketing Strategy 188
      How to Write a Marketing Plan 189
      Promoting Your Company 191
      Ways to Get the Word Out 192
      Radio: The Most Overlooked Marketing Tool 194
   Setting a Marketing Budget and Making It Work 196
      How Much Should You Spend? 196
      Opportunities for Free Publicity 197
   Hiring Marketing Experts 198
      When Do You Need Marketing Help? 198
      Where to Find Help If You Need It 199
      How Much to Pay Marketing Help 200

16 Cost of Goods Sold   **201**

   What's Included in the Cost of Goods Sold? 202
      What You Need: Raw Materials 203
      Get It Ready: Time and Labor 204
      Necessities: Supplies 205
      Buy and Resell: Purchases 206
      Operation: Factory Overhead 206
      How Does It Look: Packaging 206
      Get It There: Shipping Costs 207
      Keeping Track: Change in Inventory 208
      Everything Else: Miscellaneous 208
   How to Predict Your Cost of Goods Sold 208
   Keeping Production Costs Low to Make Profit High 209
   Making Cost Control a Team Effort 210

17 Profit   **213**

Projecting Profits 214
Figuring Out What Your Prices Should Be 215
Methods for Determining Prices *216*
How Perception Affects Price and Sales *217*
Don't Forget to Test Your Prices *219*
Sharing Profits 220
Reinvesting Profits into the Company 221

Part 4: No Man (or Woman) Is an Island   **223**

18 Your Founders Team   **225**

First Things First 225
Who Should Be on Your Founders Team? 226
Look Beyond People Who Are Just Like You *228*
Find Strengths That Complement, Not Duplicate *228*
How to Find the Best People for Your Team 229
The World Is Full of Candidates *230*
Do You Need a Consultant to Choose Your Team? *230*
Determining Who's Qualified and Who's Not *231*
Interviewing and Choosing Your Founders Team 232
How to Interview Candidates *232*
Looking Past Business *234*
Laying the Groundwork for Your Founders Team 234
Setting the Record Straight *235*
Legal Things to Think About *235*

19 Employees   **237**

Company Personality 237
Your Employees Are a Valuable Asset 238
What You Should Do for Your Employees 239
Bring Home the Bacon *239*
What Are the Benefits? *240*
How About Those Perks? *241*
Working Conditions *241*

What You Should Expect Your Employees To Do for You 242

Promote Loyalty *242*

Reward Honesty *242*

Time for the Hard Work *243*

Establishing Rules and Responsibilities for Employees 244

Don't Make Any Rules You Don't Intend to Keep *244*

Make Sure You Have a Clear Chain of Command *245*

Dealing with Discipline Matters *245*

Motivating Your Employees 246

Part-Time Employees, Temps, and Homeworkers 247

20 Board of Directors and Shareholders   249

Choosing a Board of Directors..250

What Image Should Your Board of Directors Convey? *251*

Who's Who on Your Board of Directors? *251*

What's the Role of a Board of Directors?......................................252

Just Who's Running This Company, Anyway? 253

Keeping Shareholders Happy and Still Having Time to
Run Your Business 256

21 Building a Strong Support System   259

Why Do You Need a Support System? 260

Knowing You're Not Alone...260

Who to Look to When You Need Some Help 261

Chamber of Commerce *262*

Professional Organizations *262*

Lawyers *263*

Accountants *265*

Insurance Agents *266*

Government Sources *267*

Salespeople and Suppliers *268*

Employees *268*

How to Keep Your Support System Strong 268

22 Family and Friends   271

How's Your Family Doing These Days? 271

Your Life Is More Than Your Work, and Your Work Is
More Than Your Job 273

Making Time to Be There 274
When You Can't Be There 274
Scheduling Time Away from Work 275
Dealing with Reactions of Friends and Family 276
Should You Ever Hire Family and Friends? 278

Part 5: Growing and Changing Along with Your Business   **281**

23   Keeping a Constant Watch over Your Business   **283**

Your Business Is Like a Baby 283
Evaluating Every Day Where Your Business Stands 285
The Balance Sheet 285
The Short-Term Profit and Loss Statement 287
The Cash Flow Statement 289
Reacting to the Ups and Downs 290
Get Others Involved 291
Trusting Others to Help Take Care of Your Business 292

24   Being Ready to Change as Your Business Grows   **293**

Evaluating the Rate at Which Your Company Is Growing 294
Is Your Company Growing Fast Enough? 295
Is Your Company Growing Too Fast? 296
Considering Possibilities for Further Growth 297
Buy Another Business 297
Licensing 297
Networking 298
Franchising 298
Taking Your Company Public 298
How to Predict Growth 298
How to Prepare for Growth 299
Removing Limits for Growth 299
The Limits That You Set 299
The Limits That Others Set 300
How Will You Need to Change as Your Business Expands? 301

25 Looking Ahead for Your Business 303

Knowing What's Ahead for You and Your Business 303
How Do You Know When It's Time to Expand? 304
    Time to Expand *304*
    Expanding Locally *306*
    Expanding Regionally *306*
    Expanding Nationally *306*
    Expanding Internationally *307*
What If You Decide to Sell Your Business? 309
Merging with Another Company 311
Keeping It All in the Family 311

26 Going Public 315

What It Means to Go Public 315
The IPO 317
Private Placement 317
    Be Prepared *318*
    The Deal *319*
How to Take Your Company Public 319
    Finding Someone to Help Take Your Company Public *320*
    Preparing a Prospectus *322*
    The Showdown *322*
Determining an Initial Public Offering 324
How Going Public Can Change Your Company 324

Part 6: Entrepreneurial Opportunities 327

27 The Whole Entrepreneur Thing 329

Evaluating Your Experience as an Entrepreneur 329
Learning from What You've Done 330
Feeling Good About What You've Done 333
Doing It Better the Next Time Around 334
Now That You're an Entrepreneur, Could You Work for
    Somebody Else? 335

28 Helping Other Entrepreneurs 339

Is the Person You're Helping Cut Out to Be an Entrepreneur? ... 340
Helping to Build a Better Business Plan 342

Helping to Raise Capital 343
Helping to Start Up a Business 344
Entrepreneurism Is on the Rise 345

29 Becoming an Independent Investor   349

Moving Beyond the Day-to-Day Operations of
   Running a Company 350
The Attraction of Being an Independent Investor 351
Finding Investment Opportunities 353
   Where to Look for Opportunities 353
   Knowing Which Opportunities to Take 353
Investing Is a Different Kind of Entrepreneuring 354
   Venture Capitalists 354
   Investment Groups 355
   Private Sources 355
   Small Business Investment Companies (SBIC) 355

30 Building a Reputation   357

Building the Kind of Reputation You Want 358
Reputations Are Fragile 359
Being Involved in Your Community 361
   Politics 362
   Environmental Groups 362
   Clubs and Organizations 362
   Religious Organizations 363
   Activities for Kids 363
Preserving Your Reputation Where It Counts the Most 364

Appendices

A Additional Resources   367
B Glossary   369
   Index   375

Foreword

Becoming an entrepreneur is certainly one of the most exciting and challenging career paths a person can choose.

It requires courage to be an entrepreneur. It takes tenacity, great confidence, perseverance, and incredible amounts of determination.

As fellow entrepreneurs, we fully understand and appreciate the joys, frustrations, and concerns that John Sortino surely encountered as he started The Vermont Teddy Bear Company and grew it into a successful, respected business.

Starting a new career is never easy. Starting a new career on your own, without backup from a firm, or benefit of a regular paycheck and guaranteed benefits, is an even more difficult undertaking.

When John created his first teddy bear in 1980, all he had were his hopes and dreams, and the unwavering belief that he could make it as the Teddy Bear Man. He started out with very little money, hardly any experience, and no help. But, he believed in himself, and, little by little, he grew The Vermont Teddy Bear Company into a $20.5 million company by 1994.

This is what makes John Sortino a wonderful example of an entrepreneur, and the perfect person to write this book. Sortino thrives on facing and overcoming hurdles. He's at his best when he's got his back to the wall and is looking for a way out. He never says never.

We met John when he began advertising The Vermont Teddy Bear Company on WOR Radio in New York City, where we do a daily radio show dealing with financial topics.

John was completely enthralled by radio, and we were very happy to be able to contribute to the success of his company by reading the advertisements for his bears on the air. He got great response to those ads, and set the standard for successful radio advertising.

Anyone who has met John knows that he loves to have fun, and that he has a great ability to make work fun for himself, his employees, and whoever else might be involved. He lives what he preaches—taking care of his employees, and giving back to his community.

As parents ourselves, we were always impressed by John's family values, and how he remained a genuinely nice, unassuming person after the phenomenal success of The Vermont Teddy Bear Company.

If you're serious about wanting to learn what it's like to start up, own, and run your own business, then you've come to the right place.

The Complete Idiot's Guide to Being a Successful Entrepreneur takes you through the entrepreneurial process in a manner that's extremely informative and entertaining.

John shares his knowledge, his humor, and his slightly offbeat way of looking at business and the world, in a style that's easy to read and understand. He offers real advice and information in a clear, extremely useable manner.

Good luck to all of you who dream of becoming entrepreneurs, or who have already made the leap into owning your own businesses. Enjoy this book, and keep it handy as a reference as you grow your business. We think you'll look to it often, for many years to come.

Ken and Daria Dolan

America's only husband and wife radio team, Ken and Daria Dolan are widely recognized financial experts, with more than 35 years of collective experience over a broad base of personal finance subjects. Their popular show, *"The Dolans,"* is heard weekdays on more than 170 radio stations across the country. They were awarded the only four-star rating for financial broadcasting excellence by *Newsweek* magazine, and also were named to the 1996 Radio Hall of Fame by *Vanity Fair* magazine. Ken and Daria Dolan live in Maine, and are the parents of one daughter, Meredith.

Introduction

Starting and running your own business involves more than getting a good idea and calling the Yellow Pages for a listing. There are many, many things to think about and do before you can begin operating a business. The business environment today is complex and constantly changing.

The first thing you need to do is be sure in your own mind that you're willing to do all the necessary work and that you have the commitment you need to successfully start and run your own business.

If you're sure, then you've got to think about practical matters like the type of business you'll have, where it will be located, how you'll fund it, who will help you with it, and so forth.

Once your business is operating, you've got ongoing issues such as employees, taxes, legal matters, operating systems—the list goes on and on.

Being an entrepreneur is hard work, that's for sure, but most of us wouldn't have it any other way. This book deals with all the issues raised here, and many, many more.

As much as it's intended to be a business guide, however, this book is meant to be a source of encouragement. If you really want to be an entrepreneur, then go ahead and be one. Don't let anything get in the way of your dream. Look at this book when you get discouraged, and remember that practically everyone who's started a business has encountered difficulties and roadblocks. The trick is to get around them and keep on going.

What You'll Find in This Book

Part 1, "The Heart and Soul of an Entrepreneur," starts out by looking at the qualities needed for a successful entrepreneur. The most important are persistence and confidence, in that order.

You'll also spend some time in Part 1 thinking about what it means to fail and the difference between having a business fail and being a failure. One has nothing to do with the other, you know.

And, because being an entrepreneur is a pretty intense experience, I'll offer some suggestions on how to keep a balance between your work, family, friends, and activities.

In Part 2, "Getting Down to Business," it's time to do exactly that. You'll look at different opportunities for businesses and try to figure out what makes the most sense for you. You'll examine the benefits and pitfalls of partnerships, look at things like zoning and taxes, and see what it means to incorporate your business.

Part 2 also contains, in my opinion, the most important chapter in the book, "The All-Important Business Plan." I can't stress enough how important it is to read this chapter carefully and keep it handy when you write your own plan.

Financing your business is another important area to remember and that, too, is covered in this section.

Part 3 is "Business Basics," and it deals with the nuts and bolts of running a company. You'll learn about the main cost areas of a business: general and administrative, cost of goods sold, and marketing and sales, and how to predict and control costs in each category. I'll also discuss profits, and what to do with them once you get them.

In Part 4, "No Man (or Woman) Is an Island," you'll have a look at the many different people who are involved in some capacity or another with your business. You can't keep an entire company running all by yourself, you know. There are lots of people you need to rely on, and it's important to know how to find them, work with them, and keep them happy working with you.

You'll also have another look at dealing with your family and friends because, when you get right down to it, nothing is more important than that.

"Growing and Changing Along with Your Business" is the title of Part 5, which deals with topics such as the growth of your business, taking your business public, and selling or merging your business. It also discusses the importance of understanding your business systems and keeping a close watch on what's going on.

Part 6, "Entrepreneurial Opportunities," takes you a step beyond starting and running a company. In this part, you'll look at other things entrepreneurs can do, such as helping others with their startups or becoming independent investors.

Once you understand business and how it works, all kinds of opportunities present themselves. You also look at how important it is to build and maintain a good reputation.

When you finish reading this book, you'll have a pretty good overview of what's involved in starting and running a business. You'll have a better handle on the challenges and rewards of being an entrepreneur.

Extras

In addition to valuable information on starting and running businesses, this book contains a lot of miscellaneous facts, accounts of the author's experiences, the author's particular take on what some things mean, and some situations to watch out for.

These odds and ends have been placed in shaded boxes, and given particular names. Here's how they stack up:

Bear Facts

These are interesting little tidbits about starting a business or other aspects of being an entrepreneur. Lots of them are based on John Sortino's actual experiences.

Over the Rainbow

Dream big, set your goals high, and take all the help you can get, and you'll be over the rainbow in no time. The tips offered in these areas will help you get there.

The Word According to John

Some people see things a little differently than most, and the author is one of those people. These pieces give Sortino's particular take on definitions and ideas.

Grizzly Area

There are many traps to watch out for when you're getting into business, many of which are high-lighted in these areas.

Acknowledgments

The author would like to thank the many people who provided time, information, or resources for this book, and those who have helped, counseled, and inspired along the way.

Thanks to the editors at Macmillan Publishing for making an idea a possibility, and then a reality. Especially to: Gary M. Krebs, Nancy Warner, Lisa Lord, and Donna Wright.

Thanks to Bert Holtje of James Peter Associates, and a very special thanks to Paula Gill of Gill Media, for her enduring friendship, her amazing patience, and her sound advice and direction. Also to Susan Shelly.

To my family—my parents and grandparents, who taught me the value of hard work; my brothers, Paul and Joseph Sortino; and the sweetest sister in the world, FlorenceAnn Wolfling. Also my aunts and uncles, Thresa, Marty, Franklyn, Sonny, Rose, Alice, Olivia, Don and Julius.

To all my friends and business associates, especially (in no particular order): Susan Sortino; Sen. Patrick Leahy; Jane Robbins; Frank Tornton; Nick and Cindy Zegarac; Father Holland, S.B.A.; Tom Cabot; Ray Pecor; William Ruffa, Sr.; William Ruffa, Jr.; Bonnie Phiefer, Ed Amidon, Pasquale Amadore, Herb Blumenthal, and Glen Wright.

Also, Michael Whitmer, Brain McNeil, Fish, Mark Macormack, Whit Smith, Sheryl McIenna, Luis Calperin, Larry Winters, Bobby Winston, Jack Geary, Dustin Schiavi, Orlif Speers, Ronnie Sweet, the good employees at the Vermont Teddy Bear Company, all my friends at UPS, Alen (ALDEN) Central High, SUNY at Plattsburgh, everyone who ever bought a Vermont Teddy Bear, and the kids and helpers from the Charlotte Expos Little League.

To all the people who make radio work: Robert Alden, James DiCastro, Mike Fagan, Jane McMichael, Martha Barrios, Brenda Hall, Joe Anistasi, David Wilkes, Chris Souchack, Marie Passion, Mark Seaburg and Triple X Radio, and Luie Manno and WKDR.

And, to the people who make radio fun to listen to: The Dolans, Don Imus, Bob Jones, Howard Stern, Johan Hamburg, Rick Dees, Ross Britian, Susan Bray, Russ Solzberg, Chris Russo, Mike Francessa, Kevin Matthews, Lisa Taylor, Dan Daniel, Jim Kerr, Bill Handel, Don & Roma, Greg Whiteside, Scott Shannon, John Gambling, Alan Combs, and Todd Pettingill.

Part 1
The Heart and Soul of an Entrepreneur

If you want to be an entrepreneur, you have to make sure you've got what it takes—you know, the right stuff.

So let's take a few minutes to think about your dream and why you want to be an entrepreneur in the first place. This part gives you a candid overview of what it means to be an entrepreneur and what kinds of problems and rewards go with the territory.

When you finish reading it, you can decide whether you've got the heart and soul to enter the great world of entrepreneurism.

Chapter 1

Having a Dream and Making It Work

> **In This Chapter**
>
> ➤ A dream is the doorway to entrepreneurship.
>
> ➤ Many factors can motivate someone to be an entrepreneur.
>
> ➤ Persistence is an entrepreneur's most valuable quality.
>
> ➤ Confidence is the second most valuable quality.
>
> ➤ Once you decide to be an entrepreneur, go for it!

Dreams come to different people in different ways.

Maybe you've known ever since you were a kid that someday you'd invent a fantastic machine that would do something fabulous. You probably weren't sure back then, lying on the grass and watching the clouds roll by, exactly what your machine would do. You only knew it would be something really special.

Maybe it would be a time machine, able to transport you and your friend to the past or the future. Or maybe you'd invent something capable of producing snow in your back yard whenever you felt like sledding or having a snowball fight—even if it was August.

How about a machine that could somehow zap you to school so you didn't have to walk, or ride on the bus? Or one that could get food to those kids your mom always said didn't have enough to eat? Maybe you thought you'd invent something that could help make sick people better, so your grandma wouldn't have to use that wheelchair anymore.

Or maybe your dream came to you later in life. Maybe it evolved during your college years, born of late-night, rambling conversations with friends that eventually took form and resulted in serious plans for the future.

It could have been a major life event that brought your dream to the surface—perhaps a marriage or, as in my case, the birth of a child. Perhaps a relative died and left you a business that ignited your dream. Or maybe your dream was born of necessity. You needed a livelihood, and you conjured up a dream that would allow you to produce one.

My motivation for starting the Vermont Teddy Bear Company was love for my first-born son, Graham. I became interested in teddy bears when Graham was a baby and we spent hours playing in his nursery. Surrounded by stuffed animals, I noticed all of them had been made somewhere else and imported. For some reason, that bothered me. I wanted to give him a bear that was made in a place he could go and visit, if he wanted to. I wanted the bear to be handcrafted, and I wanted it to be something he could keep forever.

Before I knew it, I was obsessed with making teddy bears. I vowed to make the best teddy bears anyone had ever seen. You know what? I think I did.

Regardless of how or when *your* dream started, the only important thing now is that you have it, and it's yours. With that dream, anything is possible.

Grizzly Area

Nearly every fledgling entrepreneur reaches a point at which he or she wonders if all the work is worth the sacrifice necessary to make the dream a reality. As an entrepreneur just starting out, you're likely to miss a lot of your kids' soccer games, not to mention family dinners, times with friends, and other activities. If you're not willing to make these kinds of sacrifices, and the others that will be necessary, you'd better think hard about how much your dream means to you. Being an entrepreneur is hard work, and it's not right for everyone.

If You Have a Dream, You Can Be an Entrepreneur

All entrepreneurs have dreams. Some are well planned and executed according to schedules, but other dreams come about almost by accident. It's a sure bet, however, that every entrepreneur has a dream that pushes him or her along toward a goal.

Of course, you need more than a dream to become an entrepreneur. If a dream is the cornerstone of an entrepreneurial effort, you still need a lot of bricks, mortar, and tools to make that cornerstone into something solid and usable.

You'll need information and knowledge, you'll need money, and you'll need boundless energy. You'll need to be willing to devote inordinate amounts of time to your effort and to put aside—at least for a while—some of the leisure activities you enjoy.

You'll need good communications skills, a fair amount of ego, and a sound reputation. You'll need to be able to work with many kinds of people and have the ability to convince others that your dream is viable. You'll need the confidence to ask people you barely know, or don't know at all, to help fund your dream. You'll need even more confidence to stand behind your dream when others question it. And you'll need great quantities of persistence and perseverance to keep on trying when seemingly insurmountable problems occur.

Without the dream, though, all these other talents and resources won't help you be an entrepreneur. The dream is the spark necessary to ignite your effort to be an entrepreneur. Without it, the fire can't burn.

Exactly What Is an Entrepreneur?

If you look in the dictionary, you'll see that an entrepreneur is a person who organizes and directs a business undertaking, assuming the risk for the sake of the profit.

Although that definition is true, it's not complete. There's more to being an entrepreneur than organizing, directing, and assuming risk. Anyone who's every started a business will back me up on that.

People have many different impressions of what it means to be an entrepreneur. Some people associate entrepreneurs with Hollywood and show business, and think of them as promoters, organizers, or musical and other acts.

Others think of entrepreneurs only as the Donald Trump types, whose billion-dollar business deals are hyped as big news in local and national newspapers.

Many people fail to realize that the guy who owns the corner grocery store is an entrepreneur, as is the woman who recently opened the nail salon in the center of town. The teenager who starts her own baby-sitting service is an entrepreneur, as is the owner of the coffee shop on Main Street. Donald Trump is an entrepreneur, along with Lee Iacocca, Bill Gates, Ben and Jerry (the ice cream guys), and the kid who comes around and shovels your driveway when it snows or sets up the lemonade stand down at the corner on hot, summer afternoons.

Entrepreneurs can be extremely wealthy or wonder if they'll have enough money to pay the bills this month. They're young and old, male and female, black, white, yellow, red, and brown. They come in all sizes, shapes, and ages. There are no restrictions on who can join the entrepreneur's club, as long as the applicant is willing to give the effort his or her very best shot.

> **The Word According to John**
>
> An *entrepreneur* is a person with extraordinary energy, persistence, and determination, who believes in himself or herself enough to follow through on a dream or idea. This person does whatever it takes to make the dream a reality and always looks for another way when encountering disappointment or failure.

What's the Motivation?

There are probably as many reasons *why* people become entrepreneurs as there are entrepreneurs.

Some motivators—such as a desire to help society or to provide the means for a wonderful life for your family—are arguably better than wanting to show that stupid cousin of yours that you can make more money than she can. Still, all provide impetus to get moving toward your goal of being an entrepreneur.

If something motivates you strongly, it can often kick-start your dream and cause you to turn that dream into a workable plan. A recent article in the *Harvard Business Review* says that psychologists believe that the strongest motivator for people who successfully run their own small businesses is "the need for achievement, the desire to do something better or more efficiently than it has been done before."

Some other common motivators include:

➤ a desire for power

➤ a desire for wealth

➤ a need to fulfill an inner drive

➤ a need to realize a dream

➤ a desire for notoriety

➤ a desire to make work fun

➤ a desire to prove they can be successful on their own

Some people are motivated to become entrepreneurs because of things they don't want to do, such as work for someone as a subordinate or be required to show up for work at the same time every morning.

Whatever the particular motivator is that drives you to be an entrepreneur, it isn't as important as the level or degree of motivation you possess. Your motivation has to work hand in hand with your energy, determination, persistence, and all the other factors that make you successful.

Motivation to become an entrepreneur is extremely important, but it's not, by itself, enough to make you a successful entrepreneur.

Deciding To Do It

If you've already decided that you will definitely be an entrepreneur, and you're reading this book to find out the best way to get started and proceed once you're in business, you can skip over this section. On second thought, go ahead and read it anyway. What can it hurt?

If you'd like to be an entrepreneur, but you're just not sure whether you're willing to take the first big steps to becoming one, be sure you read this section carefully—and probably twice.

Whether you decide to start being an entrepreneur today or 5 years from now, the decision to do it must be wholehearted. Even if you want to start a business that involves working only part-time or that you can run on the side in addition to a job you already have, being an entrepreneur requires a tremendous amount of energy and attention.

Bear Facts

Sales were very slow, to say the least, when I first started my business as a teddy bear maker. To be on the safe side, I kept my full-time job with a Vermont-based company called Garden Way. It wasn't long, however, until my fledgling teddy bear business consumed all my energy, and much of my time. I had to make a decision. Fortunately, the decision was a no-brainer. I knew I really wanted to make teddy bears, so I quit my job with Garden Way and committed all my time and energy to the Vermont Teddy Bear Company.

People compare starting and tending to a business to getting married and maintaining the marriage, but I've always thought it's much more like having, and tending to, a baby. A business requires constant care and attention. There's always something that needs to be done.

So, when you decide that you're going to be an entrepreneur, decide wholeheartedly and set forth with determination and perseverance.

Qualities of an Entrepreneur

Certain personal qualities are found in most entrepreneurs. There are certainly exceptions, and it's not wise to stereotype, but it's safe to say that most entrepreneurs possess at least some, and probably the majority, of these characteristics:

➤ Self starter

➤ Well organized

➤ Innovative

➤ Able to make decisions

➤ Able to solve problems

➤ Able to overcome obstacles

➤ Flexible

➤ Adaptable

➤ Responsible

➤ Good communicator

➤ Determined

➤ Confident

➤ Persistent

Think about the entrepreneurs you know and ask yourself how you would describe them. Chances are that many of the words listed above come to mind.

The late Sam Walton, founder of the Wal-Mart chain, said that the most important thing for an entrepreneur is "knowing where you want to go and being willing to do what it takes to get there."

Take another look at the list of characteristics, and pick out all the words or phrases that apply to Walton's quote. To know where you want to go requires innovation, responsibility, confidence, and the ability to make decisions.

Bear Facts

Charles Edward Merrill (as in Merrill Lynch), started college, but he was forced to drop out because of a lack of funds. Still, he made his way to Wall Street and was rich by his 31st birthday. Henry Ford not only didn't have much formal education himself, but he had a general distrust of college graduates, even those that worked for him. Walt Disney's education was leaving home at age 16 to join the Red Cross Ambulance Corps during World War I. Same with hamburger guru Ray Kroc, only Kroc was only 15 and lied about his age. Estée Lauder lived above her dad's hardware store in Queens and got her education by pedaling cosmetics in beauty shops and beach clubs. You get the picture. There have been lots of wildly successful entrepreneurs with little formal education.

To be willing to do what it takes to get there requires innovation, flexibility, adaptability, determination, confidence, and persistence.

The more of these characteristics entrepreneurs have, the more easily they can know what they want and be willing to do what it takes to get there.

People often ask whether a great education is necessary to be a good entrepreneur. I think education is definitely needed, and the more education you have, the better an entrepreneur you can be. I don't, however, think you have to go to a prestigious college—or any college at all, for that matter—to get an education. Sure, formal education is important, but educating yourself by observing, seeing, trying, doing, achieving, and repeating it all again and again is the best way to learn.

All these characteristics and education are important, but there are two I put at the top of the list.

Persistence: The Most Important Quality

I've already discussed some desirable qualities for entrepreneurs, such as energy, good communication skills, and the ability to deal effectively with many kinds of people. Those and other qualities are important, but one quality stands alone at the top of the list of desirable traits for entrepreneurs—*persistence*.

In my opinion, there's no single quality or trait that's more important to being a successful entrepreneur. Persistence is the quality that keeps you motivated when things aren't going the way you thought they would. Persistence can make you look for one more possible solution to the problem that has baffled you for weeks, and it makes you pick up the phone again to call the guy who told you earlier that he couldn't help you.

The dictionary says that persistence is "stubborn or enduring continuance," and I guess that definition is as good as any. I'd add to it, however, because I think there's more to persistence than that.

I don't think anyone knows for certain if persistence is a quality present from birth in some lucky people or if it's something acquired through experience and circumstance.

The Word According to John

Persistence is the determination and strength to keep going long after you feel like quitting. It's the stuff inside that makes you pick yourself up and try one more time.

Basketball great Michael Jordan is often held up as a model of persistence. Probably everyone knows that he was cut from his high school basketball team the first year he tried out, after which he vowed to work harder than anyone had ever worked before to ensure he'd make the team the next year.

As you know, the rest is history. Jordan not only made his high school team, he went on to be the greatest basketball player the NBA has ever seen. Still, he says he never forgot how he felt when he was cut from that team, and he has worked ever since to make sure he'd never be passed over again.

We don't know if Jordan was born with his great persistence or if it developed along with his speed and soaring ability, but I believe anyone can become more persistent if he or she is willing to work at it. If persistence doesn't come naturally to you, you have to make a conscious effort to develop it. Tell yourself that you won't give up. Convince yourself that you're resourceful enough to solve any problems you encounter, even if it takes more than one try. Picture Michael Jordan on the basketball court, and tell yourself that you, too, can fly. Be willing to keep trying when things go wrong, and accept that, ultimately, it's up to you to make your dream come true. Motivation is necessary to stick with your dream when the going gets rough; it has to come from within you. Other people can offer support, but this is your ballgame.

Don't think, however, that you have to solve every problem that comes along by yourself. If you find it difficult to ask for help, you'll have to learn to do that, too. Hey, nobody said being an entrepreneur was going to be a stroll in the park.

Confidence: The Second Most Important Quality

Once you've got a handle on persistence, you can start thinking about your confidence level. Confidence is the second most important quality of a successful entrepreneur. You've got to have a good measure of confidence in yourself, but also in other people and in your surroundings.

Confidence in Yourself

Self-confidence is definitely a necessary trait in an entrepreneur because you're called on almost constantly to perform tasks and make decisions that require great amounts of faith in yourself. It's nearly impossible to make any kind of decisions—especially important ones—without self-confidence, and decision making is an integral part of entrepreneurship.

Making any kind of decision requires self-confidence, but dealing with the fallout from a bad decision you've made requires an extra measure of the stuff. It's self-confidence that allows you to get over a bad decision you've made and look ahead to the good decision you know you'll make tomorrow.

Self-confident people are positive people who think they can succeed. They're not easily discouraged, and they practice persistence. If you don't think you're particularly self-confident, here are some ways to increase that quality within yourself:

Over the Rainbow

On the chance that persistence is a learned trait, do your kids a favor and start teaching them when they're young to persevere and persist in their endeavors. Our society makes it all too easy to move on to something else as soon as we encounter trouble or difficulty, so you can give your kids a good start by teaching them persistence. Remember, the best way to teach them is through your example.

Grizzly Area

You need to be aware that being an entrepreneur isn't always easy. You're bound to run into unforeseen problems, and many of them will be caused by your own mistakes. If you can't face up to your mistakes and move ahead, then you'd better think long and hard about whether being an entrepreneur is a smart move for you.

➤ Be optimistic. Believe that things will get better, even when they're at their worst. Keep telling yourself you're okay and you have the strength to hang in there until things improve.

➤ Be patient. Patient people get more respect than impatient people, and respect improves your level of self-confidence. Being patient, or at least appearing to be patient, around impatient people gives you a definite advantage.

➤ Remove any limitations you've put on yourself. You might not even realize you've done so, but if you've limited yourself in any way, you need to undo it. Ask yourself if you're doing less than you could be, and then figure out why.

➤ Be your own advocate. Tell yourself all the time that you can do whatever it is you need to, and don't be afraid to convey your strengths to people around you.

➤ Keep the faith. Believe in whatever you believe in, and make sure it includes you. Be brave and try, even when you have doubts. You'll be surprised at how often things work out even better than you had expected.

If something does go terribly wrong, you need self-confidence to try again. Think about an athlete who has been badly injured. If a skier, for example, is injured during a bad crash, he needs great self-confidence to get back on the slopes after he's healed. It will probably take some time for his confidence to be restored, and I doubt whether he'll jump right back onto the steep trail where the accident occurred. The important thing, however, is that he'll go back to the slopes and try again.

Confidence in Others

Although self-confidence is extremely important, you need to have confidence in the people around you, too. Nobody in business can get along without other people. You need to work with all kinds of people, such as employees, partners, members of a board of directors, stockholders, suppliers, salespeople, advertising people, and financial people.

I'm not saying that you should, without question, fully trust every person you come in contact with. There are some real horror stories out there about entrepreneurs being taken for everything they had because they trusted the wrong people. There's more about trust and knowing who to trust in Part 4, "No Man (or Woman) Is an Island."

After you get to know someone, however, and decide that you can trust her, then you've got to extend confidence. Did you ever work with or for

Over the Rainbow

It's a common trait among beginning entrepreneurs to want to have their hands on every part of the business and oversee everything, right down to the smallest detail. Resist these urges, however, and trust that your employees and partners know what they're doing. Keeping overly close tabs doesn't indicate confidence in others.

someone who doubted your motives or ability and expressed no confidence in you? Not a good feeling, is it? Knowing someone lacks confidence in you doesn't inspire you to work hard and do your best, that's for sure.

So be sure that you cultivate your confidence in the people around you, and don't forget to include your family and friends. A self-confident person doesn't think he's the only one who can do something well.

Confidence in Your Environment

Having confidence in your environment is having an overall sense of peace with your surroundings. It's knowing that things happen for reasons and trusting that things usually work out okay.

It's important for an entrepreneur to have confidence in her environment because it provides assurance that even the worst times don't last. It gives her a larger framework than her own business in which to operate.

Did you ever meet someone who lived in a state of constant fear, always sure that something would go wrong? His house or business was certain to somehow catch on fire and burn down. The little lump on his neck had to be cancer, he was sure of it. Bad things were destined to happen to his wife, his kids, and his dog. His car would be recalled, his computer would crash repeatedly, and the quarterback of his favorite football team was sure to be injured, ending the team's playoff chances.

That type of person is sorely lacking confidence in his environment, and that lack is certain to affect every area of his life. Besides making himself a nervous wreck, he makes everyone around him one, too.

Without confidence in your environment, you can't be self-confident or have confidence in others. Confidence in yourself, confidence in others, and confidence in your environment are closely intertwined and interdependent.

Finding the Courage to Make the Leap

It takes courage to be an entrepreneur, there's no doubt about it. It's a big leap of faith to trade in the assurance of a weekly paycheck, employer-provided health benefits, paid vacation, and your own parking space for something that maybe even you perceive as risky and uncertain.

You'll need the support of your family and friends, and you'll need the persistence and confidence I discussed earlier. It makes it easier to take the first steps into entrepreneurship, however, if you keep the whole thing in perspective.

Think about the worst thing that could happen. Your business could fail, right? Now, ask yourself how bad that really would be. You could always find another job, or try another entrepreneurial venture. You don't normally die because of a failed business, nor do you generally lose your family, your home, or your self-respect. You don't get put in jail for failing at a business, and you're not denied the chance to try again. A lot of things in life are worse than a business failure.

On the other hand, think of the best things that could happen. You'll get into a business that's exciting, challenging, fun, and profitable. You'll have a great time, you'll make tons of money, and you'll get that beach house your family has wanted for a long time. You'll meet all kinds of interesting people, and you'll be responsible for yourself, your work, and your company, and you'll learn about things you never knew existed.

When you stand back and get some perspective on your situation, the stakes don't seem quite as high, and the challenge and potential for fun become irresistible.

If you really want to be an entrepreneur, and you're willing to do what it takes to be one, then go for it. Understand that there's a tremendous amount of work ahead of you, even before the doors of your business ever open.

Keep your persistence and confidence handy, take a deep breath, and get ready to become an entrepreneur.

Over the Rainbow

Develop a mantra that you recite to yourself again and again. Make it something like, "I can do this, I know I can. I will be successful because I believe that I can be."

The Least You Need to Know

➤ A dream doesn't guarantee success as an entrepreneur, but you can't be an entrepreneur without one.

➤ An entrepreneur is a person willing to take risks, expend great quantities of energy, and work like heck to make a dream a reality.

➤ Entrepreneurs are motivated by many things; the degree and level of motivation are more important than the particular factor that motivates.

➤ Persistence and confidence—in that order—are the most important qualities an entrepreneur can possess.

➤ It's important to stand back and get some perspective on your situation before you commit to being an entrepreneur.

➤ Once you decide you're going to be an entrepreneur, you need to give it your very best effort.

Chapter 2

Are You Sure You Want To Do This?

In This Chapter

➤ Being an entrepreneur means a lot of hard work, responsibility, long hours, and an uncertain salary.

➤ Consider all the facts before committing to starting your own business.

➤ Excuses have gotten between many would-be entrepreneurs and their dreams.

➤ Keeping your dreams alive requires overcoming excuses and negative thoughts.

If you haven't already hung out your shingle, and you're reading this book, chances are pretty good you think you want to be an entrepreneur. Guess what? *Thinking* you want to be an entrepreneur isn't good enough. You've got to *know* you want to be one and be willing to do whatever it takes to get started.

It could be that you've been toying with the idea of starting your own business for years, but have never gotten around to doing it. You might think having your own business will take too much time away from your spouse and kids, or be too stressful, or require business knowledge you don't have. Maybe you've hung onto the job you have not because you like it, but because you're reluctant to give up the sure things of weekly paychecks and benefits.

Whatever your reasons have been for not getting started with your own business, you're going to have to work through them and put them aside before you commit yourself to being an entrepreneur.

If you're working for somebody else, you're letting that person be responsible for you. If you work for yourself, you'll be responsible for, and to, yourself. That scares some people, but I'd much rather be taking care of myself than having somebody else be responsible for me.

Over the Rainbow

When you decide for sure to start your own business, you're taking control of your own destiny and making the dream truly yours. Doing this gives you a tremendous sense of empowerment.

Remember when you were a kid and you couldn't wait until you were old enough to do whatever you wanted without your mom, or dad, or teacher, or *somebody* always telling you what to do? Well, when you work for yourself, you've finally reached that point. There's nobody to tell you what to do. Sure, you listen to other people and take good advice, but you're the one in charge.

Before you take the first step toward starting your own business, however, you need to make sure you really want to be an entrepreneur. You need to be sure you're willing to do whatever it takes to get a business off the ground and running successfully. If after careful thought and consideration you decide that being an entrepreneur isn't for you, that's fine. But it's better to know that now than halfway through the work of a business startup.

Take a Good, Hard Look at the Facts

At the risk of sounding like those warnings of adult language, violence, and partial nudity that the TV networks run before some of their shows, I want to tell you that this chapter contains some pretty graphic, to-the-point information.

This kind of information isn't meant to scare or discourage you. It's only intended to get you to take a good, hard look at some of the realities of being an entrepreneur. It would not be fair, or right, for me to encourage you to go ahead and start a business without considering all the facts. I think all entrepreneurs have the potential to make a lot of money and to be very successful with their businesses, but they have to be willing to work hard to pull it off.

At the end of this chapter, I'd like you to take a few minutes to really think about what it would be like to start a business. After considering all the angles, maybe you'll decide it's not really what you want to do. If that's what you decide, fine. Being an entrepreneur isn't for everybody—that's for sure. I hope, though, that you'll read this chapter and decide that being an entrepreneur is exactly where you're headed.

People tend to think of entrepreneurs as Donald Trump types. They envision tuxedos, Ivana and Marla, towering buildings, and limousines. Not everything about being an entrepreneur, however, is fun, exciting, or glamorous. Just as with any venture, there's a fair degree of less-than-thrilling, but necessary, work.

There will be countless problems, all of which you'll have to solve or know who to get to solve them for you. You'll have to be able to think on your feet to come up with innovative solutions to problems that will occur, and you'll have to know how to look for problems on the horizon so they can be avoided.

Bear Facts

Pete Slosberg, a co-founder of Pete's Brewing Company that makes Pete's Wicked Ale, learned big time about problems that can come up fast and kick you in the tail. Pete was renting facilities in a brewery and making his beer during the brewery's downtimes. He also stored his beer there. Pete got a call one Wednesday night from the owner of the brewery, who told him he'd declared bankruptcy and the place would be locked up first thing Monday morning. Because his beer was stored there, Pete stood to lose a lot more than his brewing facilities. He got about 15 friends together, and they worked around the clock for two and a half days to get Pete's beer out of the doomed brewery. He was still faced with the problem of finding another place to make his beer, but he saved his inventory.

Sure, it's okay to think about the glamorous, fun parts of being an entreprenuer—and there are some. You might not get a limousine or Marla, but you'll meet some interesting people and run into some fun situations. You can't, however, go into a business startup venture wearing blinders and thinking that everything will go smoothly and according to plan.

Betting Against the Odds

More than half of all businesses that start up fail.

Now that we've got that fact out into the open, I want to tell you something about it. Ignore it. Don't spend a bit of energy thinking about it. You need to focus on what you want to do and do your very best to make it happen, not worry about a statistic.

About half of all marriages fail, too, but that doesn't stop people from getting married or from trying again after one marriage fails.

If you go into a business or a marriage thinking that you'll fail because most people do, chances are you *will* fail. It's the self-fulfilling prophecy thing.

One of the greatest tightrope artists who ever lived, Karl Wallenda, had never thought about—or at least had never talked about—falling, until the last three months of his life. His wife said that during those last months, however, Wallenda was terrified that he'd fall. He put all his energy into being afraid of falling, she said, rather than into walking the tightrope. Ultimately and tragically, his fear became a self-fulfilling prophecy; he fell and was killed.

It takes an inordinate amount of *energy*—both physical and emotional—to start your own business. If you do it right, you'll find you have tons of energy because starting your own business is fun and exciting. No matter how much energy you have, however, you'll have little to spare. You can't afford to waste any of that energy—not even a tiny little bit—on worrying about some business failure rate statistic.

The Word According to John

There are many definitions of energy. In my opinion, *energy* is the internal force that gives you power and allows you to do what you do in a day. It's continuously renewed and replenished by enthusiasm, joy, and fun. Energy works with the brain, but it comes from the soul.

That's not to say you should never worry. Believe me when I tell you there will be plenty of things to worry about. You shouldn't waste energy by worrying about a statistic that doesn't apply to you, however, or about other things that you can't control.

Who knows whether Karl Wallenda would have been killed had he not been consumed with the fear of falling. Maybe it would have happened anyway. Maybe, though, he focused all his energy on his fear and didn't have enough left to keep him on the wire.

The next chapter deals extensively with failing, so I won't go into it in greater detail right now. Keep in mind, however, that if you start your own business, you'll be betting against the odds. But if you don't start it, you'll be missing out on the opportunity to beat the odds.

Long Hours, No Guaranteed Salary

When you work for somebody, you generally know what's expected of you. You have a contract, or there are posted rules or a manual that tells you what you're expected to do and what your responsibilities are. You know what you'll be paid in exchange for doing those things, and you know there are limits on where you can go in the job.

It's likely you have a boss who cares more about looking good to the upper management types and collecting his paycheck than he does about your career advancement. He's covering his own tail, not worrying about yours.

Done properly, a job is much more than working in exchange for money and trying to keep your boss happy. It's prestige, it's challenge, it's fun, it's fulfillment. But let's face it—there aren't too many people who work because they enjoy the challenge. Most employees work because they get a check every payday.

When you work for yourself, the expectations generally are less clear-cut than they are when you work for somebody else. An entrepreneur's guideline for hours and salary would look something like this:

➤ Hours? Until the work is finished.

➤ Salary? Whatever the business can afford.

Not very specific, is it? When you finish this book, though, you'll have a better understanding of how hours, salary, and other issues can be managed, but for now, the expectations are pretty fuzzy.

Oh, another thing about starting your own business... In addition to working long hours, you're going to have to work the jobs of more than one person. You're likely to be a worker, a boss, a secretary, and maybe even a custodian.

Recently, I read about a guy who started his own business. He always dressed fastidiously in a well-made business suit and was noted for his professional appearance. What no one knew, however, was that before he went home every night, he'd change into a coverall and clean his offices. He'd empty trash cans, clean the floors, wash windows—whatever needed to be done. He did this because he couldn't afford to pay a cleaning service, but he wanted the office to look nice and be clean.

He was determined that his business would succeed, and he did what he felt was necessary to ensure its success. That guy will probably be extremely successful, unless he falls into a dangerous trap—the trap of thinking he can or should do everything by himself.

Grizzly Area

If you saw an advertisement for the job you'll take on when you start your own business, you'd probably never consider applying for it. It would read something like this: "Great job with lots of potential; long, long hours; salary—maybe; chance to have fun along the way; will require stamina, persistence, and problem-solving skills. Be prepared to figure out how to pay yourself and to put up significant capital when starting." If you're not prepared to take on a tough job, you might not be cut out to be an entrepreneur.

I used to go into the Green Mountains in Vermont to cut my own firewood. For $10, I was granted a wood lot and allowed to cut and remove up to five cords of firewood. I would cut the wood, haul it home in my van, cut it into smaller pieces, split it, and stack it up. Eventually, it would dry out and I'd have firewood. I didn't have much experience with this kind of work, and the process took days and days. But I used wood to heat my house, and I thought this was a great deal.

My neighbor, Doug, was watching me work with the wood one day. Doug was a huge, Viking-type man, whose profession was that of a hoof doctor. He traveled all over New England, cleaning the hooves of cows and other farm animals. In his calm, solemn manner, Doug called me over and related a good piece of advice that had been passed along to him.

"You know, John," Doug said, "my father always said it was smart to do the things you know how to do and pay somebody to do the things you don't."

I've thought about Doug's advice hundreds of times since he offered it that day, and I know it's some of the best advice I've ever received. Don't get hung up on doing stuff

Grizzly Area

It makes no sense to spend time cleaning your office when you should be developing an advertising plan, and yet some entrepreneurs do exactly that. Concentrate on doing what's important and needs to be done. If that takes up all your time—fine. Hire somebody to clean the office. Keep your mind on what's important now and what needs to be done. If your priorities get screwed up, you'll find yourself in big trouble.

The Word According to John

Your *work ethic* is the thing that tells you about working, the way your *conscience* tells you about being truthful, treating people with respect, and so forth. They're both little voices inside you.

that doesn't need to be done. Get somebody else to do the little stuff, and keep yourself free to do that which only you can do.

You might have to sweep the floors in your new business, but not when there's more important work to do.

If you do find yourself staying late to sweep up, use the quiet time to contemplate and think about tomorrow's priorities. And don't worry. You won't have to do the sweeping for very long. Keep in mind that the satisfaction, excitement, and fulfillment of starting your own business more than make up for the long hours with no guaranteed salary.

This Is Gonna Be Hard Work

Nobody who's done it is ever going to tell you that starting your own business is easy. In fact, anybody who's done it will tell you that it's a lot of hard work. That's not to say it won't be fun. You'll have a great time watching your dreams coming true, bit by bit. Making dreams come true, however, requires a good deal of sweat.

If you're going to be an entrepreneur, it helps greatly if you have a good work ethic. What is a work ethic, anyway? To hear a lot of older people talk, it's the thing that young people don't have any of. Actually, though, your work ethic is a code that's programmed inside you. Your work ethic motivates you to do the work that you do, and to take pride in doing the work well.

Some people, you'll notice, have work ethics that let them do just what it takes to get by. They're the clock-watchers, always ready to be out the door at 5:00 sharp. They wouldn't dream of volunteering to take on a project that requires working extra hours, even if the project had the potential to be really great. They're not driven to do more, or do their jobs any better, than they have to.

People without good work ethics sometimes get along just fine, if they're very goal oriented. It's better to be goal oriented *and* have a great work ethic. Some people without a strong work *ethic*, however, get along strictly on their ability to meet goals, regardless of how they do it.

Employees with strong work ethics are the kind of people compelled to go the extra mile and work until the job is finished:

➤ They're the farmers you see with lights on the front of their tractors, determined to get the rest of the field plowed before they quit for the night.

➤ They're the small-business owners who work hard all day, and then spread out their paperwork on the dining room table to do before they go back to work the next morning.

➤ They're the working moms who hold down a full-time job, and then come home and cook dinner for their families, clean up the kitchen, do the laundry, and still bake cookies for their kids' school fairs before finally falling into bed.

➤ They're the athletes driven to train, to work, and to practice until they get it exactly right—the skater who spends hours and hours each day on the ice, practicing a move again and again until finally it's perfect, or the high jumper who won't stop working until he's satisfied his technique will let him jump as high as he possibly can. Baltimore Oriole player Cal Ripken was noted for his work ethic. Ripken set a major league record streak by playing 2,632 consecutive games.

People with work ethics that are just so-so often resent those who get ahead because they're willing to work harder and longer. They don't recognize, or at least they don't admit, that a lousy work ethic is what's holding them back. Instead, they blame it on their boss or circumstances.

Bear Facts

In my opinion, mothers should be applauded for their work ethics and entrepreneurial skills. I have a lot of respect for women (and the men who take on traditional mom duties) who manage homes, kids, kids' activities, kids' teachers, social lives, civic or religious work— and the list goes on and on. These women are entrepreneurs in the truest sense of the word, and they display admirable work ethics every day.

A person who doesn't have a good work ethic will probably find it difficult to be a successful entrepreneur. A poor work ethic makes the job more difficult to manage. Your work ethic is shaped and formed by what you observe when you're growing up.

If you've always been around people who work hard, chances are you'll work hard too. Hard work is what's normal to you.

But if you grew up around people who did just what they had to, never really enjoying their work or feeling a connection to it, your work ethic will probably reflect that, too.

Bear Facts

I was raised in a family of entrepreneurs and hard workers, and can hardly remember a time when I didn't work. I had paper routes, painted buildings, worked in factories, and took whatever jobs came along. Work was the normal thing to do in my family, and we all did it.

Make Sure You Have Fun

If you think your work ethic could or should be better, there's a secret you can use to improve it.

Try to find more enjoyment in your work. If you really get into what you're doing and you're having lots of fun doing it, your work ethic will improve and get stronger without you doing a thing. You'll want to keep working because you're having a great time. You'll learn that doing the very best you can makes the work more fun, and you'll be driven to work even harder.

We've all known people who have loved their work—who are never happier than when they've got a monumental project ahead of them. To them, work is fun. There's little distinction between work and recreation. In fact, recreation sometimes becomes work because it takes them away from work. Those are the real entrepreneurs.

Be careful not to confuse an entrepreneur with a workaholic. There's a big difference. A workaholic is addicted to work the way some gamblers are addicted to playing the ponies. They've got to do it, and the more the better.

Workaholics usually don't get a lot of pleasure out of working, but they're compelled to keep doing it. It's not a choice. Entrepreneurs, on the other hand, work because they want to. They know that hard work is what enables them to realize their dreams, and they know that making dreams come true is not a chore, but a pleasure.

And What's All This Talk About Responsibility?

Starting a business tends to create a ripple effect. It starts out small, affecting you and your immediate family. Soon, the ripples spread out to include people such as your financial backers, your partners, and your founder's team. Eventually, you've got employees, and they're affected, also.

It should make you stop and think for a minute when you realize how many people could be affected by your business venture. Some will be people you love and care about, and others will be people you barely know. Regardless of who they are, however, you'll bear some responsibility to them.

In addition to people, you'll be responsible for a lot of other things. You'll be responsible for paying bills on time and for making sure there's enough money available to do so. Other things you might be responsible for include the following:

➤ Complying with government regulations (a huge chore!)

➤ Filling orders on time

➤ Getting the orders right

➤ Establishing rules and guidelines for employees

➤ Making sure your product meets all standards and regulations

➤ Maintaining your property

➤ Traveling to promote your business and meet with the people who can help you

➤ Keeping up with personal relationships

➤ Juggling your schedule to fulfill all obligations

Over the Rainbow

I felt a huge responsibility to my employees at The Vermont Teddy Bear Company. The majority of them were women; some were single parents. You can't let yourself get overly involved with your employees, and you should remember that you're not responsible for *what* they do. But you've got to realize that you're responsible *to* them. In many ways, they're dependent on you, just as you're dependent on them.

I could go and on with that list, but you get the picture, right? Being an entrepreneur carries huge responsibility, but true entrepreneurs will embrace it and bear it without complaint.

When you believe in yourself, which you've got to do to be a successful entrepreneur, you have the confidence to believe you can handle as much responsibility as you need to. Sure, you'll get tired now and then of being so darned responsible, but you'll know it's part of the job and something you can handle. You'll much prefer being the one responsible over someone being responsible for you.

Stop Making Excuses

I hope you've read all the information presented so far in this chapter and shrugged your shoulders. Right about now, you should be saying something like, "Yeah, I know it's gonna be hard work, long hours, an uncertain salary, and lots of responsibility—so what? Let's get started!"

If that's the attitude you have, more power to you. You're definitely heading in the right direction. If, on the other hand, you broke out in a sweat while reading about the long hours and responsibility, you might be coming up with some excuses right now to give up your dream of being an entrepreneur.

People can come up with all kinds of reasons they can't do something. It wouldn't be hard to come up with a bunch of excuses for not starting your own business. You might say:

"I'm due for a promotion soon, and I hate to pass it up."

"My husband/wife doesn't make enough to support us if I am without a regular salary."

"I've got to save money for my kids to use for college, and I can't afford to risk what we've already saved."

"I don't have enough experience to start my own business."

"I don't know where I'd find enough money to start my own business."

"Everybody knows it's harder for women to start businesses than it is for men."

You could come up with dozens of excuses that might stop you from becoming an entrepreneur. If you buy into any them, though, your dreams are at risk.

If you can't get past the excuses, sit down and try to work through them. Remember that everybody who's ever left a job to start his own business has had concerns, but every successful entrepreneur managed to get past the excuses and move ahead with his plans. He put his dreams in front of the excuses and refused to look at the excuses anymore.

You can do the same. If you want to be an entrepreneur, stop making excuses. Use that energy to start doing what you can now to prepare yourself for starting your own business. Soak in any knowledge that might help you when you're on your own. Look around your office and see how things are run. Do they work? If so, think about how those procedures or practices could apply to your business. Relegate the excuses to the back of your mind, and concentrate on more useful and productive thoughts.

Over the Rainbow

Look, if you go for it, and it doesn't work out, it's not the end of the world. You'll find another job, or go back to your old job, or try to do something else. Don't burn any bridges while you look to the future. Everything will be fine.

Remember Why You Wanted To Be an Entrepreneur in the First Place

When your head is filled with excuses about why you can't be an entrepreneur, find a quiet place and think about your dreams. Remember all the hopes and visions you've held onto over the years, just waiting for a chance to make them realities.

Think about the scenes you've imagined in which you're running your own business. You're competent and confident, and you're having a great time. You're meeting all kinds of people and making a good living for you and your family, and you know that starting your own business is the best thing you ever did.

Motivate yourself by thinking how cool it will be to go to your next high school or college reunion and tell everybody you own your own business. Think about how great it will be to walk into an office and know that it's yours.

Remember how tired you are of having a boss tell you what to do all the time. What time to show up, what time to go to lunch, what time to go home, and what to do while you're in the office. Aren't those big reasons why you wanted to become an entrepreneur?

Think about the desire you have to do something really good, all by yourself. Remember how you've dreamed of building a business from the ground up and making it into something people will talk about.

More than anything, remember that it's your life, and you're in control of it. You can do whatever you want to, if you're willing to work and learn.

If you keep those thoughts and images in your head, you'll find that there's no room for the excuses. Stay focused on the positives—all the things that have inspired you to become an entrepreneur.

Go for It!

An entrepreneurial spirit would not be daunted by all the challenges presented in this chapter, so I'm sure yours has not been.

It's important to understand what being an entrepreneur entails, but it's also important to understand that most of those things are positive. Even the things we've discussed in this chapter— hard work, long hours, responsibility, and financial considerations—can be looked at as challenges you'll have great fun tackling and overcoming.

If you think you want to be an entrepreneur, consider all the facts, and make up your mind. If

Over the Rainbow

Think of the entrepreneurs you know. They're no smarter or more talented than you are. They probably faced the same challenges when they started their businesses as you will when you start yours. But they met the challenges and overcame them to realize their dreams. You can do that, too.

you *know* you want to be an entrepreneur, then put aside the excuses, the worries, and any other barriers that might stop you from making your dream a reality. Go for it!

The Least You Need to Know

➤ It's important to consider all the facts before committing to starting your own business.

➤ Being an entrepreneur entails hard work, long hours, an uncertain salary, and a lot of responsibility.

➤ True entrepreneurs aren't afraid of challenges; they look forward to meeting and overcoming them.

➤ Excuses can get in the way of dreams if you let them.

➤ When your head is filled with reasons why you can't start your own business, replace them with thoughts of your dream and why you wanted to be an entrepreneur in the first place.

Chapter 3

Failing at Something Doesn't Make You a Failure

In This Chapter

➤ Our society's obsession with winning.

➤ A dream not attempted is a failed dream.

➤ Failing at a business isn't the end of the world.

➤ Learn from your mistakes.

➤ What to tell others if your business fails.

➤ A look at some who have failed and then prospered.

Failure is pretty much a dirty word in America.

Winning, or succeeding at whatever we do, is considered the American way. Traditionally, we're a country of self-reliant, hard workers who might get knocked down from time to time, but always manage to come out on top. Americans have always seen themselves as winners.

This attitude has served us well. It's what fueled those scrappy American colonists when they fought the British in 1775. It's what caused explorers to blaze trails westward and settlers to follow. It's prompted restless souls to build railroads, fly airplanes, and orbit the earth in spaceships. Although it has moved us ahead, this must-win attitude isn't without a downside.

Winning and Losing

Check out a kid's Little League or soccer game sometime. Take a good look at some of the parents on the sidelines, screaming at their kids to run faster, hit harder, maybe even cheat just a little bit—anything to beat that other team of 8-year-olds.

Kids quickly get the picture. They learn that in our society, it's good to win and bad to lose. Winning is a big deal in America, and it doesn't stop with Little League. We want to win at sports, at love, at business, and at life itself.

There were a lot of empty seats in Giants stadium December 13, 1998, when the New York team stunned the Denver Broncos by beating them 20 to 16 and ending the Broncos' until-then perfect season. Why the empty seats? The Giants were 5 and 8—losers. A lot of fans, including season ticket holders, opted to stay home or go Christmas shopping instead of coming out to cheer for their losing team.

Let's face it. We want our teams to win every week. If they don't, we're quick to bail out and find a team with a better record.

We hate to fail at relationships, although nearly everybody does at some point. We dream of starting businesses that become incredibly successful, but the thought of failing at business is too scary for many people to even think about.

Our desire in this society to succeed and win is so strong that we run the risk of thinking we deserve success, even if we haven't earned it. There's great pressure on us to be winners and to succeed at whatever we do. When we don't succeed, and, inevitably, everyone will sooner or later fail at something, it can be a devastating experience.

Entrepreneurs, however, have to be of stronger stuff than the average person. We have to understand that failing from time to time is part of the package. We have to be willing to shrug our shoulders, say "Oh, well," and look for a better way to do things the next time.

This chapter comes early in the book because it's extremely important to think about the possibility of failing and to put it into perspective. I don't expect that you'll fail, but I want you to think through the *concept* of failing and come to grips with it. Most people are very much afraid of failing. Only fears that are confronted and dealt with can be dismantled.

Failing at something is not the end of the line, and all successful entrepreneurs understand that. It's simply part of the process.

Fear of Failing Is a Great Inhibitor

I've known people, and you probably have, too, who are so afraid of failing that they refuse to try at whatever it is they want to do.

This applies to all parts of life, not just business. I knew a guy whose lifelong dream was to be a doctor. All through junior high, high school, and college, he planned to go to medical school. He worked hard and got good grades, but not great grades.

Bear Facts

There was a 24-year period at Stanford University when no Fs were given. Everybody passed every subject. The policy was changed in 1994, and failing grades are again permitted to be issued. Some faculty members argued against reinstating failing grades, saying that students should be able to experiment with classes, without fear of pulling down their grade point averages. But Stanford President Gerhard Casper disagreed, saying, "Unless you dare something and admit that you may fail, you are living in an illusionary world."

He got increasingly nervous and upset, worrying that his grades wouldn't be good enough to get him into that elusive medical school he had targeted. Finally, he became so afraid during his last semester at college that he would be rejected that he decided not to apply. All his friends tried to convince him to give it a shot, but he refused. He went home to work at his father's car dealership instead. I often wonder what that guy thinks about at the end of the day, and if he still dreams of being a doctor.

There are people who are so afraid of being rejected that they won't ask somebody they care about to go to a movie or meet them for a cup of coffee.

Fear of failing causes a salesperson whose confidence is low to not even attempt to make the sale, and it causes the schoolchild to sit out of the class spelling game because he's afraid he'll get the first word wrong and the other kids will laugh. There's no question that a lot more would get done, if people weren't so afraid of failing.

The next time you want to do something, but you're hesitating because you're afraid you'll fail, think about this: If you don't do something because you're afraid you'll fail, you've already failed. This guy I knew failed to be a doctor because he didn't have the guts to go for what he really wanted. Maybe he wouldn't have been accepted to medical school, and he would not have become a doctor anyway. Who knows? But by not even applying to medical school, he guaranteed his failure. He's pretty successful in his

The Word According to John

Exactly what does it mean to *fail?* The dictionary is full of definitions, such as "to lose power or strength," "to become deficient," "to fall short," "to become insolvent or bankrupt," and "to be unsuccessful in obtaining a desired end." If I were Mr. Webster, though, I'd define it like this: "to not attempt to do what is important."

family's car business, but he's not that doctor he dreamed of being. I can't help but think he would have been better off to try, fail, and move on rather than always wonder if he could have made it.

If you're having trouble getting started as an entrepreneur because you're afraid you could fail, you're going to have to get over it. Yeah, you could fail. But to let that fear stop you from trying is to have failed without ever getting started.

Taking Risks Isn't All That Risky

Being an entrepreneur does entail risk, and nobody who knows what he's talking about is going to tell you anything different. Reality is reality, and more than half of all new, small businesses fail. That's risk.

Bear Facts

More and more Amish people are leaving their family farms and starting small businesses, usually involving woodworking or construction. For some reason, these Amish entrepreneurs enjoy a nearly unbelievable success rate with their businesses. A study in the Lancaster, Pennsylvania area showed that 95% of new Amish ventures succeeded, compared to fewer than half of all new ventures societywide. When asked about their amazing success rate, the Amish entrepreneurs attributed it to hard work, commitment, and faith.

Businesses fail for a lot of reasons. People start them without fully thinking through what they'll do or how they'll do it. They fail to set goals or even start out with sound business plans. You will not make these mistakes, however, and you have every reason to be optimistic about the success of your business.

Yes, you'll encounter risks along the way, but keep in mind that risk is not exclusive to entrepreneurs.

Downsizing: A Corporate Hazard

Think about all the people you know or have heard about who have been downsized. Many of these men and women assumed they were in safe jobs with dependable companies—companies they would be with until they retired.

Downsizing has been a common phenomenon of the 1990s—so common, in fact, that former U.S. Labor Secretary Robert Reich advised American workers several years ago to adjust their thinking and prepare for the possibility of layoffs.

"Job security is a thing of the past," Reich said. "People are going to have to get used to the idea of involuntary separations—sometimes four, five, or six times during a career."

Sounds pretty risky to me.

Risk is inherent in many jobs in other ways, too. Look at the risk that a police officer or firefighter takes on every time he or she goes on duty. Lots of jobs, such as commercial fishing, military endeavors, and high construction work are dangerous. How about a professional quarterback, who risks having his career cut short every time he drops back to pass, despite an onslaught of defensive linemen?

You might not think about it very often, but regardless of what your job is, you take a lot of risks every day. We all do. Risks are an inevitable part of life.

Life Is a Risky Business

Most of the risks we encounter daily are small and don't involve dire consequences. There are financial risks, personal risks, job-related risks, and risks with relationships.

You take financial risks each time you invest in the stock market or buy some mutual funds. Betting on a ball game is a risk, and so is attempting to talk to somebody you've just met at the coffee shop or bar.

There are some really big risks, too. We risk losing the people we love or our own lives every day. Every morning, when you send your kids off to the bus stop, you run the risk that something will happen to them, and they won't come back.

The minute you walk out your front door and climb into your car to drive to work, you're risking getting into an accident and being badly hurt or killed or of hurting somebody else.

We all live with these kinds of risks every day, but healthy people don't let them get in the way of living. You believe that your kids will go off to school, and they'll be home again that afternoon. You don't keep your money under your mattress, fearing a repeat of the Great Depression, and you smile and say hello to that attractive person next to you at the bar, even though you know he or she might not be interested.

Risk can't be, and shouldn't be, avoided. William James, an early 20th-century writer, is quoted as saying, "It is only by risking our persons from one hour to another that we live at all."

Grizzly Area

I don't think anybody loves risk—even gamblers. The biggest risk, to me, however, is to let the fear of it render you motionless so that life simply passes you by. If you let that happen, I don't see how you won't regret it later.

Risk Takers

Consider those people who not only don't avoid risk, but *choose* to take extraordinary risks for the fun or the challenge they bring. Maybe you're one of those people.

Downhill skiers who pull out all the stops and practically fly down the slopes are examples of risk takers. So are mountain climbers who won't be satisfied until they've done Everest, and kayakers who take the fastest, whitest way down the river every time. These kinds of people don't avoid risks; they embrace them. And there's at least a little bit of that attitude in every entrepreneur.

Think about the biggest risks you've taken in your life, and what the results have been.

Are you married? Getting married is a big risk. I'm sure you know that chances are about 50-50 that it won't last. Still, most people don't avoid getting married because they're afraid the relationship might fail.

Do you have a kid or two? That's a huge risk. Something could happen to them, but stable people don't forego the joys and rewards of having children because they're afraid tragedy might strike.

We accept risk as a part of life, whether it's personal risk, business risk, or a combination of the two. And do you know what? Usually, the things we do that involve risk work out okay.

It's no sure bet that trying your darndest to stay away from risk will keep you from failing. A lot of risk is unavoidable, and failures do occur. It *is* a sure bet, however, that trying to avoid risk by not pursuing your dream will prevent you from succeeding.

There Are Worse Things in Life Than Failing at a Business

Let's say, just for the sake of discussion, that you start up a business, and your business fails after 18 months. It goes under. Belly up. You're suddenly out of a job.

If that scenario scares the heck out of you, you're going to have to get a lot tougher, and adjust your attitude a little bit before you jump into an entrepreneurial effort. Failing at a business is not the equivalent of a death sentence. It's not even the equivalent of a terrible, major calamity. Sure, it will probably be hard on your ego. You'll go over and over in your head what went wrong and what you could have done differently. You might even try to blame the failure on somebody else, like a partner, a supplier, or a major customer. You'll fret about your future, your finances, and your reputation. That's all normal.

Go ahead and sulk for a little while. Lick your wounds until you feel better. Those are natural reactions to a wounded ego, but never forget that a business is only a business. If it fails, you can try again, or you can go find a job with someone else.

Real, true tragedy is out there, but it's not a failed business. Real tragedy is when the doctor pulls you aside and tells you that your 9-year-old has cancer. Or when you look into oncoming headlights on your side of the road and know you can't get out of the way in time. Or when a mudslide barrels down on a poor Honduran village, wiping out entire families and everything they ever had. Those are things that devastate.

A failed business, in comparison, is more of a big *inconvenience* than a tragedy. If you take only two or three lessons with you from this book, that should be one of them. A failed business is not the end of world, although it might seem like it for a little while.

I just finished reading a book called *Tuesdays with Morrie: An Old Man, A Young Man, and the Last Great Lesson*. The book, a real account of deathbed discussions between Detroit sportswriter Mitch Albom and the late Morrie Schwartz, Albom's former college professor, focuses on what's really important in life. Family, relationships, enjoying life, and knowing who you are ranked way up there as important issues for Morrie Schwartz. As he was dying of Lou Gehrig's disease, he was able to communicate these ideas to Albom, who was forced to confront his own shortcomings and misconceptions.

Over the Rainbow

Tuesdays with Morrie was published in 1997 by Doubleday, and it's available for sale on the Internet, at both Amazon.com and barnesandnoble.com. It's a quick read, and well worth your time.

Not to turn this into a book review, but *Tuesdays with Morrie* does a great job of encouraging readers to examine their priorities and take a look at the direction in which their lives are going. If you're not sure about those things, I'd highly recommend the book.

Chalk It Up to Life (and Business) Experience

I've never met a person who hasn't failed at something. And through my own failures, I've learned that they're hardly ever fatal.

Sometimes mistakes and failures are fatal. If you fail to follow traffic rules, or you fail to stay sober before you drive home, your failure might be fatal. If you fail to take care of yourself by exercising and watching what you eat—that failure might turn out to be fatal, too.

Generally speaking, however, failing at something doesn't kill you. Even a big failure, like a marriage that doesn't work out, is not fatal. Certainly, a business failure isn't. If used properly, failure can be a great motivator and a great teacher.

Remember the Michael Jordan failure story in Chapter 1, "Having a Dream and Making It Work"? Perhaps if he had made that school team, he wouldn't have developed the drive and motivation he's so famous for.

You learned in Chapter 1 that the two most important characteristics of an entrepreneur are persistence and confidence. These are the traits that inspire you to get up, dust yourself off, and start planning your next venture should failure occur.

I'm going to let you in on a secret: Nobody who has started his or her own business will consider you a failure if your business fails. Entrepreneurs have great respect for other entrepreneurs because they understand the entrepreneurial process. Only other entrepreneurs can really understand the energy, determination, resourcefulness, and effort it takes to get a business off the ground. Whether that business ultimately succeeds or fails is secondary to getting it started in the first place.

Bear Facts

National Public Radio reported recently on its "Morning Edition" program that a survey of top executives at several large companies shows that these top-management types have far more respect for entrepreneurs than they do for their own chief executive officers. CEOs are seen as people who have worked the system to get to the top, whether or not they really deserve to be there. Entrepreneurs are viewed as people who are innovative, creative, and smart.

You probably don't want to hear that failing is good for you because it:

(a) builds character

(b) makes you more determined

(c) teaches you a lesson

(d) etc., etc., etc.

I won't tell you that failing is good for you, but I will tell you it's not by a long shot the worst thing that can happen to you.

I'd like you to decide right now that if your business fails, you will pay careful attention to the experience and learn everything you can from it, both personally and professionally. Keep journals, analyze your records, and talk to business associates. Figure out what went wrong, and then figure out how to keep it from happening the next time. Step back and look at the whole picture. How did the business affect your personal life? Are you happier now than before you started it? Were you happier working for yourself than you were when you worked for somebody else?

If your business venture gives you the answers to some of those questions, then it was a useful and, arguably, successful experience. Even if the business failed, the process of starting it was successful.

Telling Others You've Failed

If your business fails, you can tell yourself it's not the end of the world, and you'll be right. Still, it won't feel good.

Some people describe the death of a business as similar to the death of a loved one. Susan Edwards, a psychologist from Princeton, New Jersey, said that business owners whose businesses fail go through the same stages as those dealing with a death. They experience shock, denial, anger, depression, and ultimately, acceptance, she says.

I think comparing a failed business to the death of a loved one is a little dramatic. It's safe to say, however, that nobody would consider the experience to be one of the best things that's ever happened.

Remember in Chapter 1, when I said that entrepreneurs generally have a fair amount of ego and self-confidence? These areas are usually the first casualties of business failure. If your business fails, your ego will hurt, and your self-confidence will be shaken. That's just the way it is, and those things might make it difficult for you to tell others about the failure. You'll have to explain the situation to your family and friends and tell your employees and anyone else involved in the business.

As difficult as that might seem, it's not the end of the world. You have to chalk it up to experience, and move on.

Over the Rainbow

Experts say that if your business fails, you need to set aside some time to assess the situation and decide what you're going to do. They recommend spending some downtime with your family or friends, instead of getting right back into another business endeavor. Use that time to re-examine your goals and come up with a plan for the future. Above all, experts advise, don't get stuck in a negative mindset. Keep thinking that your next effort will be a huge success.

Great Failures

If you're feeling a bit discouraged after all this talk about failing businesses, try not to. This chapter doesn't in any way assume that your business will fail. It merely tries to give you a sense of perspective on the subject.

A lot of people have started businesses, had them fail, and gone on to be successful at other ventures. So if you happen to be involved with a business that fails, keep in mind that you're in good company. Many people who are now greatly admired have some pretty serious mistakes and setbacks on their resumes:

➤ Remember Windows 1.0? It was a flop. Windows 2.0? Same thing. It wasn't until Bill Gates introduced Windows 3.0 in 1990 that his product took off and made him the entrepreneurial legend that he's known as today. Gates made mistakes and he failed, but he used the experience to make a better product.

➤ Baseball legend Babe Ruth hit 714 home runs during his career. You know how many times he struck out? 1,330.

➤ Sports broadcaster Wayne Root launched several businesses when he got out of college and watched each one fold. When he decided he wanted to be a sports announcer, he was rejected by hundreds of TV stations. Finally, Financial News Network (FNN), a cable network, offered him a job as its weekend sports anchor. From there, he leap-frogged to USA Network, and his career kept on building. Root now lives in a mansion in Malibu, California.

➤ Even Thomas Edison, considered one of the greatest inventors of all time, experienced failures, but he kept a positive attitude. Legend has it that a friend attempted to console Edison during a particularly frustrating time as the inventor was working on the development of a new electrical storage battery. Nothing was going right for Edison, but it turned out he didn't need consolation. The inventor reportedly said to his friend, "Why, man, I've got a lot of results. I know several thousand things that won't work!"

So you see that failing doesn't make you a failure. It should be viewed as an extremely worthwhile, although somewhat painful, form of education and used to your benefit the next time around.

Bear Facts

Wayne Root learned so much from his failures that he's written a book about it. Not everyone will be able to relate to his title "The Joy of Failure!" but it might be worth a read.

I hope you're a little less worried about having your business fail than you were before you read this chapter. The most important things to remember are as follows:

➤ Failing is sometimes part of being an entrepreneur.

➤ Not trying is automatic failure.

➤ A failed business should not rank as one of life's greatest tragedies.

➤ Having a failed business doesn't make you a failure.

If you remember those lessons, you should have the perspective you need to handle failure, should it occur. But remember to keep a positive attitude. We don't anticipate failure; we merely need to know how to cope with it if it happens.

The Least You Need to Know

➤ Our society loves success, but everybody experiences failures sometimes.

➤ Not trying something because you're afraid you'll fail guarantees failure.

➤ If your business fails, it's important to remember that it's not the worst thing that could happen to you by a long shot.

➤ Everyone makes mistakes. Smart people learn from their mistakes and use the experience the next time around.

➤ People who have started their own business, whether or not they've been successful, are generally understanding and sympathetic toward those whose businesses fail.

➤ If your business should fail, you might find it difficult to talk about to others, but don't assume you'll be judged harshly.

➤ Many extremely successful entrepreneurs have had businesses that failed.

Chapter 4

The Balancing Act

In This Chapter

➤ Maintaining a balance in your work and personal lives.

➤ Knowing how much time to work and when it's time to quit.

➤ Making and taking time to relax and have fun.

➤ Keeping an eye on your health.

➤ Setting priorities is a necessity.

➤ Loving to work versus having to work.

If you think that starting your own business won't affect your personal life, you're dead wrong.

I often compare starting a business to having a baby. A new business, like a new baby, needs constant attention. It needs to be carefully watched and tended. If you're a parent, I'm sure you can remember the demands of your newborn and how having a baby changed your life.

You try to plan for all contingencies, only to find it can't be done. Nobody can antici-pate a sudden fever in the middle of the night or even the sheer amount of time required to take care of a baby. Having a baby changes not just your routine, but your attitudes and priorities. Things that used to be terribly important suddenly don't seem that important at all.

The same thing will happen when you start your business. You'll become consumed with it and the demands it puts on your life and energies. Nights out with your buddies or girlfriends will move to the back burner on the priority stove. You'll find yourself scrambling just to have the time you want with your family.

Grizzly Area

It's one think to be greatly inter-ested in and excited about the business you're starting, but it's quite another thing to be consumed by it. If you don't keep what's really important foremost in your mind, you'll risk losing a lot in your life.

Over the Rainbow

A great benefit of having your own business is that you get to make your own hours. So it's possible to leave work at 3:00, coach your kids' Little League until 5:00, have dinner with your family, and come back to the office until 9:00. You need to set your priorities and work your schedule around them. Don't let anybody tell you it can't be done.

It Takes a Good Chunk of Time to Start Up a Business

I've already told you that starting your own business takes a lot of time. Once you're up and running, the idea is to find other good people and train them to do tasks like bookkeeping, sales, and shipping. When you're just getting started, however, you need to be around to either do everything or make sure someone else is doing it the way you want it done. If you're going to start a business that will be successful, you're going to have to be there for it.

For real entrepreneurs, this isn't a problem.

If we didn't like to work, we wouldn't be entrepreneurs. Most of us relish the challenges and joys that are part of starting a business. If that means some long days, we understand that's part of the package.

Starting a business is exciting. It's exhilarating and fun, and it sure doesn't seem like work. It's easy to get caught up in it all and lose track of time. I can remember looking at the clock and being amazed at how much time had passed.

Especially when you're first starting out, there's a great temptation to put everything else to the side and devote 100% of your time and energy to your business.

It's impossible to say how many hours you'll need to spend working while you're getting your business off the ground. It depends on a lot of things, such as:

➤ The type of business you're starting. Obviously, starting a full-fledged manufac-turing company takes longer to set up and requires more "be-there" hours than a business selling newspapers on the street corner.

➤ How task-oriented and organized you are. If you're organized, know what has to be done, and start the task at 8:30 a.m., you'll need to spend less time at work than somebody who thinks about the chore for a while, goes to lunch, thinks about it some more, and finally gets around to starting the task at 2:30 in the afternoon.

➤ Your priorities. If your absolute top priority is to be a parent who spends time with your family, then you'll figure out a way to get your work done and get home to spend time with your kids. If your top priority is work, I can almost guarantee that the job will take longer.

Working long hours is fine, unless it affects the rest of your life negatively.

Finding Time for the Important Stuff

There are only 24 hours in a day. That's the way it is, and that's what you have to work with. Because making more hours isn't an option, you have to accomplish as much as you can during the time you have. To do that, you've got to decide what's important to you, and figure out how to make time for it.

Recently, I read about a woman who's a freelance wedding and portrait photographer. She said she works like hell for three weeks, and then takes the fourth week off. She refuses to schedule anything for the fourth week and spends it camping, hiking, traveling, or reading. This downtime has become so important to her that she lets nothing get in the way of it.

That sounds great, but the fact is, it wouldn't work for most of us. Still, this woman figured out a way to create some balance in her life, and you have to do the same.

Make a list of the things in your life that really matter to you. It probably includes your family, your friends, maybe your church or synagogue, an activity you really enjoy, a club you belong to, or an obligation you feel you have to keep.

Whatever is really important to you, that's what you've got to figure out how to fit into that 24-hour period called a day.

When I was getting The Vermont Teddy Bear Company up and running, I typically worked every day of the week. I didn't work all day every day, and some work could be done from home (I packed a lot of bears into boxes while watching *Cheers*). In the early stages, though, I still had the pushcart and was trying to oversee a small manufacturing plant, as well. It was a seven-day-a-week job, and it never got finished.

Over the Rainbow

I keep balance in my life by refusing to give up things that are important. When I'm at home in Burlington, for instance, I coach Little League. I'm absolutely passionate about Little League and would do anything necessary to stay with it. I also make it a point to spend time with friends, check in with my favorite restaurants and coffee shops, and shoot some hoops at the local YMCA. You've got to keep yourself grounded and in touch with familiar things that mean a lot to you.

Still, I always made time for the things that were most important to me. I loved leaving work to go home to my family. Whenever possible, if I took a day trip to visit gift shops and try to sell my bears, we'd all go. And despite being short on both time and money, we still managed to take vacations and have great times.

As I'm writing this book, I'm dividing my time between Vermont and Denver, where I'm helping with the startup of a company called American Performance Products, manufacturers of Luv Feet shoe inserts.

Because my kids are still in Vermont, making time for the important things is a bit more challenging. I do, though, because I wouldn't have it any other way. I fly home to spend time with them. I watch them play basketball, find out what's going on in school, and keep up with what's happening in their lives.

Work, Work, Work

For most entrepreneurs, finding time to work isn't a problem because work naturally tends to be a priority. Normally, it's not work that suffers because we're doing other things; it's other things that tend to suffer because we're working.

If you love your work—and I hope you do—you might end up feeling guilty. The guilt isn't because you're working too much; it's because you're having so much fun doing it that you don't want to quit. You might be seeing that your work is cutting too much into areas of your life, like the time you spend with family and friends.

Sometimes you have to be at work, and that's all there is to it. At those times, you have to hope your family will understand and your other commitments will wait. But if you get yourself organized, work hard while you're there, and delegate jobs when possible, you should be able to strike a balance between work and the other important things in your life.

Family and Flextime

The relationship between work and family has gotten a lot of attention in the past few years and has become widely recognized as an area that should be carefully monitored.

The University of Minnesota's Center for Corporate Responsibility came out recently with an extensive report on "The Work and Family Dilemma." The report addresses all kinds of issues relating to work and family and cites problems caused by the strain of trying to balance the two areas.

The work and family issue is alive and well in politics, too. The debate over whether to allow flextime instead of overtime pay for workers has been a political hot potato.

The federal government has been offering flexible work schedules to employees since 1978, but the private sector has been slower to jump on the bandwagon. Those in favor of allowing employees more flexible scheduling say that it cuts down tremendously on stress and makes workers more productive in the long run.

Those opposed to flexible scheduling say it cuts down on productivity and causes confusion and great disruption in the workplace. Personally, I think flextime is fine. Most of my employees at Vermont Teddy Bear were women, and I saw the great need they have for some flexibility in their work schedules. You need to have some guidelines, and they need to be responsible for getting their work done. I found, however, that flextime created peace of mind and made my employees more productive.

Bear Facts

Although there's strong disagreement among employers concerning flexible scheduling, employees who have it seem to be pretty much in agreement that it's a good thing. Eight out of ten government employees surveyed said they like the flextime program and want to see it continued.

Flextime is less of an issue for entrepreneurs just starting a business than not-enough time is. You can be as flexible as you want, but there are still only 24 hours in the day. When you're just starting out, there never seem to be enough hours to do everything you want to.

Don't let that discourage you. Remember when the baby was first born and you thought you'd never get another full night's sleep? Remember how quickly that time passed, though?

Finding family time is going to be up to you and your family. Believe me, though, it can be done. If you don't find time for your family, I guarantee you're going to be sorry later on. I've met too many entrepreneurs whose marriages have gone down the tubes, and whose relationships with their kids have suffered, because they were so obsessed with their work.

Tell 'Em

Let the people in your family know how important they are to you. Tell them. Even if it's hard for you to put into words how much your family means to you, keep trying. It will seem natural after the first few times.

Grizzly Area

As if the about-50% divorce rate that's the national average isn't bad enough, the rate among entrepreneurs tends to be even higher. In my opinion, this is directly attributable to the amount of time and energy we tend to put into our businesses instead of into our families. Watch out! It's an easy trap to fall into. Just remember that as much as you love your business, it will never love you as your spouse and kids do. They have needs, too, and you've got to be attentive to them.

As important as it is to tell them how you feel, it's just as important, and maybe more so, to show them. Here are a few suggestions for keeping in close touch with your family. See how many more you can come up with on your own.

➤ Live as close to work as possible. When I first started The Vermont Teddy Bear Company, we moved closer to Burlington. The time I didn't spend commuting was time I had at home with my family.

➤ Meet someplace for lunch or dinner. If you can't get home, ask your family to meet you someplace close to your shop.

➤ Schedule special events, and make sure you're there. Leave a note on the breakfast table in the morning, telling your kids to be ready to go at 7 p.m. Show up on time, and take everybody to a movie, ball game, or whatever.

➤ Attend school functions and sporting events when you can. Make a special effort to get to at least some of your kids' activities. Watch carefully while you're there, and make sure to talk to your kids about it later.

➤ Don't overschedule yourself. You can't coach Little League, be an active member of the PTA, take part in your church council, and serve as vice president of the Lion's Club, while still having the time you want with your family and running a business effectively. Pick one thing you really want to do, and let others handle the rest.

➤ Make special time for your husband or wife. Plan a surprise evening out at your favorite restaurant. Leave a small gift every now and then, and remember to say, "I love you."

These suggestions might sound obvious, but the temptation to devote all your time to starting a business can be very powerful—and very destructive.

When you're with your family, it's important to leave work behind as much as possible. It's no fun for your kids if you keep interrupting your hike in the woods to take calls on your cell phone. Unless there's a good reason you can't, leave it at home when you're with them.

Bear Facts

Even as an entrepreneur, I get annoyed when I'm having lunch or dinner with somebody who can't seem to go for more than 20 minutes without taking or making a call on a cell phone. I don't know, maybe it's just me. I can understand that once in a while these calls might be absolutely necessary. Much of the time, though, I suspect they're not.

Entrepreneurs tend to drift away from what they're doing and find themselves back at the office mentally. This, too, isn't fair to your family. They spend enough time without you. It's important that during the time you have together, you're really there.

The same ideas apply to friends as well as to family. You've got to make the time available to stay in touch. When you're in business, you can't always surround yourself with the kinds of people you'd choose to spend time with, so your friends should become increasingly important to you.

If you're lucky, you have good friends. If you're smart, you'll make time to keep in touch and maintain those friendships. Even when he was at the height of basketball stardom, Michael Jordan found time to hang out with a group of guys he'd been friends with for most of his life.

Jordan would check in frequently by phone, and whenever he could, he'd head back to North Carolina, where he grew up, for all-night card games and talk sessions with these guys. These are the guys who have kept him grounded and in touch with who he is.

It's important to remember and value the people who know you and accept you, just for who you are. As you spend more and more time in business, you'll realize how nice it is to be with somebody who's not asking for anything from you, except to be with you and have a good time.

Fun and Relaxation

Too often, we give up the things we like to do to make more time for work. It's a real temptation to do this, but I've found that in the long run, it doesn't pay off.

Because entrepreneurs get energy from their work, and find pleasure in their work, they often fail to distinguish work from leisure and relaxation. However, when you're working, you're always *on*. You're geared up and ready for whatever happens. Your adrenaline is flowing, and you're prepared to handle anything that comes along. You're running at full tilt, and you're loving it.

As much fun as you might have while you're working, you're not relaxing, and any doctor will tell you that downtime is important. You can't go at top speed all the time. It's like running your car without changing the oil. Sooner or later, it's going to result in big problems.

Take the time to relax. Make sure the time you spend with your family and friends is fun and relaxing for everybody. It's not going to be a fun—much less relaxing—day if your wife and kids hate to hike, but you insist on a family outing on the trail.

Over the Rainbow

When you manage to get some downtime, avoid the temptation to overschedule. It's tempting to try to cram everything into the few hours you have off. You want to spend time with your family, see some friends, take a run, and go through a stack of magazines that have piled up. Sometimes an afternoon by a swimming pool, drinking a beer or two and playing with your kids, is the better way to go.

Most fledgling business owners don't take vacation. It's not in their natures to step away from their "babies" or hand the reins over to somebody else for even a little while.

Over the Rainbow

If you can't get away for a vacation, take a mini-vacation. Try a weekend at the beach or mountains or even a day trip to a great amusement park or another favorite place. It's important to take some time, even if you feel like you'd rather not. Your kids will remember a terrific day at the amusement park a lot more than they'll remember your sales figures.

The trouble is, if you left a company with a generous vacation policy to start your own company, you and your family are probably somewhat spoiled. Let's face it: There are some nice perks about working for somebody else, and paid vacation is one of them. Now, I'm not saying you'll never be able to take a vacation while you have your own business. One of the goals of being an entrepreneur is to give yourself some flexibility. Still, the first few years are pretty tough when it comes to getting time off.

Did you ever meet a person who never has fun? Who always seems nervous and on edge? Some people don't know how to relax or have fun, and it's really a shame. They're not people that you like to be around, so make a point of taking time for fun and for being with the people you love. Not only will it keep your relationships healthy, but it also makes you a better worker. You need to step away from work occasionally to maintain perspective about it. A day or two away can recharge your batteries and make everything seem clearer and more manageable.

How's Your Health?

The previous section on fun and relaxation is a direct lead-in to this section, which deals with health. The two topics are undeniably related. How is your health, anyway?

Not to get too personal, but are you overweight? Do you exercise? Watch what you eat? Watch what you drink? Get enough sleep? I sound just like your mother, don't I?

Too often, entrepreneurs put health issues on the back burner, just as they do with family and other important things. If you're young and healthy, you can get away with that for a while. Eventually, though, ignoring your health catches up with you.

We've probably all heard more than we care to about stress, and I'm sure you've all had your share of it. It's hard to avoid stress these days. Our lives move fast, and we face a lot of demands and expectations, both from ourselves and from others.

Starting your own business isn't going to lighten your stress load, so you have to learn how to handle it. I can't tell you how to handle your stress because everybody does it differently. I don't think there's any magic formula for making stress disappear. And frankly, I think a lot of people, myself included, operate better under a moderate amount of stress. Experts have long said that we need a certain amount of stress to keep us moving and productive and excited about life. That's the good stress—the kind that makes us excited about what we're doing and propels us from our warm, comfy beds in the morning. But there's no doubt that too much of the bad kind of stress drags you down.

When I was first starting my company, I used to give blood every 8 weeks, and I still donate as often as I can. In addition to doing something good for somebody else, donating blood is beneficial to the donor. Every time I gave blood, I had my blood pressure and pulse measured. My blood was checked to make sure I wasn't anemic, and several other checks were conducted. I always felt like I was getting a free, mini-physical exam each time I showed up to donate. It made me feel good and relieved any anxiety I had to know that my blood pressure and the other things they checked were fine.

Bear Facts

The National Institute for Occupational Safety and Health estimates that 90% of American workers claim they encounter big-time stress in the workplace at least once or twice a week. The American Institute of Stress in Yonkers, New York, estimates that between 75 and 90% of all visits to primary care physicians are stress related.

Typical symptoms of too much stress (the bad kind) include headaches, backaches, insomnia, depression, overeating, or alcoholism and drug abuse. Too much stress can make it hard to get up in the morning or make you short-tempered with your family and friends. It can take away your enthusiasm and make life seem like a drag.

Experts say that men are usually less sensitive than women to the early signs of stress, which means they tend to not do anything about them. A couple of aspirin in the afternoon and a martini or two at the end of day keeps the stress at bay—or so we think.

If left untreated, stress can contribute to problems such as heart attacks and strokes. I can't tell you how to handle stress, but I will advise you to take steps to combat it. You can find stress-busting recommendations in any magazine, but here are a few that I like:

➤ Ride a bike or walk to work, if it's feasible. Biking sometimes doesn't take much more time than driving, and it's a great way to get rid of stress. If it's impractical to bike or walk to work, try it on the weekends or after work.

Grizzly Area

Take a good look in the mirror sometime when you're under a lot of stress. Chances are you look awful. There's no doubt that stress has direct physical results, and if you don't learn to handle it, you'll pay dearly later in life.

➤ Shoot some hoops. There's nothing better in the middle of the day than working up a sweat on the basketball court. You'll go back to work with a new attitude.

➤ Meet a friend, spouse, brother, sister, whatever, for lunch, dinner, or a drink at the end of the day. Really focus on the person, and talk about anything but what you've been doing at work. Getting involved with another person's life tends to make you stop worrying so much about your own.

➤ Do something a little crazy or really fun. Go sledding with your kids, or take a ride in a convertible—top down, of course. Take a walk in the rain without an umbrella, or leave work early and go see the movie you've been dying to see, but haven't taken time for.

Even though women might handle stress a little better doesn't mean they're immune to it. No way. Most women who work, either for themselves or for someone else, still bear the lion's share of home and kid care. Things are getting better, but that's still the way it is.

You all know, I'm sure, what experts say are the most important things we can do to stay healthy. Don't smoke; get some exercise; stay away from fast food; drink in moderation, if at all; be happy; and get enough sleep.

Speaking of sleep, finding time to get enough of it is a problem for many entrepreneurs. As you know, starting a business uses up many of the allotted 24 hours we get in a day. By the time you do the other things you have to do, there often isn't much time left over for snoozing. You can go with less sleep for a while, and some people don't ever need much. Most of us, though, feel the results if we shortchange ourselves on sleep for more than a couple of days.

I know you've heard those stories about Thomas Edison sleeping only 3 hours a night, but not many of us have Tom's capacity to operate well on just a few hours of shut-eye.

I've read all kinds of stuff about how you can hypnotize yourself to drop immediately into a deep sleep and skip the part where you're sort of drifting off. If you go immediately into deep sleep, the theory is that you need a lot less because it's better quality. So you can stay up later, get up earlier, and still feel well rested.

Never having tried this deep sleep self-hypnosis trick, I can't say whether it works. I suspect a lot of us don't need to hypnotize ourselves to fall into a deep sleep at the end of a long day. To me, sleep is the perfect way to get away from all the pressure and stress, and it comes very easily.

Over the Rainbow

Everybody has their own sleeping habits, whether or not they're starting up a business. I think it's a mistake to try to stick to someone else's sleep schedule. Each person's body is different and requires different amounts of sleep. I tend to stay up for a while and then crash. Other people I know make sure they get a certain amount of sleep every night. It all depends on what works for you.

Keep in mind that starting a business is intense, but things do level off after you have it up and running. Again, you can compare the process of starting a business to that of having and raising a baby. If you have kids, you no doubt remember those first few months, when sleep was a precious, and extremely limited, commodity.

It will probably be the same way when you're starting your business. You'll be going at full speed, and there simply will be less time for sleeping and other leisure activities. But it won't last forever. Remember how fast the baby grew up? And remember that the payoff is well worth the effort.

Take a Look at Your Daily Routine

What's your daily routine like? Maybe you're one of those folks who likes everything to be predictable. You know—breakfast at 7:00, lunch at noon, the gym at 6:00, and dinner at 8:00. Or maybe you don't have much of a routine at all. Maybe you end up having dinner at 10:00 much of the time, just because you didn't get to it before that. If your daily routine is important to you, try to keep it as close to normal as you can.

But understand that running a business results in a lot of surprises and situations that have to be handled at the moment they occur. Sometimes those situations happen just as you're getting ready to leave for the gym.

You can try for a routine, but you're going to have to be flexible. Again, things will probably calm down after your business is up and running. Still, owning a business is sort of like being a doctor or a minister. You're pretty much always on call.

Establishing Priorities and Sticking to Them

If your daily bike ride is what keeps you sane and grounded, then it should be a high priority in your life. You should do your ride—every day—come hell or high water. Obviously, you don't want to cancel appointments so you can go biking, but if it's important to you, get up an hour earlier and bike to work, or take an hour off at noon to get out.

You're going to have to set priorities and stick to them. Certainly, a lot of those priorities will be related to your work. That's necessary, and the way it is. Your family time should be a priority that's not to be messed with. If your church or synagogue is important to you, then set time there as a priority.

Only you can decide where your priorities lie and what they are, but it's important to know your priorities well so that you can structure your life around them. That's not to say there won't be times when you absolutely can't make it to church or days when your family time gets shortened because of an emergency.

On the other hand, there might be days when work gets put aside because of a family emergency, or you take an extra-long lunch break to spend some time with your husband or wife.

Bear Facts

A book with great insights into prioritizing, as well as all kinds of other issues, is *The One-Minute Manager* by Kenneth H. Blanchard. I think every entrepreneur should read this book. It's not long, and it's fast and easy to read. It's available in almost any bookstore or online from both Amazon.com and barnesandnoble.com.

Because of limited time, the priorities you set have to be the things that *must* get done, as opposed to things you'd *like* to get done. If possible, recruit somebody else to do things like mow your grass or clean your house. These tasks can get to be distractions that interfere with your priorities.

When Work Gets To Be a Problem

I've already established that entrepreneurs love to work. An entrepreneur who hates work is like a doctor who can't stand the sight of blood. It can't be.

Entrepreneurs get a kick out of working, and they think it's fun. They work a lot because they have to, and they don't mind doing it because they see their work as the way they can reach their goals and realize their dreams.

Some people, though, *must* work. Their whole sense of self-worth is based on their jobs. Even when they're not physically at work, their minds are there. They are the true workaholics.

Loving to work and having to work are two different matters. If you can go home from work and enjoy the time you have with your family and friends, you don't have a problem. If you resent your family and friends because they take time away from your work, you'd better take a close look at your attitude and priorities.

If working long hours is causing problems at home, but you think the hours are necessary, you have to try to resolve the problem. Explain to your family exactly what you need to do in a day, and try to give them a better understanding of how you spend your time. Be sensitive to their needs and feelings, but try to make them understand yours, too.

Don't let your family make you feel guilty about working long hours, if the hours are necessary to make the business successful. Explain that you won't always have to spend so much time away from home and that the business you're starting will benefit everyone in the family.

If the work issue becomes a major problem, look for a counselor who deals with such issues, and get some help. No business is worth losing your family.

Bear Facts

A good book came out a few years ago that deals with the topic of workaholics and how they can cope with the condition. Written by Barbara Killinger, a psychologist, the book is called *Workaholics: The Respectable Addicts*.

The Least You Need to Know

➤ There are limited hours in every day, so you need to make the most of your time and accomplish all you can. Be productive and organized to make sure you get done what needs to be done.

➤ It's important not to fall into the "work is all that matters" trap and to make time for all the things that count in your life.

➤ When you're spending time with family and friends, give them your attention and leave your cell phone at home.

➤ Work might be fun, but it's important to have some downtime in which you can relax, too.

➤ Know how to recognize signs of stress, and take steps to relieve it before it takes a toll on your health.

➤ Because of ever-changing demands, entrepreneurs often find it difficult to establish a daily routine. It's to your advantage to remain flexible.

➤ You need to know and understand your priorities, and do everything you can to stick to them.

➤ No business is worth losing your family and friends; if your work is causing problems, figure out what you can do about it, or get some help.

Chapter 5

The Ups and Downs of Entrepreneurship

In This Chapter

➤ Good days and bad days.

➤ Entrepreneur success stories.

➤ The pluses and minuses of making lots of money.

➤ Responsibility is part of the entrepreneurial package.

➤ Social responsibility is definitely a two-way street.

➤ Handling the job of being your own boss.

As with everything in life, there are ups and downs to being an entrepreneur. Good days and bad days, highs and lows. Every now and then, something happens that makes it perfectly obvious that quitting your job with the XYZ Company and starting your own business was the best thing you've ever done. Other days, you might think you must have been out of your mind to do such a stupid thing. That boss you couldn't stand might end up looking pretty darned good some days.

I hope there will be more good days than bad days and many more highs than lows. It's important to maintain a sense of perspective and remember that highs and lows are part of the package with any endeavor—not just with being self-employed. Highs and low happen in marriages, when you work for somebody else, and even with your health.

When you get discouraged, and at times you will, just keep thinking that things will get better. Studies have proved that positive people are more successful, not to mention happier, than those who are always negative.

Let's have a look at some of the ups and downs of being an entrepreneur. I think you'll conclude that the ups far outweigh the downs. Once you get the hang of it, you'll find that entrepreneuring has a lot more peaks than valleys.

Making Money—Lots of Money

One of the reasons you started your own business, or want to start your own business, is to make money, right? And you hope you're going to make a lot of money.

The entrepreneurial world is full of success stories about people who had ideas and the guts and brains to make them work. Take Gardenburgers, for instance. Paul Wenner, a chef, came up with Gardenburgers, a meatless alternative to hamburgers, in 1985. In a year, he had deals with 70 restaurants to sell his product. Today, Gardenburgers can be found on the menus at more than 40,000 restaurants, and Gardenburger is a $500 million company.

On a smaller, but no less successful, scale, consider the story of Thanh Quoc Lam, a Vietnamese refugee who tried for 4 years to leave the oppression of his home country. Finally, after paying off some government people, he and some family members were permitted in 1979 to join others on a crowded boat for Malaysia. They spent 9 months in a refugee camp there before the Red Cross helped them get to San Jose, California.

The Word According to John

Wealth is a subjective thing. I know businesspeople who don't consider themselves wealthy, even though they're multimillionaires. Wealthy, to them, is Bill Gates and his 40 or so billion dollars. On the other hand, I know people who get a couple of hundred thousand dollars in the bank, or even a couple of thousand dollars, and think they're about as wealthy as an Arab sheik. It's all in what you perceive wealth to be.

Once in the United States, Lam wasted no time in learning to speak English and finding work. After a series of low-paying jobs, he got a job driving people from San Jose to Reno, Nevada, for gambling. He soon started organizing his own tours and making sandwiches for customers to eat during the drive.

It took too much time to make the sandwiches, so Lam started buying them from another Vietnamese businessman, Le Vo. When competition in the tour business got heavy, Lam got out, and joined Vo in the bakery and sandwich shop business. Today, they have a chain of sandwich shops and a wholesale French bakery in Honolulu. Their yearly sales are more than $4 million.

In my case, my first business, The Vermont Teddy Bear Company, had a slow start, but took off after 5 years with phenomenal growth. I opened my teddy bear cart in 1983, and my sales for that year were $35,000. That wasn't great, or even good, but it seemed okay to me because I loved being in business. When the company opened its first sewing shop in 1984, sales for that year hit $200,000. That was better, but we had a lot more expenses, and we still weren't making much money. By 1985, our sales were at $400,000. They fluctuated between $300,000 and $400,000 from 1985 until 1989, and I was losing my shirt. I couldn't think of any way to make more money or to cut expenses, and times were pretty tough. We struggled along, finally hitting the half-million-dollar sales mark in 1989. We were still losing money—big time.

Then we changed some things—specifically, the way we were marketing our product (much more about that in Chapter 15, "Marketing and Sales") and the kinds of bears we were making. That's when realized I hadn't known exactly what my customers wanted. I thought I knew, but I was wrong. Primarily because of those changes, our sales in 1990 were at $1,900,000. In 1994, my last year as chief executive officer with The Vermont Teddy Bear, our sales reached $20,500,000, and we had an evaluation of $100 million when we went public.

In 10 years, I'd gone from working 80 hours a week with practically no financial return, to running a multimillion-dollar, publicly held company. That was a wild and crazy decade!

What's Good About Making Money?

Making a lot of money is good because it gives you great freedom. You have a lot more choices when you have money than when you don't.

You might get into a business that allows you to make a fabulous salary soon after you start up. If so, good for you. I didn't make much money at all in the beginning, and the most I ever paid myself was $80,000 a year. But I thought that was great because it gave me a level of comfort I hadn't had before.

I built a nice house for my family in an area with good schools. We traded in my '78 Chevy van for a Voyager van, which I loved because it had seat belts and I felt my family would be safe riding in it. I could take my kids on some neat trips and go out to dinner when we wanted to. I even bought a used boat for outings on Lake Champlain. I was able to pay my bills without worrying. If the van needed repairs, I didn't have to wonder where the money to pay for them would come from. We were very comfortable, and I thought I was very rich.

In addition to being a personal plus, money—obviously—is great for your business. It gives you the luxury of not having to sweat too much when something goes wrong and requires capital. It also gives you options, just as it does in your personal life.

Over the Rainbow

Don't be in too big of a rush to get everything you've always wanted the minute you start making a little money. I built a nice home in a neighborhood full of $300,000 houses. My house cost $100,000. When I made more money, we added on to it. We'd always wanted a boat, so we bought one—except we bought a used one and took out a loan to get it. Start out small, but have confidence in your future.

Many entrepreneurs, like myself, thrive on the challenge of setting up a business and getting it running. I loved running my own company, too, but I quickly realized that I didn't want to spend the rest of my life as a manager. I wanted to start another company or at least be involved with the startup of another company. Fortunately, I had the money to be able to do that.

Money gives you choices. Once your business is successful and bringing in lots of money, you might choose to sell it and start another business. You might choose to stay involved with the business, but get your cash out to use it for another venture.

The point is, you can choose what you want to do, because you have money to back up your choice.

Another thing about making a lot of money is that it helps you be confident you can do it again. When you've started a business and made a lot of money from it, you don't have the same doubts when you go out to try it again as you did the first time.

What's Bad About Making Money?

If you don't have money, it's hard to imagine there's a downside to having it, but there is. Lots of downsides, actually.

Did you ever hear the statistics about people who win the lottery or get a lot of money some other way? Those people have all kinds of problems, starting from just about the day their numbers come up.

Relatives you think would be happy for the winner often are incredibly jealous and resentful. Sometimes they're downright mean. Many of the winners end up divorced, depressed, and in counseling. They have no idea how to handle a large amount of money, and some begin to fear for their safety or the safety of their children. Many of these winners say they were happier before they won.

Bear Facts

A classic example of a lottery winner gone bad is William "Bud" Post, of Oil City, Pennsylvania. Bud was a cook with a traveling circus before he won $16.2 million in a jackpot lottery in 1988. Five years later, Bud was broke. Furthermore, his brother was in jail for allegedly hiring a hit man to murder Bud and Bud's *sixth* wife, so that he could collect the lottery money. Bud lost a lot of friends and family members who felt they were entitled to Bud's money; he'd tried a couple of business ventures that failed, and an ex-girlfriend sued him. Some winner, huh?

Studies show (why do we need studies to tell us what's so perfectly obvious?) that impoverished people generally aren't happy people. They have all kinds of worries and fears that people with money don't. Some include:

➤ Not having enough food for themselves and their families

➤ Not being able to pay for medical treatment when they need it

➤ Losing the place where they live and becoming homeless

➤ Not having adequate clothing

If you give people with these worries enough money to ensure a decent standard of living, they'll be much happier than they were without money. But studies show that once people have everything they need, having a lot of money doesn't ensure greater happiness.

Bear Facts

I remember watching Johnny Carson on the *Tonight Show* when he was going through one of his divorces. I often think about what he said, which was something like "When you have money, people think you have no problems. All money means is that you don't have money problems. You still have all the others."

Sure, money gives you the opportunity to get toys. You trade in your Jeep for a Mercedes four-wheel-drive and buy a bigger boat, a bigger TV, more jewelry, more clothing, more of this, and more of that.

So you have more, bigger, and better stuff. However, because happiness comes from within, not from the stuff you buy, you'll be no better off. After the thrill of possession wears off, you're right back to where you started.

Some people say it's impossible to get a lot of money and remain the same person you were before you had it. I don't think that's necessarily true, but it's clear many people do change after they acquire a lot of money.

Some decide they need new friends and bail out on their old ones. Some go crazy and buy everything they can get their hands on. Others become suspicious, thinking that people are after their money or want to be around them only because they have money.

Surely, not every one you know is trying to get a hand in your pocket, but it's important to know there are people who want your money. Friends or relatives might want a little help getting started in businesses of their own. Every cause in town may hit you up for a handout, and all kinds of moneymaking schemes will become available for your investment.

Bear Facts

I know a woman who inherited well over a million dollars. It completely changed the way she looked at life and drastically changed her. She had a small business, which she immediately got rid of. She took up tennis, and then quit. She took up golf, and then quit that. She bought a condo in Arizona, and then sold it. She bought an apartment in Chicago, but decided she didn't like the city. She traveled, but got tired of it. She left her husband, saying he worked too much and was no fun. She completely lost her focus in life when she came into this money and became extremely discontented and unhappy.

I think it's important to support causes you believe in and to help out where you can, but only you can decide how much and to whom you'll give your money. Don't let any person or group pressure you into giving money when you don't want to. Remember, you've got to take care of your family and yourself first before you start giving money to any group or organization.

If you make a lot of money, especially if you make it fast, there's the possibility you'll get caught up in the excitement of having it. Sometimes money becomes too much of a priority and gets in the way of what's really most important.

Having money is good. Letting it become the most important thing in your life is bad.

How Others Might Perceive You

In our society, money gives you status. I know, I know—it shouldn't. But it does. Right or wrong, our society uses money as a measure for a lot of things. We assume—not always correctly—that a person with a lot of money is a successful person. We think people with money must be happy, although we know that's often not the case. We tend to gauge intelligence, power, and worth by how much money somebody has.

So when you make a lot of money, you get a status boost in the eyes of many people. Suddenly, you're a successful businessperson. People ask you for advice and want to be around you. It's an ego thing, and it's sort of fun. It doesn't last because you quickly catch onto the game and get tired of it. But it's sort of flattering when it first happens.

Although your money will impress some people, it will irritate others—generally the people who wish they had more money than they do and think they should have yours.

Bear Facts

Even entrepreneurs get jealous of each other. Karen Axelton, managing editor of *Entrepreneur's Business Start-Ups*, wrote a column about jealousy in the magazine's January edition. She recommends that the person having the envy attack use the object of her jealousy as a role model. That way, she can use the tactics of the successful entrepreneur and become successful herself. Good advice!

Some people, regardless of how hard you've worked, won't give you any credit for having earned your money. They'll say you are lucky, were in the right place at the right time, or something like that. Generally, it's because they're jealous, they don't understand what you've done, or they heard someone say something about you.

I know some people hinted that the only reason I was successful at business is because I'm Sicilian and had "connections." People look at those fortunate enough to go to good schools and say that their success was handed to them, that they didn't have to earn it. But anyone who has a successful business had to have worked hard to make it that way. These kinds of comments are nothing you should worry about. When your business is successful, enjoy the success for yourself and for your family, and don't waste your time worrying about what other people might say.

Responsibilities of an Entrepreneur

Responsibility is an integral—and inescapable—part of being an entrepreneur. The minute you open a business, you become responsible to your community. When you hire employees, you become responsible to them, and you continue to be responsible to your family, just as you were when you worked for someone else. Now, however, you don't have an employer to depend on for a paycheck, a paid vacation, or health insurance. It's all up to you.

Good entrepreneurs understand their responsibilities and accept them happily. Responsibility is just part of the package when you own your own business. If you don't enjoy responsibility or resent being responsible for others, you'd do well to re-evaluate your motives for wanting to be an entrepreneur.

Bear Facts

Entrepreneurs must be responsible in many ways. They're responsible for selling the best products and services they can make, not something that doesn't work or is potentially harmful. They're responsible for seeing that their employees get their paychecks because they have families to care for. They are responsible for not causing damage to the environment. You take on a lot of responsibility when you become an entrepreneur.

If, on the other hand, you understand that being an entrepreneur and being responsible are inseparable, you're headed in the right direction.

Responsibilities to Your Family

In most cases, the members of your family count on you to provide for them. I'm sure there are entrepreneurs out there who have spouses with incomes that could easily support the entire family or who have income from other sources. They could get along just fine without their businesses earning a cent. Most of us, though, are in business to make money and to give our families the lifestyles we want them to have.

We want to be able to pay for braces when the orthodontist says little Becky needs them. We want to be able to send our kids to good schools or to summer camps, or take them to Disney World.

If you think this puts some pressure on you, you're right. There *is* pressure involved in supporting a family, but it doesn't apply just to entrepreneurs. People who work for someone else also are responsible for providing for their families, and they, too, can feel pressured.

Bear Facts

Losing a job and feeling you're incapable of supporting your family can be major causes of depression for both men and women, experts say, because you feel that you've failed to meet your responsibilities.

Sometimes, though, when you work for somebody else, it's a little bit easier. You can count on getting a specific amount of money handed to you at a specific time. Your employer gives you health insurance or at least helps with your health insurance costs. Maybe you have a dental plan. You get 3 weeks of paid vacation time each year and a couple of days off at Christmas. You have a 401K plan that's helping out with college money.

When you're on your own, raising a business, you can't always count on those things. If you want health insurance, you've got to find it and pay for it yourself. You've got to set up your own retirement funds and make sure the money gets into them. It's all up to you now, but still, your family is depending on you.

It's important to plan for things and make sure your finances are on sure footing before you start your business. Find a professional you trust, and go over your financial position. Make sure you know exactly what you have and where it is. Don't overlook retirement accounts, bonds, and other assets.

Responsibility to Your Employees

If you think your responsibility to your employees ends when you hand them their paychecks, you'd better think again. You're responsible to your employees in more ways than you might realize.

I'm not saying that the responsibility is all yours—your employees have to hold up their end of the deal, too. But if they're doing the jobs they were hired to do, you're responsible for seeing that they're compensated and treated fairly, that their working environment is safe and pleasant, and that they are treated with dignity.

In addition to compensation, which includes benefits like insurance and paid vacation time, I believe an employer is responsible for giving employees pleasant working conditions, respect, and chances for advancement.

I'll get into this in much greater detail in Chapter 19, "Employees," which is all about dealing with employees. Suffice it to say, however, that I strongly believe business owners should treat their employees with the same respect they ask from them and, within reason, do whatever they can to make the job experience enjoyable and rewarding.

Over the Rainbow

I am deeply committed to treating employees well, both because I think they deserve it and because it's good for business. At The Vermont Teddy Bear Company, my employees were mostly women. When we built a new factory, the women had a say in what should be included, and I listened to them. We put in a lot of bathrooms and lights in the parking lot for when they left work at night. There were lots of windows so employees could look out at the mountains and a soft surface on the floor instead of cement, which is hard on the feet and legs. These things added some expense, but my employees were appreciative, and they showed it by giving me their best work. It fostered great loyalty.

Responsibility to Your Community

Any entrepreneur who doesn't feel some responsibility toward his or her community is going to have trouble.

Take a look around your community, and think about who supports its organizations, clubs, and activities. Local business owners typically are active in their communities, and for good reason. Being involved with your community does many things, including the following:

➤ Creates good will. It's a lot easier to operate a business in a harmonious community than one where every move is monitored, criticized, and challenged. Unhappy community members can make it impossible to operate a successful business.

➤ Helps keep the community strong. Business owners' participation and support help communities thrive and remain healthy. Being involved also creates a sense of togetherness and cohesiveness within a community.

➤ Provides a good climate in which to do business. A strong, healthy community with a good economy is a much better place to have a business than one that's sick and failing. It's definitely beneficial to help a strong community stay strong.

➤ Ensures that you're in on decision making. Being involved with your community ensures you know what's going on and gives you a say when issues arise. Nothing is more irritating than a person who refuses to get involved until he's directly affected by a situation, and then tries to take charge.

➤ Gives you credibility. Entrepreneurs who are involved in and who serve their communities generally are respected and admired. They have credibility, and people listen to their ideas and concerns.

Some entrepreneurs choose to donate money to different organizations within their communities. Others give their time. There are some fun and innovative way of becoming involved in your community, even if you don't have a lot of money to contribute. Consider some of these suggestions:

➤ Be a mentor.

➤ Create internships in your company for local high school or college students.

➤ Donate your product or service to an area event.

➤ Be active in local environmental groups.

➤ Get your employees involved in community efforts such as blood drives.

➤ Coach a Little League team.

➤ Sponsor a Little League team.

➤ With your employees, take responsibility for cleaning up a section of highway or portion of a creek.

It doesn't have to cost a lot of money to have a high level of community involvement. The Vermont Teddy Bear Company never gave much money to groups or organizations, but we gave a lot of time—and a lot of bears. We made special bears and sold them to the Vermont State Police at below cost so each trooper could keep a bear in his or her car and use it to comfort children. Any organization could call and request bears, and we'd give them. We gave bears to hospitals. I'd go into schools and show kids how the bears were made.

The stairway in Burlington's public parking garage was painted a horrible shade of green. Everybody complained about it. I know a woman who does murals, and The Vermont Teddy Bear Company paid her to turn the staircase into a giant aquarium that everyone loved.

There are many examples of socially responsible companies in the United States that contribute to their communities. Some notable ones are Ben and Jerry's, Starbucks, Stonyfield Farms, The Gap, IBM, and Levi-Strauss.

Most entrepreneurs tend to be socially minded, and when they are, everyone benefits. Remember that social responsibility is a two-way street; you usually end up taking as much as you give.

Being Your Own Boss

I don't think there's anyone who doesn't want to be his or her own boss—at least sometimes. Even when you have a boss you like and can work with effectively, there's definitely an appealing aspect to calling your own shots. Of course, you're never really your own boss. You're always responsible to somebody or something—like the bank, or your stockholders. Well, you know what I mean.

As with most things, there are ups and downs to being your own boss. An interesting thing is that the ups for some people are the downs for others. For example, Nancy thinks it would be great to be her own boss because then she'd be in charge of everything, but the idea of being the final word on everything scares Jack to death.

Over the Rainbow

As the business owner, you have to take the lead in getting your employees involved in community events and causes. I used to go with any employee who wanted to donate blood. We made an event of it by going out to lunch afterward. If you expect your employees to represent your company in a walkathon or another event, you'd better plan to be there, too.

Grizzly Area

When you're first starting your business, you'll have limited time for community involvement. You should be aware of the issue and sensitive to it, but understand that most of your involvement will occur later on. If you focus too heavily on community involvement early on, your company could suffer, and you won't be able to afford to be socially responsible. Sure, you should do what you can, but don't push it too much.

Bear Facts

A poll conducted by Louis Harris and Associates showed that 67% of working Americans dream of being their own bosses, to the point where they've seriously considered working for themselves.

Some of the Good Stuff

For me, being my own boss is great. There's no one I'd rather have telling me what to do, and if I screw up, there's no one but myself to blame.

Don't think, however, that I don't look to many other people for advice and guidance. Being my own boss doesn't mean I know more about everything than anyone else. It just means that I'm the one responsible for the final decisions and the ultimate success or failure of my business.

Many people like not being accountable to anyone else in terms of their work hours. They think they can show up and leave whenever they want to, without anyone bothering them about it. Although being your own boss does allow you flexibility in that regard, you're still accountable to others. You need to be around for meetings or to help solve problems or get a situation taken care of. You can, however, sneak off for a haircut or a lunch date occasionally.

Some of the Bad Stuff

I have a partner who loves being his own boss, but he isn't always very good at it. He'll leave the office in the middle of the day to visit a gift shop, taking the person who answers phones with him. He makes deposits and doesn't tell anybody, screwing things up for the person in charge of deposits. He comes and goes as he pleases, so we don't know where he is. And he's quick to criticize employees for mistakes, but can't understand why his employees don't stick around for very long.

Having the privilege of being flexible because you're the boss is great—but taking advantage of it and making things difficult for your employees or partners isn't.

You have to have a good amount of self-discipline to be a good boss. You also have to do some unpleasant things.

You sometimes have to fire people. Sometimes you need to confront them about sensitive issues, like their personal hygiene. Sometimes you need to pull an employee aside and tell her she needs to get some help for a drinking problem.

Bear Facts

We had few rules at The Vermont Teddy Bear Company, but employees knew the ones that were there were meant to be followed. I hated having to fire someone, but I knew it wasn't fair to the employees who were working hard and following the rules to let someone stay who wasn't willing to do those things.

Being your own boss means that the worries about things like the payroll, the bills, and the long-range plans are all yours.

Some people are better at being their own bosses than others. To be good at it, you've got to be willing to accept ultimate responsibility for everything concerning your business. That's a big problem for some people, and it can causes difficulties within their businesses.

What probably bothers more people than anything else about being their own boss is that it's difficult to get away from it. You tend to carry your work and responsibilities with you, in a briefcase, on a laptop computer, or in your head.

As with any job—and with nearly anything in life—there are good things and bad things about being an entrepreneur. Most of us find out that the good things far outweigh the bad, and you should expect that you will, too.

The Least You Need to Know

➤ There are ups and downs to nearly everything; being an entrepreneur is no exception.

➤ Making a lot of money is great, but there can be some drawbacks.

➤ Responsibility is a fact of life for entrepreneurs.

➤ Most entrepreneurs share a sense of social responsibility and a desire to give back to their communities.

➤ Being an entrepreneur means you get to be your own boss, but you've got to make sure you can handle the job.

➤ Being your own boss doesn't mean you can be inconsiderate or irresponsible to your business or employees.

Chapter 6

Being the Best at Whatever You'll Be

In This Chapter

➤ Making the most of the qualities and skills you have.

➤ Working to improve the areas that need it.

➤ Commitment is important for its own sake.

➤ Hanging in there when times get tough.

➤ Maintaining perspective on problems.

➤ Preparing for everything makes everything easier.

➤ Making your dream come true.

We've had a lot of general discussion about what's involved with being an entrepreneur. Pretty soon, I'll get into more specific issues, such as choosing the business that works for you, writing a business plan, finding the people you'll work with, and other areas. This last chapter of Part 1, however, deals with some of the more idealistic aspects of being an entrepreneur.

It covers, among other topics, the importance of doing your best at whatever you do and being committed to what matters in your life. Many factors are involved in being an entrepreneur. There are the financial aspects, the managerial aspects, and all those practical issues we're going to be discussing in later chapters. There are the less concrete aspects of being an entrepreneur, too, such as keeping your faith in what you're doing when times get tough and remembering that your life is more than your work. Those are the types of issues I'll be dealing with in this chapter—so let's get started.

Reaching Inside for the Best Parts of You

No matter what kind of business you end up running, how long you stay with it, or what you move on to afterward, there are a couple of things you've got to try to do all the time.

You've got to hang in there and do your best, whether your business is flying high or looking like it'll be shut down by the end of the day. Being an entrepreneur is not a job for quitters. It's a job for people who can face the biggest problems with confidence and figure out a way to fix them.

Expect that having your own business will be great. You'll wake up every morning and wonder what will happen that day. You'll be anxious to get to work to see what's going on. You'll have more fun than you ever thought work could be.

But (you knew that was coming, didn't you?) there will be times when you wonder how you'll make it through the day. Those are the times when you've got to reach inside yourself for the best parts of you and put them to work. If you keep the right attitude, even the problems that are inherent to owning a business can be fun. Challenges are fun, don't you think? Well, problems are just challenges. They're just things that need to be solved.

Remember when Ross Perot ran for president back in 1992? He bought a whole lot of airtime for his infomercials and talked about how he was going to bring the country back to its glory days through good old-fashioned hard work. One line he used all the time has stayed in my mind. He must have liked this line because he used it a lot. He'd say, "It's gonna be tough—but it's gonna be fun."

Perot could have been talking about being an entrepreneur, as well as his plans to fix up the country. That line, "It's gonna be tough—but it's gonna be fun," pretty well sums up this venture you're entering into.

No matter how much education you've had, or what schools you've attended, or how much money you have, if you can't think on your feet, solve problems, and keep a sense of perspective about what you're doing, you'll have a lot of trouble as an entrepreneur. You need to be able to think outside the boundaries and look past what you've been taught. Don't let anybody tell you something can't be done, just because it's never been done before.

The Word According to John

To my way of thinking, *mainstream education* is a process that trains people to be good workers. It teaches them skills needed to perform certain tasks. It doesn't, however, teach them to be entrepreneurs. Entrepreneurs learn (usually on their own) to think and reason and be practical managers—not to perform tasks and be good workers.

Give It Your Best

What I'd like for you to do right now is decide that no matter what happens while you're starting and running your business, you'll always give it your best shot. You're going to invest a lot of time, sweat, guts, and heart into this business venture, whatever it may be. It deserves everything you can give it.

All kinds of books are available today about reaching your potential, being the best you can be, not sweating the small stuff, habits of effective people—you've seen them. Maybe you've read some of them. Those books are great, if you take something useful from them. Sometimes they help you see things or think about issues that you ordinarily wouldn't.

More important than the stuff in those books, though, is the stuff that's in you.

Bear Facts

I've met a lot of people since starting my first business. I've met celebrities, businesspeople, very wealthy people, even the president and vice president of the United States! The best people I've met are those with strong characters, who inspire your trust and care deeply about causes and other people. They're the people who get involved with their communities and try to make the world a better place.

In the first chapter, I talked about desirable qualities and skills for entrepreneurs and picked two—persistence and confidence—as being the most important. Persistence is the most important quality. It's what makes you keep trying when you're tired or when things aren't going the way you'd like them to. It gives you the strength to overcome the biggest problems that come up and to keep your dreams alive.

Confidence, the second most important quality, is necessary for you to believe in yourself and your dream, especially when others are questioning it. The other traits I mentioned in Chapter 1, "Having a Dream and Making It Work," were the following:

➤ Good communications skills. They are essential to any job, whether or not you're an entrepreneur. People who can communicate effectively have an easier time getting what they want. Think about how vital communication is for a baseball team, for instance. All kinds of communication is happening when baseball players are on the field. They're communicating with each other and with their coaches. It's absolutely necessary to their game, as it is to all efforts that involve more than one person. Running a business requires setting up good communication systems and making sure they're followed.

➤ Some ego. Ego is tied in with confidence and believing in yourself. You've got to think you're good enough to get where you're going, even if nobody else seems to.

➤ A decent reputation. Nobody wants to work with someone who's known as a cheat or somebody out only for himself. Believe me, if you get that kind of reputation, it will spread.

➤ The ability to work with others. It's a lot easier to get along with other people than to always be working against them. Sometimes you've got to stand up for what you think is right, even if it's an upopular position. You can't let people walk all over you. On the other hand, the better you get along with people, the more friends you'll have, and you can never have too many friends.

➤ A fair amount of persuasion power. You're going to have to persuade people to lend you money, to support your idea, and to buy your product or service. A little persuasion power comes in mighty handy.

Now I'd like to add a few more helpful characteristics of entrepreneurs:

➤ The ability to think on your feet, reason, and make quick, sound decisions. These qualities are extremely important for an entrepreneur. Have you ever met somebody who finds it impossible to make a decision about anything? Indecisiveness can really hinder someone from doing much of anything, but there are a lot of people like that. They can take orders, but they have big trouble deciding anything on their own. Good entrepreneurs are able to look at a situation, make an assessment, and decide what to do about it, quickly.

➤ Being goal oriented. Being an entrepreneur is all about setting goals and meeting (or exceeding) them. You have daily goals, short-term goals, and long-range goals. All of these milestones are important to your business.

➤ Patience. You need to have patience because, inevitably, there are hold-ups and glitches that can drive you crazy if you're an impatient sort. On the other hand, too much patience can slow you down. You need to be able to wait— but not too long.

➤ Nerves of steel. Having your own business can test the nerves of the strongest entrepreneur. You'll feel sometimes as though your life is on the line (it's not, of course, but sometimes it seems so), and you've got to act like you're out for a stroll through the park. Good nerves are a definite plus!

➤ Faith. This quality is important. I believe that when things are good, you need to know you're getting help from someplace or something outside yourself. When things are bad, you need to believe they're going to get better. You need to have faith in all kinds of things, really—a higher power, yourself, your environment, your family and friends, and the belief that everything will work out and be okay.

Most people aren't blessed with every one of these qualities and skills. It would be nice if we all were, but it doesn't work that way. What you need to do is take full advantage of the good qualities you have and try to develop the ones you don't have. It's also important to be honest with yourself about negative qualities you might have and try to change them.

If you're extremely impatient, for instance, work a little harder on that area. It can be done. Characteristics such as this one are mainly habits, you know.

I have a friend who had a terrible habit of yelling at her kids and really losing it with them. She knew this was the pattern of her childhood, when her mother had yelled frequently at her and her siblings. She recognized it as being a habit that wasn't good, but she still yelled. This behavior was upsetting to her kids and to her. Often, she and the kids would all end up crying.

Over the Rainbow

It's not good to be overly self-absorbed, but you do need to take time every now and then for some introspection. If you don't do a little self-assessment of your strengths and weaknesses every now and then, you tend to let areas in which you could improve slide, and you might not give yourself credit for what you do well. Just as you would evaluate an employee, you should evaluate yourself now and then.

One day, she decided she wasn't going to do it anymore. She knew it was hurtful and served no purpose. When she felt the urge to yell at her kids, she left the room, regardless of what they were doing or what was going on. She learned to go to another room and take a deep breath, think things through, and then go back to her children. When she got back, she'd explain why they needed to stop what they were doing or otherwise handle the situation that had made her angry.

After a while, the new-and-improved calm-mom routine became her normal demeanor. Yelling isn't a habit anymore, and it rarely occurs. She lapses every now and then, but the situation is much better in her house. She relates better to the kids and certainly they relate better to her.

We all have areas that can use work. Some of us procrastinate, and others would rather make excuses than face up to a mistake. Some of us have trouble being on time for things; others find it difficult to meet new people. What we all need to do is concentrate on our good qualities as we work to improve the ones that need our attention. Reach way inside for the very best parts of you and use them to your advantage whenever you can.

Remaining Committed to What's Really Important

In the 1960s, everybody protested everything. In the '70s, we wore polyester. The '80s went down in history as the "me decade," when everybody looked out for himself or herself. During the '90s, people rediscovered commitment and started looking outward, past themselves.

I think we have a lot to look forward to as we enter the next century. Certainly, we'll see technology we never dreamed was possible. The economic forecast remains strong, and there's hope that the rest of the world will begin to share some of the comforts we've enjoyed in this country for so long.

I see many people trying hard to give something back to the community and the country that have been good to them. I see many people who are committed to making the world a better place for everyone.

Bear Facts

Folk singer and social activist Pete Seeger once said that the best people he knew were those who were committed to something. It didn't so much matter what; it was the sense of commitment that made them alive and interesting and the people he most liked to be around. Seeger said committed folks are those with "the live hearts, the live eyes, the live heads."

People are committed to all different kinds of causes and beliefs, and they demonstrate their commitment in different ways. Think about the causes currently out there: abortion rights and anti-abortion, gay rights, gun control, right to die, pornography, child abuse, treatment of elderly people, political oppression, the death penalty, and so forth. There are also smaller, everyday causes, such as helping out at the neighborhood youth center, coaching a kid's team, or being a homework mentor at the high school. The list of causes is neverending.

Some people are visible and outspoken about their commitments, and others work quietly and behind the scenes, seeking no recognition. Nearly everyone, however, has some sort of cause he or she believes in. It can be as personal and private as raising your own family in a particular manner, or as public and open as carrying signs in front of an abortion clinic.

I think that the cause or belief you're committed to is less important than being committed to something. It can be a community issue or something bigger, like gun control or the threat to the rainforests. Being committed to something makes a person interesting and forces her to deal with something other than her own life. My guess is that the really interesting people you know are those who take stands. They're the committed ones who aren't content to sit back and watch something they don't agree with pass unchallenged.

As much as you might be tempted to give up causes or, as you become busier and busier with work, lessen your commitments to what you're involved in—don't. Believe me, that's a big mistake. It's important to maintain a sense of perspective when you're running a business, and being involved with issues other than the business is what gives you that perspective.

It's easy to become wrapped up in the business and let it become the center of your world. It's an important part of your world, to be sure, but it shouldn't become the only part.

Owning a business gives you a great opportunity to be involved with your community and show your commitment to improving it. For example, Ben and Jerry's, the Vermont-based ice cream company, pays its workers for volunteer time within their communities. At The Vermont Teddy Bear Company, we held an Easter Egg hunt every year for the kids in the community. It was great fun, and most of the employees were happy to give some of their own time to help with it. Every now and then we had a community cartoon festival and donated the proceeds to the area food bank.

Grizzly Area

I've known a lot of people who get involved in so many things that they end up being ineffective in all of them. They join different organizations, but don't have time to truly get involved with any of them because they're spread way too thin. As a result, they end up standing around, not doing much of anything. It's much better to concentrate your time and energy on one activity or cause you really believe in, and let other people do the other things. If you get into too many things, you'll end up not being able to help with any of them.

There's a lot going on in life and a lot happening in this big world. To not get involved with some of it is to cheat yourself out of some great experiences and a chance to make a difference. Causes don't have to be difficult or complicated. Your cause might be as simple as mine—Little League. I'm absolutely committed to Little League because I think it does so much for kids and communities. I wholeheartedly support Little League, I coach Little League, I love Little League. When somebody tries to get me involved with another cause, and I know I don't have time to do it, I don't apologize or make excuses. I just say "My commitment is Little League. That's what I do."

Keeping the Dream in Sight When the Nightmares Begin

Having your own business won't always be a lot of laughs. I think you're well aware that there'll be tough times. You might encounter them right away. Maybe you'll have difficulty getting funding for the business, or have trouble with licensing, or something like that.

Bear Facts

Talk about having your back to the wall! The Vermont Teddy Bear Company at one point owed $300,000 to the IRS, and the IRS guys were none too friendly about it. It was around Christmas time, and the whole company was pretty depressed. We decided we'd hang in there for Christmas, which was a busy time when we stood to make good profits. After Christmas was Valentine's Day, our busiest time of the year. As bleak as things looked before that holiday season, we pulled through and came out the better for it. Don't give up!

Or you might sail right through the startup phase, but run into problems 5 years down the road. Believe me, I know all about making mistakes and having trouble with your business. I've been there, and it can be really discouraging.

When things are at their worst, you've got to pull out all your reserves of perseverance and keep going. Instead of focusing on the problems, focus on possible solutions. Accept the problem as it exists, and get busy figuring out a way to make it better.

Any problem can be solved. Try not to think of it as *your* problem, merely as *a* problem. That makes it less personal and makes it easier for you to step back and look at the problem objectively, rather than emotionally.

Bear Facts

I love this quote about persistence from Harriet Beecher Stowe: "When you get in a tight place and everything goes against you until it seems as though you could not hold on a minute longer, never give up then, for that is just the time and the place the tide will turn." Isn't that great! She's saying, I think, "Keep the faith."

When things get tough, keep thinking about what you're working for. Keep your dream in front of you, and remember how important it is. It was a dream that prompted you to become an entrepreneur in the first place. Let it carry you through the difficult times.

When it looks like your dream might be turning into a nightmare, it's easy to focus on the situation and ignore everything else. Don't. Everybody runs into problems, but believe me when I say they always get better. Don't become so consumed by what's happening that you lose sight of everything else.

During stressful times, you need to pay extra attention to your health and to the people who love you. They'll be worried, and keeping things as normal as possible makes everyone—you included—feel better.

Try to get enough sleep, watch what you eat, and avoid the temptation to drink more than you should or do other unhealthy things. When you're under a lot of stress and trying to cope with problems, make sure you get some exercise. Even leaving the office for a half-hour walk can make you feel a lot better. Getting out for some exercise clears your head so you can look at things more clearly and objectively when you come back. Better still, you might get a great idea while you're burning off those calories and improving your cardiovascular health. Who knows?

> **The Word According to John**
>
> *Perspective* is an interesting thing. It's what sets us apart from the situations in which we find ourselves and lets us step back and view them from a distance. Being able to maintain a good perspective in the face of a major problem or crisis is a desirable attribute for an entrepreneur.

Making It Work

If you have this book and you've read this far into it, you must be pretty serious about being an entrepreneur.

I've played a lot of devil's advocate up to this point. There's been a lot of discussion about issues associated with having your own business that could be considered negatives—long hours and not much money at the beginning, possible problems with balancing work and family, and so forth.

All that discussion was intended only to make you aware of what comes with the territory when you're an entrepreneur. It's easy, when you have a dream, to rush into things without fully knowing what to expect or what might be involved.

I think that if you're well prepared and equipped with information when you first start your business, you'll have an easier time with the startup and greatly improve your chances of success.

Many people who want to start their own business worry about getting funding and writing business plans. Those tasks, however, aren't that difficult because somebody can tell you exactly how to do them. I will, in fact, tell you all about those subjects a little later in this book. What's harder is figuring out how you'll manage and cope with the demands, stresses, rewards, and joys of the job you're going to do.

Nobody can give you an exact formula for handling the negatives because no two people are the same. You can get all the advice you want on how to react to certain situations. You won't know until you're in a particular situation, however, exactly what you'll do. You might think you could never survive a visit from the IRS, for example. But if it happens, you've got to deal with it, and you might be surprised how well you handle it. On the other hand, you might think a misplaced order is no big deal, and then find out when it happens that it's a huge source of stress for you.

Whatever happens, though, you'll make your dream work if you really want to. Entrepreneurs are a tough bunch. They haven't made the impact on the business world that they have by backing off from problems or giving up at the first signs of trouble.

Entrepreneurs have made possible things that other people didn't even dream of. Henry Ford's idea was to make a car that would be affordable to nearly everyone—and he did. Mary Kay Ash wanted to develop a line of skin care and beauty products that would make women feel good about the way they looked—and she did.

Over the Rainbow

Just remember that your business is your business—not your entire life. Try to keep a sense of perspective about what's most important, and don't let the inevitable problems overwhelm you. You'll do just fine.

In 1997, a 17-year-old kid from New York City named Adam Ezra Cohen developed a new method of photolithography. Just in case you're not familiar with that word, photolithography is the means by which information-packed patterns are electro-chemically etched onto microchips.

Cohen was awarded first prize in Westinghouse's Science Talent Search contest and given a $40,000 scholarship for his trouble. This 17-year-old kid dreamed of a better way of doing something and made it happen. Amazing, isn't it?

I think that being an entrepreneur is really the dream of many, many people, but most of them never accomplish their dreams because they're afraid to try.

You, however, have decided to go for it. You're going to make your dream come true.

The Least You Need to Know

➤ Figure out what your best qualities and skills are and make the most of them.

➤ Be aware of your shortcomings, and take steps to improve them.

➤ Being committed to something is more important than what you're committed to.

➤ Don't get involved in so many causes or organizations that you can't be effective at any of them.

➤ When it seems that everything is going wrong, keep a firm grasp on the dream that made you want to be an entrepreneur in the first place.

➤ Make it a habit to step back and look at problems objectively; think of a situation as *a* problem, not *your* problem.

➤ Knowing as much as possible about what to expect will eliminate surprises and make your job easier.

Part 2
Getting Down to Business

It's time to get to work, and you've come to exactly the right place if you want to know how to pick the right kind of business for you to start. Some opportunities have a greater chance of being successful than others, and you want to jump on one that has the potential to make it big.

Pay special attention to Chapter 12, "The All-Important Business Plan." Your business plan is absolutely vital to your company's startup and running, so this chapter is the most important one of the book.

Chapter 7

What Kind of Business Makes Sense for You?

In This Chapter

➤ Consider your personal criteria before starting a business.

➤ Options for home-based businesses are on the rise.

➤ Make sure your business suits your lifestyle.

➤ Keep an eye on location.

➤ Making money is great, but it's not everyone's top priority.

➤ Match a business to your personality and work habits.

➤ Varied experiences and skills are valuable ones.

Sometimes circumstances determine the kind of business you find yourself involved with. Other people spend years meticulously planning and plotting exactly what they want to do. Some entrepreneurs get talked into joining a business or get involved because they become caught up in the excitement of a new business venture.

I know a 31-year-old who was working as a mid-level manager for a large company. One day his 56-year-old father was shoveling snow and suffered a massive heart attack. He never even made it to the hospital. When the will was read, this 31-year-old manager learned—to his great surprise—that he was the new owner of his dad's real estate business.

Or how about this scenario: An old buddy of yours decides to open a pizza shop. He tells you he's sure it's going to be the best shop anywhere, and he's going to make a ton of money. He's got a great location and an unbelievable deal on some really good equipment he's getting from a guy who's leaving the restaurant business. He's so enthusiastic that his attitude rubs off onto you. The next thing you know, you're part owner of Joe and Bob's Pizza shop.

Think about the people you know who own businesses. Do you know how they got them? Go ahead and ask them when you get a chance—I bet you'll hear a lot of interesting stories. Some might have been deliberately and carefully planned, but I bet as many as not came into being through unforeseen circumstances.

Regardless of how you end up in a particular business, it's important to make sure the venture makes sense for you. Taking over, starting up, or joining someone in a business is a big commitment. It becomes more difficult and less manageable if you end up doing something that doesn't fit your wants and needs.

Identifying Personal Criteria

There are a lot of things to think about when you're trying to decide what kind of business you're going to start. You need to consider how different businesses will fit your lifestyle and your interests and meet other personal criteria.

If you inherit a business, like the guy I mentioned earlier, or get talked into joining a business with somebody you know, you're assuming a passive role. You're letting things happen, instead of making them happen.

Sometimes that works. The guy who took over his dad's real estate business has done pretty well with it and enjoys it thoroughly. He's lucky. He could have found himself stuck with a business in which he had little or no interest. People sometimes take over family businesses out of loyalty or a feeling of obligation, instead of interest or desire.

Grizzly Area

I'll get more into family businesses in Chapter 9, "Going It Alone or with a Partner?" but just a note for now: Joining a family business or getting family members to work in your business are tricky situations and should be handled with extreme caution. You stand to lose a lot more than a business partner if the arrangement doesn't work out.

The best reasons to start a business are because you really want to and because you believe you'll be successful at it.

For those things to happen, a business should meet your personal criteria, as in these examples:

➤ If you're the parent of three small children, you probably want a business that allows you to have some flexibility. You never know when a school play will pop up in the middle of the day, and those kinds of things just shouldn't be missed.

➤ If you love to stay up until 3 a.m. and sleep until 10:30 a.m., it wouldn't be a good idea for you to start up a coffee and bagel shop that opens at 6 a.m.

➤ If you're a high-powered, ambitious sort, you should look for a business with lots of growth potential.

➤ If you've retired from a job and want to start a business to keep you busy while earning a little extra money, you might want to consider something that requires only part-time hours.

➤ If you have chronic health problems or a condition that makes it difficult or impossible for you to do certain things, you have to keep that in mind when choosing a business. Health considerations can often be accommodated, but some businesses might be better suited for you than others.

➤ If you hate the cold weather, you sure don't want to open a ski resort in Vermont—or any business in Vermont, for that matter. Consider where you want to live and work when choosing a business venture.

These are just a few examples of what to think about when you're considering businesses that make—or don't make—sense for you.

Bear Facts

To me, the most important personal criteria to think about is *fun.* Is what you'll be doing going to be fun? I've never gotten involved with a business that I didn't think would be fun, and as long as I have anything to say about it, I never will. Work is a big part of life, and I want my life to be fun. Life is too short to have work that makes you miserable.

Personal criteria takes into account your personal and family situations, your financial needs, your health, your personality, your work habits, and other factors. Certainly, they aren't the only ones worth considering when choosing an entrepreneurial venture. I mean, it would make no sense to start a business that clearly has no future at all, just because you think it meets your personal criteria.

But if you want to do something you'll be happy and satisfied with, personal criteria are important to consider.

Finding a Business That Meets Your Criteria

There are thousands of business venture opportunities out there. How do you find the one that's right for you?

Some business opportunities are pretty traditional and standard, and some are as offbeat as you can imagine. As society becomes more high tech and service oriented, you'll see all different types of businesses starting up.

> **Bear Facts**
>
> Examples of offbeat business ventures I've read or heard about recently include farms that raise animals for game meat for fancy restaurants. People are raising elk, buffalo, and deer and selling the meat for high prices to restaurants. Trout farming is on the increase, too. My neighbor in Vermont is a hoof doctor, who goes from farm to farm cleaning and treating animals' hooves. One friend bought a water truck and fills up swimming pools. There are nearly as many businesses as there are ideas for businesses.

The Internet is helping to spread the word about hundreds of entrepreneurial opportunities. Personal services, such as locating and checking out day care opportunities for busy moms, arranging for groceries to be delivered to the homes of working couples or elderly people who find it hard to get out, and delivering home-cooked meals on request, are booming. In addition, there are the actual Internet jobs, like designing Web sites or Internet marketing. Opportunities are limited only by a lack of imagination.

Let's have a look at some common wants and needs of entrepreneurs and see what kinds of businesses would best fit their personal criteria.

Family Concerns

If your primary concerns are your family and your family life, then you have to find a business that makes it easy to keep them your top priority.

If you're committed to having dinner with your family every night, a 2-hour commute isn't conducive to that goal. If you live on Long Island and have to ride the train for 2 hours to get home, chances are your family will have had dinner and gone off to soccer practice, ballet class, or whatever before you hit the door at 7 or 8 p.m. If you work 3 miles from home, however, you can easily make that family dinner happen.

I felt very strongly about living close to my house while my kids were small. I wanted to be close to home and close to their schools. It gave me a feeling of security, and it sure made life a lot easier.

There were many, many times I would leave work to pick up one of my kids at school and take him or her home, or to practice, or to the dentist, or something like that. Moms and dads with small children might want to be sure their offices are as close as possible to a great day care center so they can visit at lunch or be accessible in case they're needed.

On the other hand, there might be a good reason why you should not live close to where you work. If what you do requires you to work in New York or another large city, you might choose to sacrifice time with your family so that they can live outside the city. If you don't want your kids growing up in New York City, the 2-hour commute to Long Island might be necessary.

Some people choose to start businesses in their homes. To me, that's not the best situation, but I understand that some people work well at home with their families around them. Government figures show that about 20% of American households are the sites of home-based businesses, and that about 1,200 new home-based businesses start up every day. Some of them are extremely successful.

Bear Facts

Home-based businesses often quickly outgrow the confines of the home and move elsewhere. Take Microsoft, for example, which had its humble beginnings in a garage.

You've got to do what works out the best for you and your family. Just understand that if your family is your top concern, you should consider all the family-related factors when you're choosing a business. Build the business around your dreams.

If your business is one that requires a lot of travel, will you be able or willing to do so? Being away from home can cause a strain both for the traveler and the people left at home. If there's somebody at home to pick up the slack while you're out traveling for business, that's great. But if your travel causes a real hardship at home, that's a problem.

Some people just don't like traveling. I try to make the best of it when I have to travel, but I've never liked having to follow somebody else's schedule to catch a plane. I don't like sitting around in airports, or having to rent cars, or spending nights in impersonal hotel rooms. It's often necessary, and I accept that. But I suspect there are a lot of people who, like me, simply don't enjoy it.

Another family-related concern is whether your business will allow you to live in the area you and your family want. Some businesses work better in

Over the Rainbow

If you do find that you need to travel, make the most of the time spent in planes and at airports. Laptops are great for traveling, or you can spend the time catching up with reading, replying to memos, and so forth. Travel time doesn't have to be downtime.

different areas than others do. You'll do better in Florida with a bait and sporting goods store that specializes in fancy deep-sea fishing equipment than you would in Iowa, for instance. Or if everybody in your family loves to ski, you could open a business that caters to the ski resort industry. Doing so would give you a business opportunity, as well as opportunity for a lifestyle you and your family would enjoy.

I read an article recently about a couple with three children who bought a resort on a lake in Northern Minnesota. It was 80 miles away from the closest town, and the only way to get there was to fly in.

It sure wasn't the life everybody would want, but this couple and their kids loved the lake and wanted to make a life there. They said the resort was not just their business, but their lifestyle, too.

Take a few minutes and picture *where* and *how* you want to live. Do you envision a rural setting or an urban one? Do you see yourself fly-fishing on your days off, or going to a Knicks game at Madison Square Garden? Do you like gardening? Skiing? Fancy shops? All these things have to be considered when you're deciding what kind of business you're going to have. Go ahead and dream big. Picture the life you really want, and then figure out how to make it work.

Grizzly Area

Whatever you do, resist the temptation to buy everything you need to start up a business with credit cards, and then carry the balance for months and months while the interest adds up. Beg, borrow, or steal—well, maybe not steal—but don't get yourself over your head in credit card debt before your business is even off the ground. Bad idea, especially if you're going to look for other forms of financing. Lenders won't look kindly at tons of credit-card debt.

Financial Needs

If you're the sole, or even the primary, breadwinner for your family, you probably want to start a business with a lot of moneymaking potential. If you're starting a business that your family won't depend on as their only income, you can have a little more latitude when choosing it.

I think every entrepreneur wants to make money, but it's not number one on everybody's priority list. Take a close look at how much money you need to make to keep up with your financial obligations. You still need to pay the mortgage while you're starting up your business, you know. And even though those credit card companies will be happy to let you get away with only the minimum monthly payment for a while, you'll pay dearly down the road for carrying that balance.

It's a good idea to make up a cash-flow budget, outlining all your expenses. It doesn't have to be anything fancy or complicated—just write down everything you need money for. That way, you can see exactly how much profit you need to make to keep up with those expenses. After you've figured all that out, look a little further down the road at what you'd like to be making in, say, 6 months or a year.

Don't underestimate what you can do. Set some ambitious short-term and intermediate-term goals, and go for them!

Bear Facts

I made only $8,000 in 1983, selling teddy bears from my pushcart in Burlington. Regardless of that, I set my sales goal for 1984 at $250,000—and met the goal. Think big!

Personality and Work Habits

If you can't stand being around kids, you shouldn't think about opening a toddler-time gym. If your idea of high fashion happens to be your oldest jeans and a flannel shirt, a trendy boutique obviously shouldn't be your number-one choice for a business.

I could go on and on, but you get the picture, right? You've got to find a business that suits your personality. Maybe you've always been fascinated with fashion. You love clothing. You love the designs, the colors, and the aura of the fashion industry. In that case, yeah—check out the trendy boutique idea. But if the thought of designers and their clothes makes you feel nervous and out of your element, don't even think about it.

Another thing to think about when choosing a business that makes sense for you is your work habits. Are you a person who loves to hang around the office until 10 or 11 at night? Or do you get your best work done before 6 a.m.? Some businesses lend themselves better to particular hours than others, and it's worth thinking about how business hours and your personal hours mesh.

For instance, video rental stores typically stay open quite late at night and don't open very early in the morning. Bakeries, on the other hand, are

Over the Rainbow

It's important to remember that as your business grows, you'll hire people to do parts of it, freeing yourself for other things. You might need to be there practically all the time in the beginning, but things quickly get better as you bring people on board and let them share the responsibility.

doing a brisk business before the sun comes up. Retail shops traditionally open later than places like service stations and diners, and the hours vary with manufacturing facilities. Anyway, you get the point, right?

Also, think about whether you're looking for a part-time business or full-time endeavor. Do you want something that allows you to set your own hours, or will you have to be at work at set times? These are all factors to consider when choosing a business.

Grizzly Area

A common mistake new entrepreneurs make is to open a business that relates to something they like, but isn't a fun or interesting business to have. Say, for instance, that you love baseball, so you open some of those batting cages that are popular. You'll quickly find out that your business involves more standing around watching people slip quarters into the machines and cleaning up the place when they're gone than it does anything related to baseball.

The Word According to John

Passion for what you're doing is what makes it fun, not work. Without a degree of passion, a business is just a job.

Choosing a Venture That Matches Your Interests

I believe it's important to have a business that deals with things you like. Believing in what you're doing makes you a better businessperson.

How? Well, it's a heck of a lot easier to sell something you really like than something that doesn't mean a thing to you. It's easier to sell the idea when you're looking for funding, too.

And it's a lot more fun to make something that you love than something that's just another product. I always envisioned myself as a toymaker because I love kids and wanted to do something that could bring joy to them. My dream led me to The Vermont Teddy Bear Company. When I started it, I became somewhat obsessed with the little creatures. I knew nearly everything about every kind of bear made.

I think that intense interest in, and love of, teddy bears, was part of what saw me through the first few tough years. I was working hard and making hardly any money, but I was working with these little critters I loved. My product made the disappointments a little easier to bear—no pun intended.

When I left The Vermont Teddy Bear Company, I started the Chicago Bicycle Company and developed the first bike made especially for baby boomers. Again, bikes are something I could be excited about. I love biking, and knew I could make a bike that was far more comfortable and practical than anything on the market.

My latest product, the Luv Feet shoe inserts, isn't as warm and fuzzy as bears, but like bikes, it's something I can get behind and believe in. These shoe inserts have the potential to help people avoid all kinds of injuries, and I like knowing I'm a part of that. I believe it's a good and useful product.

Being in any business requires various skills. It's not enough simply to be interested in whatever it is you're doing or to like the product you're making or the service you're selling.

Although passion for what you're doing isn't the only necessary ingredient for being successful at a business, in my opinion, it's the most important ingredient.

I loved making teddy bears. While I was making them, I thought, and still do think, that Vermont Teddy Bears are the best bears in the world. People often commented on the passion I had for what I was doing and for the teddy bears we made.

To me, those remarks were great compliments. You need to consider all the pros and cons of starting any kind of business, but you need to listen to your heart and find something that can make you happy, too.

Putting Your Experience to Work for You

One thing I've realized over the years is that every experience you have helps prepare you for something that's coming up. Skills and experience picked up along the way, regardless of where they come from or how they're acquired, will serve you well, if you let them. When you're choosing a business to start, be sure to consider all your past experiences and examine the skills and experiences you've gained from them.

Don't make the mistake of thinking that only job-related experience is helpful when you're looking to start your own business. Think about everything you've done and the skills you've acquired.

Maybe you're an avid camper, or bicyclist, or canoeist. All those activities require skills and knowledge. Anybody who participates in any kind of activity should learn from it. I mentioned earlier that I've been a Little League coach for many years. I'm sure I've learned more from coaching Little League than the kids who play learn from me.

Coaching teaches you about child (and parent) psychology, sports-related injuries, time management, politics, and scheduling—not to mention the finer points of Little League baseball and small-town life. It teaches you to remember what it's like to be 11 years old and keeps you in touch with what's important outside your own little world and your work.

Before I started coaching, I probably thought my work, other than my family, was the most important thing I did. When I started hanging around with these kids, who didn't care at all about my work, I started seeing the world through their eyes.

Remember how boring it was to be a kid and have to sit around with a bunch of adults who were talking about their jobs? It was deadly! I started to realize that these kids were seeing a lot of things I wasn't because they were looking around, not focusing on a business. It took my mind off business—fast—and made me really look at and enjoy what was going on around me.

Now think about jobs you've had over the years. Remember as many of them as you can. I bet if you think about it, you can come up with lessons or skills you learned from every one of those jobs that you can apply to whatever it is you decide to do as an entrepreneur.

For example, I was a professional Boy Scout for a while. It was great. As a district executive, I got to organize Scout events, work at camps, and do all kinds of fun activities. That job is memorable because it was fun, but it also taught me many things. I was in charge of raising a lot of money, so I learned about fundraising. I had to train a lot of people, which gave me some valuable management lessons. Most important, it taught me many, many lessons about life.

The Word According to John

Experience, I think, is all the knowledge and *skills* accumulated over a lifetime. It doesn't matter where it comes from; it just matters that you apply it whenever possible to whatever you're doing.

Another job I had was delivering packages for the United Parcel Service. That was a great job, too. In addition to being able to join the Teamster's Union and wear those cool UPS uniforms, I got in terrific shape jumping up and down and off and on the truck. The best lesson I took from that job was in time management. You've got a certain amount of time to deliver a certain number of packages, and it's up to you to get it done, or you're out the door (or out of your truck). The United Parcel Service is run like a tight, military operation, and it pays off. It pays well, but you've got to work by the company's rules.

Painting buildings taught me that doing it the right way the first time saves you the trouble and time of having to do it again. A summer job in a factory making railroad bearings, punching a time clock in and out, gave me a sensitivity about what motivates—and doesn't motivate—workers. All you'd hear at the time clock, and at most other places in the factory, was swearing and complaining about management. That was an ugly situation, and not a pleasant place to work. It was management versus union, every step of the way, with a lot of resentment on both sides. That place taught me how *not* to treat employees if you want them to do their best work.

To think that your experiences are limited to those acquired through formal training or schooling is selling yourself short. Your life has taught you a lot more than what you learned in school. Make a list of the experiences and skills you've acquired. Maybe you got good at scheduling and keeping track of other workers' hours for the payroll when you had that job at the fast food restaurant. Or maybe you learned how municipal government operates that summer you worked for the township road crew. Working in a department store might have given you a basic understanding of retailing. Each job you've had has given you experience in something.

What about other things you've done? The volunteer activities, the trips with your kids, maybe even that cross-country jaunt you took with your best friends when you graduated from college. All these things have given you skills and experiences that are useful, regardless of what you decide to do. Just make sure you use this wonderful store of experience you've collected over the years.

These personal criteria are not the only factors to consider when you're thinking about what business to get into, but they're important. Finding the right business makes it a lot easier to be excited and happy about going to work in the morning. When you find a business that you can be excited about and believe in, there's no such thing as work—just a fun and rewarding venture.

The Least You Need to Know

➤ When trying to figure out what business makes sense for you, it's important to examine your personal criteria before making a decision.

➤ If being close to your family is a top priority, consider a business that can be operated from your home.

➤ Factors such as health, your likes and dislikes, personal habits, and your personality should all be considered when choosing a business.

➤ Make sure your business allows you and your family to live in an area you like.

➤ Some businesses are more compatible with a certain lifestyle; if a particular lifestyle is important to you, be sure the business fits it.

➤ All entrepreneurs want to make money, but it's not always the most important factor for everyone.

➤ Work habits, such as whether you prefer working early or late, should be taken into account when choosing a business.

➤ Think about all the experience you've accumulated throughout your life and put as much of it to work for you as you can.

Chapter 8

Identifying Where You Can Be Successful

In This Chapter

➤ Look past personal criteria.

➤ Understand growth industries.

➤ Look at potential growth industries for the future.

➤ Stay on top of trends and opportunities.

➤ Keep away from the trends traps.

➤ Use your brain, listen to your heart, and trust your gut.

How does an entrepreneur decide what business he or she wants to start up and own? Good question. You've already done a good bit of work on this problem by evaluating your personal criteria and putting all those factors in perspective. It doesn't matter how much you want that bait-and-tackle shop if you live 500 miles from the nearest body of water and your family absolutely refuses to move. Unless you're up for a really long commute, that shop's just not gonna happen.

Once you've established your personal criteria (all the stuff I talked about in Chapter 7, "What Kind of Business Makes Sense for You?"), you've got to figure out what makes sense businesswise. Although I'm convinced a good entrepreneur can be successful in any business, some businesses and industries might be easier to make a go of than others.

People talk a lot about growth industries, glamour industries, niches, and trends. What's most important, though, is your dream. If you've always, for some reason, wanted to have a laundromat, then you've got to figure out how to open a laundromat that will be the most successful one your town has ever seen. You've got to figure out how to make a laundromat that's so cool, even people who don't have laundry to do will want to come.

Don't overlook good, solid, dependable businesses that have always been around and always will be. They're not glamorous, but plumbers, electricians, landscapers, and the like can make successful businesses.

Let's have a look at some things to consider when deciding what business you're going to start.

Growth Industries

Everywhere you look, you see articles or hear people talking about growth industries. It's sort of an entrepreneurial buzz phrase. My view on growth industries is a little different from what might be considered mainstream (by now, you've probably noticed that a lot of my views tend to vary from the mainstream), because I think that with some great ideas and smart management, any industry can be a growth industry. Let's have a look at exactly what these growth industries are and how you can find a spot within them.

What Is a Growth Industry?

Growth industries are simply industries that are expected to expand significantly. Some of them are perfectly obvious—like the electronics and computer industries. Some are more obscure and may even seem sort of strange if you're not involved with them—like the captive deer industry that has been rapidly expanding in Wisconsin and surrounding states. Just in case you aren't familiar, captive deer producers raise deer, which are eventually slaughtered, and the meat is sold to restaurants.

The trick to growth industries is that financial communities get behind them and invest in them heavily. That just about ensures they'll continue to be growth industries in the coming years.

Bear Facts

Market researchers can predict growth industries based on a variety of factors. I think, though, that smart entrepreneurs can identify and predict growth industries just by keeping up with what's going on and by listening to what people are saying.

Conversely, if the financial community perceives an industry as a non-growth or stagnant one, it's less likely to invest in it. Conventional wisdom says that this lack of support virtually ensures the industry won't grow, but I don't think that's necessarily true. Sure, some industries aren't experiencing the rapid growth that others are, but I think any industry can be a good industry for an entrepreneur who plays it smart and works hard.

Some people think you should seek out growth industries and not consider opening a business in anything that's not been targeted as one. However, I think it's much more important to have a business you like, even if it's not in a growth industry.

What good is it going to be for you to start up a software company if you don't know the first thing about writing software and, furthermore, you don't even like being around computers? It makes no sense. Sure, the software business is part of a huge growth industry. If you get into something you don't really like and you're not interested in, however, you're not going to be effective or successful. If by some chance you do manage to make a go at it and be successful, you still might not be fulfilled.

If what you like and what you want to do falls within a growth industry—more power to you. If writing computer software is as much fun for you as watching the New York Yankees in their own stadium is for me, then you've got it made. You're going to put your dream to work in one of the hottest industries going.

When you write your business plan, in effect, you're writing a sales instrument. Part of the goal of your business plan is to sell your idea for a business to the people you're asking for money.

If you have a good idea and a good, sound business plan with all the pieces in place, you can find financial backing. I think it's a big mistake to give up on something you want to do just because it might not have the growth industry approval rating of the financial community.

When you have an idea of what you want to do, gather all the information you can about it. Talk to people who are in the business you want to be in, read trade magazines, and check out library resources. Find every bit of information you can, so you know as much about the venture as possible. Your work will be apparent on your business plan, and you'll be a step ahead when it comes to knowing about the business you plan to get into.

How to Find Growth Industries

There are many ways to identify growth industries. You can go to your local bookstore and get a book that lists the best businesses to be starting now. That type of book comes out periodically and is based on market research.

If you decide to buy one of those books to get some ideas, be sure you get a current one. An industry picked for growth 10 years ago might not be considered a growth industry today. Here are just a few of the books available from a bookstore or online from Amazon.com or barnesandnoble.com:

➤ *101 Best Businesses to Start*, by Sharon Kahn

➤ *199 Great Home Businesses You Can Start (and Succeed In) for Under $1,000*, by Tyler G. Hicks

➤ *101 Best Small Businesses for Women: Everything You Need to Know to Get Started on the Road to Success*, by Priscilla Y. Huff

Magazines geared toward entrepreneurs usually contain information about growth industries and also have some good information from people who have done what you're getting ready to do and have been successful at it. It might be worth it for you to check some out.

You can read market research reports, trade journals, business newspapers and magazines, or whatever else you come across to get an idea of what growth industries are. Another way to identify growth industries is to open up your yellow pages or take a walk around your town.

If four new coffee shops have opened downtown within the past year and a half, and you guess that coffee shops are part of a growth industry, you're right on track. Now, let's look a little further. Go to your local Macy's, or whatever department store is near you, and take a walk through the housewares department. Head for the coffeemaker section and have a look at all that's available. You'll see cappuccino makers, espresso machines, fancy European coffeemakers, bean-grinding machines, and much more.

It's a far cry from your basic Mr. Coffee, isn't it? Now head over to the gourmet food section and see all the different kinds of coffee and variations on coffee that you can buy. Have a look at all the items available with the coffee selection—spoons and stirring sticks dipped in chocolate, six kinds of biscotti, flavored syrups—you name it, it's there.

Coffee is definitely a growth industry, and you don't need a book or a market research report to tell you so. But it hasn't always been one. Sit back, grab a cup of your favorite java, and let me tell you a story about an entrepreneur with a vision and a dream, who refused to give up, and now is the CEO of a billion-dollar business.

In the early 1980s, coffee sales in America were dropping between 5% and 10% a year. The industry outlook was bleak, but there was a man named Howard Schultz, who worked for a little retail company in Seattle called Starbucks Coffee, Tea and Spice.

Schultz—who from his childhood in the Bayview Projects of Brooklyn has risen to the King of Coffee—was dispatched by his company to Milan, Italy to check out an international housewares show. While walking through the streets of Milan, he noticed how many espresso bars there were. He was intrigued by their atmosphere, where people gathered to chat, catch up on the news and gossip, and enjoy each other's company.

Schultz became convinced that a similar concept would work in America. He said that the idea "seized my soul," and he came back to American with "a passion in my heart to make this dream a reality." His Starbucks partners weren't interested, so Schultz left the company and started his own. When the partners sold Starbucks a couple of years later, Schultz bought it back. It wasn't easy for Schultz to make his dream come true, but he refused to give up.

Hundreds of investors turned him down when he was looking for funding, and it took him a year to raise the money he needed. After he'd started his business and bought back the Starbucks operation and name, he still was looking at an uphill battle.

Bear Facts

Schultz was quoted during an interview with a reporter from Time Inc. as saying, "Every entrepreneur has to take a leap of faith and pursue his or her dream. I'm living proof that it can be done."

Schultz became the owner of Starbucks in 1987, and started losing money big-time. The company lost $1.2 million in 1989, not because it was poorly managed, but because Schultz invested mightily in his business. He bought the best computer system he could find and a top-notch coffee-roasting facility. He gave great benefits to his employees and hired the best management team he could find.

Schultz was convinced he knew what he was doing. Clearly, he did. The businesspeople who invested $100,000 in company stock in 1987 have stock valued at about $10 million today. Starbucks stores are now a common sight not only in Seattle, but across the country. When Schultz decided to follow his dream and start the Starbucks coffee shops, coffee wasn't a growth industry. Schultz is largely responsible for having *made* coffee a growth industry.

I hope you've taken from this story the lesson that if you believe in your dream strongly enough, you'll find a way to make it work. Schultz was convinced he saw an opportunity in an industry that was losing ground, and he turned the industry around.

Look around, and pay close attention to what's going on. What are people talking about? What are they eating and drinking? What are they wearing? Where are they hanging out? What kinds of things or services do they want but can't find? There are lots of ways to identify growth industries.

Growth Industries for the Next Century

People always want to know what's going to be hot. Our country is fascinated with predictions. I'll tell you what market researchers are saying will be the hot areas as we enter the next century, but you've got to promise me something.

You ready? Promise me that you won't toss away your dream just to get into an industry that somebody has decided will be hot. Okay?

All right, then. Here's what experts at the U.S. Bureau of Labor and Statistics have identified as the fastest-growing job areas as we head into the 2000s:

➤ Health care. Baby boomers are getting older, so health care is going to be important. The United States soon will have 76 million boomers in their 50s, then their 60s, then their 70s … you get the picture. An aging population ties in directly with the need for many services, too.

➤ Robotics. Huh? Yeah, robotics, as in robots, but a lot more complicated.

➤ Computer graphics. Or computer anything.

➤ Information technology, like the Internet and telecommunications, in case you've been asleep for the past 10 years and have missed this trend.

➤ Biotechnology, which gets into techniques like cloning. Remember Dolly the sheep?

➤ Lasers. They're being used in more and more areas, like communications, health care, and manufacturing.

Well, there they are. Remember that these are general areas targeted as growth industries, not particular businesses such as coffee shops, domestic deer farming, or fancy dog biscuit production.

Bear Facts

Just a little tidbit about robotics: LEGO MINDSTORMS, a new division of the LEGO toy company, went on a 30-city tour during the summer of '98 to introduce its new product, the Robotics Invention System. The system is based on LEGO pieces, and something called the RCX, a LEGO microcomputer that can be programmed using your computer and serves as the robot's *brain*. Users make robots out of LEGO pieces, and then create a program to make it run. The program is transferred to the RCX, giving the robot its brain. All this for about $200. Pretty cool, don't you think?

These growth areas might give you a direction to steer your dream toward, but I doubt anyone is going to suddenly decide to trade in his or her dream of owning a restaurant to start a business in the laser industry—at least I hope nobody would do that. But if you've always had a strong interest in lasers, and you've got a new idea for making them better, then by all means—go ahead and learn everything you can about this predicted growth industry.

To get a better idea of these predicted growth areas, use your imagination. Try thinking about the health care industry for a minute—what's involved with it and where your interests might fit in. The health care industry includes the following:

➤ Health care professionals, such as doctors, nurses, nurse practitioners (a growing area), physical therapists, occupational therapists, and so forth.

➤ Hospitals. Think about all the opportunities for entrepreneurs within hospitals. Hospitals require food service, laundry service, cleaning services, and lots of other services. I just read about a guy who made a fortune because he designed a computer-controlled medicine dispensing system for hospitals. It kept track of everything that was dispensed and took inventory of each kind of medicine. He got the idea while his wife was in the hospital and he was watching the nurses waste their time by recording each medicine they removed from the cabinet.

➤ Nursing homes and partial nursing homes. This business is growing by leaps and bounds. Look around at all the new facilities for elderly or sick people, and think about all the opportunities for products and services for nursing homes and the people in them.

➤ Rehabilitation services, inpatient and outpatient. There's a big need for these services and the people who provide them—not to mention products that make it easier for people with rehab needs to get around or do what they need to do.

➤ Pharmaceuticals. The development and distribution of medicines is booming.

➤ Home-care services and products. There's a growing trend toward home health care. Imagine the possibilities for products and services.

These are just a few of the hundreds, if not thousands, of opportunities with the health care system. I bet if you sat down and made a list, you'd be astounded at how many possibilities you could come up with. Try it.

Once you get an idea of exactly what's involved with an industry that's been targeted as a growth area, you might find that your interests fit right into it. Maybe, for instance, you're really interested in nutrition and food service. You always thought you'd open a restaurant that offered food for health-conscious folks, but you weren't crazy about the thought of being tied down to the night, weekend, and holiday hours involved.

When you start thinking about opportunities in the booming health-care industry, you realize there's a need for food service in hospitals and nursing homes. Then you see there's a trend toward home health care, and all of a sudden, a light bulb goes on over your head. Bingo! You'll develop and produce meals designed for people with special medical needs and deliver the food to their homes. You'll have meals for diabetics, for people with heart conditions, for people with digestive problems, non-dairy meals, vegetarian meals, and so forth. The special meals will be matched to the people who need them and packaged in microwaveable trays that are easy to open.

Bear Facts

If you want to start a business or create a product, start by identifying a need and figuring out how to fill it. I wish somebody would make a really good, low–fat salad dressing. I count fat grams all the time. It's the only thing I do for weight control, and it works. But I can't find a good salad dressing that isn't loaded with fat. If anybody has a good idea, I'm telling you there's a need for it.

Now you've managed to work your interest in nutrition and food service into a growth industry. You get the best of both worlds.

Trends and Opportunities

Within every industry, there are trends and opportunities. The trick is to be able to spot them and get in on them early. If you don't get in on the ground floor, you have to work a little harder to be better than your already established competition.

For instance, when the everything-is-low-fat-or-no-fat movement began a while back, the beef industry took a hit. It's rebounded (showing that what goes around comes around), but it was forced to take a look at what it was doing, change its advertising focus, and develop leaner cuts of beef.

While sales of beef went down, sales of chicken and fish went up. Red was out. Low-fat and white were in, hence the glut of *light*, *lean*, and *low-fat* products that you've seen on the market. All these events were trends within an industry. Fish farms started up or expanded. People started raising elk, buffalo, ostrich, and other animals for their leaner meats that were perceived as healthier.

Entrepreneurs changed the focus of their restaurants to better suit the trends of the time. Cream sauces were replaced by lighter concoctions, and no-fat sorbets were added to the dessert carts. Franchises like the TCBY yogurt places sprang up in response to the public's demand for low-fat foods.

Bear Facts

Pork producers were quick to take advantage of the trend toward leaner, lighter meats. They developed leaner types of pork and promoted them heavily as "the other white meat." It worked. Pork sales are way up from a decade ago.

Knowing When to Jump on Board

It's a smart idea to look for trends and opportunities and get in on them early—if they make sense for your business. It's important to be willing to let your business change and evolve as trends and opportunities become apparent. And the sooner you can spot them, the better.

If you own a ski resort, for instance, you've probably been keeping up with the surging interest in snowboarding—a definite trend that's presenting good opportunities. Participation in the sport has been increasing by about 20% a year since 1995, according to the National Ski Area Association in Denver. At the same time, the number of skiers has been dropping steadily since 1990. If I owned a ski resort, you can bet I'd be designating areas for snowboarders and doing whatever else I could to cater to this group, which is predicted to account for about 35% of visits to ski resorts within the next 5 years.

Trends are easy to spot if you keep your eyes open. Look around your town. If there are five Italian restaurants, and people are waiting on the sidewalk to get into them every night, you've probably spotted a trend. If, on the other hand, there are four Chinese restaurants, and the only people in them every night are the cook and waiter, you'd be correct in assuming that Chinese food is not a current trend.

What are some trends right now? Well, what's trendy? Microbrew beer. Coffee. Fancy stuff for pets. Computer games. Colored nail polish.

Over the Rainbow

If you were a ski resort operator, the best thing you could have done when you first started hearing about snowboarding was to learn everything you could about it. Sometimes business owners are too focused on what they're doing, to the point they can't see past their business to anything else. If you focus only on skiing, you're missing an opportunity to get in on the ground floor of a hot new sport. When I was making bears, if there had been a sudden, huge outcry among consumers for stuffed chickens, you can bet I would have added chickens to my product line.

Sandwich wraps. Hiking boots. Chocolate. Timberland. Bell-bottoms. Wine. Luv Feet shoe inserts (just thought I'd slip that one in). Organically raised food. Anything that's perceived as being good for the environment.

Will these things stay trendy? Who knows? Will other things come along to take their place if they don't? You bet. If it suits your business or your interests to get into trends, then go ahead. If you start making bell-bottoms, and in 2 years nobody wants bell-bottoms anymore, you can make wide legs, or straight legs, or no legs, or whatever the demand happens to be. Remember that what's *out* in one place might be the trendiest thing around in another. For instance, if a trend seems to be on the downswing in America, it's very likely it's just picking up in Europe.

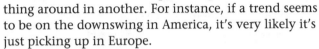

Grizzly Area

A word of caution about trends—they can be deceiving. You might think one will be around for a while when in fact it's doomed to a very short life. Trends can be pretty tempting, but you need to make sure you really understand what's going on. If you don't, you're setting yourself up to lose.

When Not to Jump on Board

I would never recommend that someone jump into a business venture solely because it's a trend. No matter how good a trend it might be, if you're not happy in the business in which the trend is occurring, it's not a good move for you.

If you're tempted by a hot trend and you have an idea of how to jump on board and profit from it, draw up a plan outlining exactly what you want to do. Get all the information you can about the trend, the business it applies to, and what else is going on with it. Then let your plan be your guide and tell you whether your idea will work.

Don't ever let somebody talk you into getting into a business just because it's a hot trend. If coffee is the hottest thing in your town (get it?), but you can't stand the smell, taste, or even the thought of it, it's a pretty sure bet you shouldn't get into the coffee business. Trends can be good, but determination and perseverance are much more important.

Your Brain, Your Heart, and Your Gut

Once you know what you want to do—what businesses you want to get into—go ahead and get going. Make up your mind that you're going to do whatever it is you want to do, and make up your mind that you're going to be the best at it.

If you want to open a gas station, then make it the best darned gas station your town has ever seen. Get all the information you can about gas stations and the business of running them.

What do people want when they come to a gas station? Good service? Cheap gas? Knowledgeable attendants? A car wash? Clean surroundings? A place to get coffee and snacks in the station? Good bathrooms? All of the above?

What else? Maybe you'll think of something different. Maybe you'll include a counter in the station where customers can buy gourmet dinners, all prepared and ready to heat up when they get home from work. Do something to make your gas station stand out from your competition.

If you want to start a software business, a cell phone business, a dance school, or a welding shop, decide that it's going to be the best one ever. And don't let anybody discourage you from pursuing your dream.

Accept that not everyone will be encouraging, but remember that some people aren't encouraging about anything. It all comes down to doing what you want to do and believing that you can make it work. It all comes down to using your brain, taking strength and courage from your heart, and trusting your gut.

You're going to have a great business because you believe that you can.

The Least You Need to Know

➤ After you've established your personal criteria, there are some other factors to consider when choosing a business.

➤ Starting a business within a growth industry might give you an advantage, but you should never choose a business to pursue just because it's been targeted as a growth area.

➤ Your attitude, willingness to work, and level of perseverance are more important to the success of your business than whether it's in a growth industry.

➤ It's good to keep an eye on trends and opportunities, but not to get into something you don't like or that's over your head just because it's considered trendy.

➤ The best thing to do when choosing and starting your business is to use your brain, find strength and courage in your heart, and trust your gut.

Chapter 9

Going It Alone or with a Partner?

In This Chapter

➤ What's good and bad about sole proprietorships.

➤ All partnerships are not created equal.

➤ Choosing a partner, or partners, can be a tricky business.

➤ Make sure everyone has similar expectations and goals.

➤ Consider a limited liability business.

➤ Protect yourself and your business.

Once you've decided what kind of business you'll have, there are still many other things to consider. Some are practical considerations, like how much money you need to get started and where that money will come from. Others are legal questions, like what form of ownership you'll have.

It's pretty amazing, but many entrepreneurs all but ignore the legal structure of their business, thinking it doesn't really matter or it's not important. Let me go on record as saying that it *is* important, and it's something you should consider carefully.

In this chapter, you'll have a look at three different forms of ownership: *sole proprietorships*, *partnerships*, and *limited liability companies*. Another form of ownership is a corporation, which is discussed at length in Chapter 10, "Basic Things to Consider When Starting a Business." For now, let's look at some of the advantages and disadvantages of these forms of ownership, some of their legal implications, and how you should—and shouldn't—choose a partner.

Advantages and Disadvantages of Going Solo

Before I talk about what's good and not so good about being solo or having a sole proprietorship, there's something you need to understand. It's just about impossible to be in business by yourself. You might think you're going to be, and others might perceive that you're in business by yourself, but really, it can't happen.

The Word According to John

Being the *sole proprietor* of a business means that you bear all responsibility for it. In my opinion, it doesn't mean that you're solo. Even as a sole proprietor, you have people to answer to and other people who are somehow involved with your business.

Over the Rainbow

You can buy insurance to protect your personal assets from liability in the event that you're a sole proprietor. If you choose to go the sole ownership route, this is something you should check out.

You're in business with, and for, whatever your source of funding may be. It might be the bank, a relative who loaned you money, or someone or something else, but as long as you've borrowed money to finance your venture, you can't truly be in business by and for yourself.

You're in business with and for the government, no matter what kind of business you have. Government regulations tell you, to some degree, how to run your business, and the government takes a good chunk of what you make through taxes.

If you have a board of directors, a founder's team, or stockholders, you're not in business by yourself. You might run the business or be the boss, but you're really not in it alone. There's nothing wrong with that, either. Personally, I'd rather have people around with whom to share ideas and concerns, commiserate when things go wrong, and celebrate when things go well.

You can, however, be the sole proprietor of a business. What that means is that you, as the proprietor, are totally responsible for all business conducted. Having a sole proprietorship is an *owner-take-all* kind of deal. You get nearly total control of the business and you get *all* the profits. That's the good news. The bad news is that you also get full liability for all business debts and actions. That's right, folks.

If Frankie's Sandwich Shop owes $30,000 to the bread and meat guys and there's no money to pay the bills, guess whose house the bread and meat guys are coming after. Sorry, Frankie. Maybe that extra room at your mother-in-law's house is still available.

The Positives

Still, the sole proprietorship form of ownership is popular and commonly used for small businesses. Let's have a look at what's appealing about this form of ownership:

➤ *It's easy to do.* A sole proprietorship is the easiest legal structure to get started. All you have to do is apply for an occupational business license in the community or municipality where the business will be located. If the business will be operating under a fictitious name—such as Tiny's Carpet Cleaning or Lucky's Lawn Service—you must have the name published in your local newspaper. Supposedly, that allows the public to know who's responsible for Lucky's business activities, although you have to wonder just how many people read those ads.

➤ *It's fast.* In most places, you get a license very soon after applying for it, and you're free to put out your shingle. There's not much waiting for approval or messing around with red tape.

➤ *It's streamlined.* If you're in business by yourself, with no employees, you can use your social security number as your taxpayer identification number. If you have employees, you need to request an employer identification number from the IRS.

➤ *There may be tax advantages.* I'll get into this in more detail in the next chapter, but when you're first starting up a sole proprietorship, there are usually some personal tax advantages you can take. Remember, that for tax purposes, the IRS treats you and your business as one. You might see some substantial tax savings because of investment tax credits.

Sounds pretty good so far, doesn't it? Well, don't be fooled.

The Negatives

There are some serious drawbacks to sole proprietorships. I already mentioned the most serious drawback—that you, as owner, are responsible for all business debt and action. Remember the trouble Frankie got into with the bread and meat guys? Or if your delivery van runs down an old lady while she's crossing the street, look out. It's all on you.

In addition to the most obvious drawback of a sole proprietorship, there are some others. Let's consider what they might be:

➤ *You'll be relying on your own expertise.* This might not be a bad thing, if you're an expert at whatever you're doing. And it's true, you can always find help and advice if you look. But people in business by themselves sometimes develop a tendency toward an "I can do it by myself, thank you very much," attitude. This attitude can make them reluctant to ask for help, even when they might know they need it.

Over the Rainbow

If you choose to have a sole proprietorship, find somebody dependable to talk to about liability and insurance. There are types of insurance you can get that help cover you if some kind of catastrophic event occurs. You could ask an insurance person you know and trust, or a good lawyer, or somebody from your area's Small Business Administration. Just be sure you get yourself covered as much as possible.

➤ *You'll be relying on your own assets.* If you go to the bank and ask for $100,000, the collateral on that loan will depend solely on your assets. If you have money of your own to put into the business, it probably wouldn't be as much as you could get with a partner or partners. The fact is, the more money of your own you have to put into your business, the more money you'll probably be able to get from a lender. A bank is a lot more likely to loan you $100,000 for your business, if you've got $100,000 to put into it, too.

➤ *If you become disabled, or die, your business ceases to exist.* Nada. Obviously, this can cause some serious problems when it comes time to dispose of the business, divide the estate, and so forth.

Over the Rainbow

Keep track of every penny you put into your business when you're starting up and include the information in your business plan. You'll have a better chance of getting a bigger loan, or getting a loan with less hassle, if you've got your own money in. Even if you've invested your money in your business and lost it, tell the bank about it.

➤ *It might be hard to attract good management people.* Many people prefer to be partners or part owners of a business they're going to help manage. A sole proprietorship won't likely be attractive to managers, and that can be serious trouble for your business.

➤ *A sole proprietor loses out on some tax breaks* that a corporation gets, such as deductions for insurance expenses and health benefits. While the government slowly is increasing the amounts you can deduct for health benefits, they're still not to a desirable level.

As you can see, there are advantages and disadvantages of being a sole proprietor. While I fully understand that sometimes it's the only way someone is able to start a business, I don't think sole proprietorships are advisable for the long-term.

Setting up a sole proprietorship is a good, quick way to get started in a business, but I wouldn't keep that form of ownership for too long. It just involves too much personal risk and isn't in the best interests of an entrepreneur.

Popular Forms of a Sole Proprietorship

The following is a list of businesses that work well set up as a sole proprietorship:

➤ Private consulting

➤ Painting, wallpapering, and decorating

➤ Freelance writing and editing

➤ Catering and/or party and event planning

➤ Services such as pet sitting or cleaning

If you are in these lines of work, it's always your choice, however. Make sure you look into the pros and cons of each type of ownership to find the one most suited to your needs.

Advantages and Disadvantages of Having a Partner

So you think maybe you'll form a partnership, do you? Well, as with sole proprietorships, there are good things and bad things about partnerships.

Before I get too far into the partnership discussion, however, I want to make sure you understand something:

> There is a difference between a business that's operated as a *partnership* and an *incorporated business* in which two or more people are partners.

The partnership form of ownership I'm going to be discussing pertains to an *unincorporated business*. Basically, the owners of a business pool their resources and share control and management of the business. They also share the liability, and their personal assets may be attached to cover liability.

When two or more people work together in a business that's been incorporated, they're *partners*, but they're not in a *partnership agreement*.

From time to time, I'll talk about people with whom I've been in business, and I'll call them *partners*. That doesn't mean, however, that we've shared partnership agreements because all my businesses have been incorporated. I get into incorporating a business in Chapter 10, so there will be more discussion about incorporation then.

There are two types of partnerships: general partnerships and limited partnerships.

Grizzly Area

People often talk about having partners, or being with a partner, but they don't mean that their business is set up under a legal partnership structure. Be aware of the difference, and make sure you understand what the person is talking about, should this come up in conversation. Otherwise, you could be misled.

Partnerships in General

In *general partnerships*, two or more people get together and start a business. They agree as to how they'll conduct the business and how the profit, risks, liabilities, and losses will be distributed among them. The partners are responsible for all business debt, and each partner is responsible for all liabilities. Partnerships don't have to be divided equally among all partners; it can be whatever percentage you agree on.

For instance, if Pat, Jose, and Jenny decide to start a carpet cleaning business, they need to agree on exactly how the business will be set up and operated. They need to determine how much money each one will invest and what share of the profits each will get. They also need to determine the degree to which each will be involved in running the business, assuming risk on behalf of the business, and so forth.

If Pat and Jose each have $100,000 to throw into the pot to get the business going, but Jenny has only $50,000, Jenny is still considered a partner. The three of them are liable for all business debts, and each of their personal assets may be attached. Jenny will still have a voice in how the company is run. However, the fact that Jenny's contributing less money is almost sure to affect her role in running the business, her share of the profits, and her responsibility.

Partnership Limits

Limited partnerships are a little different. Under this legal structure, one or more partners invest in the business, but are not involved with the day-to-day operations. The management aspect is handled by one or several general partners.

The general partner or partners are responsible for all the business debt, but the limited partners are liable only for the amount of money they've invested in the business.

A Look at the Positives

What's good about partnership agreements? The main advantage is that having a partner means you're sharing the liability associated with the business. Let's have a look at some other advantages:

➤ *Partnerships generally have more financial clout than sole proprietorships.* Because you're working with two or more personal financial statements, you've got more in the way of assets than just one person would. Investors often are more enthusiastic (that means willing to give you money) about a partnership than a sole proprietorship.

➤ *A partner's strengths can compensate for your weaknesses, and your strengths for her weaknesses.* If one of you is a great salesperson and the other is great at creating new products, it could be a match made in heaven. If both of you are great salespeople but are terrible at business management, you're going to be looking at a problem when it comes time to run the business.

➤ *A partner can make working a lot of fun.* Some people love to work alone, but it's not for everyone. I much prefer to have people around when I work—to bounce ideas around with, to talk over problems, to share some good jokes. When you have a partner, or a couple of partners, you're part of a team. Having my teddy bear cart was fun, but I sure missed the camaraderie of having somebody else around.

➤ *If one partner dies or becomes disabled, the business can continue.* Unlike with a sole proprietorship, the remaining partner or partners can keep the business up and running.

Although there are some advantages to partnerships, they can be pretty tricky to manage successfully. Lots of people advise against partnership agreements, saying they rarely work and are risky, both personally and to the business.

I think that if you choose a partner carefully (I'll get into how to do that in a few minutes), lay out the legal groundwork carefully, and be sure that you both, or all, have a solid understanding and similar philosophy of what you want the business to be, then a partnership can not only work, but also be a rewarding experience.

Get a good business lawyer, and make sure you have a partnership agreement that covers all contingencies. Especially make sure you have a good buy-out agreement and plans for what happens if one partner dies or becomes disabled. Make sure it's stated in the agreement that if one partner decides to get out, his or her share of the business must be offered to the remaining partners before it's sold to anyone else. You don't want to get to work some day and find out you have a new partner who you've never seen before and who doesn't appear to be a very nice person.

The agreement should also clearly state who's responsible for what aspects of the business and how duties will be divided. Be sure that all partners fully understand the agreement and have your lawyer go over it with everyone present. Every agreement will be different, depending on the type of business, number of partners, and so forth. Just make sure everyone is on the same page.

Grizzly Area

Entrepreneurs sometimes tend to be attracted to partners with the same skills they have. Even if you work well together and seem to be a good fit, it's a better idea to find a partner that complements your skills, not one who duplicates them. If you find somebody just like you, you run the risk of having double strengths, which is fine. But you also run the risk of double weaknesses, which isn't so great.

A Look at the Negatives

Still, there are some disadvantages to partnerships. Let's take a look:

➤ *You have to share control of the business.* You might not consider that a disadvantage. In fact, you might think that's just fine. But a lot of people have trouble sharing the control, especially if the business was their idea. Think long and hard about whether you're willing to do that before you take on a partner. If you've already started the business and are thinking of getting a partner, think even harder. You'll have to make a lot of changes.

➤ *You have to share the wealth.* Having a partner means sharing the profits. Your partnership will, you hope, generate more profits than you would have on your own, and you'll end up better off—but you won't be in a take-all situation.

➤ *You have to be accountable to somebody else.* Of course, you're always accountable to somebody (as I mentioned earlier—to banks, the government, and so on), but when you have a partner, you're accountable all the time. Courtesy and good business sense dictates that you check with your partner before you go out of town, leave work early to go to your kid's basketball game, or okay the purchase of a new machine. Some people enjoy talking things over and working as a team. Others end up resenting the accountability.

These are some of the good and bad things about partnerships. I bet you can come up with more of each. Remember that although having a partner means the liability is shared, and therefore lessened somewhat, you both are still personally liable for risk associated with the business.

I can't tell you what form of ownership your business should have. I will highly recommend, however, that you don't go out and set up a business until you've read the next chapter and gotten an idea of the advantages of creating a corporation. If you don't incorporate your business, talk to somebody good about protecting yourself in case of liability.

Choosing a Partner or Partners

If you decide you're going to have a partner or partners, you've got to figure out who they'll be. How do you choose a partner? Should it be a friend? A spouse? A sibling or in-law? There are lots of things to think about before you ask somebody to join you in a business.

If, as I've said earlier, owning a business is comparable to having and raising a baby, then choosing a partner is comparable to choosing a spouse. You're going to have to be there for each other when the going gets tough—and all that other stuff. It's certainly worth some careful consideration.

Just a note: When I talk about choosing partners in this section, I'm talking about partners in either an unincorporated partnership agreement or partners within a corporation. The process of, and reasoning behind, choosing partners in either of those situations is the same.

Family Members

Many people go into business with members of their families. I guess there are some advantages to that, but I've gotta tell you, the thought of it makes me break out in a sweat.

Although I've never worked in a business with a member of my immediate family, I have a very strong suspicion that if I did, it would change the nature of our relationship. It seems to me that it would be hard to separate the business part of your life from the family part of your life. I have these images of a family sitting around the dining room table, all chatting about what happened down at the office that day and arguing over whether to keep that new guy who started in the sales department.

Don't get me wrong; I love working, and I really enjoy my businesses, but I don't want them to be my whole life. I've known a handful of married couples who have started businesses together, run them successfully, brought their kids into them, and eventually let the kids take over. These experiences were terrifically rewarding to those entrepreneurs, and I can fully understand why they would have been. To have started a venture together, raised it, made it successful, and passed it along to offspring would be awesome. It would be almost like raising another family.

I just don't think it would work for me, or for many other people I know.

There have been lots of successful businesses run by brothers, sisters, fathers and daughters, mothers and daughters, fathers and sons—you get the idea. Maybe working together, but not living together, would be less likely to change a relationship.

All I would say is if you're doing a partnership with a family member, be sure you both understand how things will work. Define how the responsibility and authority will be divided. Talk about hours, dividing profits, putting money back into the business, and everything you can think of.

Grizzly Area

I know this sounds picky, but I've seen families absolutely collapse over problems you'd think would be the easiest to resolve. Issues such as who gets to take vacation when, who gets time off for family events, what to name the business, and hiring other relatives can turn into huge stumbling blocks. It sounds ridiculous, but watch out for similar problems if you get into a family partnership. They can turn into pretty high hurdles to get over.

Friends

Many successful business partnerships have started as friendships. It's a natural progression, when you think about it. People with similar interests often become friends, so it's likely that entrepreneurial spirits would find each other.

Once together, the subject of starting businesses is bound to come up. A casual idea evolves into a plan, and the next thing you know, you're in business. Okay, it's a little more complicated than that, but you know what I'm saying.

One of the best partners I ever had—Nick Zegarac—was a good friend before we started the Chicago Bike Company. Nick was working as a bartender in a great place in Chicago when I first met him. I'd visit him every time I got into town, and we'd sit around talking until 2 or 3 a.m.

Our conversations often turned to business, and after we'd gotten to know each other pretty well, I asked Nick to come in with me when I started the bike company. We weren't equal partners, but Nick had a significant role, and I was thrilled when he decided to join. Besides being one of the funniest people I've ever known, Nick is as good a salesman as they come. We complement each other well.

As with family members, partner-friends have to understand each other's expectations and goals. You should expect great things, but each of you should be aware of, and prepared for, the possibility that the business could fail.

You have to understand that there's a tendency to blame the other person if things don't go well, and you should be prepared to deal with that. Just understand that although being partner-friends can be tremendously fun and rewarding, there are some risks.

Grizzly Area

Although asking a friend to become a partner is fine, be sure you do it for the right reasons. You might have a great friend who's totally unsuited to be your business partner. To make him one, you risk both the friendship and your business.

Strictly Business

Some people aren't crazy about the thought of going into business with somebody they don't know. They think it's sort of like a blind date or an arranged marriage. Actually, there's nothing at all wrong with these arrangements—the business ones, that is.

Sometimes your lawyer, accountant, mother, or another entrepreneur might tell you about somebody they think would be a good match for you and who's looking for a business opportunity. Who knows? Maybe they're on to something. It wouldn't hurt to meet the person for coffee or a drink, would it? It might turn out to be a match made in heaven.

Often, after your business is established, someone will approach you about becoming a partner. This is usually for financial reasons, not because the person has a sudden, burning interest in making teddy bears, or whatever your business might be. If that happens, you have to consider all aspects of the offer and what it would mean to your business before you make a decision.

Limited Liability Companies

An interesting, and fairly new, form of legal structure for a company is called a *limited liability company*. This type of ownership started in the western states, where it's been around for 15 or 20 years. It took a while, however, for legislation to pass in all states (Vermont was one of the last) allowing this type of company.

Limited liability companies aren't much different from corporations, except they're not incorporated. The partners enjoy the same personal financial protection as they do within a corporation.

Some people choose this form of ownership because it gives them some corporate advantages (I'll get into that in more detail in the next chapter), but allows them to be taxed as a partnership instead of a corporation. There are both advantages and disadvantages to each of those methods of taxation, which I'll discuss in Chapter 10. For whatever reasons, different people prefer one method to the other.

Limited liability companies require about the same amount of paperwork to set up as corporations do. If you're thinking about a partnership for your business, I'd recommend checking out this new form of ownership. It offers some personal protection that partnerships don't. Different states have different regulations regarding it, so you need to find out what your state requires.

A possible drawback of a limited liability company is that the regulations do vary from state to state, and most people aren't familiar with the ins and outs of such a company. Make sure you do your homework if you're interested in starting a limited liability company.

The Least You Need to Know

➤ Practically no one is ever in a business by himself or strictly for himself.

➤ There are advantages and disadvantages to sole proprietorships and partnership agreements.

➤ There are two kinds of partnership agreements: general partnerships and limited partnerships.

➤ Having a family member as a business partner works for some people, but most people would do well to look carefully at the pros and cons.

➤ Many successful businesses have resulted from friendships that turned into partnerships.

➤ There are legal ways to protect yourself and your business, and you should make sure you know what they are.

Chapter 10

Basic Things to Consider When Starting a Business

In This Chapter

➤ Different kinds of corporations and how they work.

➤ The procedure of incorporating your business.

➤ Registration requirements for your business.

➤ Choosing a business name.

➤ Applying for nonprofit status.

➤ Understanding taxation methods and rules for different legal structures.

➤ Staying within zoning regulations.

Entrepreneurs tend to be idealistic, creative types. They have dozens of ideas flying around in their heads, and it gets a little hard sometimes to keep them all in order. Little tasks like keeping track of meetings, messages, and phone calls sometimes get lost in the shuffle.

I think it's these qualities that make a lot of entrepreneurs impatient with the nuts-and-bolts business stuff that needs to be done before you can actually open up shop. We're in a hurry to get going. We're figuring out how we're going to make a business happen. We want to start making, or providing, or designing, or doing whatever it is we're going to do once our businesses are up and running.

Issues such as the legal structure of the business, taxes, zoning, and other rules and regulations can seem like impediments to getting your business up and running. *Impediments* is a nice way of saying those things are pains in the you-know-what.

It's tempting to try to shortcut all that stuff, but certain steps need to be followed when you're starting up a business. Don't be tempted to take shortcuts because if you don't do what's required, it's bound to result in even more of your time, not to mention a lot of hassle.

Incorporating Your Business

In the previous chapter, I talked about three different legal structures for small businesses: sole proprietorships, partnerships, and limited liability companies.

There are occasions when those structures are appropriate for a small business, so it's good to understand what those terms mean and how businesses that operate under them are set up.

Most businesses, though, should be incorporated. Let's have a look at what that means and how corporations are different from the business structures discussed in the previous chapter.

What's It Mean to Incorporate?

When you incorporate your business, you make it something legally separate from yourself. Instead of the business being in your name, it's registered in the name of the corporation, and the corporation is responsible for all its business activities. You will be an employee and a stockholder, as opposed to a personal owner. The corporation, which is a legal entity, can enter into contracts, buy and sell, sue and be sued.

The Word According to John

If you're a bit confused about the distinction between a *corporation* and a *limited liability company*, you're not alone. Limited liability companies aren't much different from corporations, except they're not incorporated. There's no stock, shareholders, or board of directors. The owners, however, get the same limited liability advantage as those in a corporation.

When you form a corporation, it limits the liability of each stockholder to the amount of his or her investment in the business. If the business fails, or if it's found liable in a lawsuit, it's the corporation that's responsible, not the people who own it. The shareholders can lose whatever they have invested in the business, but their personal assets are protected.

There are two basic types of corporations: C corporations and S corporations. The primary difference between them is how they're taxed, and I'll get into that later in the section "What's All This Talk About Taxes?" S corporations were created with small companies in mind, and most states limit the number of investors this type of corporation can have.

Should You or Shouldn't You?

I don't think it's a question of whether you *should* incorporate; I just think it's a question of *when* to do it. To my way of thinking, it's just good common sense to incorporate and remove your business risk from your personal assets. There are some cases in which incorporating will not be beneficial—usually with very small, one-or-two-person businesses. Talk to a good business lawyer to find out what's right for you.

It does cost money to incorporate a business, and you'll probably need to have some professional help—a business lawyer, an accountant, or maybe both. Some people incorporate their businesses by themselves, but it's wise to have somebody available for guidance and to make sure everything is done properly. It's no bargain to spend a lot of time completing paperwork, only to find out it's not correct and has to be done a second time.

You should be aware that when you incorporate your business, you're putting out flags to auditors and inspectors, who might want to make sure you're adhering to municipal, county, state, and federal laws. As long as you are, you've got nothing to worry about except the possibility of some annoying and time-consuming visits.

Going through the incorporation process can be a hassle when you're trying to start a business. I think it's really important to incorporate your business, but don't let the process of incorporating get in the way of doing the other things you need to do to get your business going.

When I had my teddy bear pushcart, I wasn't incorporated. I was too busy getting started with my business. It certainly didn't hurt my business to wait until it had grown a bit, and then incorporate it. Don't, however, let it slide because you don't want to take the time to do the legal work. You'll rest better at night knowing you've done what you can to protect your personal assets in the event of business liability.

Just so you know, forming a corporation limits your personal liability, but it doesn't remove it completely. It's difficult to keep your personal assets away from your business. It's what we all try to do, but banks and creditors can make it very, very difficult. When you're first starting a business, your personal assets are often all you have. And believe me, the banks you work with will want to know all about them. Often, you're asked to personally guarantee a loan. It's a good idea not to do that, if you can manage it, but sometimes you have to.

It made me really nervous at first to have to sign personally for business deals, but after a while, it didn't seem like such a big deal. After all, if I didn't believe in my business enough to personally sign on it, how could I expect anybody else to believe in it? All this money getting and lending is a game you have to play to get your business started. Don't sweat it too much. Just do the best you can and trust that it will all work out.

Over the Rainbow

Ask your accountant or lawyer about the feasibility of putting your personal assets (home, car, and so forth) in your spouse's name. If you're not married, you might use the name of a parent or child. Some people move their personal money offshore to protect it. If there's nothing in your name, your creditors can't take it.

How to Incorporate

To incorporate your business, you've got to choose a name for it, and you've got to file articles of incorporation with the Secretary of State in the state where your company was started. That sounds kind of complicated, but it really isn't a big deal.

When choosing a name, it's a good idea to submit the one you'd really like your business to be known as, but have another one or two handy, just in case. If the name you choose is already in use anywhere in your state, you have to come up with another one. Try to pick a name that isn't likely to already be in use. For instance, calling your new business Mary's Flower Shop is more likely to result in a duplication of names than if you call it Mama Mary's Petal Parlor, or something like that.

Seriously, think carefully about what you'll call your business. You might think Mama Mary's Petal Parlor is funny, but what kind of image does it project? You don't want to limit your business because the old ladies who might buy flowers think you're a motorcycle shop or something.

Bear Facts

I think it's a good idea to choose a name that lets potential customers know what you're doing or making. It makes your business easier to locate, and I think people remember the name better if the product or service is in it. For instance, if you have a lawn care service, and you call it "Jack's," that doesn't tell prospective customers anything about what you do. If you call it "Jack's Superior Lawn Service," though, people know exactly what you offer.

Okay. After you have a name, you've got to go through the process of filing articles of incorporation. Basically, that means you have to fill out some forms.

You're asked to provide information about the nature of your business. Just what is it you propose to do once you open? Are you going to operate a restaurant? Run a manufacturing plant? A massage parlor? A gas station? Laundromat? You get the picture. You also need to give the address where your business will be operating.

When you form a corporation, you have to designate the amount of corporate stock you'll have and declare the value of the stock. There's a minimum amount of stock required for a corporation, and that amount varies from state to state. After you've set the amount of stock, it can be divided up among people within the corporation. Those people are called *shareholders* because they hold, or own, shares of the company.

The shareholders elect a board of directors, and the board of directors, typically, elect the company officers. This sounds a little complicated, but it isn't really. Here's how simple it can be, if you choose to make it so.

Bear Facts

Many investors require businesses they're involved in to be incorporated in Delaware because it's a very corporate-friendly state. You don't need to be incorporated in the state where your business is located.

You start the company, and you incorporate it. You decide on the amount of stock you're going to have. If you choose to, you can keep all the stock yourself. In some states—but not all—you can be the only member on the board of directors, and appoint yourself president of the corporation. The only thing you can't do is to serve as both president and secretary of the corporation. You have to find another person to serve as secretary, but he or she doesn't have to own any of the corporation. A lot of people recruit their spouse or a friend for that position.

I'm not saying that's the smartest way to run a corporation because everything depends on you. You'd be better off to get some good people with some business experience on your board and to earn money for the company by selling stock.

Having a corporation and running it properly requires some effort. The shareholders have to adopt bylaws, file corporate tax returns separate from their personal returns, hold shareholders' meetings on a regular basis, take and maintain minutes of the meetings, and file periodic reports with the states where they're located.

Doing these things keeps your corporation legal, which is the only way it can protect you. If your business is sued, and it's discovered that you've ignored the requirements to keep it legal, you're not going to benefit from the corporate shield. Your corporation will be in name only, and not valid. You've got to make sure you meet all the legal requirements.

Over the Rainbow

It's really important to have good people helping you when you set up a corporation. I just can't stress enough how important it is to have the best accountant and lawyer you can hire. Regulations on corporations vary from state to state, so make sure you get a professional who knows corporate law.

Incorporating as a Nonprofit Business

Businesses that provide services to the community sometimes can be incorporated as nonprofit businesses. Being nonprofit doesn't mean you can't make a profit—these businesses often make as much money as their for-profit counterparts. The difference is that their profits can't be distributed to members, directors, or officers. Nonprofit agencies are known as 501(3)s.

Bear Facts

Nonprofit organizations provide a service to the community in the following areas: religious, educational, charitable, child welfare, animal welfare, scientific, literacy, national or international amateur sports competition, or testing for public safety.

Setting up a nonprofit business, such as a day-care center or an animal rescue center, is a two-step process. You've got to apply for incorporation with the Secretary of State in your state, just as you would with any business. You've got to do the articles of incorporation, pay the filing fee, and so forth.

Then you have to file for tax-exempt status with the IRS by submitting a 1023 form and other materials. The IRS will want to see your budget, your bylaws, your articles of incorporation, a filing fee, and other items. It's a good idea to prepare by attending one of the seminars or classes for nonprofit organizations offered in some communities.

Getting nonprofit status can get pretty complicated. If you hire a lawyer, which you're likely going to need, try to find one who specializes in nonprofit incorporation. Keep the costs as low as you can by doing some of the work yourself and having the lawyer check it. It's probably a good idea to meet with a nonprofit expert before you get too far along with the application process. The expert can tell you if your venture is likely to be approved as nonprofit, saving you the time and trouble of going through the application process if it doesn't stand a chance.

Here are some books that should be useful. They're all available on the amazon.com and barnesandnoble.com Web sites:

➤ *A Legal Guide to Starting and Managing a Nonprofit Organization*, by Bruce R. Hopkins.

➤ *The Complete Guide to Nonprofit Corporations—Step-By-Step Guidelines, Procedures and Forms to Maintain a Nonprofit Corporation*, by Ted Nicholas.

➤ *Starting and Running a Nonprofit Organization*, by Joan M. Hummel.

➤ *How to Form a Nonprofit Corporation* (4th ed.), by Anthony Mancuso.

Registering Your Business

Regardless of your business's legal structure, you have to register it with your local government and perhaps with the state and federal governments as well.

All municipal and county governments require business owners to register and get a license before they start operating. This requirement allows government officials to keep up with who's running what and make sure the business complies with all the local regulations.

It's no big deal to register with your local government. You have to fill out a form or two and pay for an annual license. The fee will vary, depending on where you live. Some businesses, such as restaurants, have to be inspected by the health department. Be sure to ask if there are any special requirements that apply to your business.

If your business is retail and you collect sales tax, you have to register with your state's Department of Revenue and get a state identification number. You can get an application by calling the revenue office that's closest to you. You should also call the Secretary of State in your state to find out if your business needs any other type of registration. It might, depending on what you're doing.

Bear Facts

Don't wait for somebody to come around and tell you what registrations you need to comply with. It's up to you to find out, so contact the applicable agencies and ask. It's the old story of "Ignorance is no excuse," if it's discovered later that you don't have the proper registrations.

There's federal registration, too, for all businesses that have employees. If yours does, you need a federal identification number so you can report your employee tax withholding information. Call the IRS office nearest you to get a form for this. Other federal registration regulations might apply if your business imports or exports. Check it out with the IRS.

What's All This Talk About Taxes?

Taxes are just one of those things, aren't they? Nobody likes them, but we've all got to live with them. Taxes, and all the laws and regulations that go with them, are one of the biggest reasons you need to have the best accountant you can find.

Even when you've got a good accountant, though, it's important that you understand your tax situation. You have to know what taxes you're responsible for and how to pay the least amount possible. If something goes wrong with your tax return, it's your name on the form, and it's your door the IRS guys will come knocking at.

The way you're taxed depends on the legal structure of your business. Without getting too involved, here's how it breaks down:

➤ **Sole proprietorship** A sole proprietor is taxed as an individual. You have no separate tax return for your business, but simply attach a Schedule C to your 1040 form. You also have to pay a separate tax for the self-employed. This tax is actually your share of social security. If you were working for somebody else, you'd pay half the amount (right now, it's 15.3% of your earnings), and your employer would pick up the other half. Because you don't have an employer, you get to pay both halves. Lucky you.

Over the Rainbow

Take advantage of programs that teach you just about everything you need to know about taxes. The IRS offers tax education seminars at no charge. Call your local office to find out when and where. There's also a program called the Small Business Taxpayers Education Program (STEP) that's offered through the Small Business Administration (SBA) and other centers for small businesses. It's also a good idea to get an official tax code manual to keep in your office.

The good news for sole proprietors is that because all income is reported as personal income, you're allowed to deduct business expenses, and you may be eligible for investment tax credits, depreciation allowance, and so forth. Be sure you know what you're entitled to, and take advantage of it. This can result in big savings on what you have to pay.

➤ **Partnership** A partnership is taxed the same way as a sole proprietorship. The income or loss from the business is passed on to the partners, who include it on their personal tax returns. A Partnership Income Form is used instead of a Schedule C, and attached to the 1040 form. It requires that you report any changes in the asset and liability status of the business, making it a little more complicated than the Schedule C.

➤ **Limited liability company** A limited liability company is taxed like a partnership. The profit or loss is passed on to its members and reported on their tax returns. This means the company pays no taxes; only its members do.

This is a big plus for these companies. They enjoy the same kind of liability protection that corporations do, along with the tax advantages of partnerships.

➤ **Corporations**   As mentioned earlier, there are two kinds of corporations: C and S. C corporations, or C corps, have a double whammy when it comes to paying the federal income tax. The corporation has to pay a tax on its earned profit, and the people who get salaries or corporate dividends have to pay again. You can get around this problem somewhat by taking some of the corporation's profits in salary, commission, or bonuses, but most C corp owners continue to complain about the way their company is taxed.

S corporations are basically corporations with special tax status from the IRS. They don't pay tax on the corporate level. Profits and losses are passed on to shareholders, and shareholders include the income on their personal tax returns. If there's a loss, shareholders can write it off on their personal taxes. Many business owners like the taxation method of an S corp, but you shouldn't make your company an S corp without taking a good, long look at what it entails. There are a lot of restrictions and regulations that go along with S corps.

Grizzly Area

Don't even think about trying to figure out a way to get out of paying income taxes. The IRS doesn't look kindly on tax evasion, and you won't think much of spending time behind bars. Not everybody gets a break like Darryl Strawberry did a few years back when he was arrested for tax evasion, but allowed to play baseball while being under house arrest.

Bear Facts

The IRS has a pamphlet about S corps that you can get. It's Publication #589, called, cleverly enough, *Tax Information on S Corporations*. You can order one by calling 800-829-3676. The information also can be downloaded off the Internet. Check out the IRS Web site at www.irs.ustreas.gov.

➤ **Nonprofit corporations**   If your business is granted nonprofit status, you're exempt from paying federal income tax, and people who donate money to your organization can use the donations as tax deductions. That's the good news. The bad news, as mentioned earlier, is that getting this status is complicated and can be quite costly.

Regardless of your company's legal structure, you've got to pay careful attention to your taxes. If you don't file the right form or you're late in filing, you can be found in violation of the tax laws and fined. You might end up paying big-time late-filing penalties, plus interest.

Remember that nearly all states have state income tax, too. Some forms of ownership, specifically sole proprietorships, partnerships, and sometimes S corps, are required to pay quarterly estimated federal income taxes if the self-employment income is more than 20% of their total income.

If you have a retail business, you have to collect sales tax, which is then sent to your state revenue department along with a monthly report. If you have employees, you need to pay, and report, employee withholding taxes and social security.

As you can see, taxes are an important consideration for business owners and another damned good reason to have the best accountant you can find.

Put Some Great Players on Your Team

If you're feeling a little overwhelmed by what you've read so far in this chapter, don't be. The type of ownership you choose for your business depends on many factors. You need to consider the size of your business, what you're planning for it, whether you like to work with others or by yourself, and lots more.

The best advice I can give you is to make sure you have the best people you can find helping you. You'll need an accountant, and you'll probably need a lawyer. Hire the best people you can find, even if they cost a little more. Being an entrepreneur isn't about being able to do everything yourself; it's more about being able to find good people to do things for you.

When you're trying to figure out what type of legal structure to use for your business, think about where you want to be in five years. Plan backward, if you can. Do you plan to keep your business forever, or will you be looking to something else to do in five or ten years? This is going to affect the type of ownership arrangement you want, and many other things, too. An important part of being a successful entrepreneur is being able to look ahead and plan for where you want to be. Sure, your plans will change along the way, but you should have an idea of where you're heading.

I think the smartest and most important thing to do when you're thinking about starting a business is to find yourself the very best accountant you can. Nothing against your Uncle Bob's accounting firm there on Main Street, but in my opinion, the only way to go is with one of the Big Five firms.

Bear Facts

Here are the names and Internet addresses of the Big Five accounting firms:

PricewaterhouseCoopers: www.pwcglobal.com

Andersen Worldwide: www.arthurandersen.com

KPMG International: www.kpmg.com

Ernst & Young International: www.eyi.com

Deloitte Touche Tohmatsu International: www.deloitte.com

These firms have entrepreneur programs in their companies and can offer excellent counseling and guidance as you set up your business. I highly recommend that you contact one of these firms in your area. They can tell you how much their services will cost for a year, send you to certain banks when it comes time to get a loan, and generally steer you and your business in the right direction. My experience with two of these firms, KPMG and Ernst & Young, has been that they take great interest in entrepreneurs and are anxious to see your company grow and become successful.

When you start up a company, you're building a team, and you need the best players you can get. If you pick your friend George to be your accountant, you're getting one guy for your team. If you go to a Big Five firm, you have thousands of accountants behind you, plus the name of the Big Five firm.

Consider Your Local Zoning Laws

When you're thinking about where to put your business, remember to check out zoning laws and other factors that might affect your location choice. The most important thing to think about is where you want to be. I knew that I wanted my teddy bear factory to be near my home because it was important to me to live close to where I worked. I also knew I wanted it to be in a spot where the employees could look out and see the mountains. I wanted it to be in a place I thought was conducive to good work.

Unfortunately, zoning laws or other restrictions might not let you locate your business where you would like it to be. Make sure you check out zoning regulations and any other regulations that might affect your business. Don't think that the rules don't apply to you. I know a guy whose "I'm above the law" attitude landed him in big trouble, and one of these days will land him in jail.

Let's call the guy Don. Don, who owns a small insurance company, decided to buy himself a $1.2 million home in an exclusive, wooded community. Because the home was so large, he decided to move not only himself, but his entire insurance business into it. He figured that the business could pay the mortgage, which he couldn't afford to pay. So he partitioned off the garage and a downstairs room, turned the downstairs family room into a big office, put his CIS people upstairs in a mother-in-law's apartment, and set himself up in a large hallway at the bottom of the steps. By the time he finished, he had office space for about 15 people in a home that was zoned only for residential use.

Of course, the neighbors immediately took exception to 15 cars driving in and out several times a day, not to mention the UPS and other service vehicles that went back and forth. Undaunted, Don asked the employees to park in the lot of a church near this community and to walk across a cemetery and through the woods to his back door. I'm not kidding—this is a true story.

Of course, the employees quickly tired of the cemetery trek and of a lot of other things Don was doing. It's still not clear whether it was an employee or one of the neighbors who called the township zoning office and reported Don, but it was pretty exciting when the inspectors and the police showed up one day. Now Don is renting office space for his business and living in his partitioned-off house, which he can't sell. Real smart, Don.

Other Rules and Regulations

If you're going to own and run a business, you need to be on the lookout for regulations that apply to you. There are Occupational Safety and Health Act (OSHA) regulations for the workplace. If you own a landscaping business, for instance, you might be subject to some of the Hazardous Substance Labeling Act regulations, which require you to post warnings of potential pesticide and other chemical hazards.

Just be aware of the tons of rules and regulations you're expected to remain in compliance with. You probably don't even know about half of them, but they're there. Just as you can't avoid a speeding ticket by telling the patrolman you didn't know the speed limit was only 35, you won't impress some government inspector by saying you weren't aware of the regulation you've been found in violation of.

The Least You Need to Know

➤ Forming a corporation separates you and your personal assets from the business.

➤ There are different kinds of corporations, subject to different tax requirements.

➤ Incorporating your business requires filing with the Secretary of State in your state.

➤ Choose a name for your business that lets people know its nature and purpose.

➤ You have to register your business locally and perhaps with the state and federal governments, as well.

➤ Achieving nonprofit status can be a complicated, and expensive, procedure.

➤ It's definitely not smart to try to get around rules and regulations.

➤ You're responsible for knowing about, and complying with, rules that apply to your business.

Chapter 11

Should You Buy an Existing Business or Start Brand-New?

In This Chapter

➤ Researching the business you're thinking of buying.

➤ Taking a realistic look at where the business is heading.

➤ Pluses and minuses of buying an existing business or starting a business from scratch.

➤ Negotiating a deal.

➤ Pros and cons of franchising.

Whether to buy an existing business or start one from scratch is a common question among entrepreneurs. Sometimes the answer is obvious. If you want to own and run a company that offers rafting tours on the local river, and there's no such company, the only way to get that business running is to start and build it yourself.

If, on the other hand, you've always wanted to have a gas station, and the Citgo on the main street is up for sale, it might make sense to buy it.

In this chapter, you'll look at some of the good and bad aspects of starting new and of buying what's already in place. There are lots of considerations.

Buying an Existing Business

A lot of people think that buying an existing business is way easier than starting one from scratch. In some ways, I guess it is. Don't let anybody tell you, though, that buying an existing business doesn't take a lot of work. You have to do a lot of careful, thorough research before you agree to buy a business. If you don't, you're setting yourself up for the possibility of a big mess.

If you start a business from scratch, you can see exactly what you've got at any particular time. You're starting with nothing, and then organizing and building and creating until you've made a store, a manufacturing outfit, or whatever. You're putting the pieces together in the way you want them—the way you understand.

But when you buy somebody else's business, you have no idea what's there. Sure, you can walk through and look at the inventory, watch the employees in action, and check out the customer base. You can get the owner to tell you all about how the business started and how he's run it for the past 25 years. Unless you're willing to get down and dirty, however, you still don't have a complete understanding of that business.

The most important thing you've got to do is get a complete and thorough understanding of the place's financial statements, which should determine whether you buy the business. Financial statements are reports done in a specific manner to meet the guidelines of Generally Accepted Accounting Principles (GAAP). They're used to convey information about your company's operations and financial position. When done using the GAAP guidelines, your financials can be distributed to whoever needs to see them.

Generally, financial statements contain the following:

➤ Income statement

➤ Balance sheet

➤ Retained earnings statement

➤ Cash flow statement

➤ Notes to the financial statement

Don't take the owner's financial statements at face value unless they're audited financials, backed up by a reputable auditing firm. The type of financial statements you're dealing with are important, and it's up to you to make sure they're complete and accurate.

What you need to determine from the financial statements is whether you can make a profit from the business. Does that business make enough money for you to pay back your loan (assuming you borrow money to buy the business) and still make a profit?

You need to know the value of the business before you can decide whether it's a good idea for you to buy it. Avoid the temptation to overlook financial shortcomings of the business because you think you can buy it and quickly turn it around. Should you be optimistic? Oh, yeah. Should you be unrealistic? No way.

It's gonna take time to turn a business around, even if you're the best manager since Lee Iaccoca. You can't assume that your profits will increase by 300% the first year you have the business. Well, I guess you can assume that if you want, but you can't build a business plan on that assumption. You can rebuild a sluggish business, but it will take time and probably cost some money. Maybe you'll have to renovate or remodel the existing store or plant. Maybe you have to upgrade and update your inventory to attract more customers.

Nobody's saying you can't do it, but make sure you're realistic about what's involved and how long it will take. If possible, you want to get complete, audited financials, with everything on them verified. You should have records for at least the past three years. If the business hasn't been around that long, get records from its start.

Financial statements aren't the simplest things to analyze and understand. It's going to take some time and effort. You can get an accountant or someone to help you, but don't let somebody else do the work for you. If you don't understand the financials, you won't understand the business. If you don't understand it, you shouldn't buy it.

To determine the value of the business, you've got to look at factors such as the amount of inventory on hand, money that's owed to the business, money that the business owes to suppliers, and so forth. You don't want to find out after you've signed an agreement that the seller sent out thousands of dollars worth of bogus bills to make it look like a lot of money is coming in, or that he owes a lot more to suppliers than you realized.

You need to research the market value of the business by finding out the selling prices of similar businesses, and figure out items like the replacement and liquidation values of assets. You also need to determine whether the business is in any legal proceedings that might result in lawsuits. What if you buy that Citgo on Main Street and find out six months from now that the underground gas tanks have been leaking for the past 10 years?

If good records aren't available, watch out! Poor recordkeeping indicates poor management, and that spells trouble. Inadequate recordkeeping could also mean that somebody's been trying to hide something. Either way, it's a headache you don't want to deal with.

Grizzly Area

Be sure you don't rush into buying a business without considering all the factors. Sometimes we're so anxious to get started with something that we overlook shortcomings, thinking we can fix them once we're up and running. That might work for minor issues, but if you overlook a major problem, you're going to inherit it and likely have a hard time overcoming it.

Over the Rainbow

Many times in this book, I've strongly recommended that you look for help of one kind or another. Working with and understanding financial statements is one area in which you should seek help. Rely on your lawyer or accountant to help you with them. Read books about them. Get advice from other business owners. Take a business course, if practical. Do whatever you need to do, but make sure you know what's going on.

133

Be sure to find out why the business is for sale. Usually, there's a legitimate reason— the owner wants to retire, he's moving out of the area, he's decided to start a new business, his partner just died, or something similar.

However, if you find out the business is for sale because the roof has been leaking like a sieve and the owner doesn't have the money to put on a new one, or because the IRS has been calling to find out about a little problem with the last tax returns, look out. The last thing you need when starting out is to find yourself embroiled in legal problems that aren't even of your own making.

Over the Rainbow

Sometimes an owner who wants to sell a business might be less than honest when telling you her reasons. She might want the business to look better than it is or avoid mentioning any problems she's having with it. Be observant of facial expression and body language when you're talking to somebody about reasons for selling. Nonverbal clues can tell you a lot.

The Word According to John

Due diligence is a business term frequently bandied about. Different people define it in different ways, but all it really means is finding out every last thing you can about a company. Due diligence relates to finances, location, marketing, and every other aspect of a business.

Knowing why the business is for sale helps you determine and negotiate a buying price. If the owner clearly is under a great deal of pressure to get rid of the business, it should help you get it at a better price. Just make sure you won't be stuck with the reason the owner was so anxious to get rid of it!

The thorough, meticulous process of looking carefully at all aspects of a company you're considering buying is called *due diligence*. Due diligence is not only smart, it's necessary. Investors conduct due diligence all the time when they're considering putting money into a business, and you need to do it when you're checking out a business you're thinking of buying.

Now that you know how important it is to conduct due diligence before you buy a business, let's have a look at some of the possible advantages of buying an existing business.

Pluses of Buying an Existing Business

There are definitely some advantages to buying an existing business instead of starting up your own from scratch, such as:

➤ *You get a business.* If your goal is to get a business, buying one is quicker than starting one. If you don't particularly want to go through the process of starting a business, and you've got the money to do it, buying one ready-made puts you a giant step ahead.

➤ *You get customers and income.* There's a lot to be said for not having to scratch around for customers. To know you have a customer base and the money that comes with it can be worth a lot.

➤ *You get suppliers.* Finding good suppliers can be a hassle, but yours will already be in place.

➤ *You get a track record.* Looking at a company's financial records gives you a good indication of what your expenses, revenues, and profits will be. You'll know what to expect if you take over the business.

➤ *You might get a custom-made management course.* Often, the person selling the business agrees to stick around for six months or so to teach you how to run the business. Sure, you've got to pay a salary, or work a deal with the purchase but it very well might be worth the money. Some new owners don't like that, preferring to feel things out on their own, but a person who's run a business successfully and understands all its nuances is a valuable resource. You could benefit greatly by taking advantage of her expertise.

➤ *You might get a good deal.* Maybe the seller *really* wants to get rid of his business because he's inherited a ton of money and decided to become a surf bum in Hawaii. Even if the business isn't your cup of tea (as they say), you could buy it cheap, keep it for a few years, and sell it for a good profit. That's not a bad deal!

➤ *You might get the framework of a business that you can build up and really make your own.* Sometimes one person sees great potential in a business that another person can't. Maybe you see a business with great potential that's being poorly managed. Good ideas, enthusiasm, and a positive outlook can make it possible for you to take a not-so-great business and turn it into something that's all yours and fabulous.

➤ *You might be able to invest less money initially.* If the seller is willing to finance part of the sale, as many are to help sell the business for the price they want, you might be able to negotiate a manageable down payment and pay off the balance over time with a lower interest rate than you could get from a bank or other lender. The business is used as collateral.

➤ *You get experienced employees.* You won't have to find and train employees, because you'll already have them in place.

These are factors to consider if you're thinking about buying an existing business. It could be a good idea. Of course, there's a downside to existing businesses, too. Let's have a look.

Minuses of Buying an Existing Business

As much as you want to think everything will be rosy if you buy a business that's already out there, you've got to face the fact that some businesses just aren't worth having. The last thing you want is to buy a business and be faced with one headache after another. Putting out fires gets to be old—real fast.

Let's look at some of the possible disadvantages of buying a ready-made business:

➤ *You might have to sink a lot of money into it.* Maybe you're getting a great price on the business, but if the machinery or other equipment is outmoded and needs to be replaced, it's not such a bargain, is it?

➤ *You might be getting a losing proposition.* If the market for the business you're thinking of buying is shrinking, or there are too many competitors, you could be looking at buying a sinking ship. That's why it's so important to research all aspects of the business thoroughly before agreeing to buy it.

➤ *You could be walking into a hornet's nest.* What if you buy a company with disgruntled employees, dissatisfied customers, and an outdated product? Or, what if you want to bring in all new employees, but the present ones don't want to leave? You can get rid of them, but you'll be setting yourself up as the bad guy before you even get your business started.

Sometimes it's easier to start from scratch than to have to undo a lot of problems and then try to make them right. You've got to carefully consider all the possibilities before deciding whether to go new or used.

Starting from Scratch

Some entrepreneurs think that starting a business from scratch is the only way to do it. The thrill of the start-up is what they most enjoy. To them, that's the essence of being an entrepreneur. I must say that I strongly identify with this group. I love the challenge of starting a business and watching it grow.

Bear Facts

Some people think that starting your own business from scratch is the only way to go. Although I think there's no feeling like growing a business from nothing to something big, buying an existing business and making it your own can be equally rewarding. Either kind of business is going to require a lot of your time and energy, and the success of either one depends on you.

To me, the excitement of starting your own business is the number one reason to do it. It's fun. It's a challenge. Each day brings something different. Plus, if you do it right, you can make a lot of money.

Pluses of Starting from Scratch

In addition to the fun of starting a business and watching it evolve from a dream into a reality, there are other, perhaps more practical, advantages, too. Here are some of them:

➤ *You're not getting somebody else's problems.* You'll have headaches, to be sure, but they'll be your own headaches, not the last owner's.

➤ *You can start small.* If you don't have a lot of capital or experience, you can start your own business small and grow it as you are able.

➤ *You'll be able to grow with your business.* You'll learn new things every day as your business grows. You'll learn how to solve problems as they crop up, instead of having someone tell you how he or she would handle it. You'll do things your way, not the way they've always been done. You'll learn to be creative and resourceful because you'll have to be.

➤ *You can create your legacy.* You can start with nothing but an idea, build it into a great business, and pass it along to your kids (if they want it). You get to name your business and envision that name on trucks and signs. If you name your business after yourself—Ben & Jerry's and Burton Snowboards, both Vermont companies, come to mind—you'll be making yourself famous. That sounds pretty darned satisfying, doesn't it?

Starting up your own business is a great experience, but don't expect a walk in the park. There are lots of things to think about.

Minuses of Starting from Scratch

As much as I think starting from scratch is cool, I will admit that there are some disadvantages. A few are listed below:

➤ *You have a great degree of unknown.* You can't really know what to expect in a business until you're in it. Sure, you can read everything available, have a great business plan, and follow all the advice you learned in business school. Until you've done it, however, you can't know all that's involved in running a business.

➤ *You have a greater chance of the business failing.* Statistically, more than half of all new businesses fail within the first five years. That doesn't mean your business is going to fail, or, if it does, you won't go on to something else and be a huge success. However, the failure rate of start-ups is higher than that of established businesses.

➤ *You might be looking at some lean times initially.* It usually takes a couple of years for a new business to start showing a profit, and it's hard work. An existing business could give you a profit right away, and you don't have the actual, physical work of setting up offices and that sort of thing.

After you consider all the pluses and minuses of buying a business and starting one from scratch, trust your instinct for what would work best for you. Which sounds like more fun to you? Which option do you think you'd be more comfortable with?

There's a growing trend of buying existing businesses. Many people who have been downsized are buying businesses already in operation. People who have retired from a career are buying small businesses for some income and occupation. People in this group are called *buyout entrepreneurs*.

How Do You Find the Business You Want?

Maybe you've always wanted to own a flower shop. You love the smell and colors of flowers and how they feel when you touch them. You've just been notified that you're going to be laid off from your job in three months, and you're thinking that now might be the time to make your dream a reality. But how do you go about finding a flower shop, or another kind of business that could be converted into a flower shop, to buy?

There are several ways.

Often, you hear about a business that's for sale from somebody you know. It's just one of the topics people talk about. It's news. Your banker, lawyer, or accountant might know about businesses for sale. Maybe somebody at your local Chamber of Commerce or Small Business Administration has heard of something. Ask around.

That's a common and effective way of learning about business opportunities. You might learn of a shop for sale through the classified ads, too. Your local newspaper has classified ads, as do business and trade magazines. Those little ads don't give you much information, but they might just serve to let you know something's available. You can call the owner or stop by to see if it's a business you want to pursue.

Business brokers are like real estate agents, except they handle businesses. Hired by the seller, they handle advertising for the sale and put potential buyers in touch with the seller. They help with the sales agreement later on, and maybe even with the financing arrangements.

Sometimes the best opportunities for buying businesses are ones you make yourself. There's no law that says you can't approach the owner of that great flower shop downtown and ask if she's interested in selling it. Sure, she might say no. But if you make an attractive offer, she might consider it. Maybe she's not interested in selling now, but will be in a year or two. Who knows?

Negotiating a Business Purchase

Say you've decided to buy a business. Maybe it's the Main Street Citgo, the tool and die shop, or the cool bookstore over on the other side of town.

You're excited as can be. You've researched everything. You've conferred with lawyers, and you've checked out the deed and the mortgage on the property. You've talked to the property owner and made sure you can get the lease extended. You've been over the financial statements countless times, and you're sure that everything is in order. You really want this business, and you're ready to buy.

How do you do that?

Maybe there's a third party involved, such as a business broker. If that's the case, she'll pretty much run things. Still, you need to know the procedure and what to look for. Or you and the seller might negotiate the deal on your own. That's okay, but you probably want to consult with a lawyer before you sign any agreements or commit yourself to buying.

After carefully considering everything about the business, you need to come up with what you think is a fair price. This won't necessarily—in fact, it probably won't—be the seller's asking price.

If you don't have the money to pay for the business upfront, figure out where you're going to get it. A bank? A loan from a relative? Is the seller going to finance it?

When you know where your money is coming from, put your offer in writing and submit it to the seller. Your lawyer can help you write up an offer, or you can do it yourself. At this point, you should expect some negotiating between you and the seller. The seller will probably come back with another number, somewhere between his original asking price and your offer.

You have to do what you think is fair. If you're sure that your offer was a good one, hold firm. Explain to the seller exactly how you came up with your number and why you think it's fair. Explain your research and what you based your offer on.

Over the Rainbow

Buying a business entails a lot more details than buying a house or a car. I've seen a lot of business deals done, and no two were done the same way. Be sure you have somebody you trust to help you when it's time to buy.

Over the Rainbow

Some people are uncomfortable offering a price for a business that's lower than what the seller was asking. If you've researched it thoroughly and can back up your offer with facts, however, you've got a good chance of getting the property for less than the asking price. Be confident and persuasive when you negotiate.

You can leave yourself a little room for movement, but set a firm limit, and don't go over it unless there's a compelling reason to do so.

If you reach an agreement, have a lawyer draw up an agreement. Remember that you have to check to make sure there are no liens on the property or any other reason the sale wouldn't be valid. You need to have a final inventory count of assets, too. After you and your lawyer are satisfied that everything is in order, go ahead and sign. Congratulations on your new business!

What About a Franchise?

Franchising can be a great way to get a business, or it can be a nightmare. I've known people who swear by franchising, and others who won't get near it.

What is franchising, exactly? For our purposes, a franchise agreement means you get to sell a trademarked product, such as Pizza Hut pizza or Wendy's old-fashioned hamburgers. For this privilege, you, the franchisee, pay a percentage of every sale to the franchiser.

Pros and Cons of Franchising

Why would you sell Wendy's hamburgers and give a percentage of each sale to Wendy's instead of setting up your own hamburger stand on the corner? There are a number of reasons:

➤ *Franchises account for almost one-third of all retail sales.* People like a sure thing. If you go into Wendy's in Peoria, Illinois, you're going to be able to get basically the same food you can get in Baton Rouge, Louisiana; Spokane, Washington; Bangor, Maine; or Los Angeles, California. Sure, there's better food than Wendy's to be had in all those places, but you've got to hunt for it. When you go into Wendy's, you pretty much know exactly what to expect, and people like that.

➤ *A very small percentage of franchise operations fail.* The U.S. Department of Commerce says the failure rate is only about 5%. Franchise sales have even continued to grow during the last few recessions in this country.

➤ *You don't need a ton of business experience to run many of the franchises out there.* Most companies will set you up with a business plan. You don't have to prove your product—that's already been done. And you pretty much get a ready-made customer base. Yeah, I can see the appeal in that.

➤ *You can take advantage of the company's advertising and promotional campaigns.* Remember when McDonald's gave away those mini beanie babies with their kids' meals and people were buying 25 kids meals just for the prizes? You get that marketing expertise when you have a franchise, and you don't have to do anything but keep making the burgers. You get name recognition that would take a long time to build up if you were starting your own company. When somebody needs to have his drain unclogged, he knows to call Roto-Rooter. If you have the Roto-Rooter franchise, you'll get the call, thanks to the company's name recognition.

Bear Facts

There are franchises that sell things, like hamburgers, and there are service franchises, like pest control, lawn care, and cleaning companies. The service franchises are usually less expensive to get into, and they're great business experience. You learn how to run a business and work with customers. They provide wonderful learning opportunities and can be very good ventures.

So why wouldn't somebody want to sell Wendy's old-fashioned burgers? Why would somebody go up against the Wendy's and McDonald's and Burger Kings to start his own burger shop? I can think of a few reasons:

➤ *A franchise isn't* really *your business.* Sure, you're running it, and you're making money from it. But you can't put out a sign that says "Sortino's—serving McDonald's hamburgers." The restaurant is McDonald's, not Sortino's.

➤ *You're not really your own boss.* You've got to follow the rules and go by the regulations set by the franchiser. This limitation could tend to get on your nerves. You have to make the burgers their way, not yours. You have to use a certain sauce on the chicken sandwiches and a particular kind of roll. Doesn't leave much to the imagination, does it?

➤ *You've got to hand back a percentage of the cost of every hamburger you sell.* I'd think that could get on your nerves, too.

➤ *The popular franchises are expensive to buy and might not be available where or when you want them.* Companies might not let you franchise in a certain location, or they may allow so many franchises in your area that you'll end up competing with other franchise locations of the same company.

Top-Ranked Franchises

Speaking of popular franchises, what are some of them? There are hundreds of businesses with franchises, but the latest list of the top 20 according to *Entrepreneur* magazine are the following:

1. Yogen Fruz Worldwide (yogurt)
2. McDonald's
3. Jani-King (maintenance/commercial cleaning)
4. 7-Eleven Convenience Stores
5. Jackson Hewitt Tax Service
6. KFC (chicken)
7. Subway
8. Century Small Business Solutions
9. Wendy's
10. Taco Bell
11. CleanNet USA (maintenance)
12. Coldwell Banker Real Estate
13. Blimpie Int'l. Inc.
14. Curves for Women (fitness center)
15. Papa John's Pizza
16. TCBY (yogurt)
17. Mail Boxes Etc.
18. Re/Max Int'l (real estate)
19. Miracle Ear Hearing Systems
20. CD Warehouse, Inc.

Although it can cost hundreds of thousands of dollars for some franchise agreements, some are considered a low investment. According to *Entrepreneur*, here are the top 10 low-investment franchises:

1. Jani-King
2. Coverall Cleaning Concepts
3. Merle Norman Cosmetics
4. Jazzercise Inc.
5. ServiceMaster
6. Chem-Dry

7. Merry Maids

8. Jackson Hewitt Tax Service

9. Terminix Termite & Pest Control

10. Novus Windshield Repair

It's interesting that the great majority of franchisees have college educations and a pretty substantial net worth. A lot of them are people who have lost their jobs because of corporate downsizing.

If you're interested in franchising a business, check out some of the many magazines that advertise franchise opportunities, including *Entrepreneur*, *Franchise Opportunities*, and others. Or check out *Entrepreneur*'s Web site at www.entrepreneurmag.com, or *The Franchise Handbook* online at www.franchise1.com.

If you commit to the franchise concept, you enter a franchise agreement with whoever your franchiser will be. You have a contract that tells you what you can and can't do, the amount of time you're obligated to the franchiser, how you must prepare the site of your operation, what kind of training you need to have, and so forth. It's a good idea to run the contract by your lawyer, because it generally covers a lot of ground and can be fairly complex. For instance, some companies add a clause to their contracts that gives them the right to buy you out, if they want to. You need to be aware of the possibility for these kinds of stipulations.

You might consider visiting some franchise owners and finding out what it's like to be a franchisee before you commit to it. Ask any questions that come to your mind. After all, these are the people who are doing it. You'll probably get a good indication of what having a franchise is all about.

As you can see, there are advantages and disadvantages to starting your own business, buying an existing business, and franchising. After you consider all the pros and cons, you have to decide what you think would work best for you. That depends on what you're looking for and what you see for yourself.

Lots of people buy franchises as investments, but never get involved with running them. If you get a good franchise and good people to run it for you, it can be a good way to make some money. Just be sure to do you homework. You should at least be aware of how the people you hire are running the business, terms of the agreement, and so forth.

Grizzly Area

Watch out for companies that are just beginning to franchise. If you become a franchisee, you run the risk of being a franchise *guinea pig*. There are some up-and-coming companies, to be sure, and you could be getting in on the ground floor of a great opportunity if you sign up with them. Just be aware that there might be growing pains.

The Least You Need to Know

➤ If you're thinking of buying an existing business, you have to be prepared to conduct a lot of research, especially on the business's financial statements.

➤ Be objective about the condition of the business you're looking at and realistic about what you're getting.

➤ There are advantages and disadvantages to buying someone else's business.

➤ There are also advantages and disadvantages to starting a business from scratch.

➤ You can find a business that's for sale by talking to people, checking out the classified ads in newspapers and trade journals, or hiring a business broker.

➤ When negotiating a business deal, be confident about your offer and able to back it up with facts.

➤ Some people swear that franchising is the way to go, and others want nothing to do with it.

Chapter 12

The All-Important Business Plan

In This Chapter

➤ The goals of your business plan.

➤ Getting started with your plan.

➤ Making a business plan for your business.

➤ The main parts of a business plan.

➤ Extras you need to include.

➤ Protecting your plan.

If you take nothing else from this book (but that would be a waste of time and money, wouldn't it?), take with you the information in this chapter on your business plan. It's the most important chapter of this book.

I used the Small Business Administration's business plan as a model for my first plan, and it's the plan I refer to throughout the chapter. It's a great business plan. You can, and should, revise it to fit your needs and your particular goals, but it's a good model. To me, it's the one to use.

Before I get into the mechanics of the plan, let's have a look at why you need it and what purpose it serves.

What Should Your Business Plan Accomplish?

Your business plan should accomplish two goals. It serves as a guide to you, your founders team, managers, and employees for how you want your company to progress and grow, and it also serves as a sales document when you're trying to attract funding for your business.

You can't say that one purpose is more important than the other. They're both essential. You can't successfully run a business if you don't have a clear idea of what you're doing and what you hope to accomplish. Nor can you run a business without money.

So you can see that your business plan is an extremely important document.

Your Plan as a Working Document

Drawn up and used properly, your business plan serves as a guide to how you're going to run your business. It helps you operate more efficiently and profitably and with fewer hassles.

For one thing, it puts everybody in your business on the same page. If you, your founders team, managers, and the key employees are using and frequently referring to the same plan, you'll all have the same ideas about where you're heading and how you're going to get there.

A good business plan keeps your company grounded and on the right track. It keeps you from doing things too quickly and tells you when you're lagging in a certain area. It's tempting when you have a new business to try to grow it too quickly. Your business plan can guide you as you think about expanding.

Grizzly Area

Your business plan is the best guide you'll have, but it's important to remember that it's not written in stone. Say that somebody comes along and offers you a spectacular price for your business. You shouldn't refuse to sell it just because it's not part of your business plan. Some people get so wrapped up in the plans that they can't see outside them, and that's a danger.

When you write and update your plan, it forces you to take a hard look at what you're doing, what you want to do, and whether those goals are going to work. You might realize while writing your marketing analysis, for instance, that the market for your product or service isn't as good as you thought it was. Oops! Still, it's better to find that out while you're writing your plan than when you've gone into full production, making something you won't be able to sell.

Catching mistakes while you're writing your business plan is like discovering the person you're engaged to marry isn't really the person you had thought. It's a hard realization, but it's better to find out before the wedding bells have rung.

Another benefit of a good business plan is that it gives you new ideas about your business. New insights and inspirations should evolve as you work on it, and you shouldn't be afraid to incorporate them.

Your Plan as a Sales Instrument

Your business plan is the most important sales tool you have, other than yourself. For that reason, it must be done well.

Remember, when you give your business plan to potential investors, you're telling them how you're going to run the company profitably so that you can repay their loans with interest. You've got to have a clear plan for how to do that and be able to convey it so that investors can understand. Your plan should be easy to read and understand, well organized, and nicely presented.

Many entrepreneurs try to start their businesses without business plans, usually because they're intimidated by the idea of writing one. Believe me, writing a plan is not all that difficult, especially when you have one (like the SBA's) to use as a guide.

The most important thing is to get started and get a plan onto paper. You can always refine it later. Then show your plan to people who have started businesses or are otherwise familiar with business plans. Get all the advice and suggestions you can to make your plan better, and don't be afraid to use your business plan when meeting with investors.

Over the Rainbow

When you present your business plan to potential investors, be receptive to their suggestions and criticisms, and don't, under any circumstances, get defensive. Remember that investors have looked at a lot of plans. You can get some great ideas for making your plan better if you pay attention and are open to suggestions.

Your Business Plan Is for Your Business

Although I recommend the SBA plan as a guide for your business plan, you need to understand how important it is for your plan to be your own. Investors want to know *your* plans. They want to know your background, how you came up with your ideas, and what your company is going to do. They're not interested in the model plan; they want to know about you and your plan.

You can hire individuals or companies to write a business plan for you, but I think that's a mistake. These plans tend to look and read much the same, and most investors know right off you didn't write it.

You can tell somebody about what you want to do, but only you can write it exactly the way you want it. Don't be tempted to copy somebody else's plan. As I said earlier, writing a business plan isn't all that difficult. You've got to have a plan that's about your business, not someone else's.

What Your Business Plan Should Include

Okay. Here's where we really get down to business (no pun intended). What should be in your business plan? Good question.

The main body of your business plan can be divided into four sections:

➤ A description of your business

➤ Your marketing plan

➤ Your financial management plan

➤ Your management plan

In addition to the main body, your plan should include the following extra material and information:

➤ An executive summary

➤ Supporting documents

➤ Financial projections

➤ A cover sheet

➤ A statement of purpose

➤ A table of contents

Let's look at each of the main parts of your plan first, and then I'll get to the extra components.

I'll discuss each part of the business plan so you can see how it's important to the overall content.

Over the Rainbow

Remember that this information is based on the Small Business Administration's business plan, which is what I used as a model when I started The Vermont Teddy Bear Company. You can find the SBA plan, and lots of other good stuff, at the organization's Web site: www.sba.gov. Click on "Starting" for the business plan information.

Your Business Description

In this section, you give a detailed description of your business. You include information about the products or services you'll offer, who your market will be, and where your business will be located.

Be sure that, while describing your business, you include any unique aspects or special features, and explain how or why they will appeal to consumers.

Here's what your business description should include:

➤ Legal stuff. When describing your business, you should explain its legal structure. Will you have a sole proprietorship, partnership, limited partnership, or corporation? Explain which form you'll use and why it will work for your particular business. Note what licenses and permits you'll need and how you'll get them.

➤ The type of business. What kind of business will you be operating? Will it be a manufacturing operation? Merchandising? Service?

➤ Your product or service. Describe the product you'll be manufacturing or the service you'll be providing. Be detailed and specific.

➤ New or used? Describe your business in terms of how you got it and the type of company it is. Is it a franchise? Are you taking the business over from somebody else or starting it brand-new? Are you expanding an existing business?

➤ Profitability. Explain why your business will be profitable. Describe the growth opportunities, and how you'll take advantage of them.

➤ Describe your business hours. Will you be a 9 to 5 retail operation? A three-shift manufacturing plant? Explain why your hours make sense for your operation.

➤ Acquired knowledge. Explain what you've learned about the type of business you'll be starting from sources such as bankers, suppliers, business publications, and other business owners. All this information will clearly identify your goals and objectives. It should explain exactly why you're starting a business and what you hope to accomplish with it.

When describing the product or service your business will offer and the market to which it will be offered, try to think like a customer. Explain how your product or service will benefit your customers and what customers will like about it. Include the following:

➤ What you're selling. Describe your product or service in detail. Don't say you'll be selling teddy bears; instead, tell how your teddy bears will be jointed, made from 100% synthetic, high-quality fabric, and so forth.

➤ The benefits of, and demand for, your product or service. What will customers like about it? Get into the minds of your prospective customers and describe why they'll think your product is the best and why they'll want to have it.

➤ What's different about your product or service. Lots of companies make teddy bears, but mine were the best because they were put together with quality workmanship and first-rate materials, and came with extras like neat outfits and chocolates. Explain what makes your product or service different and better than your competitor's.

Over the Rainbow

The business description part of your business plan is really important because it defines your endeavor. It not only will tell potential investors what you plan to do, but will firm up your own expectations and plans as well.

This section of your business plan also includes information about the location of your business. Make sure the location you've chosen is a good one, keeping in mind accessibility, security, and so forth. The topics you'll address in your plan include:

➤ Your location needs. Address the physical location of the business and why it makes sense. Are you close to a major highway, thereby making it easier to get and send out shipments? Tell why you chose the location you did.

➤ What kind of space do you have or need? If you've purchased a large building, explain how you'll use the space. If it's a small location, explain why you don't need more space.

➤ Why it works for you. Explain why the area you've chosen is desirable and how it will work for your business.

➤ How's the building? Discuss the condition of the building and describe why it's just what you need.

➤ Accessibility. If customers need to come to you, can they get there easily? Do you have accessibility from good roads or public transportation? Do you have adequate parking? Handicapped entrances? How's the lighting around the building or parking lot?

➤ Market or demographic shifts. Include trends that indicate the market will be shifting to the advantage of your business. If you're opening a day-care center, for instance, note that a new housing development is under construction, with many of the houses under contract to families with young children.

The description of your business is an important part of your business plan. Make sure you include all the pertinent information and that it's stated clearly and is easy to read and understand.

Your Marketing Plan

An important part of your business plan is a sound marketing plan. I'll discuss marketing in length in Chapter 15, "Sales and Marketing," but you should know now that marketing plays a vital role in successful business ventures. How well you market your business has a lot to do with whether it will be successful.

The key elements of a successful marketing plan are defining your market and knowing your customers. Pay attention to what you designate as your market because it can affect your chances of getting funding and the scope of your business after it's started. For instance, when I wrote my marketing plan for The Vermont Teddy Bear Company, I didn't describe my market as the teddy bear market. I described it as the stuffed animal/gift/toy/mail order business. You can see how this description created a much larger market for the company.

In addition to defining your market, you need to know your customers. Get to know what they like and dislike and what they expect from your product or service. This information will help you create a marketing plan that meets their needs and gives them what they want.

Before you begin exploring the main areas of your marketing plan, though, answer the following questions. Your marketing plan should include their answers:

➤ Who are your customers? Identify them by age, sex, income/educational level, and residence.

➤ Are your markets growing, steady, or declining?

➤ Is your market share growing, steady, or declining?

➤ If you're opening a franchise, how is your market segmented?

➤ Are your markets large enough to expand?

➤ How will you attract, hold, or increase your market share?

➤ How will you promote your sales?

➤ What will your pricing strategy be?

If the answers to some of these questions are unclear, review the parts of this book that deal with those issues, or check the glossary in the back of the book for some other good reading choices.

Now let's look at the primary topics your marketing plan will address: competition, pricing and sales, and advertising and public relations.

Grizzly Area

Pay close attention to the content of your business plan. You might discover it includes some information that you don't like. If, for instance, when writing your marketing plan, you realize your markets are too small to be viable, you have a problem that needs to be addressed. Don't ignore the information you're gathering and plow ahead because you don't want to deal with it. Even if you don't recognize problems and deal with them, potential investors will.

➤ Competition. Our society thrives on competition. It's evident in many areas, ranging from sports contests to athletic scholarships to attracting members to a particular church. Competition in business is evident as well. We compete for customers, for market share, for publicity, and so on. One of the best steps you can take when facing competition is to get to know exactly who the competitor is and what it's doing. You should look carefully at your competitor's products and services, its advertising and marketing techniques, who its customers are, how it runs its operations, and so forth.

➤ Pricing and sales. There's a lot to know about determining a pricing strategy, and I get into it in detail in Chapter 17, "Profit." For the purposes of your business plan, however, you should know that your pricing strategy can be used to improve your overall competitiveness. You need to consider factors such as retail cost and pricing; competitive pricing; pricing above or below competition; costs of labor, materials, and overhead; and so forth. It's important to have a pricing strategy that's carefully thought out and planned and to constantly monitor your prices and sales to ensure a profit.

➤ Advertising and public relations. These topics are important to your marketing plan and important pieces of your business. Make a plan that uses advertising and networking as a means to promote your business. Come up with some ad copy (or get someone to help you). If you're opening a franchise, the franchiser supplies advertising and promotional materials as part of the franchise package. You might need approval to use any materials you and your staff develop. Make sure the advertisements you come up with are consistent with the image you're trying to project.

Issues relating to marketing will become much clearer as you continue with this book. It's a fascinating area and one that's important to your business. Be sure your business plan reflects your understanding of how important marketing is.

Financial Management Plan

Sound financial management is important and necessary in keeping your business profitable and solvent. How well you manage your business's finances is the cornerstone of every successful business venture. Each year thousands of potentially successful businesses fail because of poor financial management. As a business owner, you need to identify and implement financial systems that support your goals.

Your business plan should include startup and operating budgets. The startup budget includes one-time and other costs incurred before your business opens. Your operating budget includes the ongoing costs. Remember to include the following items in these budgets:

➤ **Startup budget:** Include personnel (costs before opening), legal and professional fees, licenses and permits, equipment, insurance, supplies, advertising and promotions, salaries and wages, accounting, income, utilities, payroll expenses.

➤ **Operating budget:** Make up a budget for the first three to six months of operation. Include the following expenses: personnel, insurance, rent, depreciation, loan payments, advertising and promotions, legal and accounting, miscellaneous expenses, supplies, payroll expenses, salaries and wages, utilities, dues and subscriptions, fees, taxes, repairs and maintenance.

The financial section of your business plan should also include:

➤ Any loan applications you've filed

➤ Capital equipment and supply list

Over the Rainbow

When you start to show your business plan to potential investors, make sure you take advantage of their expertise. Bankers and other investors will give you suggestions about how to improve your business plan, so be sure you pay attention and make the changes. That way, by the time you hit your third or fourth candidate, your plan will be in really good shape.

➤ Balance sheet

➤ Break-even analysis

➤ Profit and loss statement

➤ Pro-forma cash flow

The income statement and cash flow projections should also include a three-year summary that's detailed by month for the first year and by quarter for the second and third years.

This part of your business plan generally addresses the accounting system and the inventory control system you'll be using for your business. If you're experienced with such systems, you can do them on your own, or you can get your accountant to help you.

Regardless of who sets up the systems, you need to acquire a thorough understanding of each area and how the whole system operates.

Your plan should include explanations of all your projections. It's not enough to state your projections; you need to explain what they're based on, too.

Over the Rainbow

Unless you really know what you're doing, get some help in preparing your cash flow and income statements and your balance sheet. Thinking you can handle more than you really can is a danger you should avoid. Get your accountant to help you with these documents.

Your Management Plan

The last major part of the body of your business plan is your management plan, but it's no less important than any of the other sections.

Managing a business takes a lot of know-how and discipline. You've got to keep up with what's going on and be dedicated, persistent, and confident. You must believe in yourself as well as the people and systems you're managing.

The people in your business are your most valuable assets and resources. It's important that you understand the people who make up your business and know their strengths, weaknesses, and attitudes. There are many things to consider, and I deal extensively with the people you work with in Part 4, "No Man (or Woman) Is an Island," of this book.

Your management plan should address issues such as the following:

➤ Your background and business experience and how it can help you in the business you're starting

➤ Your strengths and your weaknesses and how you can make the most of them or compensate for them

153

➤ Who the members of your management team will be

➤ The strengths and weaknesses of the team

➤ The duties of your management team

➤ How these duties are defined

➤ The type of assistance you can expect from the franchiser, if you're starting a franchise

➤ If this assistance will be ongoing

➤ Your current personnel needs

➤ Your plans for hiring and training personnel

➤ The salaries, benefits, vacations, and holidays you'll offer employees

➤ What benefits, if any, you might be able to offer

These issues should be included in your management plan and used as a guide once you've got your business up and running.

In addition to these four main parts of a business plan, you need to include the extras I mentioned earlier:

➤ An executive summary

➤ Supporting documents

➤ Financial projections

➤ A cover sheet

➤ A statement of purpose

➤ A table of contents

Let's have a look at each one, and see what it entails for your plan:

➤ **Executive summary:** This is essentially a shortened version of your business plan. It allows someone to get an idea of what you're doing without reading the entire plan. It should summarize the entire plan, touching on everything that's important. The executive summary should include your company's strategy, an overview of your products and services, and how they'll be marketed. You should briefly discuss your competition and supply information such as your location, your future plans, and so forth. The executive summary is best done after your plan is completed. That way, you can look over the plan and pull out the pertinent information.

➤ **Supporting documents:** They should include tax returns of principals for the past three years; your personal financial statement (all banks have these forms); a copy of the franchise contract and all supporting documents provided by the franchiser, if applicable; and a copy of the proposed lease or purchase agreement for building space. Also, copies of all licenses and other legal documents, copies of the resumes of all principals, and copies of letters of intent from suppliers, and so on.

➤ **Financial projections:** These are based on your financial plan. Remember that you need to support your projections with explanations.

➤ **Cover sheet:** This serves to identify the business and the purpose of your business plan. Include the address and phone number of the business and the names of all principals.

➤ **Statement of purpose:** This includes your company's mission statement, goals and objectives, value statement, and vision statement.

➤ **Table of contents:** The table of contents, which simply tells what's included in your business plan, should be placed directly after the cover sheet. Use major headings and subheadings to identify the contents.

Grizzly Area

Your business plan doesn't have to be a slick publication, but make sure it's done neatly and put together attractively. It's easy to design a professional-looking plan with readily available software. To have a business plan that looks sloppy or hastily put together could hurt your chances of attracting investors.

As you can see, your business plan contains all the essential elements of your business. It is an extremely important document, one you should depend on heavily as you start and run your business.

Protecting Your Business Plan

Your business plan is a valuable document containing confidential and important information. Obviously, you write it with the intention of sharing it with others, but be careful who you share it with.

Your competitors would no doubt love to see the contents of your business plan. Can you imagine them salivating as they read your long-range plans, your financial statements, your personal financial statement, your pricing strategy, and so forth?

Take care about who has access to your plan. After all, you worked long and hard to develop it. It would be a darned shame to have it get into the wrong hands.

The Least You Need to Know

➤ Your business plan will serve as a working guide for your business and a sales instrument to attract investors.

➤ Writing a business plan doesn't need to be intimidating or daunting; the hardest part is getting started.

➤ Your business plan must be written exclusively for your business and must reflect its goals and plans.

➤ The four main parts of your business plan are a description of the business, a marketing plan, a financial management plan, and a general management plan.

➤ Extra elements of your plan include an executive summary, supporting documents, financial projections, a cover sheet, a statement of purpose, and a table of contents.

➤ Realize how important and valuable the contents of your business plan are and take care to protect it.

Chapter 13

Financing Your Business Venture

In This Chapter

➤ Looking ahead to figure out what you'll need.

➤ Using your assets to finance your business.

➤ Looking at some potential money sources.

➤ Traditional and non-traditional investors.

➤ Guidelines to follow when asking someone for money.

➤ Be prepared for what potential investors might ask you.

There are a lot of uncertainties when you're starting a business. There's one thing, though, that you can always count on: You're gonna need money.

You'll need money to start your business, and you'll need money to keep it running and to expand it. The money can come from your personal funds, loans from family members and friends, venture capitalists, banks, private placements, government funding sources, Wall Street, or wherever. Don't get stuck on the idea that money has to come from a particular source, like a bank. There are many avenues for funding your business.

Lots of people get hung up on the money thing. They don't want to ask family members or friends for a loan, but they're incredibly nervous and reluctant about asking someone they don't know.

I look at it this way: It's like asking a girl to dance in the high school gym. If she says no, you move on to the next girl. Sooner or later, you find somebody to dance with. It's the same with finding investors for your company. You ask for some money. Basically, they can say yes, or they can say no. That's it. If they say no, you move along to the next investor. Sooner or later ….

There's money out there, and you can find it if you're willing to knock on enough doors to get it.

In this chapter, I'll talk about knowing how much money you need to start your business and some potential sources for getting it. I'll examine some attitudes about asking for money and tell you what you might expect to happen when you ask some-body for money.

Raising money to start your business doesn't have to be a traumatic experience. If you approach it with the right attitude, it can be fun. At the very least, it's a great learning experience.

Figuring Out How Much You Need

How do you know how much money you have to raise? Good question. If you ask ten people, you'll get ten different answers. You might even say it's a subjective question. So you can ask others for advice, but when it comes down to it, you have to figure it out with the help of your business plan. Remember that your business plan is your roadmap. It pretty much tells you where you're going and how you're going to get there.

As you should be doing when you plan anything concerning your business, think about where you want to be five or ten years down the road. If your goals are big, then plan big. You need to borrow more money to start a company that will be worth $5 million dollars in five years than for one that will be worth $500,000.

Take yourself to where you want to be in five years, and work backward to get an idea of what you might need to do to get there. Do your plans include taking your com-pany public? Selling it? It's important to keep your long-range goals in mind as you make your short-range plans.

Examine your cash flow statements and your goals to figure out how much you'll need to get up and running. In addition to start-up funds, you should have at least a couple of months of operating cash in reserve, if possible. This helps you concentrate on running your new business and getting it off to a good start, instead of focusing how you're going to raise the money to pay the bills during your first few months.

Remember, when you talk to people about getting money for your business, you're not just talking about getting the business started. You need money to keep it growing, as well.

A Long, Hard Look at What You Have

You're going to hear about a lot of potential funding sources in this chapter because you have a lot of options about who to ask for money. Generally, though, most of the initial money for start-up businesses comes from the person starting it and from family members and friends.

Often, an entrepreneur can scrape together enough money from his own funds, with some help from family and friends, to get the business started. More money from other sources becomes necessary as the business expands and grows. But if you start small, you can usually find enough money initially.

Bear Facts

I started The Vermont Teddy Bear Company with very little money. I borrowed a lot from different sources later on, but because I started out small (the pushcart and my house), I didn't need much at first.

What you need to do is take a good, long look at your financial situation and figure out the total assets you have available to work with. You might end up with more than you think.

Savings

Your personal savings are an obvious area to look at when you're figuring out your financial situation, but it's important to realize what your personal savings include. If you've been working for a company, do you have a 401(k) or other type of retirement savings? Do you have mutual funds or money market accounts? Stock investments?

Sit down and make a list of all the money you have saved, regardless of where it is. Are there any savings accounts that were set up for you when you were a kid? A lot of money in banks is unaccounted for. It's a long shot, but you could have some money you're not even aware of. It's worth checking on, anyway.

What about savings bonds? Some families are great at buying U.S. savings bonds for birthdays. Have you put aside money someplace for emergencies? Do you have money saved for a car or a house? How about a cash-value life insurance policy? Your savings are not necessarily just the money you have in the bank.

It's pretty amazing how little some people know about their own finances. You've probably heard of instances where a spouse dies, leaving the other one completely helpless in the personal finance area. Usually, it's just because the surviving spouse never took the time or had the interest to learn about the finances. Or a couple breaks up and—surprise! John finds out that all the money Mary took care of because he just wasn't interested enough to do it has been put into accounts in Mary's name only.

Over the Rainbow

A lot of people are reluctant to use emergency money they've saved, or money they've saved toward a house or for their kids' educations, to fund their business startup. My feeling is that if you believe in yourself, using your own money isn't that scary. You're investing in yourself and in your family. You should believe your return will be great.

Be sure you have a thorough understanding of your personal finances. You're going to look pretty silly if you go to a bank or other source to borrow money, and it turns out you don't have a grasp on your own financial situation.

Basically, what you need to do is consider any sources of income and all other financial assets. You have to take your expenses into account, too. You don't want to commit every nickel you have to starting your business, and then remember that you don't have enough money to pay your home electric or water bill.

Add up all your assets, and then deduct all your liabilities. Remember that liabilities include expenses such as mortgage payments, car payments, household maintenance costs, and so forth. When you've figured out all your assets and deducted your liabilities, you'll know your net worth.

If you're surprised at the amount your liabilities added up to, it might be time to re-evaluate. If your credit-card bills are huge, stop buying so much. Buy only what you can pay for at the end of the billing cycle. If your car payment or lease is outrageous, consider what you're driving and think about getting something less expensive—same with your mortgage or rent. Some sacrifice now will be well worth it down the road. Trust me.

Credit Cards and Lines of Credit

It still makes a lot of people uneasy, but doing business with credit cards is getting to be more and more common. Credit card companies normally are perfectly willing to extend you a line of credit. If you have a bunch of cards, you can get a pretty good amount of money with little hassle. Remember what they say about payback, though.

Credit card borrowing has its place. If you know you have a source of money coming, but it won't be there as soon as you'd like, borrowing money on your credit card can get you what you need until the money you're expecting is available.

If you do this, be sure you know the terms your credit card company offers. The interest on cash advances is often higher than the regular interest rate, and there might be additional fees. Borrowing money on your credit card is an expensive way to get it, but if it's the only way, and it's short-term only, it might be what you need to do to stay afloat.

If you're going to apply to several credit card companies, do it at the same time. That way, you can truthfully say on the application that you have no other outstanding credit loans. If you've already borrowed from one, and then apply to another, you need to tell how much you owe. That could affect your chances of getting more credit. Credit cards are useful, but they're costly, and they're risky. Use them only if there's no other way.

Lines of credit from sources other than credit cards are extremely useful and something you should try to get. A line of credit allows you to borrow money from a particular source when you need it. It's preapproved, so you can usually get it quickly without a lot of hassle. Having lines of credit available is important as your business grows because if you can't get money fast, you could end up missing opportunities that have to acted on quickly.

Grizzly Area

I've been told that some people choose their founders teams based on the amount of credit each member has available. Whoa! Credit might be important, but if it's your basis for choosing the people who will be instrumental in forming and running your company, you'd better reconsider your priorities and start looking for other funding sources—not to mention other founders team members!

Collateral

Remember in those old movies when a guy wanted to borrow money from the bank and left his gold watch as collateral? Well, most of us don't have gold watches anymore, and collateral has gotten a little more complicated, but the idea behind it remains the same.

When you borrow money, especially from a bank, the lender wants assurance that it will get something of value in the event that you default on the loan. It wants the equivalent of your gold watch. It wants *collateral*.

Since you're just starting your business, it can't count as collateral. That leaves your personal assets—like your house, your car, and any savings you might have. Many people find that thought absolutely terrifying. As I said earlier, however, if

The Word According to John

The idea of *collateral* has been around for a long time, and it's nothing to get too worked up about. You can't expect a person or institution to give you money without knowing there's something of value available in case you don't give the money back. Collateral is simply the lender's insurance against you defaulting on the loan.

you don't believe in yourself enough to take a risk, maybe you don't believe in yourself enough.

Most lenders aren't interested in taking your property. They want their money back—with interest. They don't want the hassle of having to take your property and figure out what to do with it.

Who You Gonna Turn To?

If you can't come up with your own money to finance your business startup, you're going to have to look to other sources. You'll need to do this eventually, even if you take care of the start-up costs on your own. Businesses get more expensive to run as they get bigger.

There are many types of funding sources. I'll talk about some of the more common sources, but if you're creative, you can come up with lots more on your own. Don't restrict yourself to seeking funding from sources you read about in books or magazines.

Younger entrepreneurs (and some older ones, too) often complain that it's hard to find funding for business startups because lenders don't think young people are capable of starting and running businesses. You probably know, by the way, that evidence points directly opposite that belief. A lot of today's hottest businesses are being started by 20-somethings.

Smart, young (or other) entrepreneurs who have trouble with traditional funding sources learn to look outside the boundaries and find alternative sources. For example, a couple of Gen X-ers got some of their college professors to buy into their fledgling company. Another used her personal savings and her husband's moving allowance to start her business. Still another met somebody who remembered somebody who knew somebody looking to invest in a business like the one the Gen X-er was starting up.

I can't stress enough how important it is to cultivate and nurture contacts. The more people you know, the more names you have to call when you need something. Business networking might bring to mind images of people trading business cards at a cocktail party, but don't underestimate its importance. Harvey Mackay, the premier networker, gives all kinds of examples of how having good contacts can help you and your business in his book *Dig Your Well Before You're Thirsty: The Only Networking Book You'll Ever Need*.

I get to know as many people as I possibly can, and I maintain my contacts in different ways. It can be through coaching Little League, shooting hoops, visiting radio stations, striking up conversations with other entrepreneurs when I visit their businesses, making it a

The Word According to John

Knowing all kinds of people gives you access to all kinds of information, experience, and help. *Networking* gets a bad rap sometimes, billed as phony schmoozing with people you can't stand. I think, though, that networking is simply making and maintaining contacts with all kinds of people. It's a smart thing to do.

point to talk to the father of my daughter's classmate, or whatever. There are hundreds of ways to make and maintain contacts.

The point is that if you don't have enough money on your own to get started, and you're having trouble getting it from traditional sources, think about some nontraditional ones.

Some good sources of funding, but certainly not the only ones, for entrepreneurs are the following:

➤ Private venture capitalists

➤ Private placement firms

➤ Family and friends

➤ Lending institutions

➤ Government programs

➤ Other sources, such as universities, suppliers, business angels, and factoring

Let's have a look at what each of these funding methods involve.

Everyone's Rich Uncle

Private venture capitalists are companies that invest money into private ventures (hence, the name). Sounds good, huh? Well, it can be good. It can be *really* good, but there are potential drawbacks. Private venture capitalists naturally want something in return for their investments. In addition to hefty interest rates, they often want to tell you how to run your business. There are usually stipulations in the agreement that allow them to replace you and your founders team if your company doesn't perform up to their expectations. Occasionally, they want voting control of the company.

This isn't necessarily bad because it definitely gives you direction—strong direction—about how to run your business. Often, private venture capitalists give you all kinds of start-up help and what's perhaps much-needed guidance in the early stages of your business. If you don't have any business experience, you might welcome that.

These groups have high standards when selecting companies to fund and normally look for ventures that generate high profits. Your banker, lawyer, or accountant can probably put you in touch with a private venture capitalist.

Let Somebody Else Do the Work for You

Private placement firms are those that sell the idea of your business to investors to get you funding. The money doesn't come from the private placement firm, but from the investors they find. This can be a good way to go because it takes the burden of finding money off you. I used a private placement firm to help me find money for The Vermont Teddy Bear Company, and I think it's a good way to go.

Individuals who put you into contact with potential investors might call themselves financial consultants, business plan expediters, or something else, but their goal is generally the same. They want to be your *in* to investors. They're known collectively as *money finders*. Be careful, however. Some of these people are really good, have great contacts, and know exactly what they're doing. Others, though, don't have a clue. Check out credentials, and avoid paying any money upfront. Normally private placement firms will take a percentage of the money you get from investors, and/or shares of stock in your company. The amount of their fee depends on how much money they're able to get for you.

Money finders don't have to be professionals. Often, the people who help you find sources of money are people in your town you turn to for some help. Maybe you know a couple of your town's doctors and lawyers who could point you in the right direction. How about a stockbroker you've worked with in the past? Maybe she can hook you up with a New York connection. Don't overlook anybody when you're looking for funding. The more people you talk to, the better.

Family and Friends

I've already discussed this funding method a little bit, but it's worth a closer look. If you can borrow money from family and friends, and you can't get it from anyplace else, go ahead. But proceed at your own risk. It's tricky business.

Grizzly Area

If you do borrow money from friends or family members, make sure everything is done in a businesslike and professional manner. Have a legal agreement, outlining terms and the repayment plan. Unless you decide to include friends and relatives in your business, limit their involvement to that of lenders, not investors with a say in how your business is run. Make sure everyone understands the arrangement upfront, or you could be looking at a sticky situation down the road.

Contributing a little money to your business venture often makes family members, and sometimes friends, think they have the right to tell you how to run it. Their well-meaning advice can drive you crazy, and if they insist on getting involved, it can slow down or hurt your business. If you borrow from friends or family, make sure you have a legal agreement that outlines terms for repayment, and so forth. And if you don't *really* need their money, try to find it from someplace else.

Lending Institutions

Banks used to be the only game in town as far as lending institutions went, but now you have an increasing number of choices. Banks continue to dominate, but they've been joined by credit unions, savings and loans, and commercial finance companies.

Although it's certainly possible to get money from banks and other lending institutions, it's not always easy. They're usually reluctant to loan money for startups, and they normally want you to put up your personal assets to secure a loan.

Bear Facts

It can be very frustrating. You go to a bank to get a loan to start a business, and the banker says you can't get the money because you don't have enough collateral to guarantee the loan. Come back in a few years when your business has built up some collateral, and we'll talk, the banker says. You can't start the business without money, but the bank won't give it to you unless you have business collateral. I know a guy—Jack Craft—who's an author and businessman. He runs a company that remakes transmissions. Jack told me he had to try 50 banks before he finally got a yes to his loan request. Wow, talk about persistence! Way to go, Jack.

If you agree to sign a personal guaranty for a bank loan—and sometimes you might have to—make sure the guaranty expires when you pay off the loan. Banks often make a personal guaranty on a continuing basis; that means as long as you have a loan from that bank, you're personally liable for it.

Even if you pay off three loans, then run into trouble with your fourth one years later, your personal guaranty is still in effect. When you pay off your first loan, send a certified letter to the bank, insisting that the personal guaranty be revoked. If you don't, you're likely to forget about it, only to have it come back to haunt you later on.

When you approach a bank for a loan, make sure you're well prepared. Have your business plan with you when you go to an appointment (don't ever go without an appointment) and know what questions you want to ask.

I have what I call "Sortino's Five-Bank Rule." You visit the first bank, assuming it won't give you a loan, but you show the banker your business plan and hear what he has to say about it. Thank him kindly when he turns you down, and go fix up your business plan, according to what he told you. Do the same thing three more times, continuing to use the (free) advice you get from the bankers you visit to improve your business plan. By the fifth bank or so, your business plan should be sufficiently polished and you should be getting your loan. You'll be an old pro at handling bankers, too.

Some alternatives to banks include:

➤ **Credit unions**   Credit unions, which are nonprofit organizations, were imported to the United States from Germany in the early 1900s. Although they were initially created as financial institutions for the employees of large organizations and companies, membership standards have relaxed. If you want to, you can find a credit union you're eligible to join. If you need more information about how to join one, you can call the Credit Union National Association in Madison, Wisconsin. The number is 800/358-5710.

Credit unions normally don't make big loans, but their financing terms are good. You might be able to borrow $10,000 or $20,000 without too many problems.

Bear Facts

Credit union membership has extended far beyond people who work for a particular business or industry. There are credit unions organized by ethnicity, such as the Polish-American Credit Union, and even by family name. There are seven Lee Credit Unions, supported by the approximately 100,000 people in the United States with the last name Lee.

➤ **Savings and loans**   S&Ls, also known as thrifts, are another possible alternative to banks when you're looking for a lender. They've been around for a long time, but went through a rough period back in the late 1980s, when many of them failed and had to be bailed out by Uncle Sam (that is, taxpayer dollars). The cost of that bailout continues, and experts say it could ultimately cost taxpayers as much as $500 billion.

Recent legislative changes, however, have greatly improved the quality of *thrifts*, and they're considered viable lenders. They might be worth checking out.

➤ **Commercial finance companies**   You've no doubt heard of the big ones, such as The Money Store or Beneficial. These types of agencies loan money to people who can't get it from a bank. They get a higher interest rate for their trouble, but they could be worth looking into if you're having trouble finding money.

Government Loans

All kinds of government money is out there, but much of it is overlooked because people don't know about it or they think it's too much of a hassle to get. There's a lot of paperwork involved in getting government money (big surprise, huh?), but it's still worth your time to see what's available.

Let's start by taking a look at Small Business Administration (SBA) loans. There are two types of SBA loan programs. One guarantees the money that you'd borrow from a bank or other lending institution, and the other actually loans the money. It's easier to get the SBA to guarantee your loan from a bank than it is to actually get SBA money. In some cases, the agency guarantees up to 90% of your bank loan, which can be a huge help with getting funding from a bank.

Money for direct loans often isn't available because there's not enough money in the pot for everyone who wants it. If you can get a loan, though, the interest rates are usually lower than those on a bank loan.

The Economic Development Agency is another potential source of government funding for your business. This agency has a lot of regulations, but the loans are attractive.

Small business investment companies and minority enterprise companies are privately owned, but government licensed and regulated. The companies raise private money; after that, they're eligible to get low-interest government loans on a proportionate basis. The ratio is about one part private money to three parts government funds.

Bear Facts

This Web site, provided by the Center for Information Law and Policy as a one-stop shopping point for federal government information, might be useful when you're looking for information about federal money. It can be found at www.law.vill.edu/fed-agency/fedwebloc.html.

In turn, the companies loan their money to small business owners. Check out the membership directory of the National Association of Small Business Investment Companies in your library to find these agencies in your area.

Some states have start-up funds available for entrepreneurs, and regional or municipal development agencies in your area might offer loans, too. The Department of Agriculture has a program to help firms in rural areas with their start-up costs.

A lot of government programs and agencies loan money for small businesses. If it seems to make sense for you, then go ahead and check them out.

Other Sources

Although the ones mentioned so far are some of the better known and more popular sources of funding, there are many others:

➤ **Universities** Educational institutions are getting into the act with entrepreneur programs and people in the school who are willing to invest in them. Suppliers who want your business are sometimes willing to help you get started, either through a direct loan or lengthy terms of payment.

Over the Rainbow

People who have already started their own businesses can be wonderful sources of information as you work to get yours started. If you know somebody who's started a business, ask if you can take her to lunch and pick her brain. She's already done what you're getting ready to do and is sure to have all kinds of tips.

➤ **Angels** A large network of private investors, known as business *angels*, are always looking to get in on promising, new businesses. They include other business owners, professionals such as doctors and lawyers, managers, and so forth. The best way to find these people is through contacts. Ask everybody you talk to for leads. Something is sure to turn up.

➤ **Factoring** This is a system of using your accounts receivable as collateral for a loan. Places that offer money under this system are called factoring houses, and they normally loan you a percentage of your accounts receivable.

Be ingenious and innovative when you're seeking sources of funding. Remember that there's money out there. You just have to find it.

How to Approach Someone for Money

You can't just walk up to somebody and ask him to lend you some money. You've got to follow some guidelines. You can either do it yourself or get somebody to look for money for you.

I think it's best to do it yourself because nobody can sell your business like you can. However, it always helps to have a well-connected person in your corner, who's willing to introduce you to the people you need to meet.

Keep these guidelines in mind when you start knocking on doors, and always keep your goals uppermost in your mind. Don't let a negative comment or a discouraging word get you down. Remember where you want to be five years from now and go for it! The following are some ideas:

➤ *Get an introduction or referral.* If you can, get a well-respected businessperson to introduce you to a potential lender. This gives you ready-made credibility. Always set up an appointment, even if somebody has mentioned you to the person you want to see. Don't walk in assuming someone has time to see you.

➤ *Look good.* I never wore a really great suit, but I always wore a nice coat and tie and good shoes.

➤ *Be professional and know your stuff.* Shake hands, look the person you're talking to in the eye, and speak with confidence. Know what you're talking about. After all, it's *your* business.

➤ *Be prepared.* Take the most recent version of your business plan, current financials, income statements, balance sheets, and so forth. It's better to have too much than not enough. Be able to talk about your long-range goals comfortably. It won't work to make them up as you go along. Make sure you know as much as possible about the market you're going after and have a plan as to how you're going to attack it.

➤ *Ask questions.* Find out what the lender or investor might be willing to do for you. What other companies has he funded? A meeting is a two-way street.

➤ *Be yourself.* When you get right down to it, you can only be who you are. I know when I go to New York from Vermont that I'm not like New Yorkers. The trick is not to try. I play up being from Vermont. I do things like ask to look out the 33rd floor office window, while being sure to tell the person I'm meeting with that the tallest building in Vermont is only 10 stories. Remember, the main reason an investor agrees to give you funding is because he believes in you. When you ask for money, you're really selling yourself, so be sure you have a well-prepared sales pitch.

Finding money for your company is a challenge, but it can be a lot of fun. An important thing to remember is to not take the process too seriously. Remember, if one person says no, somebody else will say yes. Even if 10 or 20 people say no, somebody else will say yes. Don't lose your perspective, and keep your dream in front of you.

Grizzly Area

Make sure you find out exactly what an investor will want back from you before you agree to do business. Always review the proposed deal with your business attorney before agreeing to anything, and, listen to your gut. There are some less than reputable moneylenders. If you get into a bad agreement with the wrong lender, you could find yourself in very bad trouble.

What to Expect When You Ask Somebody for Money

I think you'll find that most lenders and investors are pretty straightforward. Naturally, if you're looking for big money, you'll be subjected to greater scrutiny. Some entrepreneurs say they've been asked all kinds of questions to test their ethics and values and to try to trick them into revealing some weakness.

For instance, an investor might tell you he likes everything you're doing, and he's really interested in working with you. But, he says, your marketing person looks pretty weak, and he wants to replace her with somebody he has in mind.

Now, do you agree that she's not the best person for the job and let him replace her? Or do you stand fast, expressing unwavering confidence in the team you've chosen? He might be trying to see exactly how much confidence you have in your team, or how willing you are to back down to his requests.

What if he tells you he has a cousin in business and asks that you use the cousin as your main supplier? He might suggest that you could (wink, wink) give the cousin a little advance information when it's time for him to submit a bid. Is he serious, or is he testing your business ethics?

Be aware of situations such as these, and think about what you would do, should something of that nature come up. Be as well prepared as you can, and be true to what you believe in and to your dream.

The Least You Need to Know

➤ You can't know what you need now without looking at where you want to be in five or ten years.

➤ Most people starting small businesses finance them at least partially on their own.

➤ There are many different potential sources for getting money for your business.

➤ Making and maintaining contacts is important in all aspects of your business, but particularly getting funding.

➤ Don't feel you're limited to seeking money only from traditional sources.

➤ Make sure you're well prepared when you meet with potential investors.

➤ Always keep your dream and long-range plans in mind when you're looking for funding for your business.

Part 3
Business Basics

There are lots of things to think about when you're running a business, but you've got to keep up with the basics.

Making money is a big deal when you've got your own business, and you've got to understand what's going on to be able to do that. You have to get good systems in place and understand how they work. These systems allow you to monitor what happens, control costs, and predict your profits.

Figuring out what to do with your profits is the fun part.

Chapter 14

General and Administrative Costs

In This Chapter

➤ Understanding what general and administrative (G&A) costs include.

➤ The differences between fixed and variable expenses and between controllable and uncontrollable expenses.

➤ Getting an idea of how G&A costs can be forecasted and planned for.

➤ Keeping G&A costs low to increase profits.

➤ Looking at ways to save on general and administrative expenses.

➤ Knowing that good spending habits have to be practiced by everybody—including you.

The best advice I can give for general and administrative costs? Start small and get smaller.

I'm going to let you in on a simple, but important, equation. It's so important that I'll mention it in every chapter of this section of the book. It's one of the key ingredients of Sortino's Business Basics.

The equation is as follows:

Sales – General and Administrative Costs – Costs of Goods Sold – Sales and Marketing Costs = Profits

If you keep that equation in mind as I discuss these different areas, it should help you understand how each one affects the others and understand how important controlling these costs is to your bottom line.

In this chapter, you'll look at some common—and some of the most troublesome—costs in the general and administrative area and get some ideas on how to reduce costs if they're too high and how to keep them down as low as possible.

What Are General and Administrative Costs?

General and administrative costs, which include bookkeeping, legal and accounting fees, insurance costs, office rent, and so forth, can be killers, and they can add up quickly if you don't keep an eye on them. They're the little expenses like office supplies that you don't think about until you look at the expense reports and see how they've accumulated.

Some of the expenses are controllable, but others aren't. The trick is to keep the ones you can control as low as possible; if the ones you can't control get too high, you might have to look at some alternatives.

Let's start by looking at some of the expenses incurred under the heading of general and administrative.

> ### The Word According to John
>
> *General and administrative costs (G&A) don't come under sales and marketing or cost of goods sold. They're all the other costs that come with the territory of doing business.*

Gotta Pay the Employees: Payroll

Some payroll expenses, but not all, fall in the G&A area. Executive salaries normally are included in this area, along with administrative salaries, unless the positions fall directly in another area, such as sales and marketing.

As the owner of your company, you no doubt wear a lot of hats. You do a lot of the work that needs to be done because you're not yet in a position to pay somebody else to do it. If your time is divided between general and administrative duties and sales and marketing work, and you help in production, too, be sure the cost of your salary is divided between those areas. If you spend 60% of your time with G&A duties, then that percentage of your salary should come out of G&A's budget. The other 40% should come from the other area or areas in which you're working.

Payroll can be considered a controllable area, if you're willing to take a cut in pay. When you own the business, there are payment priorities you've go to follow:

➤ Pay your taxes

➤ Pay the bank and other lenders

➤ Pay your employees

➤ Pay suppliers and other creditors

➤ Pay yourself

If you're willing to pay yourself less, you can cut your payroll costs. Many entrepreneurs take only enough for minimum living expenses for themselves when they're getting their businesses started. If you find yourself in this position, and then have to look at cutting your salary even further, don't be too disheartened.

Most people who start up businesses go through some lean times at first. Keep the faith that the payoff will be worth it. Before too long you'll have enough employees to do all the work and enough money to pay them.

I have a formula I call the *multiply and subtract concept*. It simply states that you start your company with one person—you. Your personnel multiplies rapidly because as soon as you hire one person, you've increased it by 100%. Soon, you've got 50 people working in your company, and you've greatly multiplied your starting personnel number. That's the multiplication side of the concept.

The other side of the formula is your financial interest in the company. You start out owning 100% of the business, but as you bring in other people and more employees, and maybe take your business public, your share of ownership decreases. You see, your partners take some shares of the stock, which are subtracted from your 100% ownership. You give some stock to your employees, and that further decreases your share of ownership. You multiply the number of your employees, while subtracting from your ownership in the business.

Over the Rainbow

When you do your budgets, include the amount of salary you would like to be earning, not the amount you think you might be able to spare. That way, you can see what your sales need to be so you can pay yourself that salary.

Gotta Have a Roof: Rent

Rent payments are pretty much unavoidable in the early stages of your business, and normally you have little control over the amount you have to pay.

It's usually advisable for new business to lease, rather than buy, property at first. A better time to consider buying property is after the business gets going, and things are smoothed out and a bit more certain. When renting commercial property, you pay for the amount of square footage you have. Rent normally is paid monthly, although arrangements can vary.

Be careful of extra charges the landlord might add onto the cost of your rent. Be sure you know when you negotiate the deal if your rent charges include items like heating and air-conditioning costs, real estate taxes, and maintenance fees. One way or another, you're going to pay for these things. Just be sure you understand the agreement.

If you want to get fancy with your accounting, rent charges could be apportioned to the applicable areas. The sales and marketing department, for instance, might pay one-sixth of the total rent costs. Most small companies don't bother getting that detailed when they're first starting up, but you should make that kind of accounting your goal. It's important to understand all the formulas so you can know exactly how your company works.

Gotta Fix It: Maintenance and Repairs

If you rent property, most of these costs may be the responsibility of the property owner. However, depending on the agreement you have, some of them might be passed along to you. If you own the property, you're responsible for these types of expenses.

There's not a lot you can do about them. When the roof leaks, you've got to fix it. When the paint starts peeling off the building, you've got to redo it. What's a property owner to do?

Gotta Pay It: Taxes and Licenses

Typically, applicable payroll taxes, property taxes, and the cost of any necessary business licenses would fall into the general and administrative category. These kinds of payments are called *compliance payments*, and there's not a whole lot you can do about them. If your municipality says you have to pay for a business license to operate, you've got to pay for it.

Gotta Have It: Utilities

It's next to impossible to do business without some telephones, electricity, water, and so forth. That being the case, it's next to impossible to avoid utility costs. These costs, however, are somewhat controllable. I'll get into a little more detail about that later in the chapter in the section "How to Predict What Your G&A Costs Will Be."

Gotta Have Those Professional Services

I've gone on about how important it is to have the best accountant you can find and a really good lawyer, too. The only bad thing about accountants and lawyers is that they like to be paid for their services.

These costs are somewhat controllable, but this is an area in which you don't want to cut expenses to the point of jeopardizing the quality of service you get. These services are too important to your business for you to let them slide for the sake of saving a few dollars. It's just not worth it.

Grizzly Area

If you lease property and are assessed utility charges, try to get a handle on exactly what you're paying for. If you don't get a bill directly from the utility company, but get one that's channeled through your landlord, ask him to explain exactly what the charges are for. Landlords sometimes try to pass off some of *their* expenses to you.

Grizzly Area

Watch out for the insurance salesperson who will try to get you to buy all kinds of extra riders and policies you don't really need. You spend enough money on insurance without adding to the cost by buying a policy in case your plane crashes on your next business trip. There are many types of insurance you need, but some that you can do without. Some salespeople are quick to play on your fears, but don't be tempted to buy more than you need.

Gotta Get Some Insurance

We all know what a big deal insurance has become, fueled by our extremely litigious society. It seems sometimes that insurance companies have more to say about our businesses than we do. You can, however, find ways to save money on insurance.

You'll need several kinds of insurance: worker's compensation, casualty insurance (in case of fire or other catastrophe), general liability insurance, and most likely product liability. These insurances are necessary, to be sure, but there are ways you might be able to decrease your total insurance costs.

There Will Always Be Miscellaneous

There always are things you need when you're running a business. Paper for the fax machines, copiers, and printers (whatever happened to that paperless society we're supposedly moving toward?). Office supplies and other necessities normally fall under the general and administrative area. It's important to keep track of small items so you know what you're spending. These types of things sometimes add up surprisingly fast.

How to Predict What Your G&A Costs Will Be

Some general and administrative costs can be easily predicted, but others can't. Expenses that you have control over are called *variable expenses*; the ones you have no say in are called *fixed expenses*.

Obviously, your fixed expenses are easier to predict. If your rent is $2,200 a month, that's an expense you can count on. You can plan and budget for it. But if your roof develops a sudden, and big, leak one night—that's not a fixed expense. You had no way of predicting it or of planning for it.

In addition to rent, payroll costs can be predicted and planned for and so can the taxes that fall into the G&A area. Utilities are reasonably predictable, as is the cost of office supplies. The cost for professional services can fluctuate greatly, depending on your needs during a particular period.

Variable expenses typically are those based on sales, such as the cost of your business license and your general liability and product liability insurance premiums.

You'll quickly learn how much money is needed for the fixed expenses, and you'll learn, to a great extent, to predict the variables. There will always be some fluctuations, but you'll get a pretty good feeling for your expenses fairly quickly.

Over the Rainbow

Don't confuse fixed and variable expenses with controllable and uncontrollable expenses. There's a huge difference. Your rent, for instance, is a fixed expense, but it could also be a controllable expense. You could move to a location that's less expensive or smaller. Consider the difference.

Keeping G&A Costs Low to Boost Profits

As part of the important equation introduced at the beginning of this chapter, general and administrative costs can have a big impact on your company's profits. You're going to have to work hard to keep these costs as low as possible in comparison to your sales figures. I'd recommend that you set a goal of having your G&A costs be no more than 20% of your total sales.

After you're comfortable at 20%, make it 15%. It might be hard to keep G&A costs at 20% or less of sales at first. Your sales will just be getting off the ground, while you're still looking at general and administrative expenses.

Bear Facts

When I was running The Vermont Teddy Bear Company, we consistently kept our general and administrative costs down to 11% of our sales. It took some watching out for, but it worked.

Give things a little time to settle out, and see where you are. Then you can go about making whatever adjustments you think are necessary.

Let's think about some ways to keep G&A costs as low as possible. Here is a quick list of the expenses I'm talking about, so you won't have to keep paging back to look:

➤ Applicable payroll expenses

➤ Rent

➤ Maintenance and repairs

➤ Taxes and licenses

➤ Utilities

➤ Professional services

➤ Insurance

➤ Miscellaneous

Payroll

I established earlier in this chapter that payroll expenses can be lowered if you choose to take a salary cut. It might be that you simply can't, however. If you have a family to support, or even just yourself, you need to have money, and you might be operating at a bare-bones level as it is. Unless you have another source of income, you're going to need to take a salary from your business.

What about saving money on your employees' salaries? Maybe even laying somebody off? If you really need to do that, be careful to pick the person least necessary to your operation. Also, don't assume that if you lay off the person who does the marketing or answers the phones, you can take over his or her duties. Many an entrepreneur has gotten into trouble by adopting the *I-can-do-it-all* attitude. While you're tinkering with a marketing plan or answering telephones, crucial business in the production area could go unattended.

If you're trying to control expenses, avoid the temptation to hire somebody who's not absolutely necessary. Remember that if you're making a 10% profit and you hire an employee for $20,000 a year, you need to increase your sales by $200,000 to maintain your profit level.

Rent

Rent can be a difficult, but not impossible, cost to control. The cost of your rent is established, and if you don't pay it, you'll get kicked out. That's not hard to figure out. There's no law, however, that says you can't try to negotiate a better rental fee.

Bear Facts

Long leases generally carry lower monthly rates than short-term leases.

If you can find a comparable building, in a comparable area, with comparable services that charges less rent than you're paying, there's nothing that says you can't mention it to your landlord and see what happens. The landlord might just offer to meet the other deal to keep you on board as a tenant.

It might not work, but it's worth a try.

Maintenance and Repairs

Maintenance is a predictable expense, but repairs are more difficult to anticipate and control. Repairs (that leaky roof, for example) are necessary, and they often have to be done quickly to avoid damage to the building or its contents.

A good thing to do is shop around *before* you need repairs and get an idea of what different contractors charge for different jobs. Of course, there are variables, but you should be able to get an idea.

Taxes and Licenses

You can't get away without paying taxes and license fees, that's for sure. But you can make sure you pay them on time so you're not penalized and end up paying more than is necessary. It's in your best interests to stay on top of compliance payments.

Utilities

There are some simple and practical ways to control utility costs, just as you would in your home. You can turn off lights in areas not in use, and make sure you don't have any water leaks. Limit air-conditioning and heat in storage areas and other places that aren't occupied by people. Don't overheat or overcool occupied spaces, either. If you have a manufacturing operation, remember that equipment startups and shutdowns use more electricity than steady use.

Watch how you use your telephones, and look around for the best long-distance plan you can find. Does a toll-free number make sense for your business? Telephone companies are extremely competitive, so you can find a good deal if you shop around. Talk to your employees about limiting personal calls and not using your phones to call their friends on the other side of the country.

You can't avoid utility costs, but you can control them, somewhat.

Professional Services

You know how important I think it is to have the best accountant and lawyer you can get. And yes, their services will cost you some money, but I look at it this way. If I get myself into some kind of financial or legal jam that could cost me my shirt (and my business), a good lawyer or accountant is likely to get me out of it. If I try to tackle a legal or financial problem that's over my head, I'm putting my company at risk. A good professional, on the other hand, will see my company through the situation unscathed.

Paying for top-notch professional services is a type of insurance to me. Sure, there are ways to cut down on the expenses associated with it. Maybe you don't need to have your lawyer on retainer, but could hire her on an as-needed basis. Maybe you know something about taxes and can do some of the accounting work yourself, and then have your accountant check and verify it.

Remember, though, that it might not be "time smart" for you to spend 12 hours struggling with tax work that a good accountant could do in 2 hours. Keep an eye on these expenses, but don't short-change your company.

Insurance

You can help control insurance costs just by keeping a close eye on your policies. Did you ever get an insurance bill and notice your premium was more than the last time, only to find out when you asked that your agent had increased your coverage—without even consulting you first?

The agent will probably tell you he had to increase coverage because the cost of replacing property has gone up, and you'd be stuck if you had a claim. Tell your insurance agent upfront that you want to be notified of any changes in your policy. If he doesn't do it, look for a new company.

If you think your insurance premiums are higher than they should be, schedule an appointment with your agent and talk to him about them. If you don't get any satisfaction, do a quick phone survey of other companies. Insurance rates vary, and, if you think you're paying too much, you might be.

If you can, it might be beneficial to set up a self-insurance fund or a partial fund, which would help keep premiums down.

Over the Rainbow

It's good to have your insurance agent feel that your business is important to him. He's more likely to feel that way if he gets a lot of business from you, instead of a little bit here and there. I used to let my agent meet with employees to talk about insurance they might want personally. Because he sold a lot of insurance within our company, he gave us really good rates. He felt invested in the company and always treated us well.

Miscellaneous

Little things add up quickly. I'm sure you know there's a tendency for supplies, especially office supplies, to be wasted. Keep a close eye on your inventory, and watch what goes out in the trash. Little savings add up.

If you think your G&A costs are too high, implement a cost-savings plan. Be sure everyone to whom the plan applies fully understands why it's being implemented and the goal of the plan. If you're careful, you should see these expenses drop and see a change favorable to the *profit* end of your equation.

Keeping Close Tabs on G&A Costs

General and administrative costs aren't like costs for materials or the cost of buying a new truck. They tend to be sneakier, harder-to-define expenses.

Make sure everyone understands what expenses fall in the G&A area, and make sure the costs are carefully tracked. You might be surprised to know just how much you're spending on paper or phone bills. If you don't know exactly what you're spending in this area, it will be difficult to control costs.

Making It Everybody's Business

A cost-savings plan should include everyone in your company. It doesn't make sense to have your office staff watching every paper clip they use, while the marketing people are getting used to $50 lunches with clients.

It's important that everyone understands exactly what they're supposed to do to get and keep costs down. You should have a written plan and get employees invested in the plan by coming up with their own ideas and suggestions. Reward the best ones by letting the employee leave an hour early on Friday afternoon.

When you ask employees to buy into a costs-savings plan, it's important that they see you and your partners making the same effort they've been asked to. Don't lecture employees about throwing away too much paper if you're going to lease a Lexus with company funds.

Strive to get your general and administrative costs as low as possible, and when they're there, avoid the tendency to let them creep upward. Watch the little things as well as the big ones, and remember that the result is a move toward increasing profits.

The Least You Need to Know

➤ General and administrative costs are all those costs associated with running a business that don't come under sales and marketing or cost of goods sold.

➤ Some of these costs are fixed, others are variable, and more are controllable than uncontrollable.

➤ Practice makes perfect, and in a short time you'll have a good idea of exactly what your G&A costs include and how they vary.

➤ Your G&A costs should be no more than 20% of your total sales, and you should work to get them down even lower.

➤ There are lots of ways to control and reduce G&A costs, and you should look for them where you can.

➤ Keep a close eye on these costs, and make sure everyone in the company understands what they are and how they're to be managed.

➤ Good spending habits have to start at the top—with you.

Chapter 15

Sales and Marketing

In This Chapter

➤ Understanding the differences between sales and marketing.

➤ Knowing the best way to sell your products or services.

➤ Finding the best salespeople and getting them to work for you.

➤ Learning the eight stages of a sales presentation.

➤ Figuring out how to market your company.

➤ Understanding the value of radio advertising.

➤ Working with a marketing budget.

➤ Getting help when you need it.

Sales and marketing are big expenses when you're doing business, there's no question about that. But if you look at these areas as just part of your financial statement, you'll be missing the big picture.

Yes, sales and marketing cost money, but without them, your business can't get off the ground. Sales and marketing are more important to your business than manufacturing. You can manufacture anything you want, but if you don't sell it, all you have is a bunch of manufactured stuff.

The point is that you can't look at sales and marketing as only items to be funded. These areas require careful thought and planning because there are right ways and wrong ways to do them. It's not like buying electricity or oil. You need to set up a sales and marketing system that's the most beneficial to your company, and you've got to pay for what you set up.

In this chapter, you'll look at the financial aspects of sales and marketing and other considerations, too. I'll discuss exactly what sales and marketing are and how to figure out what works best for your company. There are hundreds of ways to sell and market your products or services, but some work better for you than others.

Personally, I love radio. Because of that, my marketing ideas might be different from what you've heard before or read elsewhere. All I can tell you is that radio works for me, and I've seen it work for a lot of other companies, too.

I'll get back to marketing a little later. For now, let's have a look at what sales and marketing are and how they affect your company.

The Word According to John

Sales is the process of handing over your product or service to somebody else in exchange for money or another commodity. *Marketing* is the method of making people aware of your product or service and making them want to have it.

Over the Rainbow

Retail sales, consignment sales, trade shows, sales representatives, door-to-door, specialty sales, and pushcarts are all methods of selling your product or service. You'll probably have to try several methods before you find the one that works best for your business.

Marketing and Sales Are Different Things

Sales and marketing are both efforts designed to get customers to buy your products or services, but they're by no means the same thing.

Sales is selling your product. It's the actual process of getting salespeople out to show your product to potential customers and convince those potential customers to buy the product. If you do retail sales, it's the process of selling to the people who come to your store or shop.

Marketing is the advertising and promotional aspect of your business. It's determining the best way to let people know about your business and your product and executing that plan.

Let's look first at sales and some sales methods that might be effective for your company.

How Are You Going to Sell It?

There are lots of ways to sell a product or service. You can go door-to-door asking people to buy, sort of like when you sold Girl Scout cookies or magazines for your school's fundraiser. You can also send a team of salespeople out to demonstrate how great your product is. You can rent a building on Main Street or Fifth Avenue and sell your product to people who come in. You can set up a pushcart on your town's pedestrian mall and sell your product to people on the street.

I tried several methods of selling my bears before the company became successful. I wholesaled the bears for a while to stores like Macy's and Lord & Taylor's. That didn't work very well. It was during the '80s, when the retail business was generally down. I was directly competing with big companies like Gund, who had a lot of money to market their stuffed animals. I tried to keep my prices competitive with theirs, but it just wasn't possible.

I put my bears in gift shops on a consignment basis. Every time the gift shop sold one, I'd get a percentage of the sale. That didn't work very well, either.

The pushcart was good because it was such a great learning experience. I sure didn't get rich off it, though. It sometimes takes a while to figure out the best way to sell your product or service. It's an ongoing process of thinking, evaluating, and testing. "Test, test, test" is one of my slogans.

After The Vermont Teddy Bear Company was established, we sold our bears from the gift shop at our factory. Most of our sales, though, were done over the phone. Those phone sales were a direct result of our best marketing effort—radio.

Bear Facts

I've always loved radio. I grew up with radio—lying in bed, listening to the Yankees games. Everybody I know listens to the radio, so using it to promote Vermont Teddy Bears was a natural thing. I knew from the response from our first ad on Burlington's WXXX-FM, that radio would work for us.

Who Will Work for You?

Good salespeople are essential to any business. It doesn't matter if you have a restaurant, a gas station, a bed and breakfast, a chemical company, or a clothing store. If you don't have good salespeople, you're gonna be in trouble.

Some people refer to sales people as *the front line*. They're the people your customer knows, the people representing your business. So it's important to realize that everyone associated with your business has the potential to increase or decrease sales, and everybody in the business is selling himself or herself before any product or service.

Because sales were so vital at The Vermont Teddy Bear Company, everyone was trained to make them. People who answered the phone to take orders were taught not only to sell extras for the bears, but also to sell the company by being as polite and helpful as possible. Tour guides in the factory were taught how to get people excited about being there.

Everyone in the company knew how to answer phone calls and help customers place their orders. People in the accounting department could, and would, sell bears; same with the marketing and administrative departments as well as manufacturing. Everyone with a phone understood that, as representatives of the company, they were inherently salespeople.

Grizzly Area

As business owners, we sometimes tend to categorize employees as essential or non-essential, key or non-key. Don't make the mistake of putting salespeople, at whatever level, in the non-key category. Regardless of whether it's your top-notch field salesman, or the person answering your telephone, they're both salespeople, and they're both essential to your company.

If you have a wonderful waitress at your restaurant, she's helping you sell not only dinners, but your business. Customers will remember her as part of a great dining experience and come back. They might even bring their friends the next time.

If, on the other hand, you have a rude, surly stockperson in your clothing store, customers will be turned off, maybe to the point of shopping somewhere else. Neither the waitress nor the stock person is officially in sales, but each has the potential to affect your business. It's important that all employees understand that potential. Somebody who answers the telephone or greets visitors might call himself an administrative assistant or a receptionist, but he's really a salesperson.

Often you, as the founder of the business, are responsible for sales. This might be by choice, or it might be because you don't yet have any salespeople. If you find yourself having to sell your product, don't look at it as a negative experience. I had a lot of fun and got a great education while selling my bears.

Bear Facts

Just because it's your product or your company doesn't mean you can sell it better than anybody else. My sales increased when I hired somebody else to sell bears from the pushcart. That didn't bother me; in fact, I thought it was great. Nobody could sell the company to potential investors better than I could, but there were a lot of other things that other people did better.

Eight Very Important Steps

One of my best sources of information when I was starting The Vermont Teddy Bear Company was *The Entrepreneur's Manual*, by Richard M. White, Jr. This book was a goldmine to me. One of the best things in it was White's eight stages of selling. This information has helped me greatly in selling, and I think it will help you, too. Whether you're selling on your own or you have salespeople, you should consider White's stages and try to work them into your company's sales philosophy.

I used to keep a copy of White's eight stages of selling tacked up on my wall at The Vermont Teddy Bear Company. Each time I approached a Wall Street investor, I'd read through the eight steps first.

The following are Richard White's eight stages of the sales process:

1. **The Preamble.** While breaking the ice with small talk and jokes, you are actually assessing and getting a sense about your customer. This allows you to determine what sales strategies might work the best.

2. **Establishing the Customer's Need.** The salesperson has one view of the customer's need, the customer has another view, and then there is the need as it actually exists. In this stage, the customer and salesperson need to reach common ground on what the need really is.

3. **The Modular Sales Presentations.** This is the process of breaking down a sales presentation into different parts and knowing when to pull out a particular part during the course of your pitch. You've got to be able to mix-and-match the components of your presentation.

4. **Appetite Whetting.** This is simply the technique of making your customer want to buy. There are many ways to do this.

5. **The Interim Close.** This opens the door for the final close and makes the customer feel like the sale was his idea—not yours.

6. **The Final Close.** This follows immediately after the interim close, provided the interim close was successful. Once you've gotten through the final close, get the order. Never go back to your modular presentation because by doing so, you're opening the door for your customer to change his mind.

7. **The Reinforcement Stage.** This is when you tell your customer what a great decision he's made by buying your product or service. You assure him you'll be there for any reason and that he'll be hugely pleased with his purchase.

8. **Support the Sale.** When your customer places his order, he's counting on you to stand behind your product and your company and to make sure any problems are taken care of. Needless to say, you'd better meet his expectations.

White's book also includes a bunch of suggestions for sales closes, like the *ask-for-the-sale technique*, the *close-on-an-objection technique*, the *puppy dog close*, and lots more. White pretty much tells you everything you need to know about sales, and I recommend his book to everyone who's starting a business.

Over the Rainbow

Anybody involved with sales should not miss reading *The One-Minute Salesperson*, by Spencer Johnson and Larry Wilson. It's sound, useable information, presented in a user-friendly, extremely readable manner.

Different Kinds of Salespeople

I'm sure you realize that there are many, many different kinds of salespeople. There are high-pressure men and women and those so laid back you wonder how they get up in the morning, much less sell products or services.

Salespeople can be serious or funny, loud or quiet, require a lot of motivation, or be completely self-motivated. Nearly all of them, though—at least all the good ones—have one thing in common. They love to sell.

I don't know that there's necessarily one type of salesperson that's better than another. Some methods work for some people; others are successful doing something completely different.

Attracting Good Salespeople

I hope you've caught on by now to how important it is to have really good salespeople. How do you get them to come to your fledgling company when they probably could go to Bob's established plating works company down the street?

People who like your product or service will be the most effective at selling it. Remember that one of the rules of The Vermont Teddy Bear Company was to hire bear people. Fortunately, people who like your product or service will be attracted to your company. If they're good salespeople, you've got a great match.

It's important for a salesperson to believe in what she's selling. It's really hard to be selective when you don't care about the product.

Remember that, although your company is just starting out and is small, it has tremendous potential for growth. Make sure potential salespeople recognize that potential.

Finally, you've got to make it economically feasible for a salesperson to work for you. Because sales is such an integral part of your business, you've got to be willing to pay for it. Some salespeople are highly motivated and do best working solely on commission, and others are more comfortable with a salary. You need to figure out which method makes more sense for your company and your salespeople.

Determining Your Marketing Strategy

There are many, many choices when it comes to marketing your product or service. The best advice I can give you is to find out all you can about what's out there, and try to determine what will work best for you. Start small. If it's not working, try something else.

I tried a lot of marketing strategies for The Vermont Teddy Bear Company. We used public relations, television, print ads, radio, ads on buses and subway cars, billboards, catalogs, and direct mailings, a NASCAR sponsorship, factory tours, and gift stores.

To know how to sell your products or services, you need a marketing plan, which serves several purposes. It will be your strategy for developing and maintaining relationships with customers, state what you want your company image to be, and establish the character of your company. It will also be your guide as to how you're going to carry out the strategies contained in the plan.

For instance, are you going to advertise in the newspaper? Attend trade shows? Focus on direct mail? What about television? How about the Internet?

All these questions will be addressed in your marketing plan. This comprehensive plan should contain input from all the key people in your company. If you're starting out all by yourself, then you need to decide what the plan will contain. If you have partners or a management team, they should be involved in writing the plan.

Bear Facts

Your marketing plan *is* one of the most important parts of your business plan, so think about it carefully. I highly recommend that you read *The 22 Immutable Laws of Marketing: Violate Them at Your Own Risk*, by Al Ries and Jack Trout, for a good understanding of marketing and how it works.

Now take a few minutes to think about what's involved with writing a marketing plan.

How to Write a Marketing Plan

Writing a marketing plan isn't hard to do, but it requires that you have some information. Basically, you need to determine two things:

➤ Who your market is (or markets are)

➤ How you're going to go after it (or them)

After you've figured out who your market is, you'll be able to decide whether it's large enough to support your business venture. You can also learn what it wants, how much it's willing to pay, and so forth. If you don't know who your market is, how will you know what it wants?

You've got to identify your market, and then get to know it.

Bear Facts

Remember how I got to know my market? I did it by talking to lots and lots of people when I had a teddy bear cart. I talked to people about what they liked about the bears and what they would like to be done differently. It was the best marketing education I could have gotten anywhere.

Who your market is depends a lot on what kind of business you have. If you own a gas station, your market is pretty much the people who drive by it on their way down the street. If you have a grocery store, your market might be the people who live in your town. If you have a computer software company, your market is obviously much, much broader.

Your market is whoever might buy your product or service. When I started advertising on New York radio stations, my market became the entire New York listening area. If you have a gift shop on Main Street with a sign outside, and you do no other advertising, your initial market will be the people who walk past your store and see your sign. As word of your shop spreads, your market will expand.

Your market also depends on the product you're selling. If you're selling wide-leg baggy jeans, for instance, your market will be mostly pre-teens and teenagers. If you're marketing Viagra, your market will be primarily older men.

You can hire help to determine your markets. There are telemarketing firms and market research companies who will use surveys, mailers, focus groups, and other methods to help you figure out who might buy your product.

I think, though, that common sense, combined with some trial and error techniques, work as well as anything.

You've got to know what your market likes, doesn't like, and what it expects from a product. Identify your customers by their age, sex, income/educational level and residence. At first, target only those customers who are more likely to purchase your product or service. As your customer base expands, you may need to consider modifying the marketing plan to include other customers.

The Small Business Administration has a good marketing plan included in its business plan. You can access it on the Web at www.sba.gov. An actual marketing plan is included, and the SBA encourages entrepreneurs to print it out and use it. In the plan, entrepreneurs are encouraged to consider and address the following questions when writing a marketing plan:

1. Who are your customers? Define your target market(s)

2. Are your markets growing? Steady? Declining?

3. Is your market share growing? Steady? Declining?

4. If a franchise, how is your market segmented?

5. Are your markets large enough to expand?

After you've identified your market, you need to determine how you'll reach it.

Promoting Your Company

Promoting your company, or *advertising*, is an important component of your marketing plan. There are about as many different ways as you can think of to promote your company. If you wanted to, you could put a sandwich sign on your dog and send him out to the middle of town during lunch hour. That would get people's attention.

Or you can do huge billboards all over town. You could hire a plane and pilot to pull a banner promoting your business over six counties. You could do television infomercials, ads in magazines or trade journals, direct mailings to potential customers, or walk around town with a bullhorn.

All these methods promote your company and its products, but obviously some make more sense for you than others. Huge billboards may or may not be effective, but if you can't afford them, it doesn't really matter. Sending your dog out with a sandwich sign might be cute for a pet grooming business, but would be decidedly undignified for somebody trying to start up a legal firm.

Placing ads in trade journals makes no sense if your target market is stay-at-home moms, and self-promotion through a bullhorn certainly makes you seem unprofessional and even desperate.

Bear Facts

Regardless of what method of advertising you choose, don't expect immediate results. Consumers usually need to see or hear an ad several times before it starts to sink in. Be prepared to be patient.

Ways to Get the Word Out

Let's take a look at some traditional and non-traditional methods of advertising. While you're reading about these methods, keep in mind that each of these areas use sales representatives to market their product. It's a great idea to meet with a lot of sales reps and let them teach you about their products. You'll be amazed at what you can learn about marketing in general from talking with a sales rep in a particular marketing area. Be sure you ask a lot of questions and get all the information you can. Meeting with these sales reps is like getting a marketing education at no charge.

After you've finished this section, take a few minutes to think about which methods might work best for your business:

➤ **Newspapers and magazines** Newspaper and magazine advertising can be effective in reaching certain audiences, but they also can be expensive. Generally, the larger the publication's circulation, the more expensive its ad rates are. Be sure that the people reading the paper in which you place your ad are the people you want to reach. You can do that by checking out the publication's target audience. Look at the ads other companies are using. If you see one that's run for a long time, you can figure it's been successful. Be sure you pay attention to the day of the week on which the ad runs. It doesn't make much sense to advertise a weekend special at your restaurant on Monday.

➤ **Signs and billboards** Signs at your business identify it and tell people where you are. There's nothing more annoying than looking for a place and not being able to find it. If yours is the kind of business that depends on drive-by traffic, like a gas station, a noticeable sign is absolutely necessary. Signs and billboards other than those at your business can help to direct people to you. If you have a business like a restaurant or motel, billboards could be effective. However, be aware that their location, whether or not they're lighted, and how they're de-signed have a big influence on how effective they are.

➤ **Direct mail** Direct mail is a great way of keeping in touch with current custom-ers and can be effective in attracting new ones. If you don't have your own mailing list, you can rent one from a mailing house. Check your yellow pages to find one. Make sure you request very targeted lists so you can find the people you want to reach. Direct mail is an interesting business. If you're going to do it, make sure you understand how it works. Mailing lists usually cost a certain amount for each thousand names on them. Just be sure your mailing is catchy enough to get the attention of your potential customer. Otherwise, it's likely to end up in the trash without even being read.

➤ **The Yellow Pages** Nearly every business belongs here. It's the first place many people look when they're deciding where to buy a product or find a service. Think about the last time you were out of town for a business trip or vacation.

How many times did you scope out the Yellow Pages to find a restaurant, a nearby grocery store, or somebody who could repair or replace your broken cell phone? People use the Yellow Pages all the time. There used to be only one set of Yellow Pages, but now you might have to get listings in more than one directory to ensure you have the coverage you want.

➤ **Television** It used to be that small businesses didn't even bother looking at television advertising because the price was prohibitive. However, these days, with the proliferation of cable stations, it can be a feasible advertising option. Cable stations have pretty well-defined audiences, so you can target your ads to who you want to reach. For instance, if you're trying to sell a new kind of fishing reel, you can look for channels that target outdoors and sports enthusiasts. Local news programs are popular in many areas and might provide opportunities for reaching potential customers. TV stations have advertising sales representatives who will meet with you. Be sure you ask about the station's Nielsen ratings, which indicate how many viewers the channel has.

➤ **Infomercials** Infomercials are a fairly new method of advertising, but they're becoming increasingly prevalent. You've probably seen them—hawking everything from get-rich-quick schemes to health and fitness equipment to household gadgets. They tend to be pretty long, so you have a long time to tell everybody how great your product is. They're also very expensive, so make sure the people watching the program are the people you're trying to reach before you commit to an infomercial. They tend to run at odd times on less-than-network channels.

➤ **Radio** I'll be talking about radio in detail a bit later in the chapter in the section "Radio: The Most Overlooked Marketing Tool." Just let me say that it can really work if your product or service is right for it.

➤ **The Internet** It's definitely becoming a major advertising vehicle and will continue to increase in importance. The Internet Society reports that Internet use is growing faster than any communications medium in history, including fax, personal computers, and copiers. Statistics show that the demographics of the average Internet user is young (age 18–44), educated, and professional, with an estimated average income of more than $63,000 annually. Online transactions are expected to reach $3.3 billion by 2000. It looks like Internet advertising is the trend of the future. The downside at present is that it's expensive and requires close maintenance. If you're interested in getting in on the ground floor, however, there are all sorts of individuals and companies who will help you get started on the Net. A few to check out are:

➤ Timewalk Enterprises at www.timewalk.com

➤ Mallberry.com at www.mallberry.com

➤ Wallaby Web Design at www.lisp.com

➤ iMall Internet Design at www.cyberport.net

➤ Visionary Website Creations, Inc. at www.visionary-web.com

Other advertising possibilities include the following:

➤ **Coupons**   Included in mailers, for pickup at other establishments, in the newspaper, and so on.

➤ **Classified ads**   In the newspaper, in a local mailer, in the phonebook, on the Internet, and so on.

➤ **Audio or videotapes**   On television, at seminars or trade shows, and so on.

➤ **Seminars**   You can sponsor, attend, or be a presenter at seminars on various topics.

➤ **Giveaways**   At seminars, at local establishments, with the purchase of a product, and so on.

Over the Rainbow

The one form of advertising that does work for everyone is word of mouth referrals from existing customers to potential customers. Positive referrals are the surest way to get new customers, although it's a slow process.

The Vermont Teddy Bear Company sponsored a NASCAR driver and put an 800 phone number on the back of the car. We advertised on the sides of New York City buses and phone booths. We advertised in the subways there. After we identified New York City as our major market, we used every reasonable method we could think of to promote our product there.

As you can see, there are all kinds of advertising options. The trick is picking the ones that work for you. Your marketing program has to make sense for your company, and what works for one business won't necessarily work for another.

To learn more about different advertising methods and which might be the best for your company, check out *Advertising Age* and other magazines and journals.

Or have a look at one of these comprehensive books:

➤ *Advertising: Principles & Practice*, 4th ed., by William Wells

➤ *Advertising and Promotion: An Integrated Marketing Communications Perspective*, by Michael A. Belch (part of the Irwin/McGraw-Hill Series in Marketing)

Radio: The Most Overlooked Marketing Tool

I'll tell you right away that I'm biased toward radio. To me, it's without question the best way to advertise. I've sold teddy bears, I've sold bikes, and I've sold high-tech shoe inserts through radio advertising. Radio works, but it's the most overlooked marketing tool out there.

Why, you ask? I'll tell you why. It's not used as much or as effectively as it could be because advertising agencies don't stand to make as much money from using radio as they do from television. Producing radio ads doesn't give them the big, upfront costs that TV ads or even print ads do. Radio is seen by ad agencies as a distant cousin of TV, and it's not widely encouraged. If anything, radio ads might be combined with TV and print advertising, which is very effective. I'm telling you, though, that radio works on its own.

Radio is extremely effective in letting you reach a particular market. Different radio shows are geared toward different audiences, and they allow you to target just who you want to reach. Listen sometime to the variety of businesses that advertise on the radio and when the ads are run.

Bear Facts

I started advertising on the radio with a budget of $50 a week. As The Vermont Teddy Bear Company grew, our budget increased, and during peak periods like Christmas, Valentine's Day, and Mother's Day, we'd sometimes spend $100,000 a week on radio advertising. Our total advertising budget was $4 million yearly, and $3 million of it was used for radio.

Just think about radio for a few minutes. How many radios do you have in your home? Probably several. How often do you listen to the radio in your car? Probably often. Most people count on radio for at least a portion of their information, as well as their entertainment. Radio hosts are some of the most talked-about and influential people in America. Their pictures appear on the covers of news magazines. If you get a popular radio host to sell your product, you bet that people are going to listen.

That's been my radio strategy. Instead of ads that are recorded and then run over and over, talk show hosts actually promote my products during their shows. It gives the products great credibility and produces great results.

When The Vermont Teddy Bear Company first started doing radio ads, it was strictly local. We advertised our Beargram concept on Burlington's WXXX-FM, a top-40 station. People at the station

The Word According to John

Radio advertising, in addition to being incredibly effective, is the most fun way to advertise. Radio people take good care of you because they want your business. They're generally a really fun bunch of people, and they go out of their way to keep you happy. In short, radio advertising is the way to go!

helped me develop the type of advertising that used the shows' hosts to talk about the Beargrams. We saw fast results. Beargrams, by the way, are handwritten, personal messages delivered along with the teddy bears. It was Beargrams (among other things) that set The Vermont Teddy Bear Company apart from other bears.

We expanded our advertising efforts and took the Beargram concept to other radio markets. We also decided to sell our bears exclusively through radio. Before we increased our radio efforts, our highest yearly sales ever were $500,000. By the end of 1990—the first year we got big-time into radio advertising—our sales climbed to $1,900,000 and kept increasing.

I credit the talk show hosts for much of The Vermont Teddy Bear Company's great success. We used some of the best: Don Imus, Rush Limbaugh, Joan Hamburg, Ross Brittan, Jim Kerr, Bob Jones, Kevin Mathews, Don and Roma, and Howard Stern. They all talked about how great Vermont teddy bears were, and listeners bought into it. It's a format that really works.

Setting a Marketing Budget and Making It Work

As you saw earlier in this chapter, there are many, many options when it comes to marketing. Unfortunately, most of them cost money—sometimes big money. Advertising costs can add up quickly if you're not careful. Let's consider what you should be spending and how to get the most for your money.

How Much Should You Spend?

Your sales and marketing expenses take a fairly large chunk of what you make from selling your products or services, so you should be careful to keep them under control. Just as a reminder, take a look at the equation you saw earlier in this chapter:

> Sales – General and Administrative Costs – Costs of Goods Sold – Sales and Marketing Costs = Profits

Marketing expenses at The Vermont Teddy Bear Company accounted for 24%–28% of our total costs. This included the cost of advertising, the marketing department's payroll, catalogue production, mailing costs, radio and television costs, direct mailing costs, newspaper ads, and any marketing-related travel.

Our sales expenses, which included salaries for people who sold the bears over the phone, phone costs (which were huge because of our 800 number), training of salespeople, and anything else associated with the sales department, ran between 13% and 15%.

In general terms, you should spend an amount you're comfortable with on sales and marketing costs. If you're just starting your business, you probably don't have a lot of extra money for marketing. That's okay. Start small and do what you can. You can always increase your spending later on.

A 1996 study showed that advertising budgets nationwide more than doubled in the decade between 1986 and when the study was conducted. At that time, companies were collectively spending about $162 billion a year on advertising efforts. That worked out to about $635 for every man, woman, and child in the United States.

Don't worry. You shouldn't be concerned about keeping up with the big companies that earmark millions of dollars a year on marketing. Just find the marketing plan that makes the most sense for your business, and don't spend more than you're comfortable with. Keep testing your marketing plan, and don't be afraid to change it if you're not getting the results you want. Marketing is an ongoing process. Be sure you track your marketing strategies by asking customers how they heard about your company or product. This helps you determine what's working.

Remember that it's more effective to use the money you have to execute a good, well thought-out advertising plan than to throw a huge amount of money haphazardly into different advertising efforts.

Opportunities for Free Publicity

There are all kinds of opportunities available for getting free publicity, and smart companies take advantage of them whenever possible.

Say that your company is sponsoring some kind of community event. When I was at The Vermont Teddy Bear Company, for instance, we sponsored events like community-wide Easter egg hunts, cartoon festivals, and so forth. All the local papers and radio stations publicized the events for free because they were of interest to people in the area. Sure, it cost the company money to run the events, but the publicity was great, and the goodwill we generated was invaluable.

You can get somebody to write press releases about your company when it reaches a sales milestone, wins an award for being environmentally responsible, releases a new product, or moves to a new building. Or you can write the press releases yourself. Send them to area and business newspapers, trade journals, and television and radio stations. Be sure that any releases you send out are well written and to the point.

Over the Rainbow

You can get radio advertising at a reasonable cost because you don't have the high upfront costs associated with producing an ad. Sales representatives at the radio station you work with normally write your ad at no extra cost. Or you can listen to radio ads, figure out the ones you like, and then write your own ads.

Over the Rainbow

Some people subscribe to the theory that there's no such thing as bad publicity. I'm not sure that's true, but I do know one thing. If you get bad publicity at some point, remember that relatively few people pay attention to it. It seems to be the biggest thing in the world to you at the time, but unless it's about something really horrendous, you'll be surprised at what a little ripple it will make. Guess what? The same goes for positive publicity. It's nice to have, but it won't necessarily triple your sales.

Sometimes newspapers do stories on new businesses, particularly if it's something a little unusual. You can call your paper's business editor to see if there's any interest. We got a lot of media interest when we produced the world's biggest bear, a 26-foot-tall fellow that weighed 2,000 pounds.

You can't be shy when looking for free publicity, but don't be overly pushy. Media people hate to feel like you're telling them what they should do or say. Try to get to know some of the media people in your area. Do they attend business meetings? Chamber of commerce functions? Do they meet at a certain bar after work? Media people are good folks to know.

Often, events such as concerts or sporting contests look for sponsors. Although it costs something, your company can get some good publicity by sponsoring some of these events. The Vermont Teddy Bear Company sponsored a concert series in Stowe, Vermont. For a $12,000 sponsorship fee, we got tons of publicity, as well as the opportunity to hobnob with performers like Bonnie Raitt and Santana.

Go ahead and look for opportunities for *free* advertising. Usually, it's positive and fosters a good relationship between your company and the community. By all means, see what's available, and take advantage of it.

Hiring Marketing Experts

If you look in your phone book, you'll find all kinds of marketing services: market researchers, market analysis firms, and marketing consultants. There are also listings for public relations firms, graphic designers, print shops, desktop publishing companies, creative services, and on and on it goes.

Over the Rainbow

It's important to be involved with your advertising efforts. Don't hire somebody and then step back and give him free reign. You know your company better than anybody, and you know the image and information you're trying to convey. If you do hire someone, be sure you stay in the picture.

So with all those choices, who do you hire? And how do you know when you need a marketing person in the first place? How much should you be willing to pay for marketing help?

Let's have a look at these issues, and discover how all these types of companies are different—or the same.

When Do You Need Marketing Help?

It's my feeling that you can do most of your marketing work yourself or with the help of sales representatives from the various marketing areas. When you start advertising, you get an account representative who helps you plan your budget and gives you ideas. If you don't feel like you can handle the marketing on your own, however, you need to get somebody to help you.

If you want to do print advertising, you might need to hire someone to create an ad for you, but don't assume this is true until you check. Newspapers and magazines often have people on staff who can create your ad as part of the cost of advertising.

If you're interested in television advertising, talk to the sales representative at the station. He or she might be able to help you create an ad or at least answer your questions.

If you want to do a direct mailing, you might have to talk to somebody about renting a mailing list, or you might have to hire a marketing person to direct a multi-faceted marketing campaign. Often, though, I think that marketing efforts are best handled by those who know the company best—you and your partners.

Where to Find Help If You Need It

If you need help with any aspect of your marketing efforts, think about who you know. This could be a good time to use some of your contacts. Do you know anybody who works for your area's newspaper? Or an advertising representative at the local radio or television station? Even if you want your advertising to extend beyond your area, people who work in the field should be able to tell you how to proceed, what questions to ask, and maybe with whom you should work.

Bear Facts

Generally, if you're trying to determine who your market is, use market researchers, a market analysis firm, or a marketing consultant. If you want help in conveying an image of your company or getting publicity for it, you'd probably want to try a marketing consultant or public relations firm. For help with creating ads, signs, brochures, or promotional pieces, try graphic designers, print shops, desktop publishing companies, or creative services firms.

Maybe you know someone who works for a big marketing firm but does extra jobs on the side. That's not uncommon. Perhaps someone can point you toward an innovative, creative freelance graphics designer who can design and create a terrific ad for you. Always ask for costs, and meet with the person before committing to anything.

Don't feel you have to run directly to an advertising agency or marketing firm. Figure out exactly what it is you hope to accomplish, and think about what you could do to make it work. If you need help, ask around to get a feeling for who is available. Personal recommendations can be very helpful.

If you're confused by the many types of marketing-related businesses out there, check out what they do. Look for their advertising to determine what services they provide.

Ask other businesspeople who they have used and who they hear is good. If you see or hear an advertisement that you really like, call the advertiser and see who produced it.

Marketing firms should be willing to meet with you initially at no cost to determine your needs and tell you what they can do for your company. Don't feel obligated to sign on with the first firm. Meet with representatives from some different places and find out how they vary.

How Much to Pay Marketing Help

The cost of marketing help varies greatly, depending on who you get to help. Top-rate consultants might charge a couple of hundred dollars an hour, but a freelance graphics designer's rate might be only $40 an hour.

The only way to find out is to ask, but be aware of a few things:

➤ If you use an ad agency, there are different levels of employees, some of whom charge more than others. Be sure you know who you're paying for what jobs.

➤ If you're being charged an hourly fee, ask for an estimate of how much time will be involved. You might want to set a price that's not to be exceeded.

➤ Negotiate. You might not have much leverage with a one-time job, but if you plan to do more marketing projects in the future, you should be able to get some kind of deal. Don't be afraid to ask.

Set a budget for marketing costs, and make sure to work within it. You'll be surprised at how fast advertising and marketing costs can mount.

The Least You Need to Know

➤ Sales and marketing are interwoven, but they're not the same thing.

➤ There are many ways of selling your products or services, and you've got to know which method works best for your company.

➤ Offer incentives to attract and keep the best salespeople you can find.

➤ A good marketing plan is the heart of your business plan and guides all your marketing efforts.

➤ Radio advertising, if done properly, is cost–effective and accomplishes its goal of promoting your product.

➤ Sales and marketing is a big chunk of your expenses, but there are ways to keep costs down.

➤ A lot of your marketing work can be done in-house, but at times you might need to get some help.

Chapter 16

Cost of Goods Sold

In This Chapter

➤ Understanding the route between sales and profits.

➤ Determining the expenses included in cost of goods sold.

➤ Predicting your cost of goods sold.

➤ Keeping costs down to increase profits.

➤ Making cost control everybody's business.

Do you remember the equation I talked about in Chapter 14, "General and Administrative Costs"? Let's have a quick review:

Sales – General and Administrative Costs – Costs of Goods Sold – Sales and Marketing Costs = Profits

In the previous chapter, you learned about costs associated with the general and administrative areas and how they affected the bottom line—or profits.

In this chapter, I'm going to discuss the cost of goods sold and how it affects a company's bottom line. Quite simply, the cost of goods (or services) sold is how much it costs to make whatever you sell. It can be teddy bears, a dinner in a restaurant, or a service call to someone's house to unclog their kitchen drain.

With everything produced, either goods or services, there are costs associated with the production. You've got to buy the food to make the meal to sell in your restaurant. You've got to pay somebody to prepare it. You've got to have pans and ovens and serving pieces. The more money it costs you to produce your product, the less profit you'll make on it, unless you can get away with selling it for an exorbitant price to a market that doesn't mind paying it.

When I sold a teddy bear for $60, I didn't keep $60 from the sale. The money from the sale of the teddy bear had to help pay for general and administrative expenses, the cost of making the bear, and the cost of selling and marketing the bear.

Let's take a look at how the money from the sale of that one bear was used and how much was left over as profit when everything was accounted for:

Sale of One Bear	$60
Less G&A Expenses	($7)
Less Cost of Goods Sold	($24)
Less Sales and Marketing Costs	($22)
Profit on the Sale of 1 Bear	$7

This, of course, is a simplified explanation of how money from sales of products is used. However, it should give you an idea of what's involved between sales and profit.

Now, back to the cost of goods sold. Let's take a look at what kind of expenses are involved, how you can predict what these costs will be, and how you can keep them as low as possible to increase profits.

What's Included in the Cost of Goods Sold?

The cost of goods sold includes raw materials, time and labor, supplies, purchases, factory overhead, packaging, shipping, change of inventory, and some miscellaneous expenses. As with costs in the general and administrative area, some of them are easier to control than others, and some vary more than others. Obviously, it's important to keep your costs as low as you can to increase your profit. You don't, however, want to cut corners to the point that you jeopardize the quality of your product and make it unsellable. That's a sure way to put yourself right out of the market.

It's also important to keep good financial statements so you know what's happening with your company's money. Keep your accounts in categories. Your chart of accounts for cost of goods sold might look something like the following example:

Account Number	Account Name
5000	Cost of Goods Sold
5100	Raw Materials
5150	Time and Labor
5160	Supplies
5200	Purchases
5250	Factory Overhead
5300	Packaging
5350	Shipping
5360	Change in Inventory
5400	Miscellaneous

For instance, all expenses that fall in the cost of goods sold category might be identified with a 5000 number. The category (cost of goods sold) is identified as 5000. Raw material is 5100, time and labor 5150, supplies 5160, cost of manufacturing 5200, and so on. This makes it easy to identify where you're spending and keep track of how much money is going to different areas.

What You Need: Raw Materials

Raw materials are what you need to make a product. If you're a restaurateur, your raw materials are vegetables, meat, grains, and spices. If you're a teddy bear manufacturer, or at least a Vermont Teddy Bear manufacturer, your raw materials are fabric, plastic joints, stuffing, eyes, and thread.

Some people call raw materials *direct materials*. Whatever you call them, they're the materials that end up as part of the product. The needles used to sew teddy bears, on the other hand, aren't considered raw materials. They don't end up as part of the bear. They're one of the supplies used to *make* the product, but not actually a part of the product.

If the cost of your raw materials remains the same or drops, you don't have to worry. If, for some reason, the cost of your raw materials increases, you have to look for ways to cut costs and save money in other areas, or find a different supplier.

Over the Rainbow

Keep your financial statements consistent to make sure you know where you're spending your money. You need to build formulas that clearly explain your business. Keeping accurate, consistent records allows you to identify where you're spending more than you want to. Those are the areas where you need to make spending cuts. If you don't have an accurate understanding of where your money is going, you won't know where you're spending too much.

Bear Facts

Raw materials found in nature tend to fluctuate in price more than those that are man-made. For instance, when silk was the primary material for stockings and underwear in the early 1900s, manufacturers had a difficult time predicting profits because of the drastic changes in the cost of their raw material. The silk, nearly all of which was imported from Japan, could double or triple in price from one shipment to another. Sometimes it wasn't available at all. It's no wonder nylon was hailed as the wonder fabric!

The advantage is that raw materials are usually available from a variety of sources. If you think you're paying too much for them, you can try to get them for less from somebody else. The price of raw materials can be pretty volatile, and although your business might be able to absorb small increases, major cost jumps can really hurt your profits. It's a good idea to ask your suppliers how long they can guarantee their prices for raw materials.

Get It Ready: Time and Labor

Needless to say, time and labor are big costs involved with getting a product ready to sell. Fortunately, there are many ways you can work on reducing these costs.

Labor costs can be a big chunk of your overall budget. Many manufacturers have gone offshore in search of cheap labor, but that doesn't always work. Maybe you'll end up paying less for labor, but the quality of your goods won't be as high as it should. If that happens, you have to decrease your price, find another market, or do something to deal with your problem.

You could end up with less expensive labor costs, but lose out time-wise. What happens if your product ends up sitting in a dock warehouse someplace, only to be practically outdated by the time you finally get it and distribute it? Just be aware that there are potential disadvantages to offshore production.

Business owners often complain that their labor costs are too high, without realizing they could be responsible for the problem. If you're trying to keep your cost of goods sold as low as possible, think about how your production time is being spent. Do you see employees sitting around waiting for work? If so, you're wasting time and money. Is there inventory in your shop that's not moving? If so, you're wasting time and labor taking care of it and storing it.

If you have a restaurant, and customers are sitting around waiting to be served, you need to hire more help. Time that customers spend sitting around is time they could spend eating and drinking, which means they'd be spending money.

If you can modernize your equipment to make your workers more productive, you'll save time and money. Maybe you can find a better tool that makes work faster and easier. Look for any ways or methods that can help decrease production time.

A milestone in the production of Vermont teddy bears occurred when I figured out a way to eliminate an expensive piece of hand sewing. You see, Vermont teddy bears are jointed bears—far superior to non-movable teddies. The difficulty in making these bears, whose limbs are attached to their bodies with plastic joints, was that each of the six pieces—a head, two arms, two legs,

Over the Rainbow

Stay attuned to solutions for problems. You never know where you'll be, or what you'll be doing when they come to you. If your mind is active and open, you'll eventually figure out how to solve your problems.

and the body—had to be hand-sewn after they were stuffed. You could machine-sew the majority of the bear, but you needed to leave a small hole in each piece in which to insert the stuffing, and that hole had to be stitched together by hand. It cost about 35 cents in labor costs for each hole that had to be stitched.

I was worried about this cost. We were paying $2.10 in labor costs just for one small part of the overall production. I started thinking maybe we'd have to send some of our work overseas to get it done less expensively, but I really, really didn't want to do that. So, I started trying to figure out an alternative.

One night, while I was sitting around drinking Italian wine, a solution came to me. We would leave the hole where the joint was inserted, and then overlap the fur back onto the joint. This eliminated the need for hand sewing and actually made the bear stronger and longer lasting. It saved us all kinds of money, and produced a better product. You see what a little ingenuity (and wine) can do?

In some businesses, high labor costs are inherent and unavoidable. If you're a stained-glass maker, for instance, the cost of your labor is high because it's a labor-intensive process. Still, you might be able to develop techniques that would help you work faster—and better.

Be sure that you, or your employees, have materials available and within reach. Encourage and reward high production. If an employee made 15 teddy bears one day, I made sure he or she had materials for 20 or 25 the next day.

Be sure your operation is set up efficiently. If employees have to go looking for supplies and materials, their production level screeches to a halt.

I'm going to spend a whole chapter in Part 4, "No Man (or Woman) Is an Island," talking about how you should treat your employees and how valuable they are to your company. Still, if you're paying too much in labor costs, it affects your profit. Be aware of all the variables that can affect labor costs and do what you can to keep the costs as low as possible.

Grizzly Area

Be careful how you set up your manufacturing systems. Make sure they're practical and that employees won't have to spend time looking for and getting materials to work with. Your manufacturing system can greatly affect your labor costs. Compare it to this: If you're cooking a meal in your downstairs kitchen, but all your food is stored upstairs, you're going to spend an awful lot of time running up and down the stairs when you could be cooking! Be careful where you put the materials needed for production.

Necessities: Supplies

Supplies are items necessary to your product or service, but unlike raw materials, they don't end up as part of the product.

For example, if you're running a restaurant, your supplies include plates, cups, and linens; if you're running a dog-walking service, your supplies include the leash and items needed for cleaning up after the dog.

Buy and Resell: Purchases

Purchases are items you buy and then resell. At Vermont Teddy Bear, we included chocolate truffles with our bears if customers wanted them. We bought the truffles from a local company, and then resold them to our customers. The chocolates were purchases.

If you're running a retail business, as opposed to manufacturing, your entire stock is purchases, unless you're making the items you sell yourself.

Operation: Factory Overhead

The cost of factory overhead varies, depending on the type of operation you have. It includes the cost of rented space, depreciation on equipment, the cost of utilities, and so forth.

These costs are somewhat controllable and, obviously, something you should look at carefully if you're trying to keep down your expenses for cost of goods sold.

How Does It Look: Packaging

You can have the best darned product in the world, but if you throw it into a brown paper bag and put in on the shelf, chances are it's going to sit there for a while. A long while.

Bear Facts

Pay attention to how the things you use are packaged. Check out your cereal box and think about why that particular package was used. What's the box that your toothpaste came in look like? A classic packaging example is the move in the past few years to make tissue boxes part of your decor, instead of just a box. Kleenex started with its Expressions line, and other companies quickly followed. Now you can get tissue boxes with birds, entire gardens, herbs, animals—whatever you want (well, almost).

Packaging is a big deal in our society. We want what we buy to look nice. Often, packaging is what initially attracts buyers to a product. Packaging says a lot about the product it contains.

And it can be expensive. The cost of materials varies, along with labor costs associated with packaging. Look around at all types of packaging before you decide what to do. While you're looking at different packaging products, remember this:

➤ Packaging should *enhance* the product and give consumers an idea of what the product is about. You wouldn't put fancy perfume in a brown, recycled box, for instance, and you wouldn't package hiking boots in a delicate, floral-patterned bag.

➤ Packaging is about *image*. It's important because it's often the first thing customers see. The way your product is packaged says a lot about the product and about your company, but your packaging has to be practical, too. Corn flakes are packaged in cardboard boxes instead of bags because they're corn *flakes*, not corn crumbs, and they're packaged in boxes because boxes fit nicely on the shelves in the grocery store.

➤ Packaging can contain *hidden expenses*. If you ship your product, overly heavy packaging can add shipping expenses. Packaging materials can vary greatly in price and add to your costs if you're not careful.

Get It There: Shipping Costs

If your product doesn't get to where it needs to go, you've got big trouble. Reliable shipping—both to and from your business—is essential.

You can do everything else right—produce the best clothing, or bikes, or beer there ever was. However, if you can't get your product to the point of sale on time, it does you no good. If you sell through the mail, as I did with the teddy bears, good shipping is equally essential. I used United Parcel Service for shipping. Because I shipped so many items and used only UPS, the company gave me a good rate and excellent service.

Shipping can be expensive, but you've got to find someone you can rely on. A customer doesn't want to hear that the teddy bear he ordered didn't get to his girlfriend on Valentine's Day like it was supposed to because the delivery truck didn't show up on time. That's not his problem; it's yours.

If you're paying a lot for shipping and you ship all the time, maybe it would make sense to have your own truck or trucks and do it yourself.

It's important to make sure you work with suppliers who give you dependable shipping, too. If your supplies of free-range chicken and organic goat

Over the Rainbow

All sorts of shipping options are available. To determine which is best for your business, you should sit down with both incoming and outgoing shippers and go over rates, services, obligations, and so forth. A customer service representative should be available to visit your office and give you all the information you need. Consider all the facts before you make a decision.

cheese don't arrive when they're supposed to, you're going to have to change your menu for the evening. If the fabric you ordered from New York is two weeks late getting to your shop, your customer isn't going to get her new dress on time.

Keeping Track: Change in Inventory

Your inventory affects your cost of goods sold. Check your inventory each month to see how much you're purchasing in relationship to how much you're selling.

Everyone has a different method for keeping track of inventory. It matters less *how* you do it than *that* you do it, and do it accurately. If you need help setting up a good system for tracking inventory, check with your accountant.

Just remember: If you're buying more than you make or more than you sell, your cost of goods sold is going to be too high.

Everything Else: Miscellaneous

Miscellaneous costs in the cost of goods sold category include expenses such as trade journals, special promotions, and the cost of training employees.

Anything that doesn't seem to fit under another account can usually be considered miscellaneous.

How to Predict Your Cost of Goods Sold

The cost of goods sold varies from company to company, depending on the type of product you're making. Some products cost more to make than a comparable one. For instance, a meal prepared using only organically grown or raised food costs more to prepare than the daily special at Al's Diner. The cost of goods sold for the organic meal will be higher, so the owner of the restaurant must charge more than Al does for lunch.

Although you can check with colleagues about where they buy supplies and raw materials, be sure you're comparing apples with apples. If you ask Al how much he pays for his lettuce, for example, he might tell you he gets it for 89 cents a head down at the Publix. You want something a little more upscale than iceberg for your restaurant's salads, and it's got to be organic to boot, so you're going to end up paying a lot more for your lettuce than Al does.

Be sure you consider all the expenses you'll incur in this category. If you overlook some, you might end up being surprised at the total cost. When you're trying to predict your cost of goods sold, work backward from the price of whatever it is you're selling. Remember the chart at the beginning of this chapter? Figure out how much you can spend in each of the categories (general and administrative, cost of goods sold, and sales and marketing) and still have a profit.

Bear Facts

The rule of thumb is that your selling price should be at least four or five times what it costs to make a product. Ideally, it should be 10 times as much. If you're selling flowers for $25, but it's costing you $21 to buy, arrange, and deliver them, then something's wrong. You either have to spend less to make the arrangement or charge the customer more.

Keeping Production Costs Low to Make Profit High

Keeping your production costs down should be a constant goal that gets constant attention. One of the most important things you can do to keep your production costs down is to find a good, dependable supplier. A good supplier makes sure you get what you need on time. He's willing to work with you on payments. Generally, he'll take care of you. If you find a supplier you really like, try to make him part of your team. Let him know you're interested in a long-term relationship that's beneficial to both of you.

Just a word of warning, though. After you've established a good relationship with a supplier, keep an eye on it. In many instances, business relationships go bad for one reason or another, and somebody ends up getting hurt.

Another point to remember is to keep your inventory to a minimum. A quick turnaround is more cost-efficient than having a lot of stuff sitting around that doesn't move.

Keep your labor costs down, too. Make sure you're making it possible for your employees to work to their full potential. Remember, everything each person does is a spot on your general ledger. Take a close look at what the employees you have are doing. How are they spending their day? Is there one who appears to have a lot of time on his or her hands? Make sure you're utilizing your employees fully. It doesn't make sense to hire six people to do the work of four.

The Word According to John

Outsourcing is getting somebody outside your company to do some work or perform a service for you. You might outsource your accounting work, for example, instead of having an accountant on board. Outsourcing is expected to become increasingly popular, although a recent survey by Dun and Bradstreet and *Entrepreneur* magazine showed that less than 1% of the total sales of small businesses is spent on outsourcing now.

If your labor costs are too high, you might consider outsourcing work or using temporary workers. This alternative controls your benefits costs because you're not responsible for supplying them.

Sometimes it's a good idea for you to do some tasks yourself, but avoid the temptation to take on every job that comes along so that you can get away with fewer employees. I mean, it doesn't make sense for you to spend time sweeping the floor when you could be out selling your product.

If your cost of manufacturing is out of whack with your other costs, you need to figure out why first, and then look at what you can do about it. Some suggestions for doing that include the following:

➤ Keep a close watch on what you're spending. Identify what's costing more than it should. Prioritize the areas where you need to save money, and then figure out how to do so.

➤ Think about your prices. If you're buying chocolate truffles, for instance, for $1.50 a piece, and you're reselling them to customers for $2, think about raising your price to $3. Will the extra dollar cause customers to stop buying the truffles? Or will it generate a little extra profit? Keeping a good record of what you're spending allows you to pinpoint areas such as the truffles when you're looking for ways to cut back.

➤ Look at your raw materials to see if you could get equal or better quality for less money. Consider buying bigger quantities for better prices.

➤ Look for better, less expensive ways of doing things. Come up with systems for reducing your costs. Be innovative.

➤ Manage your packaging costs by shopping around to get the best buy you can on materials. If you want a certain look, you have to buy a specific product, but you might find variations in its price among suppliers.

Look at your overall operation, and try to think of other ways you could reduce your costs. Remember, the lower you can keep your cost of goods sold and your general and administrative costs, the more money you can put into selling your product. That should result in more sales, which generate greater profits.

Remember:

Sales – General and Administrative Costs – Costs of Goods Sold – Sales and Marketing Costs = Profits

Making Cost Control a Team Effort

There are plenty of ways to get people motivated to do something, and I'll talk more about that in Chapter 19, "Employees." I'll just say now that if you can make your employees understand they're an important part of a team, they're much more likely to pitch in to save costs, cut back on waste, and use their time and work energy effectively.

Just as with general and administrative cost-control efforts, the attempt to hold down expenses in the cost of goods sold category has to start at the top. Employees who see a buyer paying way too much for raw materials because he's too lazy or uninterested to go out and find a better price can hardly be expected to go out of their way to find less expensive manufacturing methods.

If you're initiating or following up on a cost-control effort, make sure everyone in the company is informed about it. Make sure each employee knows he or she has an important role, not only in the efforts to control expenses, but in the company in general. Tell them that higher profits can mean higher wages, and let them come up with their own ideas for reducing costs.

Be sure to record and share the results of your company's cost-cutting efforts and to celebrate milestones with employees.

Over the Rainbow

You can get your employees really involved with cost-cutting efforts by asking for their ideas and suggestions, then recognizing the top tip each month. Throw in a gift certificate to a nice restaurant for the winner.

The Least You Need to Know

➤ The money you get from selling your product or services has to pay for many things. The idea is to minimize the cost of all those items so that there's more money left over at the end.

➤ The cost of goods sold includes expenses such as raw materials, time and labor, supplies, manufacturing, packaging, and shipping.

➤ To predict what your cost of goods sold will be, you need to identify the expenses for each area and add them together to get a total.

➤ The less money required for cost of goods sold, the more there is to sell the product.

➤ It's in everyone's best interests to keep the cost of goods sold as low as possible to have higher profits.

Chapter 17

Profit

In This Chapter

➤ Making a profit is what you want to do.

➤ Working backward from your selling price to project profit.

➤ Fully understanding your expenses is a key ingredient to making a profit.

➤ Figuring out how to price your products or services.

➤ Making the most of the profit you have.

➤ Sharing the wealth.

➤ Putting profit back where it belongs.

Profits. I bet you're rubbing your hands together at the thought, aren't you? After all, profits are where it's at when you're running and growing your own business. Because that's how it is, I'm going to spend this whole chapter discussing profits and exploring the best ways to put your profits to work for your company. I'll talk about how you can maximize profits, project profits, and some ways to share profits.

The big thing to get straight, though, is that all this talk about profits is a moot point if you don't have any. You can't maximize, share, disperse, or give away profits that aren't there.

It's your goal, of course, as a business owner to make a profit. If it's not, you won't stay in business very long. Even nonprofit businesses can realize profits, and the majority of them aspire to do so. Making a profit was one of the five goals of The Vermont Teddy Bear Company, and it was posted along with the other goals on signs throughout the building. Here are the other goals, just in case you're wondering:

➤ To be the best company

➤ To make the best bears in the world

➤ To have fun

➤ To hire only bear people

Anyway, let's get on with the discussion about profit. Just to refresh your memory, have one more look at the equation you've been working with in this section of the book:

Sales – General and Administrative Costs – Cost of Goods Sold – Sales and Marketing Costs = Profits

If your costs exceed your income, you don't make a profit. If your income exceeds your cost, you do make a profit. And if your income *big time* exceeds your costs, you make a *big* profit. That's the bottom line.

Projecting Profits

To project what your profits will be, you've got to:

➤ Know what profit you want to make

➤ Have a thorough understanding of all your costs

When you're trying to project a profit, start with the selling price of your product or service, and work backward. Say you want to make a 10% profit. To do that, you've got to make sure the selling price of your product or service is 10%, or more, than the cost of all your expenses. It's a good idea to give yourself a little profit leeway and to keep your selling price, after all expenses, a little higher than what you plan to make.

Knowing what your expenses are is a big must. If you don't know where you're spending, you won't know where your controllable areas are. Some parts of your financial statement are pretty much out of your control, but in many areas you can increase or decrease spending to favorably affect your profits.

Remember the selling price of a teddy bear (from Chapter 16, "Cost of Goods Sold") and the costs for general and administrative expenses, cost of goods sold, and sales and marketing? That example was simplified, but it gave you a general idea of how spending broke down, as follows:

Over the Rainbow

Remember that your profit is important to the long-term stability of your business. By contributing a portion of your profit back into the business, you're making sure it can continue to grow and remain profitable.

Selling price of a Vermont Teddy Bear	$60
General and Administrative Expenses	$7
Cost of Goods Sold	$24
Sales and Marketing Costs	$22

After you add the amounts of those expense categories, you could see that the profit on one bear was $7, or about 12%.

In addition to knowing the total expenses of each category, we knew exactly what each category entailed and how much money was going to different items within each category. I can't tell you how important it is to have a complete understanding of where the money from your sales is going. It's the only way you can determine how to adjust your spending to increase your profit.

Over the Rainbow

The better understanding you have of every aspect of your financial statement, the easier it is to find areas where you can control spending.

Usually, you can find fat in your budget and figure out ways to save money. If, however, your expenses are at an absolute minimum and you're still not making any profit, chances are you're not charging enough for your product or service.

It's important to realize that underpricing often happens. Many people just starting businesses have a tendency to set their prices too low. They mistakenly think they can't sell their products if they charge what they'd really like to. That's a common fear, but often ungrounded. If your product is well made and something people want, they'll buy it.

If you think customers are willing to pay more, you can increase your price. If not, you need to rethink your operation. Maybe you're trying to sell something for which there's little market, or maybe your market isn't upscale enough to pay what you need to realize a profit.

Figuring Out What Your Prices Should Be

Just how do you know what to charge for your products or services? That's a question many entrepreneurs ask, and it certainly warrants some explanation.

I imagine that way back when relatively few products and services were available, pricing was more clear-cut than it is now. Operating in today's business environment means that when establishing prices, you have to look at factors such as fluctuating costs, demanding customers with clear ideas about what they'll pay for particular items, and some stiff competition.

Pricing is a tough call, there's no question about it. One of the main reasons for the difficulty is that it's hard to know what consumers are willing to pay for a particular product.

I remember when Ben & Jerry's ice cream first came on the market; the perception was that it was outrageously priced. It quickly became clear that Ben and Jerry knew what they were doing with their pricing because people stood in line to buy their ice cream—even if they thought it was outrageously priced.

There are basically three price categories: cheap, mid-range, and expensive. Everything you buy or sell fits into one of those categories. To decide in which pricing category your product or service falls, you have to think about how much profit you want to make, the nature of your market, and how much that market is willing to pay.

You need to consider how saturated the market in your area is for the product or service you're going to sell. How much competition do you have? And what can you do to get the edge on your competition?

I made the mistake of undercharging for teddy bears the first few years I had the company. I started out charging $37.50. Four years later, the price was $60. When I found out that people were willing to pay more for my bears because they recognized them as high-quality items, I started selling bears in different price categories. They were all of the same quality, but some were bigger and came with more *stuff* than others did. You could buy a bear for $50, $75, or $100.

Methods for Determining Prices

There are several basic methods for determining prices:

➤ **Cost-plus pricing**   With this method, you figure out how much it costs to make your product, and you tack on the amount of profit you want to make. If it costs you $10 to make, market, and sell an item, including your general and administrative costs, and you want to make 30% profit, you sell the item for $13 (or to be on the safe side, charge $14 or $15 to give yourself some cushion). Easy, huh?

➤ **Demand pricing**   This method combines your sales volume (the number of dolls or whatever that you sell), and your desired profit (the amount you make on each of those items after all expenses have been subtracted). The price you put on each doll is based on how many you can sell at a specific price and how much it costs to make them.

➤ **Competitive pricing**   If similar products or services are already selling within an established price range, it's smart for you to operate within that range. This method requires that you find out what your competitors are charging. You should also try to find out to what degree customers are aware of the prices of products similar to yours. If it's general knowledge that a quart of milk costs 89 cents, most people aren't willing to pay $1.49 for it, unless there's a special need or something that makes the product different from the competition's.

➤ **Markup pricing**   Some manufacturers, wholesalers, and retailers simply add a set amount to a product's cost to reach the final price. This prescribed increase, which is usually a percentage of the cost of the product, is called *markup*. If it cost $1.50 to make a truffle, for instance, and the truffle is sold for $3, the markup is 100%.

Often, you'll find that you use more than one method, or a combination of methods, to determine your prices. You might, for instance, check out what your competitors are charging and then figure out, based on how much it's costing you to make your product, what amount of profit you want to make. That approach combines the cost-plus and competitive pricing methods. The price you come up with should fall within the price range of your competition.

You can use whatever method you want to help determine your selling price, but when you come right down to it, you can't charge more for your product or service than your customer thinks it's worth. You can't exceed its perceived value. You have to recognize that because people have different ideas about what something is worth, some people will buy your product for $100, while others wouldn't pay half that price.

Where you sell your product plays a big part in how much you can charge for it, too. If you can convince somebody that your special lawn service treatment is worth $500, then you can charge $500 and get it. However, if the rule of thumb for lawn service in your area is that it's worth only $200, most customers won't be willing to pay two and a half times that price.

Bear Facts

In certain situations, you can set just about any price you want on a product or service and get it. One example is providing excellent service and finding a market that values service over price. Another is having a product or service with status-appeal to people who are influenced by that factor. If you hit the right combination of product and market, consider yourself very lucky. If you've got the hottest restaurant in town, and everyone is dying to get in, you can pretty much charge what you want for your dinners. Your customer will pay.

How Perception Affects Price and Sales

Many factors influence the perceived value of goods and services. Location and customers' attitudes affect your selling price. You could sell your specially flavored cappuccino for $4.50 a cup in a metropolitan area, but take it to a little farm town in middle America and see how many people line up for it.

Did you ever see what Christmas trees sell for on the sidewalks of New York City? The same tree I can buy in Vermont for $15 might cost $80 in downtown Manhattan.

How you position your product or service also affects your selling price. If you're making chocolate bars, for instance, you can position your product in the Hershey bar category, the Godiva category, or someplace in between. Naturally, being positioned in the Godiva category allows a higher selling price than the Hershey category.

Grizzly Area

Understand that you can't just haphazardly decide to charge Godiva prices for your chocolate bars because you want to make a big profit. You've got to make sure customers will perceive that the candy is worth the extra money. You do this by making a great-tasting, high-quality candy bar with neat packaging. If you try to sell an ordinary candy bar at Godiva prices, you'll quickly put yourself out of business.

Over the Rainbow

There's a lot of pressure on starting businesses from investors to make serious money in the first few years. Wall Street investors are putting out the word that they want their money to triple in two years, although the standard used to be five years. If you're pressured to make a lot of money right away, pricing on the high end might make sense.

Pricing is a vitally important part of your overall marketing strategy. How you price your product in large part determines how your product or service is perceived and where it is positioned within the industry.

This becomes clear with professional services. A consultant who charges $75 an hour is perceived by many people as being only half as good as one who charges $150 an hour. We all know that's not necessarily true, but that's a common perception. If someone can get away with charging extraordinarily high prices, people will think she must be extraordinarily good.

I heard a classic example recently of how the market's perception of a product affects its price. The story goes that Totes brand umbrellas used to be sold through high-end department stores. When the retail crunch of the 1980s rolled around, the manufacturer started selling them in discount stores like K-Mart and Wal-Mart.

The umbrellas became popular in the discount stores and were a big seller. So the discount stores started importing similar umbrellas because they could buy them cheaper and make more profit. Totes was out of luck. The discount stores didn't want its umbrellas anymore because they were selling the imports, and the high-end department stores didn't want them either. The perceived value of the umbrellas had dropped during the time they were sold in the discount stores, and the department stores were no longer interested.

The lesson is this: Your pricing structure and your marketing plan must be compatible with the image you want to create.

Another important factor you've got to consider when establishing your selling price is your competitors. If Joe, Bob, and Annie are getting $60, $62, and $65 respectively for their deluxe lawn-treatment services, you have to demonstrate that you're something really special to get much more than that. If you're going to charge $75 for your deluxe lawn-treatment service, you darned better have something that significantly sets it apart from Joe, Bob, and Annie's services. You have to convince your customers that your service is worth the extra $10 or $15.

On the other hand, pricing your product or service too low can be just as damaging as overpricing. A low price might attract customers initially, but it could also convey the idea of inferior quality. After all, if Joe, Bob, and Annie aren't having any trouble getting between $60 and $65 for their lawn-treatment services, how good could yours be if you're charging only $50?

Sure, you'll attract some customers whose only concern is price, but assuming your costs are about the same as Joe, Bob, and Annie's, you're going to seriously affect your profit margin. Even if your lower price attracted three times as many customers as your competitors were getting, you'd have to hire more people and buy more equipment to get the work done.

If you force your competitors to lower their prices to match or beat yours, you could risk damaging your whole industry. Take a longer-term approach, and realize that you'll be successful by supplying a quality service or product at a reasonable, fair price. Give your customers a better reason than your price to buy from you.

Don't Forget to Test Your Prices

When you think you've decided what you're going to charge for your product or service, you should do some market research and testing on a sample market before you go all out to launch your product into the marketplace. If you can get a picture of whether your product or service will sell at the price you're asking, you can make adjustments to the price, if necessary.

Find a place that will sell your product, and see how it goes over. I sold my bears in gift shops, and even in major department stores for a while. That was a good way to do price testing because they were being sold alongside competing bears, and I saw how people perceived my prices, compared to competing brand.

If you're offering a service, like lawn care, you can do a couple of things. You could do a survey before you set a price, finding out what people are paying, and what they're willing to pay for specific

Grizzly Area

If you decide to make your prices lower than everybody else's to attract customers, be aware that some of the customers you attract are likely to leave you as soon as one of your competitors nudges his price down below yours. Some people are driven by price and price alone.

Over the Rainbow

Don't forget one of the most important ingredients of setting prices—common sense. I've seen people set some pretty outrageous prices for no apparent reason. Common sense goes a long way toward helping you decide what prices you can charge.

services. Or, you could simply offer a price, and determine from the response that you get if it needs to be adjusted. Either way is price testing, just different methods.

Over the Rainbow

Make it a point to give your customers a little more than they expect for their hard-earned money. We used to pack our bears in really cool boxes and enclose a game. Customers always felt like they were getting something extra.

Finally, remember that pricing is an ongoing process. Just because you start out your lawn service business charging $60 per treatment doesn't mean you'll charge $60 forever. After you establish a price, especially for a service, it's smart to guarantee it for a specified time. If you find it's not working, though, change the price when that time expires.

Pricing can be a tricky process. However, if you research the market and your competition, know what your expenses are, and know how much profit you want to make, you should be able to set prices that work.

Sharing Profits

After you've earned profits, you have to figure out what to do with them. Many employers look to share their profits with their founders teams and employees, but that doesn't mean you write out checks to everybody in the company, divvying up the profits.

You can share profits by improving the working conditions for your employees. Maybe now's the time to upgrade the ventilation system to make the building more comfortable.

You can give them better benefits, maybe adding some kind of dental or vision plan to their basic health benefits. You can get as creative as you want. How about an on-site day-care center? I know a doctor who hired a full-time nanny, converted the basement of her office into a day-care/nursery facility, and encouraged her employees (all women, and most with small children) to bring their kids to work with them. There were about nine babies and toddlers there on any given day.

The employees ate lunch with their kids, the mothers of the babies were able to nurse them, the nanny had all kinds of games and activities for the kids to do, and everybody was happy. The employees contributed to the center to offset expenses, but the doctor paid the bulk of the costs as an extra benefit for her employees.

I quickly learned that what my employees wanted most was more money. So when our profits increased, we increased wages.

Bear Facts

One way that I shared the profits at The Vermont Teddy Bear Company was to give employees (the majority of whom were women) an option to contribute part of their wages to pay for child care for their kids. They'd send the kids to the child-care center of their choice, and the company would match the amount they had taken out of their wages. The employees really appreciated this benefit, and I always thought it made them more productive because they knew their kids were being cared for, and they weren't worrying about them.

There are all kinds of ways you can share your profits. Some owners put a share of the profits into specially designated vacation funds for their founders teams. Others allocate a percentage for their spouses. You can set up a 401K plan for your employees, increase wages, or give stock options.

What are the benefits of sharing profits? Here are a few:

➤ It makes your employees feel that their work is valued.

➤ It reduces your employee turnover.

➤ It makes it possible to attract better people to your company.

➤ It gives everyone a sense of accomplishment, having made enough in profits that it's possible to share them.

➤ It clearly states that your company has reached a milestone.

➤ It makes you, as the owner of the business, feel good.

Reinvesting Profits into the Company

It's always tempting to spend money when you have it. We see examples of that all the time, and most of us are personally familiar with the concept of money burning holes in our pockets.

That concept holds true when your company makes a good profit—especially at first. The temptation is to spend it. However, although you'll have plenty of occasions to put out money, you should avoid spending it just because it's there.

Always spend profits based on your business plan and your goals for your company.

The Least You Need to Know

➤ It is the goal of nearly every company—even nonprofits—to make a profit.

➤ To project a profit, you need to know what your product sells for and how much it costs to make it.

➤ The better you understand your financial statements, the easier it is to find areas where you can save money and increase your profit.

➤ There are several methods for setting prices on your products or services, but none of them is more important than common sense.

➤ It's important that you maximize your profits to get the most out of them that you can.

➤ There are numerous ways you can share the company's profits with partners and employees.

➤ Don't be tempted to spend profit money just because it's there.

Part 4
No Man (or Woman) Is an Island

Many entrepreneurs suffer from the "I can do it by myself, thank you very much," syndrome. We thrive on making decisions, calling the shots, and being in charge.

Although delegating and sharing responsibility doesn't come easily to many of us, we quickly learn that it's impossible for one person to do everything by himself or herself. We need people around us to help with the work, offer advice and support, and serve as our sounding boards.

This part deals with the people who are important to any business: the founders (or management) team; the board of directors and shareholders; your family and friends; and all the people you count on, such as your lawyer, accountant, banker, insurance agent, suppliers, and so on.

Without these people, and others, we couldn't run our businesses. We could make noble attempts to do everything by ourselves, but it wouldn't take long for our efforts to crumble.

Chapter 18

Your Founders Team

> **In This Chapter**
>
> ➤ Making your life easier with a good founders team.
>
> ➤ Looking for the very best people you can find.
>
> ➤ Places to look for members of your founders team.
>
> ➤ Figuring out who's qualified to serve on your team.
>
> ➤ Establishing ground rules and a framework within which your founders team can work.

Some things are best done on your own. Many things, however, work better with help and input from others. Starting up a business is one of them.

You should have an idea by now of the amount of preparation it takes to get a business up and running. There's financial, legal, personal, and all of kinds of issues you've got to deal with and sort out. This can be time-consuming and overwhelming if you don't have the right people to help you.

To ensure that your business gets off on the right foot, you need to get the best people you can find to help you.

First Things First

If you're working to start up your first business, you might be suffering from what I call the "know-it-all syndrome." It's not until you've had the opportunity to make a bunch of mistakes that you realize you don't know everything you need to about starting a business.

If you are afflicted with this syndrome, don't be alarmed. It's extremely common and completely curable. What you need is a *founder's team.*

Your founders team is the group of people who help you, from the very beginning, implement good operating systems and offer necessary expertise. These people give you support, encouragement, and direction and are invaluable to you and your company.

A strong, capable founders team impresses investors and makes it easier to get funds for your business. It makes sure that all the bases for starting a company are covered and that everything gets done that needs to be done.

The Word According to John

Your *founders team* is a body that serves as an extension of you and your talents. All the skills and knowledge you need to start a company should be present in your founders team.

Over the Rainbow

Picture your company as a pie and each department as a slice. In the very center of the pie, where all the slices meet, picture a smaller circle. That circle, which includes a part of each slice, represents your company's goals and philosophies.

I've talked about different areas of a business, such as sales and marketing, general and administration, and manufacturing. Other areas might include research and development, quality assurance, and finance. All these areas are separate entities, but if there's no overlap, you're in big, big trouble. In fact, if there's no overlap of these areas, you might as well pack up your business plan and head home.

The overlapping area of all these disciplines should be your company's goals and philosophies. If all disciplines don't have these ideas in common, your business will be pulled apart. The very center of your company—its goals and philosophies—should be shared by and common to all areas.

If your company's goal, for example, is to reach $10 million in sales in three years, every area of your company, and every person in every area, must understand and buy into that goal. If your company's philosophy is to strive for excellence in everything it does, it must be understood and practiced by all.

By the same token, your founders team also must share common goals and philosophies. No matter how varied your backgrounds or areas of expertise, each member of the team must fully understand, and buy into, the company's objectives.

The strength of your business depends on the strength of your founders team.

Who Should Be on Your Founders Team?

Now that you know how important it is to have the best founders team possible, you're probably wondering how to go about assembling it. Obviously, you've got to give some thought to who the team should include. You can't go out and round up the first five or six people you see.

It would be easier if there were a set formula for founders teams. I'd love to be able to tell you, for example, to go out and find one lawyer, one engineer, two financial people, and a helluva-good manager type. That would make it a lot easier.

Unfortunately, though, there's no set formula for founders teams. There are, however, two primary requirements:

➤ Get people who can supply all the necessary skills and experience necessary to start a business.

➤ Get the best-qualified people you can find.

Bear Facts

It's important to understand that founders teams are fluid. The team that starts your business might not stay intact after the company is up and running. If you plan a major expansion a couple of years down the road, you might form another founders team to help reach that goal. Some of the same people could be involved a second time around, but that's not always the case.

Let's have a look at who might be on your founders team. Because it's your business, you'll be on the founders team. However, you shouldn't expect to take the dominant role in all situations. If you get a top-notch lawyer on your team, don't presume to know more about business law as it applies to your company than he or she does simply because it's your company.

You should have the chairman of your company's board of directors, or another director, on your founders team, along with your chief financial person. You probably want the person who's handling your sales, the person in charge of setting up the general and administrative systems, and the person in charge of manufacturing, too. If you can get a couple of high-powered businesspeople on your founders team, you stand a better chance of attracting investors.

As it becomes obvious where your company needs some help, it will become equally obvious what kind of people you need for your founders team. Just think about what skills you need to get your business up and running.

227

Do you need somebody to help find investors and raise money? Or someone who can set up manufacturing systems? What about a marketing expert? Consider everything that needs to be done, and find strong, qualified people with the appropriate skills.

Look Beyond People Who Are Just Like You

It's a common tendency to surround yourself with people who are similar to you. I guess those are the folks with whom we feel most comfortable, most at home. It's a big mistake, however, to compile a cookie-cutter founders team. You need different viewpoints and people with different areas of expertise to make your team successful.

Some people think that a founders team should contain only one entrepreneur. The thinking behind this is that the entrepreneur will lead the team and the other members of the team will follow. The more talented the entrepreneur, this theory goes, the more successful the business will get to be.

Grizzly Area

Using a team approach to run your business makes the most sense to me, but you should know it won't always be smooth sailing. Several people working toward a common goal favor different methods for getting there. There are bound to be clashes with the team approach, but a strong team works out its differences for the good of the company. A weak team, however, with egotistical members who have their own agendas, will have a hard time doing so.

I see a couple of flaws in that theory. The first is that not every entrepreneur is a natural leader. Many are, but I'd bet there are plenty who make much better sheep than shepherds (or however the saying goes). I've known entrepreneurs who were smart businesspeople, but they weren't leaders.

The second flaw is the assumption that one strong person is better than a team of strong people. People who are really strong and confident cooperate with one another to make a business operate in the most efficient and smartest way possible. They can see past their own wishes and goals to the greater wishes and goals of the company. If you have these kinds of people on your founders team, it seems to me that's better than one leader and a bunch of followers.

If I had put together a founders team of seven people who knew everything there is to know about teddy bears, but had no knowledge of management, finance, law, bookkeeping, or so forth, The Vermont Teddy Bear Company would have been one sorry place. Can you imagine the meetings we would have had, or the techniques we might have employed to run the business?

Find Strengths That Complement, Not Duplicate

You might know four great accountants. They're all big shots in Big Five accounting firms, and they're all well known and highly regarded within the industry. You certainly want one of them for your founders team, but you don't need all five.

Bear Facts

I gotta be honest. When I was first starting The Vermont Teddy Bear Company, I suffered from a considerable case of the "know–it–all syndrome" I mentioned earlier. I was trying to do everything myself because I thought I should be able to. When I finally admitted that I needed help, then went out and found a good founders team, my life became infinitely easier. There was an incredible drop in the pressure level. I only wish I had done it earlier!

Even though they're high profile and well respected, you'd do better to diversify and find people with other skills. It takes a lot of components to create a successful business, and you need to find people with expertise in each area.

Think again about the primary areas of your business, and consider the types of people who could best set up the necessary systems:

➤ The financial area

➤ The manufacturing area

➤ The sales and marketing area

➤ The general and administrative area

Make sure the knowledge and expertise that different members of your founders team bring to your company is complementary. Their combined knowledge and experience should add up to what's needed to make the business successful.

How to Find the Best People for Your Team

There are plenty of people out there who love to get in on the ground floor of promising new businesses. They're people who thrive on challenges and on making something out of nothing. They're people who want to be involved and to know what's going on.

If you get top-rate people for your founders team, chances are you'll attract better people for your entire operation.

Bear Facts

There's a theory in business that first-rate people attract and hire first-rate people, but second-rate people hire third-rate people. Third-rate people, the theory goes, hire fourth-rate people. So you see, the only viable choice you have for your company is to find first-rate people for your founders team.

The World Is Full of Candidates

You might not realize it, but you probably know plenty of people who would be good candidates for your founders team. What about that guy down at the bank who gave you advice about your business plan? He really helped you out and showed a lot of interest in what you were doing.

Or how about your sorority sister Debra, who's now the vice president of marketing for a major New York advertising firm? She's always told you she wants to be involved when you finally get around to starting that business you've been talking about since college. There's your dad's friend, Bob, who's been involved with business startups for 30 years, and your brother's fiancé, who's a lawyer with one of the area's top firms.

As you shop around your business plan, you'll meet people who can help you get your company started. Pay attention to what these people say. Somebody who's willing to help you might not come right out and say so. If you're listening carefully, though, you'll get the sense that they're interested, and you can ask for help. Try never to be afraid to ask for help. The worst somebody can do is say no.

Grizzly Area

If you do hire a consultant to help you find your founders or management team, be sure the consultant fully understands your business goals and aspirations. There have been too many instances of completely inappropriate placements because the consultant didn't understand the company's philosophies.

Do You Need a Consultant to Choose Your Team?

There are individuals and companies that can help you find people for your founders team. You pay them a fee, and they come up with names for potential team members. Is this the best way to go? Well, it might be if you don't know people you think would fit on your team. I'd rather choose my own people, but I see why consultants might be a good idea. I'm more comfortable putting people I know on my founders teams or people who have been referred to me by business acquaintances.

If you're having trouble finding people for your team, consider these sources:

➤ Other companies that manufacture similar products or provide similar services

➤ Professional associations and societies

➤ Colleges and universities

Some owners look for their management people at businesses they'll be competing with. That's okay, but be sure you have the person's complete loyalty. There's some information about your business you don't want your competitors to know.

Remember to ask everybody you meet for referrals. Your banker, lawyer, accountant, doctor, minister, friends, relatives—even that friendly bartender down the street might know people who would be valuable members of your founders team.

Determining Who's Qualified and Who's Not

After you identify the people you think might fit on your founders team, you need to figure out whether they're qualified. After all, the person at the bank you like so much might be a really nice guy, but not at all qualified to be a vital part of your business.

Obviously, qualifications vary from position to position. Some desirable qualities, however, are the same for everyone. In no particular order, here are some of those qualities:

➤ Honest and ethical

➤ A good communicator

➤ Energetic

➤ Flexible

➤ Creative and innovative

➤ Fun

➤ Hard-working

➤ Organized

➤ Able to make decisions

➤ Wealthy

These are the qualities I would look for in potential members of my founders team. And, of course, I'd look for business experience. I wouldn't necessarily rule out somebody as a possible member of my founders team because he or she has no business experience, however.

You can tell that someone you've met is a natural salesperson, even though she's had no experience in selling. If she's willing to learn, maybe experience isn't the most important quality in that particular case.

Be attuned to different personalities and attitudes. Someone who's inexperienced, but a natural salesperson, can be trained in the methods of selling. Somebody who can't relate to people on any level is difficult to work with and probably not much of an asset, regardless of training.

Sometimes you just have to trust your gut.

Interviewing and Choosing Your Founders Team

You will, you hope, have several candidates for each position on your founders team. This is especially important for positions like the head of sales and marketing or the general and administrative chief.

After you've identified candidates, you need to meet with them and get to know them better. You can call these meetings whatever you want—interviews, get-acquainted sessions—but they're for the purpose of checking out candidates to see whether they have the potential you're looking for.

How to Interview Candidates

Before you start interviewing people, make sure you have a clear idea of what each position is intended to be, and what the person who fills the position is expected to do.

Keep in mind that when you meet with a potential founders team member, many times that person ends up interviewing you. If you've called in a high-level person in hopes of attracting him as an investor or founder, you're going to have to sell him on your ideas!

For now, though, let's focus on meeting with somebody who will be more of a management person than an investor. You know he wants the job. When you first meet with this candidate—let's say his name is Danny—give him a thorough overview of your business and what it is you want to accomplish. Make sure he understands that you're looking for top-notch people and that everyone involved with the company is expected to work hard and do the very best they can.

Grizzly Area

I think that personal chemistry is very important. If you're getting big-time vibes off of someone you're interviewing, chances are that the chemistry between you is bad. If you ignore it, you may end up paying the price later on.

When you're sure Danny understands what's going on, ask him a few general, but important, questions. Asking questions such as "What are your goals for the next 10 years?" or "What things are most important to you in this life?" gives you a chance to observe Danny as he answers. Some of the qualities you should be observing include:

➤ His comfort level. Is he relaxed, or does he seem particularly nervous?

➤ His level of mental organization. Are his thoughts organized, or scattered all over the place?

➤ His confidence level. Does he seem unsure of himself and what he's saying, or does he appear to be well in control of himself and the situation?

➤ His level of maturity. Do you get a sense that he has some experience under his belt? Idealism is great, but a level of maturity is important.

➤ His communication skills. Does he express himself clearly? Do his answers seem logical? Do they make sense?

Listening and watching carefully as Danny speaks can give you some good insights into who he is and what he thinks about. After you've got a sense of Danny, you can start hitting him with some more specific questions. Get his ideas on a wide range of topics, which might include the following:

➤ Inventory control systems

➤ Controlling purchasing

➤ Hiring and firing employees

➤ What he wants from the company

➤ What he'll bring to the company

➤ How to carry out an effective quality assurance program

➤ The best manufacturing methods

➤ Motivating workers

➤ Raising capital for the company

➤ Dealing with sensitive issues concerning employees and management

➤ His financial expectations

➤ Office management

Danny's thoughts and ideas about these and other applicable topics should give you an indication of not only his business experience, but also his attitudes and concerns.

If, at the end of this first meeting, you like Danny and think he'd be valuable to your company, tell him so. Tell him to think about what you've discussed and to call you the next day if he's interested in joining up. That doesn't mean you're committing to giving him a spot on your team; you're merely keeping the possibility open. When he calls, set up another meeting to continue the interviewing process.

Over the Rainbow

Many people like to meet with candidates over a meal so they can observe their table manners and social graces. If you get somebody on your team who slurps his soup and wipes his mouth on his sleeve, you have a little remedial work to do before you take him along to meet with investors.

Looking Past Business

While Danny talks, observe his body language. You can tell a lot about a person by watching his expressions, the way he sits, and so forth. Smarts and experience are big factors when you're thinking about hiring somebody, but you can't overlook the importance of chemistry.

Bear Facts

There will inevitably be clashes among managers in a business. It helps to have good chemistry among your managers and have everybody get along, but it doesn't happen all the time. When conflicts occur, make sure there's mutual respect and a level of etiquette displayed. People can't always like each other, but they can respect each other.

Do you feel comfortable with Danny? You know there are some people you're comfortable with right away, and others who make you feel edgy and nervous. Does he seem to feel comfortable with you? How do you think his personality would mesh, or clash, with those of other people you're thinking of bringing on board?

Chemistry is important. You're going to be spending a lot of time with the people you bring on board. If you hire people you don't like, it will make the entire experience less enjoyable than it should be. It's no fun to work with people you can't get along with.

Laying the Groundwork for Your Founders Team

After you've identified the people you want for your founders team, bring them all together. If they don't already know each other, provide ample opportunity for everyone to get acquainted. Watch how the different people interact and how responsibilities are delegated and handled. You should be able to get a good idea of how your team will work together.

Don't expect a lovefest, but if it becomes obvious that two or more members of your team don't get along and can't work together, you'd better think about getting rid of one of them.

It will take some time to establish procedures and get things at your business running smoothly. The quicker the members of your team get to know each other, however, and what's expected of them—both as individuals and as a team—the more smoothly you can proceed.

Setting the Record Straight

When you've got your team in place, make sure everyone is on the same page about things like stock, payment, responsibility, and risk. Each member should understand that there is risk involved with starting a new business.

Each member should also understand that a high degree of trust is necessary among the team, and everyone needs to know the role of each member of the team.

If you make sure at the very start that everyone has the same expectations, you're less likely to encounter surprises down the road.

Legal Things to Think About

After you have a founders team lined up, you've got to think about how you'll handle the legal aspects.

How will you pay your founders team? Often, members are paid with company stock, instead of a salary. Some members, however, might need salaries.

What about contracts? Some companies have one contract for everyone on the founders team. I think, though, that it's better to have a separate contract for every member. For one thing, the length of employment varies from member to member. Maybe you've brought in somebody to set up all the general and administrative systems. Once the systems are in place, somebody else can take over the day-to-day operations. Many founders teams are set up on a temporary basis; once the business is up and running, some of the founders move on. It doesn't make sense to have everyone following the same contract when circumstances are so varied.

If each founder has a separate contract, an agreement can be enforced with one person, without having to involve everyone in the company. That way, no one is bound by terms that don't really apply.

You might want to limit the spending abilities of each founder, set up some sort of confidentiality agreement to protect information the candidate has been given about the company, and get a non-competition agreement in place. A non-competition agreement prohibits Danny, who's been with you for three months now, from getting bent out of shape with you and your company, taking the information and experience he's gained from working for you, and going off to start a company just like yours that will compete with you.

These are just a few things to think about. Your business lawyer can advise you on other legal aspects of your founders team.

Grizzly Area

Beware of the tendency to promise more than you can comfortably deliver to the members of your founders team. Because you want to get the best possible team together, it's tempting to promise the moon to the people you hope to attract. If you do that, however, you're likely to find yourself in big trouble a few years down the road.

The Least You Need to Know

➤ A good founders team makes setting up and running your business much easier than doing it by yourself.

➤ It's important to be choosy and find the best people available for your founders team.

➤ Make sure potential members have all the skills and experiences you need to get your business up and running.

➤ Ask everyone you know for recommendations and referrals for possible founders.

➤ Although business experience is important, pay attention to potential and chemistry, too.

➤ Watch and listen carefully as you begin discussions with potential members of your founders team; you'll learn a lot about a person by the way he or she responds to questions and discussions.

➤ Set up good guidelines under which your founders team can operate, and consult your business lawyer about agreements and contracts.

Chapter 19

Employees

In This Chapter

➤ Creating a healthy personality for your business.

➤ Giving your employees what they deserve.

➤ Getting what you deserve from your employees.

➤ Setting rules and sticking to them.

➤ Motivating your employees to do their best.

Every smart business owner knows how important his or her employees are. Your employees are the people who make the business work. They're the real machinery of the operation—the guts of the thing. How you work with and treat your employees makes a huge difference in how your business runs.

I firmly believe in treating all employees with respect and consideration. I believe you should let them know, in no uncertain terms, how valuable they are to the company. Employees respond positively to these attitudes, and you get loyalty and their best efforts in return.

Company Personality

Every company has a personality. You can tell when you walk into a business what kind of place it is. When I was there, The Vermont Teddy Bear Company, with its 200 employees, was a happy company. It was painted in bright, cheerful colors, and we had music playing all the time. We celebrated the first day of spring every year with a game of softball in the parking lot. Visitors often commented on the atmosphere and how the employees seemed to like being there.

Some companies, though, aren't happy, and you can tell the minute you walk into them. You see miserable, bored-looking people sitting in cubicles. You hear people whispering about other employees, or their bosses. These companies are not happy places, and I'll bet they're not productive places, either.

This attitude, or personality, of a company is known in the business world as *company culture*. It's the attitudes and beliefs that form the basis on which you run your company. It's the way you do things.

Your goal, as the owner of your business, should be to have productive, happy, loyal employees and a positive business personality. If you have those things, your company runs more smoothly, you enjoy it more, and you have infinitely more satisfaction.

Your Employees Are a Valuable Asset

Let's face it. Without employees, we couldn't have our companies. We might be able to get them started by ourselves, but as a company grows, it's impossible to do everything yourself. We need employees.

I've worked for more than one boss with the attitude that they were doing me a big favor by giving me a job. They made sure the employees knew whose company it was and went out of their way to let them know they were just minor players in the game. These employers didn't realize the value of their employees; as a result, they had high turnover rates and employee productivity stank. It just wasn't there because the employees had no incentive to work hard. They weren't made to feel as though they were part of a team or of any value to the company.

Bear Facts

I worked for one summer at a factory that made railroad bearings. I lifted or moved 20 to 40 tons of bearings a day by myself. I distinctly remember punching in and out every day and the loud "thunk" the machine made. I remember working like an animal in a hot factory and hearing about the problems my co-workers (all members of the Iron Workers Union) had with the management they despised. I vowed that when I had my own company, I would never treat my employees like that, and I'd never have a time clock machine.

Because they weren't treated with respect, they showed no respect back. Because they were offered no incentive, they showed no interest. The attitude of employees in these places was to put in the hours and get out of there.

Maybe you've worked for people like this, too. Maybe that's why you're going out on your own now and starting your own business. If so, you can understand the importance of treating your employees with respect and letting them know that they're appreciated. Let's be sure we never repeat the mistakes of those employers we so disliked.

In addition to being valuable to your operation, your employees are a big, big expense to your company. If you hire an employee for $15,000 a year, she actually costs you about $20,000. Multiply that by the number of employees you have, and you can see what you have invested.

Never forget that your employees are your most valuable asset, and never neglect to let them know that you think so. Some employers are afraid to do this because they think it makes them less authoritative and doesn't get them the respect they feel they deserve. They think it gives the employees too much power. I'm telling you, though, that's not the case. Your employees are vital. The more they hear and understand that, the better they'll respond.

What You Should Do for Your Employees

Some business owners hate to talk about what they should, or could, do for their employees. They think that giving them a job and a paycheck is enough. Throw in a couple of holidays, and they think they've gone way beyond the call of duty. Smart business owners, on the other hand, know that's not the case.

The first thing you should do for every employee is give them a clear picture of your company's goals and visions. This feedback immediately makes them part of the effort to reach those goals. It tells them they're part of the team.

You should also empower your employees. Let them have a say in how their jobs should be done. Involve them, when appropriate, in decision-making opportunities. Invest them in the company, and they'll work hard to make it succeed.

Make it clear your company has open lines of communication, and encourage employees to use them. Every employee should feel free to discuss a problem with a superior without fear of recrimination.

Over the Rainbow

Managing employees is just like coaching a Little League team. If you establish workable guidelines, make your expectations clear, teach what needs to be learned, motivate and encourage, and let everybody have a turn at bat, you'll have a good Little League team—or a great group of employees.

Bring Home the Bacon

The salary you pay an employee is compensation for work performed. It can also motivate, or it can discourage. Employers hate it when employees talk to each other about how much they make. It's bad for morale when you get into the "How come she makes $20 more a week than I do?" dilemma. On the other hand, even a small, weekly raise can make somebody feel that her efforts have been noticed and appreciated.

Most entrepreneurs with new businesses can't afford to pay employees as much as big, established firms can. Fortunately, some employees understand that their salary is not the only benefit of a job. If you get your employees to believe that your company is headed for great things, they might be willing to buy in on your dream and accept lower wages now, with the expectation of more pay down the road.

You can also make your company a pleasant, employee-friendly place to work. To many people, those intangibles are worth taking a lower initial salary.

Over the Rainbow

Be honest with your employees. If you can't afford to pay them the going industry rate at first, explain why that's the case. Then you can lay out a plan for how salaries will gradually increase until they meet or surpass those offered by other companies. Offer other incentives, too, such as flex time if a child is sick.

You can't, of course, expect to offer only half what other businesses are paying their employees and still get top-notch workers. Here are some questions to consider when you're figuring out what to pay your workers:

➤ What kind of salaries are comparable businesses giving employees for the same kind of work?

➤ How much demand is there for the type of employee you need? If you need people with specialized skills, and there aren't many of them around, you need to pay more.

➤ How much can your company afford to pay for employees? This affects how many employees you hire and what you pay them.

➤ What, besides money, can your company offer employees as an incentive to work there?

What Are the Benefits?

Benefits cost an employer about 30% over and above an employee's salary. So if you're paying an employee $400 a week, you're actually shelling out $520 a week to cover the employee's salary and benefits.

Benefits pay for health care, pensions, vacations, and personal time. Obviously, employees love benefits, and smart employers realize that and offer the best benefits they can afford.

Don't make the mistake, however, of being overly generous with benefits that cost your company a lot of money. If you can't afford to offer dental coverage, then don't. You might give employees the option to co-pay on their health plans for items like dental and vision coverage, but don't overextend yourself and promise more than you can afford to give.

Consider offering benefits that help the company in the long run. You could chip in on tuition costs for employees who take courses or go back to school. These educational experiences will most likely enhance their potential to the company. Or pay for part of an employee's child-care costs. Knowing that their children are being well cared for makes for more productive and happy employees.

How About Those Perks?

Perks are fun. They're a little different from benefits because they're not as structured. They're often events such as employee lunches once a month or the annual company trip to the ballpark. They can even be opportunities to join a company bowling team or baseball team.

Bear Facts

I loved giving perks to my employees. We had a spring trip every year to celebrate getting through the Valentine's Day rush. We started out taking an overnight to New York, and ended up a few years later at Disney World. The company threw in the bulk of the expense, and employees figured out the rest. They loved it, and so did I. We had some great times and a lot of fun.

At Vermont Teddy Bear, we had bocce tournaments and the winners got a couple of days off with pay. We had competitive skits at our Christmas parties. The winners got three days off, and runners-up got two days or one day.

Perks don't have to cost your company much, and they're great motivators for employees. They can do wonders for morale, and help ensure that your company's personality is what you want it to be.

Working Conditions

This is another area where you can show employees that you're respectful of their needs. There's nothing worse than a company in which the owner has a great office and the employees are cramped and uncomfortable.

Think about what your employees need, and try to meet those needs. If they're sitting for long periods of time, buy the best chairs you can afford. If they work at computers for hours on end, consider some of the equipment available to make that work more comfortable and healthful. If they stand for long periods of time, think about some floor padding. At the very least, make sure they have shoes with good padding.

What about working hours and schedules? If you have a lot of employees with school-aged children, maybe you can let them create their schedules around school time. Allow some flex time so they can attend school events or take their kids to doctor appointments.

Within reason, you should make working conditions for your employees as pleasant as possible.

Grizzly Area

Don't assume that your employees know your expectations if you don't tell them. People carry over ideas from previous jobs and previous employers, and might assume your expectations are the same as what they encountered before. If you don't make yourself clear, you're risking a lot of frustration on both your part and that of your employees.

What You Should Expect Your Employees To Do for You

Like just about everything, employee-employer relations are a two-way street. If you go out of your way to create a pleasant, happy, productive work environment, you expect that you'll get something back.

That's perfectly reasonable. What you need to do, though, is make those expectations very clear to your employees. There's nothing wrong with laying out what you've done and what you expect them to do.

Promote Loyalty

If you treat your employees fairly and respectfully, it's nearly guaranteed that they'll be loyal. That doesn't mean all of them will stay with your company forever, but you can bet they'll be loyal to you while they're there.

Loyalty to a job, a company, or an employer is more than just sticking around. It's when employees play by the rules because they respect you and the company. It's when they stay late for four days in a row to help you through your peak season, or even come in on a Saturday to finish up some work.

A lot of companies destroyed any shot they had at fostering employee loyalty during the big layoffs of the '80s and '90s. You can't expect an employee to be loyal when his two best pals have just been downsized, and he's reading the writing on the wall that he might be next. But if you're straight with your employees, do your best for them, and treat them like people instead of just workers, you're sure to be rewarded with their loyalty.

Reward Honesty

It's a funny thing, but even basically honest people in many cases seem to think it's okay to take home a few legal pads from work, or to stick a couple of pens in their pockets before they leave, or to say they worked five hours when it really was only four.

Maybe they think it's different to be dishonest toward a company instead of a person. They somehow separate the two things, even though a company really is the people involved with it. For whatever reasons, a lot of companies have problems with dishonest employees.

Employee theft accounts for 75% to 80% of all loss in business. It's estimated that employee theft increases the cost of consumer goods by 15%. Some employers try to take care of the problem by locking up all the supplies, having lunch sign-ins and sign-outs, or making employees punch a code into the phone to establish a record of calls.

I never did those things because I think distrust breeds more distrust. If your employees know you don't trust them, they have no incentive to be trustworthy. All my companies have had strict rules against stealing and other dishonest acts and serious consequences for breaking the rules. But the inventory and supplies aren't locked up, and employees are trusted to come and go as they're supposed to.

Again, if you state your expectations clearly, most employees prove to be trustworthy and honest. Those who don't have to be dealt with.

Time for the Hard Work

We've always had a lot of fun in my companies, but everybody knew that when the fun was over, it was time to get back to work. It was clearly understood that we were there to work, and each employee knew exactly what he or she was expected to accomplish in a day.

You really set the tone for how hard your employees work. If they see you working hard every day, it conveys the message that hard work is what's done here, from the top of the company on down. Make sure your expectations are known concerning the amount of work each employee is expected to do in a day, and make sure you work as hard as you expect your employees to.

The Word According to John

Honesty is a valuable attribute in an employee. It's what makes him come back from lunch on time, even if the boss isn't around. It's what compels her to charge long-distance personal calls to her phone card instead of letting the company pay for them. Honesty is a quality to be sought after and valued.

Over the Rainbow

When hard work pays off—and it will—let your employees share in the pride. The Vermont Teddy Bear Company was named the Best Company in America in 1994, and every employee was as proud as I was of that award. The same year we won the Best Customer Service Company of New England. That award had gone previously to companies like Ben and Jerry's and L.L. Bean. People in the customer services and sales departments were positively beaming for days, and I made darned sure to let them know how proud and pleased I was with them.

Establishing Rules and Responsibilities for Employees

Every company needs to have some rules. Rules establish guidelines for employees and let them know what you expect from them. They set limits and convey what you, as the owner of the company, believe is important. Have an employee handbook that clearly states all the rules and guidelines so that everyone gets the same story.

Many companies, however, have way too many rules. When your company rules take longer to read and digest than your financial statements, it's time to streamline. Get to the heart of things. Having too many rules dilutes the important ones.

Don't Make Any Rules You Don't Intend to Keep

Some people who run businesses thrive on rules. They want to tell their employees how to dress, when they can eat, how much coffee they can drink, how many cigarettes they can smoke, and when they can go to the beach with their kids.

The risk these people run by making so darned many rules is that to maintain respect and credibility, they've got to enforce these rules—*all* of them. That can get to be a huge task. Do you really want to do clothing checks or keep tabs on cigarette breaks? Don't you have better things to do?

Bear Facts

We had few rules at The Vermont Teddy Bear Company, but they were strictly enforced. Our rules were no stealing, no lying, and you had to follow the law and not discriminate or anything like that. We had a three-letter rule when it came to firing. A supervisor having problems with an employee had to write a letter stating what the problem was. The letter also stated that if the problem was not corrected, the employee would get a second letter. If the problem was not corrected after that, the employee would get a third letter, at which time he or she was dismissed. This system gave employees a chance to correct problems before any disciplinary action was taken.

If you make 100 rules, you're ultimately responsible for enforcing 100 rules. You can pass off the job to somebody else, but it always comes back to you eventually. So remember that when you're tempted to get out your pad and pencil and start jotting down notes like "Bathroom breaks are limited to three per day," or "Only vegetarian meals may be consumed in the lunchroom."

Make Sure You Have a Clear Chain of Command

It's important to have a hierarchy, or chain of command, in place. Make sure everyone knows what it is and how it works. It's a lot easier to deal with a problem if you know who to talk to about it. A clear chain of command immediately tells your employees who to turn to and gets the problem-solving process underway quickly.

You don't want to have to deal with every employee complaint or problem that pops up. By having several people in your chain of command, you're still responsible for the barn burners, but you don't have to fight every little brush fire that comes along.

Make sure, however, that the people in your chain of command know you're available when needed and that you're ultimately responsible.

Dealing with Discipline Matters

It used to be a lot easier to deal with discipline matters than it is today. I'm not sure how we got so lawsuit-happy in this country, but a lot of people who get fired end up suing their former employers. A lot of them win, too.

When you have to deal with discipline matters, use some common sense, and keep these guidelines in mind:

Grizzly Area

Being the boss requires doing some pretty unsavory tasks, and dealing with employee problems is among them. I've had to talk to employees about hygiene problems, drinking problems, and family problems. I know a guy with a moving business, and one of his workers was killed on the job. He had to go to the guy's house and tell his wife what had happened. Desirable? No. Necessary? Yes. Don't think you can avoid these responsibilities. They're part of the territory.

➤ If you anticipate trouble with an employee down the road, document anything applicable about his behavior, attitude, or work. Keep records of all events, such as raises, promotions, reprimands, performance reviews, and so forth.

➤ Don't be the only evaluator. If you're having trouble with an employee, have a supervisor or other management person conduct separate evaluations. Of course, if management begins and ends with you, you'll have to be solely responsible for the review.

➤ Make sure the employee knows what the problems are, and make sure he's notified of them in writing. Be very specific about what's going on, and inform him of possible consequences. Get him to acknowledge in writing that he's been informed.

➤ If you have to fire somebody, make sure there's a third person in the room when you do it. State the reasons for the termination clearly, and don't get into a nonproductive discussion or debate.

Over the Rainbow

Dealing with employees' problems and discipline matters is a lot like parents dealing with kids or teachers with students. Any perception of unfairness is grounds for big trouble. You need to be consistent. And rules must be enforced because some employees, kids, and students always try to get around them.

➤ Don't lose your cool. Nobody likes to fire someone. Unfortunately, it's sometimes part of the territory. Be as calm as you can, and don't let the employee bait you or get you upset.

➤ If you think there's a potential for legal trouble with an employee, run it by your lawyer.

When you've got to deal with discipline problems, stand firm in your decisions. Make sure you're consistent with how you deal with problems, and treat all employees the same. It's probably a good idea to get a legal guide about dealing with employees and keep it handy.

A book that might help is *The Complete Collection of Legal Forms for Employers: All-Inclusive Sample Contracts, Forms and Checklists for Hiring, Firing, and Day-To-Day Employment*, by Steven Mitchell.

Motivating Your Employees

The topic of motivating employees could be a book in itself. It's a big issue and an important one to anyone who has a business.

There are hundreds of ways to motivate your employees, but you have to remember that what motivates one person might not motivate another. Some people respond to simple praise. Others are motivated by the possibility of promotions or raises. Others like bonuses. Some employees are motivated by responsibility.

Motivating employees isn't hard. If you're motivated and enthusiastic yourself, your attitude will be contagious. Getting employees involved in efforts to reach goals is motivating. Be sure to keep them posted on the results, and reward their efforts when the goals are met.

Bear Facts

We used to celebrate milestones at The Vermont Teddy Bear Company with 10 a.m. champagne breaks. It didn't happen very often, but when we hit a big milestone, we popped some corks and toasted to our success.

The perks I talked about earlier can be sources of motivation. So can salaries and benefits. So can stock options. Letting your employees know they're important to you and appreciated is motivating them.

During our peak seasons (Valentine's Day, Christmas, and Mother's Day) at Vermont Teddy Bear, I frequently asked employees to stay late and work. That meant I was taking away from the time they had with their families. Of course, they got overtime pay, but to further motivate them to work the extra hours, we had dinner brought in for them. We played music. We stocked coolers with all kinds of sodas and juices. All this was meant to let them know that their loyalty and extra help was appreciated and to motivate them to do it again, when necessary.

Motivating people comes easily to some. Others have to work a little harder at it. Fortunately, there are tons of ways to do it, and it's not that hard to learn.

Part-Time Employees, Temps, and Homeworkers

Those who study these things say there's a growing trend toward using part-timers and temporary workers. This is supposed to save the employers money on benefits and allow them to vary the number of employees they have according to how busy the business is at a particular time.

Of course, if you hire temps through an agency, you have to pay the agency's fee in addition to salary. Still, if you need someone for only a short time, it's less expensive to hire a temp than to hire an employee, train him, pay salary and benefits, and then lay him off.

At our peak seasons at The Vermont Teddy Bear Company, we hired almost as many temporary workers as we had full-time workers. Things got a little crazy and crowded, but I discovered an interesting thing. Hiring temporary workers brought out the best in the permanent employees. They all became trainers. They took great interest in making sure the temps were performing up to standard. The permanent workers were the big shots, and they rose to the occasion with style.

Bear Facts

Temporary employment agencies are getting specialized to be able to supply the workers that companies ask for. I understand that you can hire a sales force, computer experts, human resource specialists, and even CEOs—all through your friendly temp agency. What a world!

When you're first starting out, you might not need very many employees, and part-time workers might make sense for your company. Part-timers may or may not get benefits, depending on how you work it out. Having someone start as a part-time worker gives you a chance to see if she'd work out on a full-time basis without making much of a commitment.

Many people welcome part-time work. Don't be afraid to look at options like job sharing, either. A lot of good people want to work, but can't make the eight-hour-a-day commitment because of family or other considerations.

If it's conducive to your company's business, don't overlook the possibility of using sub-contractors. We had about 200 sub-contractors who worked from their homes for The Vermont Teddy Bear Company. It gave us the extra help we needed without having to expand our production facilities or hire more full-time employees.

There are many options for getting good employees, and you shouldn't hesitate to explore them. Remember that you don't have to run your business exactly the way the guy down the street runs his.

The Least You Need to Know

➤ You'll get the most from your employees if they understand that they're valued and appreciated.

➤ Salaries, benefits, perks, and good working conditions are important for employees, but intangibles like respect and understanding are just as valuable.

➤ You have a right, as an employer, to expect loyalty, honesty, and hard work from your employees.

➤ Make sure your employees know and fully understand your expectations.

➤ Don't make more rules than you care to enforce.

➤ There are hundreds of ways to motivate employees; being motivated and enthusiastic yourself is one of the best ways.

➤ Full-time, permanent employees aren't the only option, especially when your company is just getting started.

Chapter 20

Board of Directors and Shareholders

In This Chapter

➤ Looking at the structure of a company.

➤ Advantages of having a board of directors.

➤ Choosing board members to promote your company's image.

➤ Putting celebrities on your board of directors.

➤ Tackling the control problem.

➤ Pleasing shareholders while running the company.

What's all this talk about directors and shareholders? If your business is incorporated, it's owned by its shareholders, and you're required by law to have a board of directors. The board of directors is elected by the shareholders.

If this sounds complicated, it really isn't. All it means is that the people who invest in your company have partial ownership. You already knew that. They hold shares of the company, and they're known as *shareholders*. The board of directors, when done right, is a group of people who serve as resources of many sorts. Its members will bring valuable experience and know-how to your company. Some business owners look only to satisfy the legal requirements of having a board of directors and appoint anyone they can find to serve on it—spouse, friends, or siblings. This gives them a board of directors, but it doesn't give them the know-how that a carefully chosen board can give.

If you're the full owner of the company, then you're the only shareholder. If you don't elect anyone else to your board of directors, you can be the only person on it. You can be president of your company, too, but someone else must be secretary. Things are pretty simple if that's the case, but your company's growth will be limited.

A lot of corporations start out as one-person companies, but expand fairly quickly to include other shareholders and directors. The makeup of these groups can have a huge effect on your company.

Choosing a Board of Directors

Having a good, experienced, active board of directors is a great way to give your company some stability and set it up for growth. When you name a board of directors, you're bringing on additional expertise, perspective, and help for your business.

It might seem like a bother to find a board of directors when you're trying to get your business rolling. I think, though, that you're shortchanging your company by not bringing on some valuable help.

Think about who you want on your board of directors before you start talking to people about it. Decide what you're looking for in directors and what role you see them having in your company.

Grizzly Area

Many small business owners don't bother to set up a board of directors. They think nobody would want to serve or that it's too much trouble to get one established. That's not a smart move. Without a board of directors, you're pretty much on your own, without help when you need it.

Most small companies start out with three members on their boards and go to five or more as the business grows. Regardless of how many members you have, it must always be an odd number for purposes of voting. Be sure when you're appointing board members that the majority of them support your general position. You don't want to be surprised and find out that your plans for your company are thwarted because you've appointed board members who see things completely differently than you do.

It's probably a good idea to set fairly short terms for your board of directors. You can always re-elect someone, but at least you have the option of getting rid of somebody whose not doing his part or who you feel is not working in the company's best interests. And make sure the terms are staggered so that you have some continuity. It's not a good idea to have every member up for reelection at the same time.

Be aware when you're looking for directors that people assume personal liability when they agree to sit on your board. This makes some people reluctant—and with good reason—to agree to serve on a board. To combat this, you can buy board liability insurance to limit their liability, but it's an extra expense. In response to this problem, there's a growing trend toward using advisory boards instead of boards of directors.

Advisory boards serve many of the same functions as boards of directors, but their members can't be held liable the way directors can, and their members can't vote. Its purpose is primarily to, as the name implies, advise and offer suggestions.

If you have other shareholders, they'll want to name some of the initial board members. After a board of directors is established, members are elected and re-elected during an annual meeting of the company's shareholders.

Often, when somebody invests in your company, one of the stipulations for investing is that the investor gets to sit on the board or appoint a member or several members to your board. That's fair. Just make sure the shareholder understands what the board's role is and the image you expect it to convey.

What Image Should Your Board of Directors Convey?

I'd think you want your board of directors to convey an image of maturity and experience for your business. A new business can greatly benefit from the perception of maturity. Members should also be smart and progressive, just like your company.

Retired men and women who have owned and run their own companies, or who have held high positions in other companies, generally make great board members. They're experienced, they've got perspective, and they are known and respected in the community. They've also got excellent contacts from their years in business. Other good choices for your board are community leaders.

Who's Who on Your Board of Directors?

Many companies look for at least one high-profile person to sit on their boards. This usually isn't as hard as you might think. Think about the people you know, and then think about the people they know. It's possible to get introduced to people you want to meet. Just find someone who already knows them.

Business owners look for people who are well known in the business community, in government, in the arts, and so forth, to serve on their boards. It gives the company pizzazz and makes it seem more interesting to outsiders.

Remember, though, that a board of directors with a bunch of celebrities might be a real kick, but you don't want to overload it at the expense of experience that helps your business.

Bear Facts

I belong to the board of an organization called Dishes, which raises money to help kids. It uses supermodels to attract publicity and help get funds. I love the board meetings because several supermodels are among the other members, including my personal favorite, Cindy Crawford.

251

Many celebrities love to lend their names to causes and organizations. Don't be afraid to ask someone you think is famous to join your board. She might say no, but who knows? She might say yes.

What's the Role of a Board of Directors?

A good board of directors can do a lot for your business. It can help you attract investors. It can introduce you to potential customers and to important members of the business community. It can give your company instant credibility and recognition.

Imagine the response you'll get when you happen to mention to the guy at the bank that one of the best-known and most respected businesspeople in the county sits on your board of directors. I guarantee the guy at the bank will think of your business a little differently from then on. Believe me when I tell you that investors and lenders take you much more seriously when you have a good, strong board of directors than they do if your board is a collection of your relatives and sorority sisters.

Your board members serve as consultants, in many ways. They provide balance and perspective. It's easy for you and your founders team to get wrapped up in the company's day-to-day operations. That's what you're expected to do. Sometimes, though, when you're extremely close and involved with the business, you lose some of your perspective on it.

A board of directors, at least those who are not members of the founders team actively involved in the day-to-day running of the business, can step back and look at the situation, and offer advice as to how it should be handled. Don't make the mistake, however, of involving those board members in the company's daily operations. That's not their role.

A board of directors should set the overall company policy and make sure management follows those policies and follows through on its responsibilities. It should look at ideas for growing the company, look down the road to anticipate possible problems, and give management its feedback on how the company is run and where it's headed. It should offer whatever assistance it can to management.

Because board members typically are experienced people, they often know ways to get things done. You might spend hours trying to convince your major vendor to extend you a little more credit, but perhaps one of your board members could pick up the phone, exchange pleasantries with the vendor, and wind up with an extended credit line.

Another important function of your board is that members can serve as references for banks, lawyers, and so forth. This asset can be invaluable when you're starting up a new business. Board members should

The Word According to John

Generally speaking, the role of a *board of directors* is to improve the quality of your company's stock. There are many ways that purpose can be accomplished, but basically that's what the board of directors should do.

approve hiring key employees, such as chief financial officer, chief operations officer, chief executive officer, president, and so forth. They should hear the reports of the chief financial officer and be aware of the activities of the chief executive officer. A good board is an active board.

As you can see, the role of a board of directors is varied and important. Make sure your board is experienced and accessible when you need it. It doesn't do you any good to have people on your board who have the potential to help you, if they're never available to talk or meet with you.

On the other hand, I don't want to discourage you from recruiting experienced, busy people for your board. Remember that the busiest people typically are the ones who find time to get the most done. Most people enjoy serving as directors. It's a little bit of an ego thing, I guess, plus most people genuinely enjoy helping someone who's just starting to do what they've already done.

If your board members are very busy people, you might want to consider holding some of the meetings over the phone. Phone meetings aren't as satisfying as face-to-face get-togethers, but if something needs to be dealt with in a timely manner, then the phone is better than nothing.

Many companies pay their board members a small amount for attending meetings or pay for their travel expenses. It all depends on your company's financial status. I always tried to make our board meetings fun, so that members would want to come. We normally held our board meetings in the office of The Vermont Teddy Bear Company's lawyer. Although the lawyer wasn't part of the board, he advised the board, and it was good to have him available to answer any legal matters that arose during the meeting.

You'll find that most of the people you speak to about serving on your board of directors are supportive and helpful, whether or not they're able to join.

Over the Rainbow

Lots of new business owners say they don't want a board of directors because it causes them to lose control of their own businesses. Shareholders, not board members, control businesses. Although a board of directors is powerful because it has decision-making powers, it works for what it sees as your best interests. Your board works with you, not against you.

Just Who's Running This Company, Anyway?

Ah, the control thing ... what fun.

The shareholders run the company, but the board of directors is involved in decisions that affect the company. The president, or chief executive officer, is in charge of the day-to-day stuff but must answer to the board.

The chief financial person has control over the company's books, but the chief executive officer almost always has control over the company's money. Of course, he has to report financials to the board, and normally has checks and limits imposed on him by the board.

So who's in charge? Good question. It's an important issue to think about. Power struggles are dangerous, and many companies have been brought down from within by the control question. Establishing and keeping control of your company is easy when you're the only player. But when you've got other officers, a board of directors, a founders team, shareholders, and you name it, the control issue can become muddied—and sometimes dirty.

Bear Facts

Many entrepreneurs have been fired from their own companies by their boards. Usually, the board and the person who started the company can find ways to resolve differences, but not always. If there's no alternative, and the person who started the company no longer has more than 50% of the stock, the board just might decide to kick him or her right out.

When you, or you and the other shareholders, choose members of a board of directors, you generally choose people you think will support your position and your ideas. As your company grows and more people become involved in it, however, you might find out that your position isn't very popular anymore, or that the people who used to support you suddenly don't.

Over the Rainbow

You can find *Roberts Rules of Order* online at this site: www.arts.state.tx.us/library/roberts.htm. But be sure to buy a copy of the book, too. You'll find it's invaluable.

The founder of a company typically serves as the first chairman of the board and as the president or chief executive officer. At that point, he controls the company (except, of course, he's always being watched by people who invested in the company). He has the power. That happens for a good, and very important, reason.

At that point, the owner should spend a lot of time and effort setting up bylaws under which the company operates. *Roberts Rules of Order*, that wonderful book covering every imaginable topic related to the roles of officers, bylaws, conducting meetings, and so forth, should become the entrepreneur's bible. If you don't have a copy, make sure you get one. In my opinion, you can't run your company without it.

After you've established bylaws, using Roberts Rules, you have set the groundwork under which your company will operate. You can build in a lot of control for yourself by understanding how a board of directors operates and the role of each member.

For instance, as chairman of the board, under Roberts Rules, you have the right to restrict the business that comes before the board. You can do this by declaring it exceedingly frivolous or requiring that it be submitted a certain period in advance of the meeting. Knowing what you're entitled to do as chairman gives you a lot of power.

When you set up the bylaws, you can require that votes on issues like hirings and firings have to pass by a two-third or three-quarter majority of the board. This builds in protection against a small portion of the board gaining control.

There are many, many things you can do to stack your company's bylaws in your favor. A good lawyer can help you. Some people get uncomfortable with this discussion, but I can't imagine why. It's your company, and you want to be safe in it. There's nothing wrong with that.

I mean, you start up your company from nothing, right? You grow it and tend to it and raise it as you would a baby. Other people get involved, the company grows, and the balance of power shifts with stock purchases. All of a sudden, you could be wondering what's going on and realizing you don't have control of your company anymore.

If your shareholders and board of directors don't agree with what you're doing, they have the power to stop you from doing it, unless you've protected yourself through your company's bylaws. If you, at some point, give up the position of chairman of the board, be aware that the new chairman has the potential to control the company, depending on how effectively he or she uses the bylaws.

Let's get one thing straight about control. It belongs to the person who owns the most shares of the company. Or it can belong to the person who can convince those with the most shares to do what he or she wants.

Bear Facts

The most powerful person in a company is the one who has the most shares or the one with the most influence over those who hold the shares.

This gets really tricky sometimes, as you can imagine. Power is a big issue in business. It's sought after by an awful lot of people. Sometimes those people don't much care how they get it, as long as they do.

Over the Rainbow

Pay attention to who gets elected secretary of your company because that person assumes the role of legal historian. Many business owners have found a different version of what really happened recorded in the company minutes by a secretary who either didn't understand what was going on or had a personal agenda. The minutes of previous meetings often are consulted in the event of a dispute or disagreement. You need to know that what's in them is an accurate accounting of event and not what your secretary would have liked to occur.

It's likely that your board of directors, most of whom are shareholders, will control the bulk of company stock. This makes the board of directors very, very powerful. If you're running the company, you hope that you and the board of directors see things in pretty much the same way. Your goals and visions for the company will be pretty much the same, you hope, and the board will support you in your decisions.

If not, look out. A lot can happen in a business to change the entire way it operates and completely alter the dynamics. It's ironic that you can start a company, appoint a board of directors, and give the business 150% for three years, only to find one day that the tide has turned and the board of directors no longer supports you.

School district superintendents, who are pretty much at the whim of a school board whose members are always changing, know all about this situation. A school superintendent told me that every one of them knows that sooner or later, he or she will come up against a school board that, for one reason or another, just doesn't like him or her. When that happens, the superintendent says, you can expect that your contract won't be renewed. Better start polishing up your resume.

Keeping Shareholders Happy and Still Having Time to Run Your Business

Corporate officers have been accused the past few years of spending all their time and efforts trying to please the company's shareholders, at the expense of employees and sometimes even the company itself. The truth is that every company has to please its shareholders. True, it shouldn't be done to the extent that everything else goes down the tubes, but pleasing shareholders is pretty much the name of the game.

Don't make the mistake of thinking of the board of directors and the shareholders as completely separate groups. Many, if not most, of the members on your board will be shareholders.

Shareholders, for obvious reasons, are extremely important to a company. When you're just starting up, the shareholders are usually your key employees, your investors, your board of directors, and yourself. At this point, your company is pretty small and manageable, and your efforts are primarily directed toward getting it off the ground and running smoothly.

As your company grows, it will acquire other shareholders who might have different goals and objectives than the original shareholders had. They might put more emphasis on your quarterly earnings than on whether you're making great teddy bears or providing the highest quality lawn care of any company around. Their top goal could be getting a return—a big return, they hope—on their investment.

Bear Facts

I was a math major in college, and I'm convinced mathematics is really the universal language, particularly in business. The whole world speaks math when it comes to earnings, expenditures, salaries, and so forth. It all ends up as math.

You know, it's impossible to predict what will happen with your company. You can't foresee who will get involved by investing in it, or who you might hire to help run it, or other things like that. I'd say that the best thing you can do is to be as well prepared as you can for whatever might happen. You can do that by becoming very familiar with *Roberts Rules of Order*, keeping a close watch on your financials, and paying attention to what's going on around you.

The Least You Need to Know

➤ A corporation is run by its shareholders, and it's required by law to have a board of directors.

➤ A good board of directors can be a huge source of support and expertise to a starting business.

➤ Your board of directors has a direct bearing on the image your company will have.

➤ A well-placed celebrity or two on your board will go a long way toward getting attention and giving your company some pizzazz.

➤ The person with the most ownership is generally the most powerful person in the company.

➤ It can be tricky finding time to run your business effectively and still keep your shareholders happy, but it probably can be done.

Chapter 21

Building a Strong Support System

In This Chapter

➤ Planning ahead for when problems occur.

➤ You're not the first entrepreneur to face a crisis.

➤ Finding the best people to help with your business.

➤ Sources of help for you and your business.

➤ Maintaining a strong support system.

As the song says, we all need somebody to lean on. When times get tough in the business world, and from time to time they will, it's nice to have people you trust to look to for help.

The best thing you can do is anticipate the help you might need as early on in the game as possible. That way, you can get a support system in place before you actually need it. When you need some help, you'll know exactly who to turn to. Legal problem? Call your business lawyer. Tax problem? Call your accountant. Insurance problem? Call your agent. You get the picture.

If you're having a problem selling your stuff, you might need to hire a good salesperson to get you back on track. Of course, the sooner you realize your sales are in trouble, the sooner you can hire somebody to help you.

Now, just to see if you've been paying attention, let's see if you can answer this question. How do you know as early as possible that your sales are slipping, thereby giving yourself a chance to do something about it? If you said by paying close attention to your financial statements and taking immediate steps to correct any problems the financials reveal, you're right. Keep up the good work!

A problem becomes a far bigger problem when you have to spend hours or days looking for somebody to help you solve it, or when it's ignored while it's still small.

Why Do You Need a Support System?

Nothing can fully prepare an entrepreneur for what he or she will encounter in the course of setting up and growing a business. There's absolutely no way to anticipate all the possibilities.

One thing you can be sure of, though, is that stuff will happen. Lots of stuff. You'll have all kinds of questions, need help with different problems that crop up, and want to benefit from all the available help that's out there.

Because you realize that you can't run a business all by yourself, you understand that you need a support system. Who should the system include? It should include all the people and organizations that are important to your business, both as you're getting it started and in the future, such as:

➤ Chamber of commerce

➤ Professional organizations

➤ Lawyers

➤ Accountants

➤ Insurance agents

➤ State and federal sources

➤ Salespeople and suppliers

➤ Employees and management team

I'll show you why each of these people and organizations is important a little later in the chapter.

Knowing You're Not Alone

When you're working hard to get your business started and off the ground, you're bound to have a lot of questions and need a lot of information and advice. If you don't know who to turn to for help, all the regulations and considerations can seem pretty overwhelming. Being an entrepreneur can be a lonely endeavor if you try to do it alone. Fortunately, you don't have to.

Most start-up ventures are small and don't have the capital to hire employees to handle all the management functions. Because you don't have your own people to do all these management tasks, you depend on your lawyers, accountants, insurance agents, and other professionals to help you.

Competent, experienced business lawyers, accountants, and so forth have helped many people in the same position as you. They understand the complexities of business law and finance and are tremendous resources.

Another source of help when you're first getting your business started is other entrepreneurs. I don't know anybody who's started a business who wouldn't be happy to talk with a fellow entrepreneur about his or her experiences.

Most people welcome the chance to help somebody starting out. Speaking from personal experience, we love to talk about the ins and outs of starting and owning a business. So go ahead and call up the guy who started that shop down the street. Invite him to meet you for a drink, dinner, or just a cup of coffee and pick his brain. I bet you'll get all kinds of good advice and tips.

No matter how frustrating and overwhelming getting started can seem, remember that you're not alone. Tap into the knowledge and resources of people who have already done what you're trying to do. You can save a lot of time, expense, and frustration if you understand that you don't have to reinvent the wheel.

Grizzly Area

A big mistake many entrepreneurs make is to hire professional help because they know the person. If your friend is an accountant with one of the nation's top firms, that's a good reason to hire him, if you want to. A bad reason to hire him is because he's your friend. Friends are great, but when you're starting a business, you need the best professional help you can get.

Who to Look to When You Need Some Help

One of the best things you can learn and remember when you're starting your business is that it's perfectly okay not to know about something or not to know how to do something.

Bear Facts

Remember the movie *Star Wars*? You know, Luke Skywalker, the "force," and all that stuff? I often think of that movie, which happens to be one of my all-time favorites, when I'm doing business. We would do well to remember to "go with the force." By that, I mean learn about the system, and then go with it. The system, for all practical purposes, is the "force" in our society. Learn all you can about the programs and opportunities available, and then go with the force to figure out what businesses would work in your community. Going with the force and working with existing systems make a lot more sense than trying to force your plan into a scenario where it doesn't fit.

It's sort of like building a house. After the foundation is poured, you have carpenters come in to frame the house. They basically build the house and give it shape. When they're done, you pretty much know what the house will look like. But the carpenters don't do everything. It takes a lot of people to get a house into move-in condition. You have people who do drywall or plastering, people who lay tile, electricians, plumbers, landscapers, decorators, painters, carpet layers, and appliance people. It takes a lot of people to build a house and a lot of people to build a business.

Nobody expects the carpenters to do everything. Nobody expects you, as the person starting the business, to do everything, either. As long as you know where to find help, you can handle whatever comes your way. The trick, as I said earlier, is to have your systems in place *before* it's necessary to use them.

Chamber of Commerce

The Chamber of Commerce, which operates to assist and promote community businesses, is a great resource for starting entrepreneurs. It can give you statistical and demographic information for your market research, advice on where to locate a business, industry trends, and other useful advice.

Getting involved with your local chamber of commerce is a great way to meet other businesspeople in your area, too. In almost any chamber of commerce, you can find people with business experience who are more than willing to help out other members.

Remember that it never hurts to know the other people doing business in your community. You're likely to end up associating with many of these people in one way or another. Most chambers also offer educational opportunities for businesspeople about topics such as taxes or laws affecting business. The nationwide chamber, which was started in 1912 and represents more than 5 million business firms and individuals through its member organizations, is a powerful lobbying group for small business interests.

Look for other sources in your community, as well as the chamber of commerce. Many communities have economic development associations set up to attract business into the area. Some are subsidized with community and state funds and may offer limited financial support, or they might be able to advise you about other lenders and investors.

Some colleges and universities also offer start-up help to small businesses. You've got nothing to lose by checking out any potential sources of help and information.

Professional Organizations

There are all kinds of professional organizations for different segments of business and industry. In fact, there are thousands of them, representing advertising, accounting, higher education, chemistry, astronomy, dairy science, geology, fisheries, industrial hygiene, aeronautics, architecture, physics, library science, agriculture, and so forth.

What these organizations do is hook you up with other people in your industry. They have good opportunities to share ideas and get help or suggestions from people who know where you're coming from and what you're talking about. Some people don't like belonging to professional organizations, but they can be good places for making contacts and sharing experiences.

Lawyers

A lot of business owners hire a lawyer because she's a friend or someone they know from around town. That's a bad reason to hire a lawyer. So is hiring her because she's represented everybody in your family for three generations, or because she's a relative, or your best friend's cousin, or great to look at. Your choice of legal representation should be based solely on the person's qualifications and experience as a lawyer specializing in business.

Over the Rainbow

For a mind-boggling list of professional organizations and other career and business-related Web sites, check out the career center homepage at www.rpi.edu/dept/cdc/homepage.html. You won't believe some of the organizations listed there!

Our society is a legal minefield. One false step could land you in legal trouble without you even knowing how it happened. It's important to find a good, competent lawyer who understands your business and business law in general.

You won't need your lawyer every day. I hope you won't need her very often, but when you do, you've got to be confident that she can do the following:

➤ Be available when you need her

➤ Have a consistent level of competency

➤ Represent your best interests

Over the Rainbow

People often call their local legal societies to ask for recommendations for lawyers. That's not the smartest approach. Many legal societies won't recommend lawyers; those that do might have a few lawyers they recommend to everyone who calls—not necessarily the lawyers who are best for your business.

To find a lawyer like that, start by talking to other successful entrepreneurs. If you talk to 20 people, and 14 of them use the same lawyer and think he's the greatest thing that ever came to town, you might be on to something. On the other hand, you'll also hear about those whose reputations are less than sterling.

The public library has directories with information about lawyers and their credentials. Some of them list major clients, information about the lawyer's firm, and so forth. Here are a few directories to check out:

➤ *Martindale-Hubbell Law Directory*

➤ *Directory of the Legal Profession*

➤ *Attorney's Register*

➤ *The Lawyer's Register by Specialty and Fields of Law*

You can also get information about area lawyers from your county's bar association or from your state's Blue Book of lawyers.

Some business owners prefer to work with a lawyer who's on her own or part of a small firm. Others like big firms with lots of resources. Nobody can tell you what's best for you. If you're more comfortable with a small firm, then maybe that's the right kind for you. Large firms tend to have more connections and contacts that can come in handy from time to time. On the other hand, large firms might not be overly anxious to represent you, the owner of a fledgling business.

Also, large firms often, but not always, charge more than smaller firms. Be aware that legal fees can be quite costly, and they add up fast. Here are a few ways to keep your legal costs under control:

➤ Do the preliminary work so that the lawyer won't have to. Get as much information about the matter at hand as you can. Anticipate your lawyer's questions and try to come up with answers in advance.

➤ Don't get your lawyer involved prematurely. If you're looking at buying property, for instance, there's no point in putting your lawyer on standby before you've fully investigated the situation. It might turn out there's an obvious reason why the property isn't right for you, and you'll discover it through a little bit of investigation. There's no point in paying your lawyer to do something that you can.

➤ Forget about retainers. Unless you've involved in complicated, ongoing legal proceedings, you probably don't need to have a lawyer on retainer. Just be sure you have one who's available on an as-needed basis.

Over the Rainbow

It's important that you and your lawyer share the same basic philosophies on business. For instance, if you're determined to be fair, honest, and responsible, you don't want a lawyer who's willing to run roughshod over everything and everybody in sight to get ahead. Think of some questions to ask that will help you determine the lawyer's business philosophy.

Many lawyers offer free, get-acquainted sessions, at which time you can meet them, discuss your needs, and ask questions.

Choosing a lawyer means doing your homework and finding out who's good and who's not. It's a lot about matching up a particular lawyer's expertise with your business needs, and it's somewhat about trusting your gut. A lawyer can have great qualifications, but if you feel as though you can't work with her, you won't have an effective business relationship. There are times your lawyer will be the most important person in the world to you, so he or she has got to be someone you trust completely and are comfortable with.

Accountants

You've read several times already in this book how important I think it is to have the best accountant you can. As far as I'm concerned, the Big Five accounting firms are the way to go. If you get one of these accountants, you're getting the power of the entire firm. The big firms have lots of resources available that smaller firms just don't have access to.

The firms in the Big Five have entrepreneur programs in their companies and can provide excellent counseling and guidance as you set up your business. They can advise you on what banks to use as lenders and give you other helpful information.

These are the Big Five accounting firms:

➤ PricewaterhouseCoopers

➤ Andersen Worldwide

➤ KPMG International

➤ Ernst & Young International

➤ Deloitte Touche Tohmatsu International

I've used two of these firms, KPMG and Ernst & Young, when starting businesses. They both showed a lot of interest in entrepreneurs and were anxious to help in any way they could.

Bear Facts

It's been my experience that accountants generally go out of their way to help you and make matters go smoothly for your business. They're often portrayed as lacking in people skills, but the accountants I've worked with have been great.

Having a Big Five firm on your team is an asset when you're looking for investors. You have thousands of accountants, plus the name of the company behind you when you sign up with one of these companies.

Everybody knows an accountant, and it's natural to want to give your business to a buddy or a relative or a friend of a friend, but do yourself a favor and resist the temptation.

Insurance Agents

Business insurance is a definite necessity, and an agent you can count on is a big plus. Basically, there are two kinds of insurance agents:

➤ An independent agent, who sells insurance for many different companies

➤ An agent who represents only one insurance company

What kind of agent you get is not as important as the agent's qualifications. Ideally, you want to find somebody who has experience insuring your type of business. Agents usually specialize in insuring a particular kind of business or industry.

In addition to telling you what kind of insurance you need for your business, your insurance agent should be able to tell you how to reduce your risk. Some insurance companies have risk management specialists who come to your company and tell you what changes you can make to reduce the chance of something bad happening.

For instance, if you own a pest control business, your insurance company should insist that all pesticides be stored in a separate area or building, away from all other supplies. It should insist that all containers be clearly marked, that no smoking is permitted where the pesticides are stored, and that access to the storage area be limited.

Your business might be periodically inspected to make sure you're in compliance with your insurer's specifications. If so, remember that these recommendations are for your benefit, as well as your insurer's. Nobody wants to file an insurance claim because it means something bad has happened.

To get recommendations for insurance companies and agents, you can check with the following groups or individuals:

Over the Rainbow

These two books might help you in buying insurance for your business: *Insuring the Bottom Line: How to Protect Your Company from Liabilities, Catastrophes and Other Business Risks*, by David Russell, and *Insuring Your Business: What You Need to Know to Get the Best Insurance Coverage for Your Business*, by Sean Mooney.

➤ Industry associations. Not only do these groups most likely have recommendations about agents, but they might also have group insurance plans with brokers or agents who specialize in your industry.

➤ Other business owners. Find out who other people are using and what they think. Are the agents there for their customers when they need them?

➤ Your personal insurance agent. This is a good starting point, but you shouldn't feel obligated to buy business insurance from your personal agent. Find out what types of business insurance your personal agent has available and what his prices are. Tell him your business needs, and let him tell you what kinds of insurance you need. Then you can shop around for the best coverage, prices, and service.

➤ Chamber of commerce. Ask your local chamber of commerce for recommendations and suggestions on insurance agents with different areas of expertise.

➤ Your lawyer, accountant, and banker. Professionals know about other professionals in areas other than their own and might be able to recommend someone you can work with.

It's a good idea to meet with several insurance agents before you choose the one you're going to work with. Be sure you're comfortable with the person. Ask him to walk you through the claims process and give you prices for all the types of insurance you need. See if you can get discounts for loss control measures you've taken, such as fire and theft alarms, sprinkler systems, and so on.

Don't necessarily go with the agent who has the best prices. Take the time to compare policies, and pay attention to the rapport you have with agents. If you need different types of business insurance, you might end up with more than one agent. That's okay. Just be sure you get the coverage you need and an agent you can work with who will work for you.

Government Sources

Many entrepreneurs rely on government sources of funding and on other types of government assistance, as well. The United States Small Business Association (SBA) is probably the best known of all the government agencies that assist entrepreneurs. It can be of tremendous help to those starting small businesses.

The SBA is the nation's largest single financial backer of small businesses. In 1998, it provided management and technical assistance to more than a million owners of small businesses. It also makes low-interest recovery loans to small businesses through its disaster relief funds.

The SBA can help an entrepreneur with a business plan or supply information on marketing, taxes, and so on. At the risk of sounding like an SBA advertising piece, I'll just say it's a good place to look to if you need advice or information.

Grizzly Area

Always ask a potential insurance agent what you should do if something happens at your business and you need to file a claim. If he gives you an 800 number for somewhere in Iowa that eventually puts you in touch with a claims representative of the insurance company he's selling for, move along to the next prospective agent. An agent should represent you in the event of a claim and be available when you need him. If he's not willing to do that, the claims process will be a big hassle. Find somebody else.

Over the Rainbow

The SBA recently started a series of online business classes, covering topics such as the Y2K problem, writing business plans, and raising capital for a small business. Check out the classes at www.sba.gov.

The SBA is one of the better known government agencies, but by no means the only one. Every state has programs for small businesses. You can find out what's available in your state by calling the National Association of State Development Agencies at 202/898-1302.

Over the Rainbow

SCORE (Service Corps of Retired Executives) is a nonprofit group that offers education and services to small businesses. This group works in cooperation with the Small Business Association and sometimes with area chambers of commerce. Retired executives meet with people looking to start small business and share their experiences and advice. Call your local chamber to see if there's a SCORE group in your area.

Check the government listings in your phone book, or look at the Center for Information Law and Policy's list, which includes descriptions of federal government agencies on the Internet. You can find it at www.law.vill.edu/fed-agency/fedwebloc.html.

Salespeople and Suppliers

Salespeople and suppliers are often overlooked, but they can be invaluable sources of information and help. They are the people who get around in an industry. They know what's going on and who's doing what, and they're often among the first to spot emerging industry trends.

Having a supplier you know and can rely on can make doing business a lot easier. If you need something fast, it's nice to be able to make a phone call and know that what you need is on its way. Make it a point to get to know the salespeople and suppliers who come into your company.

Remember that good service and good information are valuable, and sometimes hard-to-find, commodities. If you have salespeople working for you, be sure to remind them how important it is to keep abreast of what's going on.

Employees

Employees have particular, and often unique, insights into the companies they work for. I think business owners should make it a point to sit down with employees and get their take on what's happening in the company. How do they feel about particular issues? Are they satisfied with their working environments? How can you help them make their work more enjoyable and rewarding? And, most important, what ideas do they have to improve the business?

Are there better or faster ways to make the product? Do they have good ideas for sales? Maybe an innovative new way to market the product? Business owners too often over-look employees as people who understand the company and can be of real value to it.

How to Keep Your Support System Strong

As with nearly all relationships, good communication is a key ingredient to maintaining a strong support system. Keeping your system strong requires attention. It means maintaining contact with the people in your support system, even if you have to go out of your way to do it.

I've known people who were constantly having lunches or dinners with the people in their support systems. That's fine, but there are other ways to do it, too. Maybe your accountant is in the group that shoots hoops at the local YMCA, or maybe your lawyer's kid is on the Little League or soccer team you coach.

Bear Facts

A friend was telling me about her friend Dave, who got into rehabbing houses with a Habitat for Humanity Group. The group, which turned out to include his lawyer and a key contact from the bank he worked with, met every Saturday for a month to rehab a building. While getting the satisfaction of being involved with a worthwhile project, Dave also got a lot of unplanned (and unbilled) time to know his lawyer and banker a lot better.

Support system maintenance doesn't have to be formal or structured. It can be as informal as a Saturday morning golf game or an employees' outdoor lunch on a beautiful spring day. Some people make it a point to send birthday or holiday cards. Others invite members of their support systems to parties or company outings. You can do whatever works, as long as you keep up a level of communication.

Maintaining a support system is about keeping up contacts. It's about helping out when you can and asking for help when you need it.

The Least You Need to Know

➤ You should aim at having a support system in place before you need it.

➤ Lots of people would be happy to help you find solutions to problems or provide information you need.

➤ Members of your support system should be hired strictly on their business qualifications, not because they're friends or someone to whom you owe a favor.

➤ People and agencies that can help with your business run the gamut from lawyers and accountants to government agencies to employees.

➤ Maintaining a strong support system requires good communication and networking.

Chapter 22

Family and Friends

In This Chapter

➤ Working at things that aren't really work.

➤ Being there when you say you will.

➤ Making it okay when you can't be there.

➤ Taking time off is A-OK.

➤ Understanding how your friends and families might react to your success.

➤ Deciding whether to work with family and friends.

I know I discussed some issues about family and friends in Chapter 4, "The Balancing Act," but it's so important that I'm going to spend a whole chapter on it here.

If you can't reconcile your work with your family and your friends, that work comes to you at a great expense. By this time, you're probably engrossed with running a business, starting a business, or thinking about a business. Any of those processes can get in the way of life with your family and friends.

In this chapter, I'm going to review how you can find more time to spend with the people you love and how to make the most of the time you have with them. You'll also look at dealing with family and friends who might not be as happy as you'd think they'd be about your business venture and your success.

So let's get started. These topics are too important not to cover.

How's Your Family Doing These Days?

If you meet up with an acquaintance at a restaurant or in the gym, and he asks you how your family's doing these days, what's your answer? Unless there's a problem

Over the Rainbow

This isn't my tip, but one I heard someplace and liked. Pretend that each area of your life—family, work, leisure activities, your faith, possessions, and so forth—is a ball you're juggling. All the balls are rubber, except for the ones that represent your family, friends, and faith. Those are made of fragile glass. So go ahead and juggle away, but be careful about which balls you drop.

going on at the time, you probably say everything's just fine, thank you very much. You probably say it automatically, without giving much thought to your answer.

If that little scenario rings true with you, stop right now. Sit down someplace where it's quiet and take a few minutes to *really* think about what's going on with your family these days. Do you know? Be as honest with yourself as possible as you answer the following questions. I'm not asking these things to make you feel bad or to lay a guilt trip on you. It's just that your relationship with your family is so important, and it so often gets put in jeopardy when we get wrapped up in business.

Think about these questions, and answer them as honestly as you can. Their purpose is only to make you think about what's going on in your life. Not all the questions apply to everyone, but I think you'll get the idea. Again, this exercise isn't meant to make you feel bad, only to get you thinking.

➤ When's the last time you sat down and *really* talked to your kids about what's going on with them? To go a little further, when's the last time you sat down with your kids and really *listened* to them about what's going on with them?

➤ Do you know who your kids' teachers are? What classes they have in school? What books they've been reading?

➤ Who are your kids hanging around with these days? What are their friends' names?

➤ Do you know what your kids' after-school routines are?

➤ How many nights a week does your family get to sit down and have dinner together?

➤ What's up with your spouse these days? Who does your wife eat lunch with? What are the names of her friends from work?

➤ When did your husband last get his hair cut? Did you notice?

➤ What do your kids want to be when they grow up? That changes at about the same rate as the weather, you know. When's the last time you checked?

➤ When's the last time you and your spouse talked about your long-term plans and dreams?

➤ What shows do your kids like to watch on TV these days?

➤ Do you and your family go to church or synagogue together? Or do you try to sneak in a couple of hours of work while they go?

➤ When's the last time you spent some time with your parents? How about your siblings?

➤ How many nieces and nephews do you have these days? Do your kids know their cousins?

➤ Do holidays come and go, practically unnoticed, or do you take time out to really celebrate and enjoy them with your family and friends?

The older I get, the faster the time seems to go. Everybody I know says the same thing. Each year seems shorter than the one before. As important as it is for us to get our businesses running successfully and to realize our dreams as entrepreneurs, let's not forget what's really important in our lives. Only your family and friends love you back. Your work never will.

Your Life Is More Than Your Work, and Your Work Is More Than Your Job

Your life is more than your work. We all know that, although sometimes our families probably aren't aware that we know.

If you're like me, you know how fast time flies when you're involved in a work project or problem or when you're just working. You get caught up in whatever's going on, and before you know it, you're late getting home for dinner—again. Be late enough times, cancel enough times, or just don't show up enough times, and you'll hardly be able to blame your spouse and kids for thinking your work is more important to you than they are.

Sure, your work is important. It's really important. I'm the last person in the world who's gonna tell you otherwise. I do know, though, that it's not the only important element in your life. Studies have shown over and over again that people who are well balanced in terms of how they divide their time between family, work, community activities, religious activities, and so forth, are healthier and happier than those who obsess on work and do little else.

Okay, so your life is more than your work. But what does "your work is more than your job" mean? Well, what do you do in your community? Coaching Little League is part of my work. It's also one of my greatest joys. Organizing and sponsoring the Easter egg hunt for the community was part of my work when I had the teddy bear company. Maybe your work is teaching classes at your church or synagogue or building houses for Habitat for Humanity. Maybe your work takes you to the soup kitchen or the homeless shelter on a winter night. Maybe you volunteer every now and then to read in your kid's classroom.

Grizzly Area

I know we've discussed this before, but keep in mind how important it is not to overschedule yourself when it comes to community work. I've seen too many people who volunteer to do everything and end up doing nothing well. It's far better to concentrate on one or two activities and let other community members take a turn at something else.

Whatever work you do and wherever it takes you, realize how important it is. It's important not only because of what you're doing for somebody else, but also because of what it does for you.

Working for the greater good is an excellent way to heighten your sense of self-worth, to give back to the community, and to help people who need it.

Making Time to Be There

Regardless of whether you're making time to take your kids to the beach, to drive the soccer team to its away game, or to help your neighbor fix the shingles that blew off the roof in the last storm, it's important to be dependable.

Lots of people use work as an excuse for not doing other things. It's easier sometimes to stay at your desk to finish up that paperwork than it is to rush over to see the second half of the softball game. It's tempting to stay and get that last order sent out instead of getting home in time to have dinner with the family and then having to come back and finish the work later. However, it's essential that you make time to be there when people are counting on you—especially when you've promised.

The bad thing about missing a game or a dinner or a night out with your spouse is that it gets easier the next time. Do it enough times, and your kids will stop telling you when their games are. Your spouse will stop asking if you want to see a movie together. There won't be a place set for you at the table anymore.

All this sounds dramatic, I know. But starting a business is tough, and it's consuming in terms of time, emotions, and energy. We have only a certain amount of those resources, so it's important to make sure you use them in the right places, not just for your work.

Over the Rainbow

It doesn't hurt to ask if it's possible to schedule a meeting for another time. Maybe it won't be. Maybe the only time the investor willing to give you $100,000 can meet with you is during your son's game. If that's the case, there's nothing you can do. It doesn't hurt to ask, however, if there's another time that would be convenient. You never know ....

When You Can't Be There

Sometimes work takes over and you simply can't be with your family and friends, even though you would like to be. It happens more often than anyone likes.

Say that you've finally managed to get a meeting with a potential investor. You have a feeling this guy is going to help you out. If he does, it would be the break you've been waiting for. The trouble is that the only time Mr. Big-Shot Investor can meet with you is Tuesday at 4:30 p.m.—when your youngest son has his first soccer game.

What to do, what to do? Only you can decide, but sometimes, things happen that preclude you from being where you really want to be.

If your absences are infrequent, and your family knows you feel bad about missing their events, an occasional miss shouldn't be a big problem. Be sure you take time to explain to your son why you won't be at the soccer game. Tell him you're looking forward to hearing all about it when you get home, and make sure you take time to listen. Maybe your spouse could videotape part of the game for you to watch afterward. It doesn't matter how you do it, but you've got to let your family know they're your first priority.

Scheduling Time Away from Work

Every now and then, it's a good idea to walk out of your office, close the door, and take a couple of days off. In fact, it's a great idea. As difficult as it might be to do that, it's beneficial and makes you a better worker in the long run.

Just as it's important to have a good board of directors to guide you and provide perspective, it's important to step back every now and then to regain your perspective on your business and how it's running. When you're so closely involved with something day in and day out, as you are with your business, it's impossible to maintain the same perspective that those not as closely involved have. You're too wrapped up in it. Problems that wouldn't ordinarily seem too bad can become monumental in your mind. Little tasks can become huge obstacles. We get too close to our work, and our perception of it becomes distorted.

It's amazing, however, what a couple of days away from work can do to restore your perspective, not to mention your sense of humor. If the thought of taking time off puts a knot in your stomach and fear in your heart, think of a way to combine business with pleasure. I used to take my family along when I went over to Cape Cod to try to get gift shops to sell my bears. I visited the shops while they went to the beach or found something else to do. Afterward, we met up for an afternoon together and had a great time. I could relax because I'd done my work and devote my full attention to my family.

When you do schedule time away, get away as completely as you can. Leave the cell phone at home, or at least in your car. Don't take it along to the beach. Don't be tempted to take your calendar, or the trade journal you've been meaning to read, or the last set of orders that came into the office.

When you're away, get away and enjoy the place and the people you're with. You'll be back at the office soon enough. Trust your founders team, or whoever you left behind, to handle matters until you get back. If you didn't leave anyone behind, trust that the business will be waiting for you when you return.

Over the Rainbow

It sounds funny to say this, but watch where your mind gets to when you're taking time off from work. We frequently drift back to the office mentally, leaving the family on the beach without us. If you don't have much free time with your family, enjoy what you do have and make sure you're really there for it.

Dealing with Reactions of Friends and Family

One of the hardest things to deal with, I think, is when you first realize that some of the people you consider friends, and maybe even some family members, don't really want you to succeed. It could be that they're jealous; in fact, I guess it usually is that reason. Or it could be they perceive that success is changing you, and it scares them. Maybe their perceptions are correct.

Business success is a funny thing. It changes your situation. All of a sudden, you're not just the guy down the street anymore. You're the guy who owns the teddy bear (or whatever) company. Your kids might get treated a little differently in school now than they did a couple of years ago when you were just getting started.

Grizzly Area

It takes a secure person to resist the temptations that come with growing a successful business. It's tempting to start thinking you're something special for getting a business off the ground. It's tempting to let people treat you differently than they did before. It's tempting to jump into the fast lane and leave your family behind for a while. If you succumb to all the temptations that present themselves, however, you could find that you're giving up far more than you're gaining. Be careful!

People ask you for advice about business-related stuff. Some people are nicer to you than they were before. People ask you to do things like serve on boards or be the spokesperson for a cause. It's fun. It's flattering, to a point.

For the people who know and love you best, though, it can be scary. Your kids might be afraid you're going to get too busy for them. Your spouse might feel jealous that your life has changed, while his or hers has remained pretty much the same. Success can upset the equilibrium and knock things out of balance. Sometimes the balance can be restored when everyone adjusts to the new situation. Often, though, it never returns.

Your friends might be resentful that you've been more successful in business than they have. If any of them had a chance to get in on your business in the beginning but declined, get ready for a cold shoulder. It doesn't make a lot of sense, but you can't expect everybody you know to be happy for you when your business starts doing well.

Success might threaten relationships you have with family and friends. You'll be meeting a lot of new people, and you'll have different things to talk about and think about than you did before. Your life will be moving quickly as you struggle to keep up with your growing business.

It's not hard to understand why your friends and family might feel as though they have little in common with you anymore. So what do you do about it? As difficult as it might be, you have to accept some of the responsibility for their attitudes and actions. You're likely to feel hurt and angry if friends and relatives don't express the same excitement you're feeling about your business.

Bear Facts

I always say that the only person you can ever be sure truly wants you to succeed is your mother. Most of your employees will, too, because they're riding on your coattails. Other family members, like siblings, might want you to succeed, too, but you never know when jealousy or resentment will rear its ugly head. You can always count on Mom, though.

If you look at it from their viewpoint, though, you can understand their concerns. Maybe you *have* changed. It's likely you're feeling more confident than you did a few years (or even months) ago. That could change the dynamics of your relationships. Maybe your friends and family resent that you've been too busy and not able to spend more time with them.

Bear Facts

I've gotta say that I was lucky to have supportive family and friends. Not everyone was supportive, but most were. My parents and siblings have always been proud of me (well, almost always). My immediate family was supportive. My real friends have cheered me on since the start, and the ones who didn't turned out to be not very good friends, so it didn't really matter. I hope you're all as lucky in this department as I've been.

If that's the case, I think you've got to ask yourself just what it is you've been so busy with and why you've allowed it to get in the way of your relationships.

If you and your buddies used to go fishing every other Saturday, but you've been working every weekend and haven't been out with them for four months, you're risking losing out on more than a few hours and beers on your buddy's boat. You're risking those friendships, and believe me, it's not a good tradeoff.

If your brother stopped talking to you after the last family get-together, try to figure out why. Maybe it's just sour grapes. Maybe he's resentful because you're getting ahead and he's not. Maybe he still thinks Mom likes you better than him. Or maybe he got sick of hearing you brag about how much money you made the previous quarter.

If your wife stopped talking to you the day after you stayed out until 2 a.m. celebrating the successful meeting you had with the investors, try to understand where she's coming from. You're out partying with she-doesn't-know-who until 2 a.m., while she's lying there not able to sleep because she's wondering where you are and worrying about you. Maybe she's threatened by your success, fearing that you'll lose interest in her as you meet new people. Maybe she's resentful because she's home minding the kids, while you're out for drinks and dinner with interesting adults.

Over the Rainbow

If you don't like it when people are resentful toward you, make sure you try your best to be happy for people you know who do well and are successful. It's easy to feel a little jealous when somebody gets ahead, but you shouldn't. We're all in this life together, and when somebody does something good, it should be a credit to all of us.

We expect that everyone will be happy for us, but we quickly find out they're not. Maybe we'd do well to think about why they're not, and figure out a way to save the relationships. Most people are resistant to change, regardless of whether it affects them directly. If your family and friends see you changing, it scares them, and they react with anger or resentment.

If you're experiencing problems with your family and friends, talk to them to see if the problems can be resolved. If not, you might think about getting some advice from a counselor or psychologist. When you come right down to it, relationships are the real essence of our lives. Remember to be careful of which balls you drop when you're juggling.

Should You Ever Hire Family and Friends?

I'm sure that when the very first person started the very first business, he was stumped by this question. Should you hire family and friends to work in your business with you? I don't know. Should you? It's a question nobody but you can answer.

Bear Facts

Bomberg's is a sixth-generation jewelry store in Birmingham, Alabama. In order to include all the family members who wanted in on the business, it opened more stores. All eight of its stores are headed by a family member.

There certainly have been, and are, successful family businesses. There are many examples of husbands and wives who work together for most of their lives, building up businesses that they retire from and leave to their kids. Plenty of businesses are run by siblings or parents and children. Lots of businesses have been started by friends and operated very successfully.

But (you knew that was coming, right?) in many cases attempts at family or friend businesses have had disastrous results. I've heard of cases where family members or friends became completely estranged after being involved in ill-fated businesses. I've heard stories of friends starting businesses, only to have one of the partners steal the other's investments. There are all kinds of horror stories around:

Sorry, but I can't help you out much with this question. I would say you should be extremely careful if you decide to work with or hire family or friends. I'm not sure whether there have been more stories of successes or disasters, but I'm pretty sure it's close.

Try to remember, in all areas of your life, what's most important. When you get right down to it, it's not the investors, or the lawyers, or the financial statements, or the inventory, or even the teddy bears. It's the people who are there to share your successes and failures—to cheer you on or to console you.

Without them, what would all the rest mean?

The Least You Need to Know

➤ It's important to examine your relationships with your family and friends to see if they need to be improved.

➤ Many things in life are more important than your work.

➤ If you say you're going to be there, be there.

➤ When spending time with friends and family, leave your work behind, both physically and mentally.

➤ Take extra pains to make sure the people you love understand when you want to be there but can't.

➤ Stepping back and taking some time off can greatly improve your perspective on your business.

➤ Many factors figure into how your friends and family might treat you after your business is successful.

➤ Only you can decide whether you want to work with your friends and family.

Part 5

Growing and Changing Along with Your Business

Nothing stays the same—not people, not businesses, not even rocks.

Because your business will be growing and changing, you've got to be prepared and know what to do to facilitate those changes. You'll be faced with different decisions about your business, all of which could affect its future.

Maybe you're finding out that you don't like running a business as much as you liked getting it started. Maybe you're thinking about selling or merging your business. Whatever you want to do, it's important to understand the effect it will have on your business and your future opportunities.

Chapter 23

Keeping a Constant Watch over Your Business

> ## In This Chapter
>
> ➤ Businesses and babies have many common traits.
>
> ➤ The importance of constant vigilance.
>
> ➤ Understanding your financial statement.
>
> ➤ Keeping problems at bay by paying close attention.
>
> ➤ Reacting, not overreacting, to ups and downs.
>
> ➤ Learning to trust others to help.

If you think you can get your business started and then stand back to watch it run, please pay close attention to this chapter. Starting your business required, among other qualities, ingenuity, energy, stamina, persistence, and smarts. Running your business requires all those traits and a healthy measure of something else: diligence.

A business bears close watching—all the time. In this chapter, you'll look at two of the best tools for evaluating how your business is doing: the balance sheet and the profit and loss statement. You'll figure out what the difference is between the two and how you should react to the ups and downs nearly every fledgling business experiences. You'll also examine the issue of trust as it applies to those who help you run your business.

Your Business Is Like a Baby

The more I think about it, the more comparisons I find between growing a business and raising a baby. There are so many similarities. Just for fun, let's have a look:

➤ Babies and businesses both require constant watching.

➤ You need to find people to help you take care of your business or your baby.

➤ Babies and businesses cost a lot of money.

➤ Raising a baby or a business is hard work, without much immediate gratification. Most of the rewards happen later on.

➤ Things go wrong with businesses and babies, and because you're learning as you go along, it's hard to know what to do about them.

➤ Babies and businesses develop personalities as they grow and mature.

➤ How babies and businesses turn out depends a lot on the person or people raising them.

➤ Babies and businesses keep you awake at night.

Like babies, businesses are easy to get caught up in. You become engrossed sometimes to the point that you don't want to do anything else. It's easy to lose perspective.

To successfully monitor and watch your business, you have to know what you're looking for. Comparing your business to a baby again, you know that if your baby cries, she wants something. If for some reason you don't have a clue what her crying might mean, you can't do much to help her.

If, on the other hand, you realize it's been four hours since she last ate, you know she's probably hungry, so you can try feeding her. If that doesn't stop the fussing, you can change her diaper, or rock her, or burp her. You know what to look for, so you know how to help.

The Word According to John

Your company's *financial statement* has three basic parts: the balance sheet, the profit and loss statement, and the cash flow statement. Those three elements make up your financial statement.

It's the same thing with your business. If things aren't going the way you'd like, you've got to know what's going wrong. If you're losing money, you must be able to look at your financial statement and see what's going on. You have to take a step back, look at the big picture, and see what's happening.

It sounds obvious, but it's not always that easy to do. When you're looking at your business, your financial statement is the best indicator of what's going on. It tells you all kinds of information you need to know about the day-to-day operations and the long-term financial situations in your company.

When you fully understand your financials, you'll have a good understanding of your company's systems and how it's running.

Evaluating Every Day Where Your Business Stands

It's not enough to take an occasional look at where your business is or how it's doing. You've got to be watching it every day.

To know what you're striving for, you must have financial goals. You should have monthly, quarterly, and yearly goals. Use your monthly financial statement to help you track your quarterly goals. Your quarterly statement helps your track your yearly goals.

Learning your way around your company's financial statement is the best way to understand what's going on. You've got to know where to look for particular items. After you learn how to read and fully understand your financial statement, you'll have a good day-to-day take on your business.

As you learned earlier, there are three parts to a financial statement:

➤ The balance sheet

➤ The profit and loss statement

➤ The cash flow statement

Each of these parts has a different purpose. Let's have a look at the function of each part and how it can help you keep track of what's happening in your business.

Over the Rainbow

Your financial statement should get to you by the 15th of each month for the previous month. In other words, you should have May's financial statement on your desk no later than June 15. If it's any later than that, you lose some of your ability to control your company's financial situation.

The Balance Sheet

Your company's balance sheet is what gives you the big picture of how you're doing. Another name for the balance sheet is the *statement of condition*.

Your business's balance sheet is similar to your personal financial statement. It tells you how much you own and how much you owe. When you subtract what you owe from what you own, you come up with the net worth of the business.

The following table shows a balance sheet from a real company. The names of people and institutions have been changed for purposes of confidentiality. The first part of the balance sheet lists the company's assets:

Assets

Current Assets:

Cash—State Bank	15,014.66
Cash—First American Bank	3,779.91
Cash—Bank of America	2,763.81
Cash—State Savings	72,804.06
Petty Cash—Union Bank	200.00
Accounts Receivable—Trade	17,576.75
Raw Materials Inventory	1,475.12
Work in Process	2,534.52
Finished Goods Inventory	5,023.02
Supplies Inventory	48.16
Total Current Assets	121,220.01

Fixed Assets:

Equipment	73,957.47
Computers	3,074.24
Furniture and Fixtures	710.78
Leasehold Improvements	694.31
Total Fixed Assets	78,436.80
Accumulated Depreciation	–1,409.00
Fixed Assets (Less Depreciation)	77,027.80

Other Assets:

Refundable Deposits	3,225.00
Deposits—Equipment Construction	23,400.00
Prepaid Expenses	17,850.00
Trademarks	245.00
Total Other Assets	44,720.00
Total Assets	242,967.81

Okay. There you can see the assets. Now let's have a look at the liabilities and equities:

Liabilities and Equities

Current Liabilities:	
Accounts Payable—Trade	11,759.25
Deposits on Stock Subscriptions	3,000.00
Accrued Interest	21,906.39
Total Current Liabilities	36,665.64

Long-Term Liabilities:	
Mountain Lake Pension	132,300.00
John Smith	113,639.38
American Capital, LLC	–1,603.32
John Jones	200,000.00
Total Long Term-Liabilities	444,336.06
Total Liabilities	481,001.70

Stockholders Equity:	
Common Stock	59,445.42
Beginning Retained Earnings	–115,500.10
Current Period Profit (Loss)	–181,978.79
Total Stockholders Equity	–238,033.89
Total Liabilities and Equity	–242,967.81

You'll notice that the categories on a balance sheet are fairly general. That's because the balance sheet is intended to serve as a *general* financial overview of the company.

The profit and loss statement, also known as the *income statement*, contains more detailed categories.

The Short-Term Profit and Loss Statement

Your profit and loss statement is what keeps you on track from month to month. It shows the expected profits or losses of your business, the expected revenues, gross profits, operating expenses, and the net profit or loss.

An actual income statement contains the percentage of the expense in relationship to the overall income. For instance, if you spent $20,000 on advertising, and your total income was $100,000, then the advertising percentage is 20%. It also lists the percentage for the year to date or the quarter to date. The statement is set up like the following income statement:

Income Statement

	Current Period		Year To Date	
Revenues:	**Amount**	**% of Current**	**Amount**	**% of Year**
Sales, T-Shirts	4,500.20	25.41	17,598.36	60.21
Sales, Tank Tops	2,296.32	69.67	9,321.20	34.79
Shipping Income	520.15	4.92	2,062.15	5.00
Total Revenues	7,316.67	100.00	28.981.71	100.00

*Note: The type of products sold has been changed for purposes of confidentiality.

Categories other than revenues, and the items listed under each category, might be as follows:

Cost of Goods Sold:

Materials
Wages—Production
Materials Freight
Supplies COGS
Rent COGS
Change in Inventory
   Total Cost of Goods Sold
   Total Profit

Operating Expenses:

Accounting
Advertising
Bank Charges
Commissions
Consulting
Consulting—Media
Depreciation
Freight and Postage
Internet Services
Late Fees
Legal
Miscellaneous
Moving—Employee
Office Supplies
Outside Services

Operating Expenses:

Packaging Materials

Postage

Rent—Office

Repairs

Supplies—Other

Travel and Entertainment

Telephone

Utilities

Wages—Accounting

Wages—Administration

Wages—Marketing

Wages—Sales

Wages—Systems

Other Tax Expense

   Total Operating Expense

   Net Profit (Loss)

Interest Income

Interest Expense

   Net Profit (Loss) After Tax

Keep in mind that every business has its own income statement. Yours won't contain exactly the same categories and items as those shown here. It depends on the type of business you own and other factors.

The Cash Flow Statement

The third part of your financials, the cash flow statement, explains the cycle of money that comes in and out of your business every month. The income statement shows how much profit or loss occurs over a specific period, but the cash flow statement shows exactly when those profits or losses happen.

If you ship out $100,000 worth of T-shirts in May, it gets recorded as a sale in May. Payment for the shirts, however, might not reach your company until September. Your cash flow statement tells you exactly when the money goes out of your business and when it comes in.

Your cash flow plan tells you at the beginning how much money you need to raise to get your business started and when you can expect to get the money back in sales or other income. It's an incredibly important part of your financials and an excellent means of keeping track of what's happening financially at your business.

Reacting to the Ups and Downs

If you keep close watch on your balance sheet, profit and loss statement, and cash flow statement, you'll have a good understanding of what's happening with your business.

It's important to remember that you won't always like what you see. The numbers on your financial statement tell you what you *need* to know, not necessarily what you *want* to know.

Maybe one of your customers owes you $17,000 for merchandise you sent him three months ago. You need $10,000 to meet your payroll that month, and your financials are telling you the money isn't there. Because you have all the numbers in front of you, you know that you need $10,000 you don't have so you can pay your employees. That's not great news.

You also know, however, that your customer owes you $17,000 for the merchandise you sent him. Because you have all the facts you need, you can pick up the phone and politely (or otherwise, depending on how many times you've already called) ask your customer to please send you $17,000 at his earliest convenience—like today! If you didn't have a handle on your financials, you might not be able to quickly determine who owes you money or figure out a way to pay your employees.

If your financials are telling you things you don't want to know, like you're losing money, the common tendency is to overreact. Your first instinct is to panic. You're sure the company is going under. You're going to be just another statistic in the failed business report. You'll never be able to borrow any more money. Your future is looking a lot more grim than it was just yesterday.

Well, feeling panicky the first few times you see numbers you don't like on your financials is perfectly normal. There's probably not an entrepreneur around who hasn't felt that way at one point or another.

Bear Facts

Most of my best thinking gets done in my car. If I have a big problem or need to figure out something important, the car's the place for me to be. I often travel from Vermont to New York City—about a five-hour trip. I've solved many problems and sifted through a lot of important stuff during those rides. Maybe your best thinking time is while you're hiking, jogging, or talking things over with a friend. Whatever works for you is fine.

You've got to resist the temptation to panic, though, because you've got to figure out a way to improve the situation. It's hard to think well when you're in the middle of a panic attack, so try to tone it down and figure out what you're going to do.

The most important thing to do when you've got a financial problem is to be proactive. You can't sit around stewing for a few days, wondering how the hell you got into such as mess. You have to quickly figure out what you're going to do and take action to correct or improve the situation. If you read your financials thoroughly all the time, you'll know early on when there's a problem. That's a great advantage in being able to do something about it.

Don't feel like you've got to solve these kinds of problems by yourself. Get on the phone to your accountant and ask his or her advice. Contact the members of your board of directors. Call a meeting if you have to. Trust me, board members won't think less of you because you asked for help. One of the roles of a board is that of advisor, and your board members should be happy to help. A good board of directors helps you avoid financial problems in the first place by keeping an eye on, and questioning, spending.

If your financials are telling you that you've had a lousy quarter, figure out what you can do to improve the situation for the next quarter.

Get Others Involved

I used to get my employees involved, and they loved it. Some of the best suggestions for how to cut expenses, save money, improve production, and increase sales came from employees.

I think it's a good idea to involve everyone you can when you're tackling financial problems, or nearly any kinds of problems. Letting others know about problems keeps them in perspective and provides opportunities for you to get help solving them.

If you obsess over problems but don't ask anyone to help you solve them, they get bigger and bigger in your head. That kind of behavior can make a hangnail proportionate to a heart attack in no time. On the other hand, if you've had a great quarter, resist the temptation to overreact to that, too. It's tempting to rush out and spend the money you've made, but you know what they say about saving for a rainy day.

It's sort of like the stock market. It's best to figure that you're in it for the long haul and not react

Over the Rainbow

When you've got to cut expenses, start with the areas that represent the highest percentages of the total budget. If wages are eating up 70% of your total budget, it makes more sense to start looking for ways to save in that area instead of spending hours shopping around for a cheaper Internet service provider, an area that represents less than 1% of your total budget.

too drastically to the peaks and valleys along the way. There will be a lot of ups and downs during the course of owning your business. It's part of the territory. Be confident that with diligence you'll be able to solve the problems, and it will all work out just fine.

Trusting Others to Help Take Care of Your Business

Because running a business is hard work, at some point most of us get others to help us. You know what? That's not always an easy thing to do. Getting back to the baby analogy, it's like the first time you leave your kid with a babysitter or drop her off at the daycare center. Remember that? Or the first time you go away overnight and leave her at Grandma's house?

You're sure nobody else can take care of your baby as well as you can. You worry constantly that she'll fall and bump her knee, or that she'll miss you, or that the babysitter won't heat her formula to the temperature she likes best.

It's the same situation when you trust somebody else to help you run your business. You fret and worry until eventually you figure out there are other competent people in the world and your business will survive, and maybe even prosper.

It's important to find people you trust to help you run your company. Trust is one of the most important parts of any relationship; without it, the relationship can't survive. Many people, myself included, have learned the hard way that you can't always trust the people you thought you could. It's a hard lesson, one that often carries considerable expense. Sooner or later, though, you've got to take a leap and find others to whom you can entrust your business. It's all part of growing.

The Least You Need to Know

➤ Businesses, like babies, bear constant watching.

➤ Fully understanding and using your financial statements is the best way of knowing exactly where your business is and where it's heading.

➤ Your financial statement has three parts: the balance sheet, the profit and loss statement, and the cash flow statement.

➤ Each part of the financial statement has a different role, but all are important in understanding your company's total financial picture.

➤ Being proactive is the best way to stave off potential problems.

➤ Overreacting to problems is a common tendency, but should be avoided whenever possible.

➤ Trusting others to help care for your business isn't always easy, but becomes necessary as your company grows.

Chapter 24

Being Ready to Change as Your Business Grows

In This Chapter

➤ Preparing to change as your business changes.

➤ Using backdating to get to where you're going.

➤ Balancing your life with the growth of your business.

➤ Preventing a business from growing too fast.

➤ Methods of growing your business.

➤ Being willing to change as your company grows.

Everybody who starts a business plans for it to grow.

All right, maybe not *everybody*. You could argue, I guess, that there have been people over the ages who have started businesses with the idea that the operations would remain exactly the same from day one until the doors closed for the final time. *Nearly* everybody who starts a business, however, plans for the business to grow.

As you anticipate the growth of your business, you need to prepare yourself for the changes that might occur as a result. No growing business remains the same; that's one thing you can be sure about. The systems you have in place might need to be changed to keep up with the growth. You'll need more employees, more supplies and suppliers, maybe more manufacturing space. You've got to be ready to make important decisions, to deal with problems, to anticipate situations, and to predict what might occur.

Judging whether the rate at which your business is growing is appropriate can be difficult. You'll question whether you're growing fast enough or perhaps too fast. You'll wonder if you're keeping in line with your goals or falling short. Maybe you'll find you're exceeding your goals.

Being prepared for the growth of your company and judging the rate of growth require you to put your entrepreneur's vision to work. You need to be your company's visionary. Fortunately, you have—or should have—some tools that can help you in that position.

Evaluating the Rate at Which Your Company Is Growing

Two important tools for keeping on top of your company's growth are your business plan and your backdating system. These tools are important throughout the life of your business, particularly when evaluating its progress. They show you whether you're on track for reaching your goals.

I didn't get into backdating as extensively as I discussed the business plan in previous chapters, so I'll cover it in a bit more detail now. *Backdating* is simply the process of figuring out how you're going to get from here to there. You set your goal, and you plot steps for how you're going to reach it. It's simple, and it works.

Backdating can be done in any time increment you want. I think everybody should have at least a five-year financial plan. You should also have a one-year backdating plan that gets reviewed on a regular basis.

Backdating is a great way to get organized before you start your business, too. Let's have a quick look at a couple of different backdating plans so you can get a better idea of how they work. You'll be surprised at how easy they are.

The Word According to John

Backdating is a plan that works in reverse. You start at where you want to be in, say, five years, and work backward, filling in intermediate goals along the way.

Your own backdating plan doesn't need to be done in the same format as the one shown here, and it can include different kinds of, or more, information. The important thing is to know what you need each month until it's time for your business to open.

A five-year financial plan would look something like this:

Year 2005:	Earn salary of $100,000
	Company goes public
	Company reaches sales of $10 million
Year 2004:	Earn salary of $70,000
	Company reaches sales of $4 million
Year 2003:	Earn salary of $60,000
	Company reaches sales of $2 million
Year 2002:	Earn salary of $50,000
	Company reaches sales of $500,000

Year 2001:   Earn salary of whatever the business will bear.
                   Company reaches sales of $100,000

Year 2000:   Open business

Today: Start business plan
                   Read all available information
                   Meet with people who have started businesses

After your backdating plans are in place, you have a means of checking to see whether you're moving along according to schedule. Your rate of growth is easy to evaluate because it corresponds to the backdating plan.

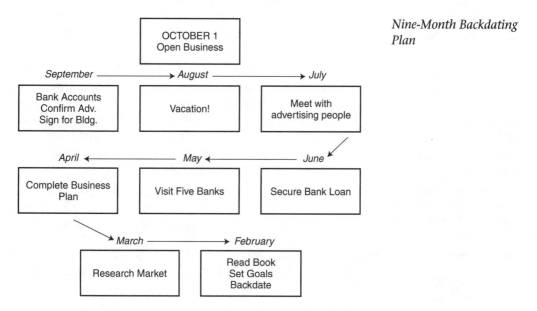

Nine-Month Backdating Plan

Note: This method would be a big help in planning what you need to do to get your business off the ground. One-year plans should also be used after your business is established.

Is Your Company Growing Fast Enough?

You can tell from your backdating and business plans whether your company is growing at the rate you'd like. Remember, however, that you can't get hung up on your plans to the point where you lose sight of what's really going on.

Remember that your plans are guides, not guarantees. You know as well as I do that the best-laid plans of mice and men often go awry (or something like that.) We've all made plans that don't turn out the way we had anticipated, and your business certainly could fall into that category. If it does, there are times to worry about it and times to kick back and enjoy what's going on.

Let's say you had planned to be earning $200,000 a year five years after you open your business. It said so, right there in your business and backdating plans. Well, here you are. Five years have passed, and your best year was $150,000.

Should you be upset? It depends. Are you enjoying what you're doing? Are you having fun? Do you have time to hang out with your family and friends? You taking some cool vacations? Tending to that little garden in your back yard? Taking in a Yankees game every now and then? If you answered yes to those questions, then why would you be upset? You're having a great time and pulling in $150,000 a year. That's not bad, you know. In fact, that's pretty darn good.

On the other hand, if you're spending 18 of every 24 hours working and fretting and getting yourself crazy, you haven't spent any time with your family and friends in two years, and vacations are just a distant memory, then I think you should be plenty worried.

If you're not reaching your goals and it's a problem, then you need to figure out why you're not reaching them and do something about it. If you're not reaching your goals, but it's not a problem—who cares? As long as you're doing well and you're enjoying the process, you're succeeding, aren't you? I think so.

Sure, you want your business to stay on track and grow at an anticipated rate. You have a certain responsibility to your founders team, your board of directors, and your shareholders to grow the business as you'd planned and stated. But it makes no sense to grow your business at the expense of your life and happiness. Finding balance in your life is important, too.

Is Your Company Growing Too Fast?

Some people think there's no such thing as too-rapid growth, but that's not true. In fact, it happens all the time. It could happen if the founders aren't smart enough or don't acquire the necessary skills to keep up with the growth. It could happen if the company doesn't have good systems in place. It could happen if the board of directors isn't doing its job.

There are lots of ways a company can grow too fast. When it does, the company actually outgrows the management, its systems, or its board, and things start to break down.

Over the Rainbow

It's vital to balance your personal goals with your business goals. Be flexible. If you haven't quite met your business goals, but your personal goals are right on track and you've never been happier, then life is good and you should enjoy it. If not meeting your business goals is making you and everybody you know miserable, however, then you should figure out how to reach those goals.

Grizzly Area

I've known people who have watched their businesses fail because they were too proud to ask for help when their businesses outgrew them. If you're floundering in your business, get help right away. If you lose control of what's going on, it's going to be hard to get it back.

It's important to watch for signs that your business might be growing too fast. If you feel like you're in over your head or things are moving too quickly, then you'd better address the issues you don't understand. Sometimes we stumble along, trying to act like everything is okay, because we don't want other people to know we don't have a clue about what's going on.

A business is only as good as the people and systems running it. If you suspect your business is growing too fast for you to handle, you're going to have to get help or slow its growth.

Considering Possibilities for Further Growth

Thinking about how your company will grow is a fun part of being an entrepreneur. It's payoff for your hard work, sweat, and worry.

In what ways, though, might your company grow? There are different methods you can use to grow your business, listed in the following sections.

Buy Another Business

Buying another business is a quick way to grow your business, but it's not a walk in the park. Remember that when you buy a business, you get all the good things about it, and all the problems as well. Still, buying a competing business, or one that complements your existing business, is a definite possibility for growth.

Licensing

You know how everybody loves T-shirts with images of the Rugrats, their favorite team logo, their favorite beer logo, or something like that? All those T-shirts happen through licensing.

Maybe you've invented a way to grow the biggest, best tomatoes ever. If you sell your invention to someone so that he or she can actually grow the tomatoes and sell them, or sell seeds for them, or sell the process to other people, you've licensed your invention. If you invent the cutest little toy—say, a bear—and allow T-shirt manufacturers to make shirts with its image, you've licensed your product. You make money from licensing by getting a royalty on the sales that result from your product or idea. Sometimes you get an upfront fee, too.

On the other hand, you can make money by buying licensing rights from someone else and producing something with what you purchase. If you buy licensing rights to a monkey toy, for instance, you might agree to make hats with the monkey on it or create books about the monkey. You make money from the sale of your product.

The Word According to John

Licensing is selling a copyrighted, trademarked, or patented product, idea, or process to someone else, with the knowledge that the buyer intends to make a profit from what he's purchased.

297

Networking

Simply, *networking* is referring parts of your business to somebody else so you can concentrate on doing what you do best. Say you have a landscaping and lawn service company. You're a genius at garden and landscape design, and you can make a lot of money at it. But you don't have time to do all the designing you're asked to because a lot of your customers want you to mow and fertilize their lawns.

The smart thing to do is network. Give all the mowing and fertilizing jobs to Dave's lawn care service, and concentrate on your landscape design, which is what you like best and where you can make the most money. Just be sure the companies you network with are reputable and good because your customers are still going to associate your name with the job.

Franchising

If you've got three great restaurants that have been packed every night for the past two years, you might consider franchising as a means of expansion. Franchising is when you allow someone to do business under your name and sell your products—you know, like Papa John's pizza or TCBY frozen yogurt.

If you sell someone the right to use your name and sell your products, you make money because you get a percentage of the franchisee's gross sales. You don't want to rush into franchising, though. It can be tricky. Remember you're taking a chance by allowing someone else to use your name.

Taking Your Company Public

You can grow your company by taking it public, but you've got to know what you're doing. I spend all of Chapter 26, "Going Public," covering the fine points.

How to Predict Growth

If you've kept track of your goals and plans, you should be able to predict how fast your company will grow.

If you're planning on buying another company, or licensing, or using another growth strategy, you have to carefully analyze the market, and then consider the implications of the method you plan to use to predict how it will affect your company's growth.

For instance, if you own a restaurant that's doing $2 million in sales, and you buy another restaurant, does that mean your company will start doing $4 million in sales? Maybe. Maybe not. It depends on a lot of conditions and circumstances, such as:

➤ the location you choose

➤ the customer base for the new restaurant

➤ market conditions

➤ name recognition in the new area

These are all factors to consider before expanding your business. If you analyze all the contributing factors carefully, you'll be able to predict the growth of your business.

How to Prepare for Growth

As your company starts to grow, you need to sharpen up your visionary skills and put them to work.

What does your business need to grow? You always need money. Your visionary talents come into play when you see early on that you're going to need more money and set about finding it before it gets to be crunch time.

You need good people to help your company grow. Getting a good team lined up from the beginning is a great way to prepare for growth. Keeping an eye on that team and making adjustments when necessary is another good way to prepare.

Anticipating what you will need and getting it lined up before it's absolutely necessary are the best ways to prepare your business for growth. Keep your systems running at peak performance, and keep good, dedicated people on board. When growth occurs, you'll be ready for it.

Over the Rainbow

All these ideas for expansion are just that—ideas. Be sure to thoroughly research any possible means of expansion, and get advice from your business lawyer.

Removing Limits for Growth

Many things can keep a company from growing. I've already gone over some of them. Lack of money is a big deterrent to growth. Not having the right people is a limiting factor. Not having the right board of directors can hurt.

If you have any of those problems, or other factors limiting the growth of your company, you have to get rid of them if you want the company to grow.

The Limits That You Set

You could, perhaps without even knowing it, be limiting the growth of your company. Are you still trying to do everything yourself two years after you started the business? If you are, you're probably severely limiting your company's growth.

Maybe you're consciously holding back growth because you don't want the business to become unmanageable. If you're doing that, you need to make a choice. You can continue to limit the growth, and you can comfortably manage a small business. There's nothing wrong with that, mind you. But if you want to have a big business, you've got to change your mindset, find some good people, set up some good systems, and go for it!

If you're putting limits on your company's growth because you've thought it through and that's what you want to do, fine. If you're doing it without realizing it, though, or because you don't know how to get the business growing, you need to address the problem.

Talk to your founders team, your board of directors, your accountant, and your business lawyer. Ask your employees for ideas. If you want your company to grow, you're capable of removing the limits you're placing on it.

The Limits That Others Set

Other people can limit the growth of your company, too. Your board of directors can stop that growth cold if it decides it doesn't agree with what you're doing. Your investors can stop your growth by refusing to give you any money. Your founders team can limit the company's growth by not establishing and maintaining good systems or not paying close attention to what's going on.

Bear Facts

I've always had the attitude that given a choice between growing a company or not growing it, you might as well go ahead and do it, as long as it fits into your plans. If having a small company is fun, why wouldn't having a big company be more fun?

Grizzly Area

The manner in which you run your business shouldn't be static. Keep the systems that work, but know when it's time to make changes. If you don't, you'll be stuck with techniques and systems that don't work simply because you're unwilling to move ahead.

The biggest thing you can do to prevent others from limiting or stopping the growth of your business is to be vigilant and know what's going on. Many times, business owners find out about a problem way too late to fix it.

Keep a close eye on what's happening. Remember that it's important for everyone to know what's going on. Keep in touch with the board of directors, and watch that you don't become alienated from its members. You've got to be able to work with the board to run the business the way you want to.

If your board has faith in you and what you're doing, it normally gives you pretty much of a free reign in running the company. If it loses faith, however, look out. Board members will watch you like so many hawks, questioning every thing you do.

Don't be afraid to move people around within the company or to bring in new people as necessary. Nobody wants to be the heavy, but if you have an employee or manager who's not working out, the smart thing to do is to talk to the person and reach some kind of agreement about what will be done. Maybe there's another area within the company where the person can be successful. Maybe the employee will agree that he or she's not a good match with the company and will look for work someplace else.

How Will You Need to Change as Your Business Expands?

When you start your business, you'll be learning new things all the time. You'll be amazed at how much you get to know about every aspect of your company. Manufacturing, marketing and advertising, communications, administration, you name it. You'll learn how to fix the copier, soothe disgruntled employees, and maybe even how to organize a bocce tournament.

If you're not willing to learn what you need to know, your business will suffer for it. I'm not talking about the bocce tournament or fixing the copier, but if you don't keep up to date with industry and business trends, you'll soon be in trouble.

Another important lesson you've got to learn is know when it's time to delegate. If your business is growing quickly and you don't have the skills to manage that growth, you'd better be willing to hand over the reigns to somebody who does. It's hard to do that, sometimes, but it's necessary for the health of your business.

The Least You Need to Know

➤ You've got to be ready to change and to make changes as your business starts to grow.

➤ A backdating system and your business plan are the best methods for evaluating the growth of your business.

➤ Don't let anyone pressure you into thinking your business has to be bigger than what you want it to be.

➤ Watch out for a business that grows too fast or not fast enough.

➤ Don't let unnecessary impediments stop your business from growing.

➤ You've got to be willing to move ahead and grow along with your business.

Chapter 25

Looking Ahead for Your Business

In This Chapter

➤ Knowing when it's time to expand your business.

➤ Choosing the method you'll use for expansion.

➤ Pros and cons of expanding across town or across the world.

➤ Reasons for selling, or not selling, your business.

➤ Deciding whether to merge with another company.

➤ Passing along a family business.

You look ahead for your business the same way you look ahead for your kids. You wonder what the company will be like in 10 years, just the way you try to visualize your children a decade down the road. You might second-guess yourself about what you've already done, and you're bound to have questions about what you should be planning for the future.

There are a lot of ifs when you're running a company. There's no way you can know exactly what will happen, anymore than you can know if the Yankees will win the World Series in 2020 or whether your hair will be looking good a week from Wednesday.

One thing you *can* be sure of is that no growing business remains the same.

Knowing What's Ahead for You and Your Business

You can predict the future of your business to some extent by using your business plan and backdating charts. Of course, these are only plans.

Unless you have a crystal ball and know how to use it, there's no way you can accurately foresee the exact future of your company. You can, however, plan for the future, and do the best you can to make it happen the way you want. To keep your company growing and healthy, follow these rules:

➤ Follow your business plan, and update it as necessary. Business plans tend to become obsolete if you don't pay attention.

➤ Put the company's goals first and the goals of individuals last.

➤ Keep on top of your systems so you can anticipate problems and act early to correct them.

➤ Resist complacency. Keep your company innovative and open to ideas and changes.

How Do You Know When It's Time to Expand?

So, you're sitting around with your founders team one night, drinking a few brews and catching up on what's been going on with everybody. It's a laid-back kind of meeting, just for the purpose of talking things over and making sure everybody's on the same page about what's been going on within your growing company.

Over the Rainbow

Expanding a business has many similarities to starting a business from scratch. You have to follow a lot of the same steps you did in the beginning. The good thing is that it's usually easier the second time around.

After an hour or so of casual business talk, somebody mentions that maybe you ought to think about expanding the company. You talk about it some more, and everybody starts getting excited. It turns out everybody's been thinking about expansion, but no one threw it out onto the table, until just now.

Thinking about expanding your business is exciting, all right. It can be a little scary, too. How do you know the right time to expand? How do you go about doing it? How do you know how far to go? Are you talking about local expansion? Regional? National? International? The possibilities seem unlimited, and your planned two-hour get-together ends up going on long into the night.

Time to Expand

So how *do* you know when it's time to expand your business? You know it's time when you decide to do it. I don't think there's any formula that tells you exactly when. Sure, you can look at your business plan. That might tell you when it's time to expand. Or you might have set an expansion goal in your backdating system.

Expansion might be prompted by an outside factor, such as an investor who decides she wants to put money into your venture and help you expand it. Or it might be prompted by a gut feeling you have. Regardless of what makes you decide to investigate the possibility of expanding your business, there are a few points you should remember.

There are different ways to expand your business. I talked about this in Chapter 24, "Being Ready to Change as Your Business Grows," remember? You can buy another business, you can license a product or process, you can franchise your business, or outsource parts of it so you can concentrate on the things you do best (and make the most money doing).

You can also take your company public (more on that coming up in the next chapter) or expand a part of your business. Say you've been selling bears in gift shops, which have been your only means of selling. Well, maybe it's time to think about a direct-mail component that would give you another sales avenue. Maybe you want to expand your business by using the Internet.

Any of these expansion methods require careful thought and planning, just as getting your business started did. You've got to go about it logically.

You need to look carefully at all your numbers, and make sure you understand exactly what's been going on in the company. Are all the systems where you think they should be? Have you been meeting your different goals?

You have to figure out how much money you need to expand and where that money will come from. You need a timetable and probably a revised business plan.

Set up a meeting as soon as possible with your board of directors to discuss the expansion plan. You need their input and approval to make it happen.

The following is an expansion checklist:

Grizzly Area

Remember that expanding a business requires time and careful planning. It might be tempting to rush into it, but if you don't get your systems in place and know exactly what you're doing before you take action, you could risk hurting your existing business as well.

➤ Evaluate the position of your business.

➤ Decide whether or not to expand.

➤ Decide to what degree the expansion will be.

➤ Make up a backdating system for what needs to be done to facilitate the expansion.

➤ Revise your business plan to include the expansion.

➤ Meet with the board of directors and present your expansion plans.

➤ Start meeting with potential investors and advisors.

An important part of your plans is deciding to what extent you're going to expand. Are you thinking about another store on the other side of town or a factory in Mexico?

Let's have a look at some of the pros and cons of expanding locally, regionally, nationally, and internationally.

Expanding Locally

Local expansion is probably the easiest way to go because it's convenient. You're right there to see what's going on. If you're the owner of Molly's Coffee and Cookie shop, and you've been doing great business ever since you opened a year and a half ago, another shop in a different location is probably a good idea.

You already have the name recognition, and you already know that people like your pizza and sandwiches. The advertising you do could be revised to include the new location without costing any more than you're already paying. Of course, you have to choose a second location, keeping in mind all the factors you considered when choosing your initial spot.

Remember to think about items such as taxes, parking, cost of leasing, security, availability, competition, population, growth patterns, traffic patterns, personal considerations, and so forth.

Expanding Regionally

Regional expansion has many of the same advantages as local expansion. It's manageable because you're right there to keep an eye on things. You can use some of the same advertising without incurring extra costs.

When you're known within a certain area, it makes it easier to expand regionally. The Vermont Teddy Bear Company, for instance, was known in the New York–Pennsylvania–New England region. We were very successful within that region but, when we tried to expand outside the region, we found we didn't do nearly as well. I think that's because people in New York, Pennsylvania, and New England equate Vermont with good quality, good products, and a fair price. People in California, for instance, don't have the same perception of Vermont and its products. We got phone calls (I'm not kidding) from people who asked our sales representatives to explain what Vermont was! It's no surprise, then, that most of our sales were from within a particular region, not too far outside Vermont.

Expanding Nationally

National expansion is a big-time operation. If you're going to expand nationally, you've got to get a whole country to know about your product, and that's not easy. It can be done, of course.

If you have millions of dollars to spend on advertising, all you have to do is buy some air time on Super Bowl Sunday. Get a top-notch ad agency to make you an ad that has everybody around the coffee machine talking about it Monday morning, and presto!

You've got national recognition of your name and product or service. Alas, most of us can't do it that way because we don't have millions of dollars allocated for advertising. We have to be content to move a little slower.

Ben and Jerry used a terrific public relations campaign to successfully expand from a regional company to a national one. Papa John Schnatter started his pizza business in a broom closet in Louisville, Kentucky in 1983, and today is causing major headaches for every Pizza Hut executive around.

So you see, it can be done, and it's not just food places, either. Nearly all national businesses were local or regional when they first started.

Understand that national expansion is tricky for various reasons, including regional differences you might encounter. You could get a very different reaction to a product or service when you market it in Miami than you do in New York City. What's a real hit in Los Angeles might fall flat in Philadelphia. A product or service might appeal to urban people much more than rural folks, or the other way around.

There's a lot to think about when considering national expansion. You've got to consider the attitudes and opinions of people in different areas, distribution, advertising expenses, logistics of manufacturing, and so on. If you do decide to try national expansion, I'd say the best way to gain recognition for your company is through direct advertising by mail, radio, television, or the Internet.

Grizzly Area

Be sure you do careful market research before attempting a national expansion. If you don't, you could end up wasting your bait on an area with no fish. It makes no sense to open a shop on Madison Avenue if New Yorkers aren't going to buy your product. Market research is an absolute must before you start your expansion.

Expanding Internationally

International expansion is getting easier, but it's still difficult. We tested the British market one Valentine's Day season when I was with The Vermont Teddy Bear Company. It was an interesting endeavor, and I think we all learned a lot from it.

The first thing to understand is that every country has its own laws and regulations, and you've got to be sure you know what they are. You can't expect to set up shop in, say, Istanbul, and operate as you would in Chicago. Setting up shop in a foreign country is pretty close to starting over. You can't do it the same way you did at home.

If you want to expand internationally, you need a good chief executive officer or chief financial officer who has significant international business experience. You also need a lawyer who's versed on international business law.

Bear Facts

Our bears sold well in England; people loved them, in fact. The problem was that we ran out of money for the expansion and had to come home. But it was fun while it lasted.

Logistically, international expansion is difficult. It's not what you'd call convenient to go check out your company when it's operating in Belgium and you're in Denver. It can be done, that's for sure, but I bet it gets to be a real drag.

I would think the most logical international expansion, if your business is in the United States, would be into either Canada or Mexico, our two biggest trading partners. It would also be easier to expand into a country where English is widely spoken, instead of one where it's not used.

Although global expansion used to be pretty much in the hands of major companies, that's changing because of technology. Some of the technology that's making it possible for small companies to compete with large ones includes:

➤ The Internet. A Web site can give you global presence, just like the big guys.

➤ Electronic mail. E-mail lets you be in touch with customers and suppliers in other countries nearly as easily as with someone in your own building.

➤ Network databases. Databases can give you information on just about anything, anywhere in the world.

➤ Laptops and modems. Have laptop, will travel, and will stay in touch from practically anywhere in the world.

➤ Satellite systems. These systems, which can be leased from vendors, allow your company to receive broadcasts from major manufacturers and suppliers in your distribution channel.

Global expansion requires extensive research. You've got to target the country or region where you want to do business. You need to understand how business is done there to develop your marketing plan and budget. You need to make sure your product will be accepted in the country or area where you plan to sell it. It wouldn't do, for example, to try to sell bikinis in a Muslim country where women are encouraged to cover themselves at all times.

Bear Facts

A fast-food company—read my lips: H-A-M-B-U-R-G-E-R-S—tried to expand into Malaysia, where about two-thirds of the population is vegetarian. It failed. Duh.

Some other factors you've got to think about when considering global expansion include:

➤ The tax structure of the country and how it will affect your business.

➤ The availability, or unavailability, of supplies that you need for your business.

➤ What competition exists for your product.

➤ The stability, or instability, of the country's currency.

➤ The political climate of the country. It's normally best to stay away from places that are politically unstable because you can't predict what will happen.

➤ The condition of the country. Are there good roads to permit transportation of your product? Are there available workers?

All these factors, and many more, are important to think about when you're considering international expansion. I'm not trying to be discouraging, but global expansion is difficult. You might do well to hire a consultant who specializes in international business and global expansion. He would serve as your troubleshooter and could make life much easier.

Regardless of the type of expansion you're planning, make sure you're expanding for the right reasons. Expanding your business can be something of an ego trip, but that's not a good reason to do it. Be sure you have the financial capacity you need to be successful in the expansion, and that you're looking at good market opportunity.

What If You Decide to Sell Your Business?

Just because you start and grow a business doesn't mean you have to keep it forever. In fact, the eventual sale of your business could well be your goal. It could be included in your business plan or noted in a backdating system.

Or it might happen unexpectedly. You might be enjoying business as usual one day when somebody comes along and offers you far more for your company than you'd ever thought about getting. You might decide to turn down the offer and keep the company, or you very well might decide to sell it. Whether you decide to sell your business depends on considerations like these:

➤ Your personal goals. What is it you want to do? Sell this business and start another one? Hang onto this one? Go back to working for somebody else? Move to another area? All of these goals could be reasons for selling, or not selling, your business.

➤ Your employees. You do have some responsibility to your employees, you know. What will happen to them if somebody else takes over your business? If you do sell, you can try to protect your employees by writing into the agreement that they'd stay and adding other stipulations. You'd have to talk that over with your business lawyer.

➤ Your vendors. You've probably spent a lot of time and effort building relationships with vendors. People often are reluctant to alter relationships they've worked hard to establish, and sometimes that plays a part in whether they sell.

➤ Circumstances. Sometimes people sell their businesses because they get sick and can't run them anymore, or a partner dies and the business loses its appeal to the remaining founders. Or the owner of the company gets divorced and can't keep the business going, or running a company turns out not to be what the owner expected. Maybe the owner is getting older and wants to retire, spend a little time traveling or fishing. Maybe it's just no fun anymore.

There are all kinds of reasons why somebody would sell his or her business. Many entrepreneurs have become wealthy from repeated starting, running, and then selling businesses at a profit.

Just as many have probably missed great opportunities by not selling their businesses at the right time. Businesses tend to be cyclical. They go through a development stage, a growth stage, and a maturity stage, and then they begin to decline.

It might be that the product or service they're producing is no longer as desirable to consumers, the management has become outdated, or the company hasn't kept up with technology.

If an opportunity to sell your business comes along when it's at its peak, but you refuse to sell and the business begins to decline, you might be stuck. I'm not telling you to sell your business. I think you should, however, be receptive to any offers you get to buy your business and consider them carefully.

If you do decide to sell your business, be sure to get the advice you need about how to do it. There are all kinds of ways to negotiate a business sale. Do you want to stay on board for a year as a consultant or officer? Do you want to make sure you can compete with the business after it's sold? What kind of financial arrangement will you have with the buyer?

All these questions, and many more, must be considered if you're going to sell. Unless you happen to be an expert in business negotiations, depend on your accountant and your lawyer to help you.

Bear Facts

Selling your company is one area where it's not like your child. You can sell your company and start up another one without feeling bad about it at all.

Merging with Another Company

Merging with another company is like selling your company in some regards and like taking on a partner in others. There are all kinds of different ways a merger can be set up.

If the company you're merging with is taking control of your company, you've basically sold your company. Maybe you'll stay on in some management capacity, or be a board member, or something like that. You can't however, have two people in charge. It doesn't work.

If your company merges with another one and your company takes control, that can be good. You get to increase your sales and assimilate the strengths of the company you've merged with. Remember, though, that you also get the company's problems.

If you're considering a merger, think about the personalities of the two companies. Will the attitudes and cultures clash or mesh? Some companies are far more formal than others and might have trouble getting along with a casual company.

Also consider whether merging the companies will make one company that's better than either of the existing companies. If not, all you'd be doing is making a company that's bigger, but weaker, than what you have now.

You have to know everything about the company you're planning to merge with, which requires extensive research. Be sure you do your homework carefully, if you're thinking about merging with another firm.

Keeping It All in the Family

Like many family situations, passing along a business can get complicated. I don't mean to be discouraging. It could work out just fine. More times than not, however, there seem to be problems.

For one thing, a son or daughter might not even want your business. That's difficult for some people to even imagine, much less accept. Some people start and grow businesses practically for the sole purpose of handing them down to offspring. When the time comes to do it, a few different reactions can happen:

311

➤ The son or daughter is happy to get the business, and the transition is smooth.

➤ The son or daughter feels pressured into taking the business, even if he or she doesn't really want it.

➤ The son or daughter refuses the business and risks damaging his or her relationship with the parent.

There's also the possibility that an offspring will take the business without being properly prepared to run it. Having a business in the family doesn't necessarily mean everyone in the family is qualified to run it.

If the plan is to hand down the business to the kids, you've got to be sure the kids know what they're doing. I think you should insist they work for another company in the industry first to gain experience and some perspective. Then have them work in every department of your company so that they get to fully understand the business. In my opinion, a child should work in every department, from receiving to sales to bookkeeping, until he or she's familiar with everything going on in the company.

Grizzly Area

Sometimes a business that's been handed down from parent to offspring fails because the son or daughter doesn't have the respect of customers and the community that the parent did. It's a difficult thing to judge when you're considering turning over your business to a son or daughter, but if you don't, you're putting your company at risk.

It's a good idea to start them in the trenches. Let them work part-time around the shop while they're in high school. After they've had some experience with another company, bring them on board in a position they're qualified for. Move them around. Don't make the mistake of putting them in a higher spot than what they're qualified for. All you're doing then is setting them up for failure.

Be careful if you have more than one child, too. Family businesses have been the cause of much stress and bitterness. Will you offer everyone who's interested a piece of the business or just those who you think are qualified? There are some tough decisions concerning family businesses, and they must be carefully addressed. Don't assume or take anything for granted when you're dealing with a family business.

The Least You Need to Know

➤ There are many factors you can use to determine whether expanding your business is appropriate.

➤ There are different ways you can expand, each with advantages and disadvantages.

➤ Local and regional expansion is usually easier and more manageable than national or international expansion.

➤ Just because you start a business doesn't mean you'll keep it forever.

➤ There are many reasons you might want to sell your business, and there are times in the business's life cycle when it makes more sense to sell.

➤ Merging your company with another requires significant research and preparation.

➤ Handing down a business to a child can be extremely rewarding but is often the cause of many problems.

Chapter 26

Going Public

In This Chapter

➤ The implications of taking your company public.

➤ Choosing between a private placement and an initial public offering.

➤ Dealing with the expense and time of going public.

➤ Preparing to take your company public.

➤ Negotiating the price of your company's stock.

➤ Changes that result from taking your company public.

It's a difficult, expensive, and time-consuming procedure, but taking your company public can be great fun. Despite all its travails and trials, I thoroughly enjoyed the experience of taking The Vermont Teddy Bear Company public, even though it did result in a lot more gray hair, a temporarily elevated blood pressure, and probably a few wrinkles, too.

Talk about a learning experience! I'll tell you the story of The Vermont Teddy Bear Company going public a little later in the chapter, but first, let's look at what it means to take your company public and whether it might be a good idea for your company.

What It Means to Go Public

Taking your company public means you're offering its shares, or little pieces of your company, for sale to anyone who wants to buy them. It's a means of generating capital for your company by letting any interested party buy its stock through federally registered and underwritten sales.

Going public is accomplished through an initial public offering (IPO). The founders and shareholders agree to sell part of their company to the public by filing with the Securities and Exchange Commission (SEC) and listing the stock on one of the stock exchanges.

The Word According to John

To me, *taking your company public* means that, in addition to generating capital, you're making your company liquid. If somebody owns stock in a public company and they want to sell it, it's no big deal. The ownership of the company can move freely from one person to another.

Seeing my company's name listed on the stock exchange was worth all the trials of taking The Vermont Teddy Bear Company public. What a thrill it was to look in the *Wall Street Journal* and see my company's name listed with the big boys in the stock exchange section.

It's important to realize, though, that taking your company public can be a great way to raise big chunks of capital, as well as something of an ego trip, but it is not without risk. There's no guarantee you'll be successful in taking your company public. If you're not, you could be worse off financially than before you started. Just because your stock is offered to the public doesn't mean the public will buy it. But if the stock issues aren't successful, you still have to pay the expenses incurred in the attempt.

Bear Facts

The major stock exchanges are the New York Stock Exchange, the American Stock Exchange, and the NASDAQ (stands for the National Association of Securities Dealers Automated Quotation system). The Dow Jones Industrial Average is the measure of the stock market, not a stock exchange.

It can be serious trouble if your stock is issued, but the public doesn't buy the entire issue or even a major part of it. You still have to pay the legal and accounting fees and filing fees with the SEC and your state. There's still the cost of the audited financial statements, pro forma statements, a SEC registration statement, official notices, and other expenses.

It's a general rule of thumb that 13% of the money you raise in a IPO will go to cover the cost of your legal, financial, and other expenses. The banking investment firm that handles your IPO normally takes a 10% commission, and your legal and accounting fees make up about 3%.

Believe me, it's a lot of money.

So how do you know whether it's a good idea to take your company public? How do you know if you and your company are ready, and how do you get a sense of whether you'll be successful in your efforts?

The good news is that taking your company public isn't something you have to do by yourself. In fact, it's possible, but not advisable, to do it yourself. Taking a company public is a complex procedure. It's better to find a qualified underwriter from an investment banking firm to guide you through the process.

I'll get into more details about the process later in the chapter. First, though, let's have a look at whether an IPO makes sense for your company or you'd be better off with another means of raising capital.

The IPO

A public offering might be the splashiest way of raising capital for your company, but it's not always the method that makes the most sense. I already went over the expense involved in taking your company public. It also takes a lot of time. Even if an underwriter from an investment banking firm handles your IPO, you've got to comply with all kinds of SEC regulations and reporting requirements.

When I was preparing to take The Vermont Teddy Bear Company public, I had to travel to Philadelphia, Boston, New York, Los Angeles, San Francisco, and San Diego to meet with investment bankers and present my company to them. That's called your "road show." Fun, but time-consuming.

Something else to consider is that to take your company public, you're required to disclose information about its products, performance, and financial conditions. There could be reasons why you'd rather keep that information private, instead of putting it out there for your competitors to see.

Of course, if you decide to go public and you're successful at it, then all the compliance and work is worthwhile at the end of the day. But if you're not sure, you might want to consider another means of raising capital—a private placement.

Private Placement

A *private placement* is identifying qualified people and asking them to invest money in your company by buying its stock. In that way, a private placement and an IPO are similar. Both involve selling your company's stock. The difference is that in a private placement, you choose to whom you sell your stock. In an IPO, your stock goes to whoever is willing to purchase it.

A private placement is less complex than an IPO because you don't have to comply with all the SEC regulations. Simply put, a private placement is quicker, easier, and cheaper than an IPO.

Don't get the idea, though, that doing a private placement is just a matter of waltzing into somebody's office, drinking a cup of coffee, asking for some money, and waltzing on out again with a big check in your hand. It's a bit more complicated (unfortunately) than that. There are still rules and requirements. Most private placements are handled by business lawyers, investment bankers, or others skilled in this area.

The Word According to John

A *private placement*, like an initial public offering (IPO), is a way to raise capital for your company by selling its stock. With a private placement, however, you get to control who buys it. With an IPO, your stock is fair game for whoever wants it.

Over the Rainbow

There's more than one way to work a private placement. It can be made for debt or equity financing or a combination of both. Debt financing is borrowing money and repaying it with an agreed-upon interest rate. Equity financing is an investor giving you money in exchange for something you have—shares of your company, control of the company, or something else. Business deals are great fun because there are no set rules. Every one is different.

Most private placements fall under the rules of Regulation D of the Securities and Exchange Act of 1993. The rules vary depending on the amount of funding you're looking for and other factors.

I recently initiated a private placement for American Performance Products. To do so, I worked with a New York City consultant who specializes in setting up companies with investors. I'd heard that he was good, and he was.

The consultant put me in touch with eight different private investors or investment banking firms, with the understanding that he'd give me more names if it became necessary. I met with each investor, or a representative from the investment banking firm, and presented my case for American Performance Products.

One of the investment bankers, Bob Winston, referred me to somebody he thought would be interested. I ended up working with the guy Bob sent me to, and Bob worked out the deal for me. Bob earned 7.5% of the money I got for American Performance Company, plus some of the company's stock for his role in the private placement.

Be Prepared

If you're thinking about doing a private placement for your company, you need to be well prepared before you start meeting with potential investors. Once the meetings begin, explain carefully what it is you're hoping to accomplish from a private placement. Potential investors want to know about your plans for the money you raise.

You need to present your business plan, which should include all the pertinent information, including the names of people involved, your marketing plan, and so forth.

Be prepared to have potential investors visit your company, and be sure your lawyer meets with the investors and/or their lawyers. My meetings with the eight representatives, a couple of whom recommended other people who might be interested in investing in American Performance, resulted in four or five offers for deals.

The Deal

An important thing to remember is that you don't have to take the first deal you're offered. Somebody might offer to give you $200,000, but they want to put three people on your board and control 50% of your stock. Another investor might offer to give you $300,000 and ask for control of only 25% of your stock. Consider all the deals before making a decision.

After you've reached a deal with the investment banking firm or the venture capitalist, you need to get a letter of commitment and a copy of the deal you negotiate. You also need an agency agreement, which states, among other things, that you agree to pay the agency or consultant who arranges for you to meet with potential investors.

The consultant's fee who referred me to the eight investment bankers was $10,000. We ended up raising $400,000 for American Performance Products. Half of the money that went to the consultant was his fee, and the other $5,000 paid for the legal fees associated with the private placement. The process took about two and a half months from start to finish. Always count on three months for private placements.

Over the Rainbow

Don't be rushed into deciding whether to accept an offer from a potential investor. Tell him that you'll get back to him, and wait until you've got all your cards on the table before you make a decision.

How to Take Your Company Public

Although doing a private placement makes sense for a lot of companies, it isn't always the best option. Sometimes taking a company public makes the most sense.

Often, the investors you work with in a private placement are interested in taking your company public. They might believe that by going public, your company can make a lot of money, in which case they can get their investments back quicker. The expectations of investors are moving toward getting their investment back tenfold within a year. In that sense, a private placement can serve as a valuable tool for meeting people and moving toward going public.

Don't be talked into going public, though, if you don't think it's the right time or your company is ready for it. As you learned earlier, going public requires considerable time and effort and is a major expense. Having said all that, it can still be the best thing for your company.

If your company is in good financial shape because you've done a private placement (or more than one) or you've had great sales, for example, it might make sense to go public. However, if you've got investors, your business lawyer, or someone you work with advising you to go public, it's something you should think about carefully.

The following list is the major steps you need to accomplish to take your company public. Details for each item are covered later in the chapter. Here's how you prepare to take your company public:

1. Revise your business plan and get updated financial statements from your Big 5 accounting firm.

2. Make sure all systems are in place and everything at your company is running the way it should be. Make any necessary changes.

3. Shop your business plan around to investment banking firms until you locate an underwriter to help take your company public.

4. Get a letter of intent from the investment banking firm. This letter documents the firm's intent to conduct due diligence to determine whether your company is suited to go public.

5. Get an agency agreement. This agreement establishes the agency's fees, sets timetables for going public, states your responsibilities and their responsibilities, and so forth.

6. Get acquainted with the other members of the banking firm, and assist in any way you can with the due diligence being conducted by the underwriter.

7. Determine, and be prepared to negotiate for, a starting price for your stock.

8. Prepare your prospectus, as required by the SEC.

9. Respond to the SEC's questions about your prospectus within the specified time period.

10. Prepare to go on the road to acquaint investment bankers with your company. This step might involve travel around the country.

11. Prepare to deal with anything that can possibly go wrong—because it just might.

Finding Someone to Help Take Your Company Public

The first thing you need to do, if you decide you want to take your company public, is to find somebody who can lead you through the process. Usually it's an underwriter from an investment banking firm. Be sure you have your business plan in order before you go, and get a financial statement from your Big 5 accounting firm to present when you meet with the underwriter. You'll need two years of audited financial statements.

Audited financials cost some money, which many entrepreneurs are reluctant to spend. You need audited financials before you can go public, but there's a way you might be able to get around having them done before the fact. If you get them done ahead of time so they're ready when you meet with the underwriter, you could end up not going public after all, but still having had to pay for the financials.

To avoid that, get your accounting firm to verify your inventory at the end of each of the two years before the time you plan to go public. If you're not sure when you'll attempt to take your company public, play it safe and have the verification done anyway. If you do this, you can put off having your financials audited until after you have a commitment from an underwriter. If you don't have the inventory verifications, though, there's no way you can go back and get audited financials.

Be advised that the underwriter typically requests $50,000 upfront. This fee covers the initial costs for the work he does to prepare your company to go public. It does not, however, give you a 100% guarantee that your company will go public. Even if you don't, however, the document stating you've gone through the initial process often makes it easier to borrow money from a bank or other source. It's a powerful document.

The underwriter does something called *due diligence*, during which he evaluates all aspects of your company to determine whether it's qualified to go public. He'll spend some time at your company, meet with people, and go through records and files. If he finds reasons why your company can't or shouldn't go public, he doesn't refund your upfront money.

If he agrees to take you public, the fun really starts. Normally, at this point, you meet the other members of the investment banking firm and get to request the price at which you'd like to sell your stock. You base that price on how much money you want to earn for your company and some other factors. The next section of this chapter deals with determining an IPO.

What you need to do, regardless of the amount you request, is start high and negotiate hard. If you're not good at negotiating, take along your lawyer, a member of your board of directors, or somebody who knows your company and is comfortable being tough. Remember that underwriters are used to this approach. They expect to negotiate. If you're not willing to, they'll walk all over you.

Grizzly Area

It's possible to take your company public without using an investment banker, but I think it's a bad idea. Security laws are complicated and picky, and as careful as you might be, I think it would be easy to be in violation of some regulation. If you were, the management of your company, and its principal equity holders, can be held liable.

Over the Rainbow

Always, always, always start high when requesting the price at which your stock will be sold. This is a game with investment bankers. To get the price as high as possible, you've got to start high and negotiate hard.

Preparing a Prospectus

After you've met with the underwriting firm, you need to create a prospectus to send to the SEC. The prospectus is like a business plan, but it contains more detail and leaves out some of the items usually included in a plan. It's an important document and should be drawn up with assistance from your lawyer and accountant.

Your prospectus will contain all kinds of information, including:

➤ The history of your company

➤ Who owns your company's stock

➤ All the officers of the company

➤ Members of your board of directors

➤ Risk factors

➤ Your financial statements

➤ Your marketing plan

➤ Your competitors

➤ What you manufacture

It must be detailed and exact and should be bound in book form before you send it to the SEC. The SEC can keep your book for up to 30 days before responding. When it does, it sends back what's known as a "red herring." The name comes from the red ink the SEC uses to write its responses on your prospectus. You then have a specified amount of time to respond to the SEC's questions on your prospectus. The questions could deal with specifics about your board or officers, your product, your financials, or anything else mentioned in the prospectus.

After you finish your prospectus, your underwriter might want you to shop it around to investment bankers in different parts of the country. The idea is to get as many people as possible to know about your company before it goes public.

Over the Rainbow

Going public takes between two and four months, so plan accordingly. You can work out a backdating system to help you plan what you need to do at particular times.

The Showdown

When all the necessary legal and financial work is done, you and the underwriter have to reach a final agreement as to the price your stock is listed at when your company goes public. It might not be finalized, as happened in my case, until the day before your company is scheduled to go public. By this time, everybody's nerves are on edge, and everyone is anxious to see what happens.

I have a great going public story I'll share with you here, as a lesson about holding out for what you want. With all due respect to investment bankers, keep in mind that they know you're anxious to go public and get the process over with. They might be counting on you knuckling under and agreeing to what they recommend. But, as you'll see from this story, you don't have to.

We were set to go public in November 1993. I had requested that the price of our shares be set at $15 per, hoping to get $12. The underwriter had agreed all along that $12 was reasonable and assured me that we would come very close.

Finally, it was the day before The Day. I was with the chairman of the board of The Vermont Teddy Bear Company and two board members. At 4 p.m. we got a phone call from the underwriter we had worked with, saying his company had set the price per share at $5.50.

Well, there was one angry Sicilian (me) at the teddy bear company that day, let me tell you. No way was I going to let our shares go at $5.50. I flat-out refused the deal, and the underwriter said he'd get back to me. The board members handled the negotiating for a while, but by 7 p.m., the best offer they had managed was $6.50. I took over the negotiations, and the underwriter said they'd go to $7, but no higher.

Again, I said absolutely not. This nonsense continued back and forth for six hours from the time it started. There was screaming and yelling, there was incredible frustration, there was incredible tension. After a while, there was beer and pizza, which helped tremendously.

I can't really describe how it felt to have months of hard work and hundreds of thousands of dollars seemingly about to go down the tubes. I was determined that we weren't going to start our stock at $5 or $6 or $7 dollars (remember that the value per share determines the value of your company), and the investment banking firm seemed just as determined that we were going to start there.

Bear Facts

Investment bankers have gone through dozens of IPOs, but they know you're doing it for the first time. The whole thing, I'm convinced, is carefully orchestrated on their part. Why do you think they waited until 4 p.m. to call with their offer the day before we were supposed to go public?

Finally, I told them to forget the whole deal. I would have been willing to take a wash on the time and fees instead of setting the price of my stock that low.

I guess the investment guys finally realized I was dead serious and not about to go along with their offer. At 10:00 that night, they came back with an offer of $10 per share. We took it. We opened the next morning on the big board, and sold 1,150,000 shares of stock at $10 per share.

Determining an Initial Public Offering

A big advantage of an IPO is that you can normally get a higher stock price than you can from a private placement, venture capitalization, or other methods of raising capital.

Companies that go public generally become more financially stable than they were before. That stability makes it easier for them to borrow money. Because the price at which your stock is offered determines the value of your company when you go public, it's important that you get the highest price possible for your IPO.

To determine a starting price, you determine how much money your company needs. That gives you an idea of how much you need to raise. Then you find out what the investment banking firm you're working with evaluates your company to be worth. It's sort of like a realtor recommending an asking price when you go to sell your house.

After that, you need to confirm how many shares of your company stock are outstanding and how many shares you plan on selling. Then you look at whether the price per share that you reach is a reasonable one. It should probably fall somewhere between $5 and $15 for the best results.

It's a complicated procedure, and you'll need help from your lawyer or accountant. Remember that you should negotiate high when you're setting your IPO. You'll most likely end up coming down on your price.

How Going Public Can Change Your Company

Changes are inevitable when your company goes public. Some of the changes are caused by outside forces, like the SEC, and others happen from within. Often, changes occur because management tends to focus more on the value of the company's stock than on what it did before the company went public. This tendency can change the focus of the entire company. Management is often accused of putting aside the company's goals in its haste and worry to keep its shareholders happy.

Certainly, this is a concern for any company, but it can be controlled somewhat if management is aware of the potential for problems and willing to work at avoiding them. If it doesn't, the danger is that long-term goals might be overlooked in exchange for making big short-term profits. Sometimes it makes more sense to temporarily slow down the growth of your company to strengthen it for the long haul. When you're worried about this year's profits, that becomes difficult to do.

Once you've gone public, you're stuck with the SEC forever. You're required to file quarterly reports and comply with other regulations. There's expense and time involved with these processes, which could require expanding your staff.

On the up side, being a publicly held company has more status than being a private company, and status is worth money. It's easier to borrow money, so you can do things and get things for the company that you weren't able to before.

When you go public, the investment banking company that helped you usually puts people on your board of directors as part of its deal with your company. This addition can change the nature of your board, which can have a big effect on your company.

These factors all need to be anticipated and thought out before your company goes public. The better prepared you are to begin with, the fewer problems you'll have as things progress.

Grizzly Area

Beware of the kid-in-the-candy-store syndrome. It's easy to get carried away and overextend your company when more resources become available to you, just because you can. Many management teams have found themselves in big trouble because of this.

The Least You Need to Know

➤ Taking your company public can be a great way to raise capital, but it's not right for every company.

➤ Your company should be in good financial shape before you even consider taking it public.

➤ Private placements often make more sense than initial public offerings.

➤ Taking your company public takes time and effort and is very expensive.

➤ There are many things you need to do to prepare your company for going public.

➤ Be ready to negotiate hard to get the price you want for your stock.

➤ Change within your company is an inescapable byproduct of going public, so be prepared for it.

Part 6

Entrepreneurial Opportunities

Once you're established as an entrepreneur, you face all kinds of opportunities. Suddenly, people come to you for help, advice, and money. The shoe is on the other foot, and now you're the one with experience and wisdom you can share with others.

This part looks at some of the ways in which you can do that, and also tells you how to build a solid reputation that stays with you and enhances your business future.

Chapter 27

The Whole Entrepreneur Thing

In This Chapter

➤ Looking at the big picture to evaluate your entrepreneurial experience.

➤ Gaining knowledge and experience from every part of your business endeavor.

➤ Being satisfied with what you've accomplished.

➤ Using your business experience to do it better the next time.

➤ Thinking about working for somebody else.

This last part of the book assumes you've had your business for a couple of years or longer. You might be happily involved with running it, not thinking about anything except growing it bigger and growing it better.

Or maybe you're getting a little restless, thinking it might be time to look for something else to do. Lots of entrepreneurs start a business, build it up, and then pass the reigns to somebody else and go off to start another one. Many entrepreneurs, in fact, do that repeatedly. It's the challenge of getting the project off the ground that they thrive on, not the day-to-day operations of the company.

Maybe you're even thinking you've had enough of the responsibility that comes with being an entrepreneur, and you might be happier working for somebody else—at least for a while. Regardless of what point you find yourself at right now, let's take a look back at what's happened with your business and where you might go from here.

Evaluating Your Experience as an Entrepreneur

Evaluating your experience as an entrepreneur should be an ongoing process. Monitoring your progress against your business plan and your backdating system helps you evaluate how you're doing along the way and gives you perspective on what you've accomplished and how you've done.

Over the Rainbow

If you're at a point where you want to evaluate what you've done and take a look at the big picture, the best thing to do might be to take a vacation. A week or so away from the business can give you a clearer picture of it and make your options seem clearer.

Sometimes you have to take a mental step or two backward, however, so that you can look more objectively at what you've done. We get so involved in the details of our businesses that it gets hard to remember the overall scheme. You've got to get out of the thick of things sometimes to see the big picture.

When you try to evaluate your experience as an entrepreneur, think about the following questions:

➤ Overall, has owning the business been an enjoyable experience?

➤ Have you achieved most of your personal goals?

➤ Have you achieved most of your financial goals?

➤ Have you gained experience and knowledge from owning and running the business?

➤ Have you maintained a close relationship with family and friends while you've been involved with your business?

➤ Overall, is your family better off than it was before you started the business?

➤ Have you made a name for yourself as a reputable, ethical businessperson?

➤ Have you been able to "give back" to your community by becoming involved in a positive, productive manner?

➤ Have you cultivated a good relationship with your employees, board of directors, and founders team?

➤ Overall, do you feel good about the business, and the time you've spent with it?

I'll look more closely at these questions in this chapter and in some of the chapters later in the book. If you answered "yes" to most or all of them, though, you can be pretty darned sure your efforts as an entrepreneur have been successful.

Learning from What You've Done

To me, along with having fun while you're working, learning is the most important benefit.

The fourth question in the previous list—about gaining knowledge and experience—is a no-brainer. I don't think it's possible to set up and run a business without gaining knowledge and experience. I don't care how many times you do it, you'll continue (or at least you should) to learn and gain experience with every business venture.

Your first business, though, should be an incredible learning experience. From the time you sit down with a stack of books in front of you, or start talking to somebody who has already started a business, looking for advice and ideas, the learning process kicks into high gear.

Think of everything you did to prepare for opening your business. The first thing you did was put your dream into action. You took an idea, probably one that was in your head for a long time, and began to make it a reality. Right there, you accomplished something many people spend a whole lifetime wanting to do, but never quite get around to it.

Once you decided to go for it, you expanded the learning process by doing your homework. You probably studied various types of businesses, looked at the market for the particular business you had in mind, and took a look at the regulations pertaining to it.

You wrote a business plan and figured out goals and objectives. Doing that forced you to put on paper all the thoughts and strategies you've had and take a broad look at many aspects of your business. Your business plan put your goals and objectives in front of you in black and white, taking them from the abstract to as real as you can get.

After it was written, you had to identify possible sources of financing for your business and present the plan to those sources. By doing that, you should have learned several things.

You got to know who's who in your community, and perhaps beyond. You learned who the people are with money and who might be willing to invest in a sound, well-thought-out business venture. You should have gained a lot of confidence as you met people and became more sure of what you were doing.

You probably learned a lot as you talked to potential investors. They might have given you tips on improving your business plan or shared some of their business experiences with you. You might have gotten a taste of government programs and red tape, too, by exploring possible sources of government funding.

Once you figured out how to finance your business, you had to get down to the basics of getting it set up and running. You needed to find a place from which to operate the business and make sure you were in compliance with all the local laws and regulations.

Over the Rainbow

Once you make contacts, do all you can to maintain them and cultivate a friendly relationship. Keep in touch with people who have helped you along the way because you never know when you'll need their help again.

Over the Rainbow

Think of yourself as a baseball player with a baseball card that lists your stats. Your value increases along with your experience, all of which is listed on your card. Pretty impressive!

You had to look at the costs of all areas of your business, set up systems, and figure out who would do what. You probably took a hard look at projecting profits and setting prices on your products or services.

331

No doubt you learned a lot about marketing and advertising your product or service. You found people to help you—a founders team, a board of directors, shareholders, and employees. You learned about hiring professionals such as your lawyer and accountant, and what makes one professional more valuable than another in regard to your business.

When you take a minute to think of everything you've done, you begin to realize the tremendous amount of knowledge and experience you've gained.

Bear Facts

The German poet Heinrich Heine said experience is "a good school, but the fees are high." A Portuguese proverb calls it "the fruit of the tree of errors." But my favorite definition comes from Oscar Wilde. He said experience is "the name everyone gives to their mistakes."

In addition to learning business skills, and gaining an understanding of the whole business process, starting and running a business probably has given you a better look at yourself. Some self-examination was necessary before you started the business, and no doubt it was often needed along the way, too.

Grizzly Area

You meet a lot of people when you're starting a business, and it's easy sometimes to overlook the knowledge and experience they can offer. Try to look at each person you meet as a potential source of information and help. If you don't, you could miss out on the opportunity to get some valuable assistance and support.

You find out a lot about yourself when your back is against the wall and you're facing a huge, seemingly insurmountable problem. You discover you're a lot stronger and more resilient than you thought was possible when you figure a way to get out of the jam you're in and back to business.

Remember way back in Chapter 1, "Having a Dream and Making It Work," when I talked about the two most important qualities an entrepreneur can have, preferably in massive doses?

They were:

➤ Persistence

➤ Confidence

You've got more of those qualities now than you did before you started your business. Even if you haven't realized all your goals (and remember, it's rare when somebody meets *all* of them), you should be feeling pretty darned good about yourself.

Your confidence level is probably higher, and if you didn't realized it when you started, you now know that persistence is what makes things happen and keeps you going when you feel like throwing in the towel and going to work for your brother-in-law's widget company.

Feeling Good About What You've Done

If you answered "yes" to most of the 10 questions earlier in this chapter, you should be feeling good about what you've done since you first conceived and started up your business. You made something out of nothing and did what you'd thought about doing for a long time.

Your business was, I hope, a huge financial success, and you've got some money now to expand the business or move along to something else. You've been able to provide some financial security for your family, and you're not worrying too much about your retirement fund at the moment. Maybe you got to buy that Jeep you wanted for a long time. Maybe you even got to build the new house you and your spouse had dreamed about. And I'm hoping you never became too wrapped up in the business to spend time with your family and friends and enjoy what life has to offer.

Becoming a reputable businessperson within your community is certainly something to feel good about. I always get a kick out of being asked to speak to community groups or civic organizations. It's great to be recognized.

Building and maintaining a good reputation in your community and beyond is so important that I spend the entire last chapter of this book discussing it. After all, when you come right down to it, only a few things in life are really, really important. Your family is one. Your health is one. Your reputation is one.

You should feel good about what you've done if you've given back to your community. I talk more about this topic in the last chapter, too, but being involved in the community does as much for you as it does for the groups you work with. Helping out in some way is a great thing, something all entrepreneurs should do.

You can never expect that running a business will be without snags and rough spots. Running a business involves ego, and anytime ego is involved, you can bet there will be clashes. Figuring out how to resolve the ego problem, however, is something to feel good about. Sometimes you have to swallow your pride and do things you'd

Over the Rainbow

I'm sure there are tons of books about fostering cooperation, handling conflicts, and building good relationships with people you work with and live with. Stephen Covey's *The 7 Habits of Highly Effective People* covers those topics in a broad-based, thoughtful way. It's worth the read.

rather not. Remember that as soon as you get other people involved with your business, you're going to be answering to them.

That's not to say you have no control, but if you've got a founders team, a board of directors, shareholders, even employees, they want to know why you do things in certain ways, what you based a decision on, or what you plan to do about a situation.

There's nothing wrong with having to answer to people. It doesn't diminish your authority or your role in the company. It just makes you accountable, which isn't bad at all.

When you're running a business, you're faced with making decisions. Many of them have to be made quickly, and many aren't easy. I think this is where the confidence factor comes into play. If you're confident about yourself and your ability to run your business, you can make decisions when you have to. If you make a wrong one—and everybody does—you don't agonize over it. Just figure out what to do about it, and then move on.

If you look at decision making as a fun, challenging part of running a business, you'll be fine. Take charge of what needs to be acted upon, and don't shy away from making decisions. Some people are terrified to make decisions because they're afraid they'll make the wrong ones.

Over the Rainbow

Remember that it's better to be proactive than reactive. If you know you're looking at a decision that needs to be made, go ahead and make it. Making a decision, even if it turns out to be wrong, is better than doing nothing and letting circumstances or somebody else dictate what happens.

Remember that hardly any decision can't be revised or worked around. It's a safe bet that 99.999% of all the decisions you make do not fall into the category of life and death. Keeping this in mind might help you relax a little and make your decisions with confidence. Don't waste time or energy feeling bad about bad decisions. When you step back and look at everything you've done and accomplished, you're likely to see that most of them worked out okay.

It's like being a baseball player. Sometimes you make a great decision and hit a home run. Other times you make a really bad one and you strike out. When it's all said and done, though, it's the average that counts.

If, at this point, you have a sense of satisfaction about the business you've started and the time you've spent running it, then you should be feeling good about what you've done.

Doing It Better the Next Time Around

No matter how well you think you've done, or how pleased you are with the business you've started, don't think it can't be done better the next time around. No matter if this business venture has turned out just the way you had hoped, there's always room for improvement. The knowledge and experience you've gained will make continuing to run your business, or starting another business, easier.

If your business is going just the way you had hoped, go ahead and be pleased, but don't get complacent. There are still things you can do to make it better. Maybe you can figure out how to cut your general and administrative costs just a little more to boost the profits higher. Or maybe you can make your employees more productive by offering them some really cool incentives. Whatever. The point is, you should never think you've got the business of running a business nailed. There are always ways you can do it better.

If your business is not going as well as you had hoped, you need to put your knowledge and experience to work for you. Maybe that experience tells you that you can't do it by yourself and you need to find a consultant or somebody else who can help you.

That's not failing. That's being smart. You're recognizing a problem and figuring out what to do about it. That kind of action stems from knowledge and experience, and there's certainly no shame in it.

If you're looking ahead to starting another business, you're definitely better off than you were when you started the first one. You can't buy the kind of experience you've gained from building a business from the ground up. Even if you don't ever start another one, you'll use that experience in other areas of life.

Bear Facts

Starting another business is a piece of cake compared to doing it the first time. Sure, there are still challenges and obstacles to overcome. But you know the steps to take and how to do things logically and effectively.

No matter how good an education you've had or how many degrees you've earned, there's no better source of knowledge than starting and running a business. You'll realize that fully if you just think about everything you've been through and all you've done to get your business up and running.

Now That You're an Entrepreneur, Could You Work for Somebody Else?

Not to worry … if you get tired of running your own business, you could always find a job working for somebody else.

Or could you?

Some people can start and run their own companies, figure it's time to go on to something else, and comfortably go back to working for an employer. Others can't stand the thought of giving up the independence and challenges of calling the shots and making the decisions. The thought of working for somebody else fills them with a sense of dread.

After I left Vermont Teddy Bear, I was contracted by the owners of the Denver-based American Performance Products to get their business on the right track. The challenge of getting another company going, even one that I didn't start, is fun, but it's frustrating sometimes, too. I spend a lot of time training people. My business experience sometimes alienates me from the company's owners and perhaps makes them feel threatened. It's difficult to watch people make bad decisions, but not be in a position to make the decisions myself.

All in all, it's been an enlightening and informative experience. It's given me a chance to see what it's like to be a chief executive officer, working for an entrepreneur with his own company. The experience has put me in a lot of different shoes.

This CEO stint of mine won't last forever. There are better ones than me out there, and I'd miss the thrill of the startup too much to stay put in one place. Although I'll continue to be involved with American Performance Products, it will probably be in the capacity of a board member or as a sort of watchdog.

If you're thinking about going to work for somebody else, remember that there are varying degrees of doing so. Yeah, if you get a job in a office, and you have to sit in a cubicle all day, talking on the phone and doing paperwork, only to have your work assessed by a supervisor at the end of the day, that might be really hard to take. But if you get a position as a salesperson for a great company that you really like and believe in, and you're given all the autonomy you want as long as you keep selling the product, that could be a pretty cool job.

Bear Facts

Above all, entrepreneurs are dreamers. For obvious reasons, dreamers don't normally make the best students in a conventional school setting, nor do they make the best employees in a traditional work setting. This quality can make it difficult to fit into a "normal" job.

Maybe you'd find a position on somebody's founder team. Think of the experience you'd bring to the table. Or maybe you'd welcome a job where you go to work at 9 a.m., get time off for lunch, and are home with your family by 5:30 p.m—you know, a job that you don't have to think about until you get back to it the next morning. There are some appealing aspects to that, don't you think?

Maybe you'd enjoy a physical job for a while, like doing construction work or delivering packages for United Parcel Service. Those kinds of jobs can be fun to do while you regroup and figure out what your next entrepreneurial venture will be. Or, you could think about consulting or training. Heck, maybe you'll even write a book!

Many, if not most entrepreneurs, however, find it extremely difficult to get back into a "real" job. For one thing, we have certain qualities and desires that made us want to be entrepreneurs in the first place.

Remember in Chapter 1 when I talked about the factors that motivate people to become entrepreneurs? Just as a refresher, here they are:

➤ A need to achieve goals

➤ A desire to do something better or more efficiently than it has been done before

➤ A desire for power

➤ A desire for wealth

➤ A need to fulfill an inner drive

➤ A need to realize a dream

➤ A desire for notoriety

➤ A desire to make work be fun

➤ A desire to prove they can be successful on their own

Those qualities are positive because they give you the drive and desire to go outside the boundaries of traditional jobs and come up with your own definitions of what it means to work and be successful, but they can make it difficult to work for someone else.

Motivators such as the desire to make your work be fun, the desire for wealth and power, and the desire to do something better than it's been done before don't go away, even after you've started 10 companies on your own.

If you do start working for somebody else, be aware that you might not be in a position to make the business work better, even though you know you could. Some bosses are threatened by people with good ideas and experience.

Grizzly Area

It's common for entrepreneurs who try to go back to working for somebody else to end up frustrated and unhappy because they feel stifled and underutilized. If you decide to go to work for somebody else, be alert to signs that you're becoming one of those people. If you see that you are, you'd better re-evaluate your decision.

If you're lucky, you might find a position in a company where you're free, and actually encouraged, to offer suggestions and have as much input as you'd like. If you're thinking of going to work for somebody else, you might try to negotiate such a position, if you can find a boss who's willing to go along with it.

Some entrepreneurs who have gone back to working for somebody else do just fine. Others who have started and run their own businesses find they're unable to work for anyone else. Whether *you* can is purely a personal decision.

The Least You Need to Know

➤ It's extremely difficult to evaluate your experience as an entrepreneur if you don't take a step back and look at the big picture.

➤ Every aspect of starting and running a business teaches you something.

➤ If you're generally satisfied with what you've done, you should feel good about your experience as an entrepreneur.

➤ The experience and knowledge you've gained from starting a business make it a lot easier to start another one.

➤ Many entrepreneurs find it difficult to go back to work for somebody else after they've started and run their own companies.

Chapter 28

Helping Other Entrepreneurs

In This Chapter

➤ Giving back by helping other entrepreneurs.

➤ Determining whether someone's cut out for the job.

➤ Helping with a business plan.

➤ Leading the way toward raising money.

➤ Contracting your services to help start a business.

➤ Advising others as they start businesses.

Part of the fun of being a successful entrepreneur is to be able to help people who are trying to get businesses off the ground, just as you were not too long ago.

I like it when people call to ask for my advice or help. I don't think I've ever turned down a request to talk to people about what kind of business might make sense for them to open, or how they should go about raising money to fund a business, or what kind of business plan they need to have.

If you've already started and are running a business, think back to when your company was just an idea and you were filled with doubts and questions. Remember how grateful you were for the people who helped you when you were looking for advice? Or for the guy who made a phone call on your behalf and got you a meeting with that investor who wouldn't have given you the time of day otherwise?

What about the investors who looked at your business plan and told you what you needed to do to make it better? If you were smart, you listened to everything they told you and used the advice to your advantage.

I remember the people who helped me when I was first starting out. There were a few people, like Ray Pecor, the owner of the Lake Champlain Ferry Company; Frank Tornton, an IBM patent attorney; and Tom Cabot, an architect and entrepreneur, whom I could always count on to sit down and talk to me about ideas, problems, and concerns. I'll always appreciate the time those people gave me, and I can repay some of the kindness they showed me by doing the same for somebody else.

After your business is up and running, you too have the opportunity to provide help and support for just-getting-started entrepreneurs. It's a means of giving back, just like coaching Little League or sponsoring an Easter egg hunt for the kids in your community.

In this chapter, you'll take a look at some of the opportunities available for you to help people who are trying to get businesses started. As somebody who's been there, you know the difficulties associated with starting a business. You know how and where to direct somebody to get help, and you know how important it is to get a good business plan and some means of financing.

Your help can mean a whole lot to somebody who has a strong desire to start a business but isn't sure how to go about doing it. Let's look at some of the ways you can be of assistance.

Is the Person You're Helping Cut Out to Be an Entrepreneur?

Chances are, if somebody comes to you asking for your help in getting a business off the ground, he's going to have the necessary motivation and desire to be a successful entrepreneur.

Whether he's looking only for advice or looking to hire you as a consultant to help get his business started, he took the time and initiative to seek you out. He's obviously aware that starting a business requires planning and all the help you can get. That means he's going into the venture with his eyes open.

As you know, although motivation and desire are important factors when you're starting a business, being a successful entrepreneur also requires a certain degree of talent. This is what you have to evaluate when somebody asks you for help. I'm not saying you shouldn't do what you can to help somebody—just the opposite. I'm all in favor of helping out, whenever and however you can.

Say that Tom comes to you and asks for a little help. He says he's been doing a lot of yard work on the side, and now he wants to start a landscaping business. He really needs some advice, not to mention some help with his business plan, and he thought maybe you'd call a few people about lending him some money.

Now, Tom's a nice guy you've known for a long time. He's bright, and he's got a lot of energy, but he's got a few shortcomings as well. Tom happens to be completely disorganized, and he's unreliable, too. In fact, he was supposed to do some yard work for you a couple of weeks ago, and you had to call him twice before he finally showed up.

Bear Facts

When somebody asks me to help them, I always make sure right away that they've got the two most important entrepreneurial characteristics. Remember what they are? Right! Persistence and confidence.

In short, he's not the kind of guy you're going to send down to your bank with the recommendation to your banker that she lend Tom some money. After all, you're sticking out your neck for somebody by doing that. You'd actually be endorsing Tom by sending him to your bank, and your name and reputation would be associated with him.

If somebody obviously doesn't have what it takes to start and run a business, you should help him by letting him know he needs to find someone with the skills he doesn't have to work with him. You'll be doing him a favor by offering advice, but you shouldn't feel as though you have to get more involved than that.

For one thing, helping somebody get a business started can be quite time-consuming. It's not reasonable to expect that you'll be able to invest a lot of time helping everyone who comes along to get their businesses up and running. It's just not practical.

If you do think someone—Nancy, this time—who's asked you for help has what it takes to start and run a successful business, explain exactly what she must do to get prepared. Don't, however, do the work for her!

It's sort of like helping your kids with their homework. Sometimes it's tempting to grab the sheet of paper and fill in the correct answers yourself because it's quicker and less agonizing than watching them trying to figure it out. By doing that, though, you take away their chances to learn.

You should tell Nancy the processes she needs to complete as she works toward starting a business. You can guide her on her business plan, backdating charts, finding a qualified lawyer and accountant, looking for financing, and many other tasks. You can't, however, do those things for her. If Nancy wants help in deciding what kind of business to open, have her consider the following questions:

Over the Rainbow

If you suggest that the person who comes to you for help look for a partner who has the strengths he lacks, and he refuses to acknowledge his weaknesses, I'd be polite, but not go out of my way to help him. You can't help somebody who doesn't want to listen.

➤ What business am I interested in starting?

➤ How do I like to spend my time?

➤ What are the skills I have, and which do I enjoy most?

➤ Do I want to work from home or away from home?

➤ How much time do I want to spend working?

➤ Do I want a job that requires travel?

➤ Do I have any marketable interests or hobbies?

The answers to these questions will help her figure out what kind of business she should be considering.

After the basics are taken care of, you can get down to business—the business plan, that is.

Helping to Build a Better Business Plan

Many starting-out entrepreneurs are scared to death about writing a business plan. They have no idea what it should contain. It sounds intimidating. They don't know what to do with it once they have it. Well, it's your job to make them understand that writing a business plan is not that big a deal.

Get a copy of the Small Business Administration's business plan and go over it, step by step, with the first-timer you're helping. Explain why particular items are important and what investors look at most closely when they start shopping around their completed plan.

Above all, be reassuring. Writing a business plan seems like an overwhelming task if you've never done it before. You'll be doing your protégée a favor if you can convince him or her that the most important thing about writing a business plan is to get it started and get it done.

It doesn't need to be perfect; you can always work on it more later. A business plan serves the important role of turning ideas into concrete plans. Plans seem more real when they're on paper than when they're floating around in your head.

A business plan is really the starting point for a business, so you should insist that the person you're helping gets started with it as quickly as possible. The SBA offers an online tutorial for writing a business plan that might be helpful.

The SBA advises that before starting to write a business plan, you should answer the following questions:

Over the Rainbow

You can pull a copy of the SBA business plan right off the SBA's Web site at www.sba.gov, or copy the SBA plan in this book. Review Chapter 12, "The All-Important Business Plan," for more information about the SBA.

➤ What services or products will I sell?

➤ Is my idea practical, and will it fill a need?

➤ What is my competition?

➤ What is my business's advantage over existing firms?

➤ Can I deliver a better quality service?

➤ Can I create a demand for my business?

➤ What skills and experience do I bring to the business?

➤ What will be my legal structure?

➤ How will my company's business records be maintained?

➤ What insurance coverage will be needed?

➤ What equipment or supplies will I need?

➤ How will I compensate myself?

➤ What are my resources?

➤ What financing will I need?

➤ Where will my business be located?

➤ What will I name my business?

Once the person starting the business has answered all the questions, he or she can use the information as a basis for the business plan. If someone comes to you with a plan already in place, you can review it and offer suggestions. It will be easy for you to see the plan's strengths and weaknesses.

Helping to Raise Capital

Another way you can help somebody who wants to start a business is by advising her on, or assisting her with, raising capital.

This doesn't mean you have to give money to everyone who comes along, although becoming an investor is an option. Just a word of caution if you do invest: You never know how the company you're supporting will turn out.

I gave a young guy $5,000 to get started in a company that makes lawn mowers. I had serious doubts about the venture, but I liked the guy and wanted to help him. He got the business started a couple of years ago and is still going with it. He's not rich yet, but his company is growing, and he's doing a good job with it.

Grizzly Area

After your business becomes successful, be prepared for many requests for help—and money. If you believe in what somebody's doing and you want to help them by investing some start-up money, by all means, go ahead. But don't feel pressured to do so. You can't get too involved with everyone else's businesses and still do a good job running your own.

On the other hand, I invested $100,000 in the business of one of the people who was on the board of directors when I was at Vermont Teddy Bear. I had confidence in that business and felt pretty good about the investment. The company went bankrupt a short time ago.

Go figure.

If you're not going to be investing money, maybe you can steer her to somebody you know who's looking to invest in a business or put in a word to your banker that the person you're helping will be stopping by.

You can also advise her on how to talk to potential investors, how to act, what materials to take along when you go to talk to somebody, and so forth.

Helping to Start Up a Business

If you're running your own business, you don't want to get so involved with helping everybody who comes along that you don't have time to do your own work, spend time with your family, and take care of other priorities. There just aren't enough hours in a day.

Unless there's a special reason why you want to help, you probably won't get involved with the actual mechanics of starting up a business. Do feel free to advise and steer the person you're helping toward others who might be in a position to help.

If you're no longer actively involved in the day-to-day operations of running a business, then you might be looking for another kind of opportunity. Many people starting or building their own companies want to hire entrepreneurs with proven track records to help them. I was hired not too long ago by American Performance Products, manufacturers of LovFeet, a high-tech shoe insert. The deal is that I come on board for a specified amount of time and help get the company on track and operating efficiently. The job involves setting up systems, planning marketing strategies, and all the other tasks involved with growing a company and getting it ready to take public.

Bear Facts

It wasn't long after I let a couple of headhunters know I'd be willing to consider some consulting jobs that I got calls about entrepreneurs looking for help. There's definitely a market out there for this kind of work.

Even if you're being paid to help somebody start up a business, don't overlook opportunities to help people who are just looking for advice and support. Sometimes an encouraging word means a lot to someone who's struggling to get a business going.

Entrepreneurism Is on the Rise

Entrepreneurship is a booming business, no doubt about it. There are several reasons for the increasing number of people who are starting out on their own, instead of going the route of working for someone else.

Mistrust of the corporate way is certainly a big reason for this recent surge of entrepreneurism. People who have been laid off, downsized, or otherwise terminated from the companies they expected to retire from are understandably skeptical of corporate life. Instead of risking a repeat of what's happened to them, many of these folks decide to start their own businesses. This option allows them to have more control over their lives. It's said that corporate dropouts are largely responsible for the franchise boom of the past decade or so.

The mood of the United States is also a contributing factor for the increasing popularity of being an entrepreneur. Surveys have showed that entrepreneurs are admired more than corporate big shots. I think that starting and growing your own business captures the collective imaginations of many people. They admire those who are willing to take risks to achieve their goals and realize their dreams.

Bear Facts

The number of sole proprietorships owned by women is growing 50% faster than the total number of such businesses. Women make great entrepreneurs; they've had the best experience managing because they've been managing one thing or another nearly all their lives.

Flexibility is another reason why entrepreneurship is on the rise. Owning your own business allows you to work unsupervised, to be independent, and to make your own decisions. Being an entrepreneur means that nobody can tell you you'll have to pick up your family and move three states west to keep your job. With some limitations, you can choose wherever you want to live when you have your own business. A high proportion of entrepreneurs who graduated from Harvard Business School, for example, live in the mountain states, the Southwest, or the West Coast. Surveys of this group revealed that they chose to move to these places and start their businesses there.

Women are particularly attracted to entrepreneurship, which allows flexibility with work schedules. The companies women are starting tend to be smaller than those owned by men, and many women choose to work part-time. But having their own businesses provides great opportunities for women who want fulfilling, rewarding careers.

With so many people catching the entrepreneurial spirit, it's no wonder I get frequent phone calls from friends and acquaintances, asking for advice on starting up a new business or about businesses they already have. I've spoken to civic groups, community groups, and business classes at universities. With so many people interested in becoming entrepreneurs, there are many opportunities to help.

I offer advice whenever I can. I recommend books, as I've done throughout these chapters. I also recommend other sources of help. Entrepreneurs helping entrepreneurs has become more than just one person sitting down with another and looking at a business plan. It's become an organized effort across the country.

Bear Facts

In addition to the community and university groups that have started up to help entrepreneurs, some entrepreneurs have made businesses of assisting others with business startups.

Towns, universities, states, and businesses have come up with dozens of ways to help entrepreneurs get started. One town in Connecticut designated an old manufacturing building as a startup place for young companies. People just starting out can get cheap space and support services for their businesses.

An innovative new program has been set up to help youth from low-income housing communities learn to start and run businesses. The programs, which started in Los Angeles and Philadelphia, are funded through grants from the U.S. Department of Housing and Urban Development. Participants get training, low-interest loans, and mentors as part of the program. They're coached on how to market themselves, write a business plan, manage finances, and everything else they need to know to get a business started. It's too early to tell how the program will work, but it's another example of the support that's become available for entrepreneurial hopefuls.

Many universities are offering support for entrepreneurs, usually through their business departments. They review business plans, help get systems set up, and provide other services. Universities are teaching entrepreneurism, too. Many schools now have centers for entrepreneurial studies, with full-time faculty members teaching the classes.

Bear Facts

A fun way to get to know and help out beginning entrepreneurs is to speak in classes, civic groups, and so forth. I've had a great time guest lecturing at Columbia University, the Dartmouth Business School, the State University of New York at Plattsburg, and the Florida Institute of Technology.

Roundtable groups have cropped up all over the country, giving entrepreneurs forums for discussing problems and opportunities. There's tons of support for entrepreneurs now that wasn't there a decade ago. You can help people tremendously just by letting them know what kind of support and services are available.

As you've seen in this chapter, there are many ways you can help other entrepreneurs. Regardless of the scope of your involvement, you can be encouraging and supportive of people who are just getting started.

The Least You Need to Know

➤ Helping other entrepreneurs is enjoyable payback for the assistance you received when you were just getting started.

➤ Be encouraging, but don't waste a lot of time—either yours or his—working with someone who is obviously not cut out to own and run a business.

➤ It's great to guide someone through the steps of getting a business started, but don't do the work for her.

➤ Helping out with the business plan is a great way to help a beginning entrepreneur.

➤ An option for entrepreneurs with proven track records is to work as a consultant, helping someone who's starting a business.

➤ Giving advice is fun, and it's much appreciated by other entrepreneurs.

Chapter 29

Becoming an Independent Investor

In This Chapter

➤ Thinking about doing something else.

➤ Being an independent investor.

➤ Looking for investment opportunities.

➤ Knowing which ones to take.

➤ Entrepreneurial opportunities for investors.

Picture this. You've started up and are running your fourth company. You've done pretty well with all of them, although some, of course, have been more successful than others.

The company you're with now, which manufactures, say, shoe inserts, has done particularly well. In fact, you never dreamed you would be as financially sound as you are now. You've taken care of the important financial matters. Your kids have enough money to go to college, and you're in the kind of house you wanted for a long time. You've got enough money designated for some nice vacations, to pay the orthodontist, maybe think about that place at the beach. And you still have money left over.

Nice image, isn't it? Well, keep it in the front of your head, and remember that's what you're working for. Keep your dream in front of you, and you'll get there eventually.

The benefit of getting to this point is that it gives you a lot of options. You can choose what you want to do. If starting companies is what you like to do best, you can keep doing it until you run out of types of companies to start. When you've got a proven track record of being highly successful, it's not hard to find investors for your ventures. You can start up as many companies as you'd like, run them for a while, and then get out to do something else that interests you.

Or you can take some time off. Maybe you've been starting up businesses for 25 years now, and you've got it down to a science. Maybe it's not quite as much fun as it used to be, and you're a little tired of it. Well, then I say, if your financial and personal situations allow it, take some time off.

Take a couple of months off and do that trip to Australia you've always dreamed about. Or stay at home for six months and work on the book you started three years ago, but never wrote past Chapter 3. Drive across the country and check out all the national parks. Take that class on building Windsor chairs. Just do *something* you've been putting off for years because you couldn't find the time.

If time off doesn't appeal to you (it does make some people incredibly nervous, you know), you could think about doing something completely different. You could get some teaching certification credits at a nearby college and land a job teaching first graders how to read and write. You could get into real estate development or deliver flowers for your daughter's expanding florist business. There are hundreds of things you could do, and you're lucky enough to have the means to choose some of them. It's a great position to be in.

Another option, and it's the one you're going to spend this chapter exploring, is to become an independent investor. Let's have a look at what that means and if it might be something that would appeal to you.

Moving Beyond the Day-to-Day Operations of Running a Company

Entrepreneurs who have started and are successfully running their own businesses sometimes ask me how they'll know when it's time to do something else. I always tell them the same thing: You'll know when it's time because the thought will be in your brain, and you won't be able to get it out. You'll have frequent thoughts, fantasies almost, about changing your focus—about doing something new. Even if you try to ignore it, thinking you should be satisfied with your current venture, the thought of doing something new will keep sneaking back into your head.

Bear Facts

I think that to most entrepreneurs, *running* a company just doesn't have the same sizzle as *starting* a company does.

There are excellent reasons why this desire for change happens. My best theory is that for most entrepreneurs, starting the business is the most fun. It's starting a business from nothing, or starting any kind of new venture, that's exciting and challenging. Running a business is good, but it's not the same as starting it.

When you're running a business, you're a management type, a CEO or a president. It still is challenging, and you're always learning new things, but it just doesn't hold the appeal that starting a business does.

Entrepreneurs are sometimes reluctant to move from a comfortable running-a-company position into another startup situation. This reluctance can be caused by family considerations ("You're going to do WHAT?"), financial considerations, or whatever.

They try hard to be happy and contented with the business they've got, and some do very well at that. Many people start businesses and stay with them until they retire. Others, though, can't get past the lure of trying something new, whether it be starting a new company or doing something completely different.

When you find you're in a position where you have extra money, don't just stick it in an account someplace and forget about it. Plan for it. Think about what you want to do.

Maybe you know exactly what it is you want to do, or maybe you have to start looking around for something. Let's see … what to do?

Grizzly Area

A reasonable ratio of safe money to speculative money is 80:20. That means 80% of your money should be in safe investments. The other 20% is the fun stuff. That's the money you should be able to invest in risky enterprises, with the chance of making it big or losing it. Don't, however, mess around with more than 20%, especially if you have a family who depends on you financially. Speculation can be tempting, but it's also risky.

The Attraction of Being an Independent Investor

Some entrepreneurs find they're attracted to the idea of being an *independent investor*, someone who puts money into a company with the intention of making back more money than he or she put in.

Say you're starting a bagel shop. Everybody in town loves bagels, and you're convinced you're going to have the best shop in town. If I agree with you, and I think there's something special about your bagels and the shop you're opening up, I might agree to invest $40,000 or $50,000 in your company.

Now, even though I'm a pretty nice guy, I'm going to want something back for that investment. Maybe I'll want to be involved with your business somehow, especially if I really love bagels. More than likely, though, I'll just want a big return on my money. I'll be pushing you like crazy to make your shop profitable, so I can start taking a cut of those profits.

Being an independent investor is a pretty powerful role. You've got the ability to help people realize their dreams, and that definitely carries power with it. If you're an independent investor, people will court you. They'll treat you like you're somebody special because you've got the means to help them get what they want. It's sort of like when you wanted something real bad from your parents when you were a kid. You stayed on your best behavior for days—maybe weeks—hoping they would be impressed enough to give you what you'd been asking for.

If you're the independent investor, you've got the same power to make or break the dream as your parents did when you were a kid. Lots of people like that feeling. They like being able to do something that gives people a chance to move ahead, especially when they anticipate getting something back in return.

Being an independent investor also allows you to get involved with companies that appeal to you. You can ask to be named to the board of directors or an advisory board, if you want to.

Over the Rainbow

Boards, regardless of what kind, are great places to meet people. If you're named to a board, be sure you take advantages of the networking opportunities that present themselves.

You can, with your investments, support companies you believe in or are particularly interested in. Nobody says you can put money only into high-tech companies that seem poised on the cutting edge. If you believe in a company that's making 100% cotton, environmentally friendly, unbleached, hand-sewn clothing, then go ahead and invest in it. It's your money. And who knows? It could be a huge hit.

If you're not particularly interested in the company in which you're investing, but you think it will pay off big for you down the road, then invest your money and watch it work for you. You're not doing a thing except letting your money work.

Bear Facts

I always think that an investor who puts money into a company only to get more money out of it is like a baseball club owner who doesn't know anything about the game, but sees the team as a big moneymaker. Yankees owner George Steinbrenner is close to hero status in my eyes because he doesn't do that. George makes important decisions for the Yankees that are based on baseball, not the bottom line. There's nothing wrong with investing for the sake of investing, but sometimes it's nice to get involved.

These reasons for investing appeal to many people. They're some of the reasons people (maybe you) become independent investors.

Finding Investment Opportunities

That heading is rather misleading because when you're an independent investor, you don't need to find investment opportunities. Believe me, they'll find you.

If you're successful and people know you have money, you get on somebody's list. When you're on the list, you don't have to look for companies to invest in or people to whom you can give your money. If you're on the list, you can expect to get calls and visits from people who would like to talk you into parting with some of your cash.

You'll get calls from stockbrokers, wanting you to buy whatever stock they're selling. You'll get calls from business owners, looking for money to start up or expand their companies. You'll get calls from more people than you can imagine.

What you need to understand is that you can't take care of everybody who comes along. If you see an investment opportunity you like, go ahead and invest, but don't think you have to give money to everybody who asks.

Your responsibility is to your family. You can't bail out every friend who gets in a bind or that long-lost cousin who got back in touch with you last year after a 20-year hiatus.

Where to Look for Opportunities

If by some chance you're not swamped with requests and actually find yourself looking for investment opportunities, I don't think you'll have a difficult time. Put the word out to other investors and have them refer promising entrepreneurs to you. Investors do that all the time.

Or you could circulate your name at nearby universities, which are usually ripe with smart, eager, poor entrepreneurs, who have terrific ideas but no money to set them in motion.

Get involved with industry groups, investment groups, or entrepreneur groups. Believe me, if you have money to invest, finding places to invest won't be a problem.

Over the Rainbow

If it's high-tech, computer-related companies you're looking for, colleges are a great place to search. It's estimated that one-third of all high-tech companies are started by entrepreneurs in their 20s.

Knowing Which Opportunities to Take

Locating opportunities and knowing which ones to take advantage of are two completely different matters. You'll find investment opportunities, no doubt about it—probably lots and lots of opportunities. Getting a feeling for what they're about, however, and judging whether they're good opportunities, is more difficult.

Just because you've started and run a company, doesn't mean you're a smart investor. If you're unsure about what kinds of companies to back, look at what other successful investors are doing. What companies are getting the money? What are the growth and glamour industries attracting a lot of attention?

Watch stock prices, and keep an eye on which ones are going through the roof. Do you know of any similar companies that are looking for some funding?

Be sure to look carefully at the business plan of each company that asks you to invest. Is it well thought out and organized? Are the company goals ambitious? What are the profit projections?

Don't get pressured into investing in a company you don't like or don't feel good about. You won't be happy with it, and even if it does well, it won't be a satisfying experience. Plenty of starting companies out there could benefit greatly from your investment, and you'll benefit, you hope, from the success of the businesses you invest in.

Over the Rainbow

When you're looking at someone else's business plan, remember the most important elements of your own. That gives you an idea of which areas you should pay the most attention to.

Investing Is a Different Kind of Entrepreneuring

Please don't let anyone tell you that investors aren't entrepreneurs. Many people are making money by investing in business opportunities. In fact, plenty of people are making money by telling entrepreneurs how to find investors. There are as many entrepreneurial opportunities as your mind allows you to come up with.

Let's take a look at a few of the different kinds of investor entrepreneurs and see how they're making money.

Venture Capitalists

The term *venture capitalist* can be a fancy name for an investor or refer to one of the many privately owned firms that invest millions of dollars each year in small businesses that are starting up or expanding.

Venture capitalists expect big returns on their investments, and they expect them quickly. I mentioned earlier that a tenfold increase in a year is not an unheard-of expectation from a venture capitalist.

The money in a venture capitalist firm can come from the firm's founders. Often, though, it trickles in from elsewhere, including cash-rich countries, companies, and individuals. This kind of funding usually occurs when someone wants to invest in entrepreneurial ventures but doesn't know how to go about it, or when someone wants to invest anonymously.

Venture capitalists usually have tight investment objectives. They look for big, rapid growth. Most insist on getting involved with the businesses they invest in. Many offer essential services to startups and continue to be involved as the company grows. If that's the case, and your company is funded in its startup, consider yourself fortunate. The same firm is likely to fund your expansions down the road.

Investment Groups

These groups of cash-rich people or companies usually have more money than they care to pay taxes on, and are looking to invest in companies so they can take advantage of some tax breaks. If the companies in which they invest are successful, the investor wins twice—through tax breaks and profits from the business.

Private Sources

Lots of individuals, wealthy families, consortiums, and so forth look for good business opportunities to invest in, with the hope of increasing their investment. These sources normally gather information about promising startups and contact the founders, instead of having hopeful entrepreneurs contact them.

Small Business Investment Companies (SBIC)

There are about 300 SBICs in the United States, which have invested upward of $13 billion in about 80,000 businesses since they were authorized by Congress in 1958. These privately owned groups are funded by individual investors and by their owners.

All SBICs have to be licensed by the Small Business Administration, and each owner of an SBIC has to put up at least $5 million of his own capital before he's approved. Some SBICs target special groups, usually minority firms.

Although SBICs are prohibited from having controlling interests in the companies they fund, they can participate in ownership investments. Some companies funded by SBICs that have made it big include America Online Inc., Federal Express Corp., Outback Steakhouse Inc., and Apple Computer. Any of those names sound familiar?

These are a few of the many investment opportunities available to entrepreneurs. If the idea of being an independent investor is appealing to you, maybe you want to check out the possibility more thoroughly.

You probably know some investors from when you were looking for money for your own

Over the Rainbow

You can get a list of all the SBICs in the United States from the Small Business Administration's Web site at www.sbaonline.sba.gov, or write to Associate Administrator for Investment, U.S. Small Business Administration, Washington, D.C. 20416.

company. There's nothing wrong with calling and asking if you can meet for a few minutes to ask for some advice. Don't call just the investors who gave you money, either. Go back to everyone you had talked to, and get all the information you can.

The Least You Need to Know

➤ There comes a time when most entrepreneurs start thinking about doing something other than running their business.

➤ If you've been successful with your business, chances are you're in a financial position that affords you some options you wouldn't otherwise have.

➤ Being an independent investor is a powerful position because you have the opportunity to help people make their dreams come true.

➤ Investment opportunities aren't hard to find; in fact, they'll find you.

➤ Just because you're a good entrepreneur doesn't necessarily mean you'll be a good investor.

➤ There are many opportunities for entrepreneurs who want to get into investing.

JOHN'S A GREAT OWNER!

Chapter 30

Building a Reputation

In This Chapter

➤ Molding your reputation to what you want it to be.

➤ Keeping reputations intact.

➤ Getting involved with the community.

➤ Choosing a means of giving back.

➤ Remembering what's most important.

Somebody once said that a good reputation is more valuable than money. I think, when you're talking about entrepreneurs, that a good reputation *is* money. Your reputation, both personal and professional, can have a big effect on your business—and your bottom line.

When it's all said and done, I believe that people prefer to do business with somebody they can trust, like, and admire. We're sometimes forced to buy from or work with people we don't like or aren't sure we can trust. I don't like that feeling, and I don't think most other people do, either.

I remember a husband and wife who owned a restaurant. The husband was the chef and the food was great, but their during-business-hours fights were legendary. Some people stayed away because of them, but like I said, the food was really good, so they managed to do a pretty good business. The situation really got out of hand, however, when the husband was shot to death in his home. The wife and their son were the only other people in the house when it happened. The wife, who claimed her husband had shot himself (in the back) was accused, but later acquitted. She tried to re-open the restaurant (with a new chef, obviously), but her business was ruined, along with her reputation. She sold the restaurant soon after.

We've all read about financial advisors who bilked clients out of thousands and thousands of dollars, doctors who have sexually abused patients, lawyers who outrageously overcharge their clients, and the list goes on and on. I understand that a lot of these situations are prompted by underlying problems, such as addictions or psychological disorders. Still, I believe that if people thought about how easy it is to damage or destroy a reputation before they acted, they'd be less likely to do some of these things.

Hey, I'm not saying I'm perfect or anything like that. Don't get me wrong. But when you're an entrepreneur, you have only your name, and the name of your company, on which to build a business. You don't have the Microsoft or Westinghouse or Chrysler name behind you, holding you up if you go a little astray. It's just your name and your company's name. It's vitally important to recognize that and do everything you can to protect those names and the reputations that accompany them.

Building the Kind of Reputation You Want

People and companies have different goals, strive for different achievements, and want to be known for different reasons. Henry Ford wanted to make it possible for everyone to own a car. He came close to that goal, developing the moving assembly-line system of manufacture and selling his Model-T for $500 in 1913 (during the depression of 1920–21, Ford lowered the price to $280).

He also felt it was important for his employees to have good buying power, and he was willing to put his money behind his ideals. Ford shared his tremendous profits with employees by paying an unheard of $5-a-day minimum wage. Ford established his reputation and his company's reputation on these ideals, and he's still remembered for them more than half a century after his death.

Bear Facts

Hardly anybody's reputation is impeccable, and Henry Ford was no exception. He did some pretty goofy things, including publishing an anti-Semitic newspaper in the 1930s. This damaged his reputation at the time, but seems to have pretty much faded away.

Sam Walton, the founder of Wal-Mart stores, built his reputation around his humble lifestyle and down-home management approach, despite his great wealth. Walton, who used to visit each of his stores at least once a year, meeting with employees, giving sales tips, and leading Wal-Mart cheers, lived in a modest home in Bentonville,

Arkansas until he died in 1992. His name was on the mailbox outside his home, and his phone number was listed in the local directory. He drove an old pickup, often with a couple of dogs accompanying him. Walton ate in local restaurants and went to the local barber for his haircuts. His lasting reputation is that of a common man who built an empire.

Ben and Jerry, the ice cream guys, work hard, and have succeeded at creating for their company a reputation of being socially responsible and environmentally aware.

I worked hard to build The Vermont Teddy Bear Company into a place that was friendly, fun to be around, and family oriented. Yeah, it was warm and fuzzy, but come on. We were making teddy bears!

Take a minute to think about the people you admire and respect. What are their reputations? If they're businesspeople, what are the reputations of their businesses?

You can mold an image for your company through public relations, advertising, and marketing, but if you don't build up a reputation that supports the image, it falls apart.

For instance, a company could use skillful public relations to create an image for itself as being committed to human rights, equal opportunity employment, and so forth. But if the company's reputation is that it discriminates regularly against minorities and hires kids to work in sweatshops overseas, it can kiss its purchased image goodbye.

Image is smoke and mirrors. Reputation is the real thing. It's fairly easy to create an image. It's harder to build a reputation and even harder to rebuild it, should it become damaged.

Grizzly Area

It's curious that celebrities can do some despicable things that badly damage their reputations, but still maintain the public's admiration. I don't think non-celebs could get away with that.

Reputations Are Fragile

It takes considerable work to build a good reputation, but it takes considerably less work to damage it. Think about it. A respected businessman gets arrested for soliciting an undercover cop pretending to be a prostitute. Oops! There goes his reputation. Yeah, maybe he can rebuild it. Maybe.

Athletes have a tradition of tarnishing or wrecking their reputations:

> Albert Belle, the Baltimore Oriole's outfielder, is a darned good hitter, but his reputation stinks. He refuses to sign autographs, he trashes the clubhouse, and he gained notoriety for harassing some kids who came to his house for trick-or-treating at Halloween.

Mike Tyson, well … what can I say about Mike Tyson? Here's a guy who went from being the undisputed heavyweight boxing champion of the world to a convicted rapist who, after he got out of jail, bit off part of Evander Holyfield's ear. Geez!

Companies and organizations, too, can suffer serious damage to their reputations. The International Olympic Committee is struggling to salvage what's left of its reputation. IOC members were found to have betrayed the Olympic spirit in a big way by accepting all kinds of gifts—cash, college educations for their kids, freebies at posh hotels—from the cities vying for the honor of hosting the Olympic games.

In addition to damaging the reputation of the committee, the scandal has threatened to affect corporate sponsorship of the 2002 Winter Olympics in Salt Lake City. US West, a regional telephone giant, is withholding millions of dollars in sponsorship payments until the scandal is resolved.

This is a classic example of how a damaged reputation can lead to a damaged bottom line. Another example is Texaco; executives there suffered a blow to their reputations after tapes were released on which they were heard using ugly, racist language. The disclosure resulted in a Jesse Jackson–endorsed boycott against the company.

Texaco also has a history of discriminating against qualified blacks and women by passing over them for promotions. In addition to economic implications of a boycott, Texaco had to spend big bucks trying to undo the damage done to its reputation.

Same with Nestle Foods, which was the target of a boycott in the 1970s when it sold infant formula to poor women in underdeveloped nations. It was considered a status symbol in those countries to feed babies infant formula instead of breast feeding, but poor women diluted the formula (often with unsanitary water) to make it last longer, and their babies suffered. The effect of that boycott, supported by many well-educated, affluent people in this country, affected Nestle's bottom line for years.

Public relations people say that companies don't do enough to prevent damage to their reputations. If more was done to prevent damage, experts say, companies would spend less time trying to mend and rebuild their reputations.

Bear Facts

Just when you think you've heard it all: Some companies are instituting "reputation management processes," designed to help them get a handle on and control their reputations.

I think we all know what flies and what doesn't when you're dealing with people. You don't lie. You don't steal. You don't do something that hurts someone. You know, we didn't have many rules at The Vermont Teddy Bear Company, but the ones we did have included just those things.

It's not hard. I mean, those are the rules nearly every parent teaches his or her kids. They are some of the first lessons we learn in school, along with the ABCs and how to count to 10.

Bear Facts

As a former professional Boy Scout (I was a Scout leader from 1974 until 1997), I developed a deep and abiding respect for the Boy Scout laws. Just in case you never got into scouting, a Scout is trustworthy, loyal, helpful, friendly, courteous, kind, obedient, thrifty, brave, clean, and reverent. Words to live by!

You build a reputation, either personal or professional, by getting involved and doing things right. You shouldn't take shortcuts or mislead your customers. If you do things right, stand by your product, and be honest with your employees, customers, suppliers, and everybody else, you'll build and maintain a fine reputation.

Sure, you'll make mistakes. But a person with a good reputation who makes mistakes and then admits to making them, is nearly always forgiven, and his reputation remains intact.

Being Involved in Your Community

An important component to building a good reputation is being involved in your community. This lets people know who you are and what you and your company are about. There are many ways to get involved in your community. You can join clubs and organizations, coach Little League, sit on the school board or town council, join an environmental group, or get on the committee to restore the town green.

Each of these things might be equally important, but remember that you can't do them all. There's a danger of spreading yourself too thin, which many eager-to-serve entrepreneurs fall into.

Politics

Politics is sort of a dirty word these days, disdained by many as we're subjected to one political scandal after another. Still, political involvement is important to people who are in business. The political climate can greatly affect how you do business and how your business finances are affected.

Over the Rainbow

People who serve on local government groups, such as a town council or township board, have the advantage of knowing everything that's going on. And local government sometimes wields significant power. You're involved in all kinds of important issues, including taxes, zoning matters, and so forth. If you're interested in politics and want the advantages of getting information early on, serving on a local board might be a good option to consider.

It's not enough to help out with somebody's campaign or lend your name to a popular cause. You need to get to know what's going on and be willing to fight for what's most favorable to your community's entrepreneurial climate. This could take some time. You might have to serve on a committee or take a seat on your town council or county advisory board.

Local politics can be a lot of fun. Remember, if you don't get involved, somebody whose political views are 180 degrees away from yours just might.

Environmental Groups

There's no shortage of environmental groups, if you feel that's your calling. Most communities have groups committed to preserving open space, wetlands, a local biking trail, and so forth. There also are watchdog groups, many of which monitor businesses to make sure they're in compliance with environmental regulations.

There are hundreds of local, state, regional, and national groups, all dedicated to preserving or restoring the environment. If you're interested, you can jump in at any level, although local is probably the easiest. Many communities hold annual environmental happenings, where people turn out to clean up a creek, de-litter a roadway, or do other environmentally responsible work.

Grizzly Area

You can serve on every environmental group you can find, and pick up litter along the highway every Saturday morning. But if your business doesn't set a good environmental example, your words and actions won't mean a thing. You've got to put your money where your mouth is.

Clubs and Organizations

There are dozens of clubs and organizations in any given community. Some are special interest groups, like a biking or investment club. Others are community service groups, such as the Lion's or Kiwanis clubs.

These kinds of clubs and organizations are great places to meet people and give you an opportunity to get involved and help your community.

Businesses can sometimes work as partners with community groups to sponsor events or projects or contribute to a community-related cause.

Religious Organizations

Religion is such as personal matter, I hesitate to mention it here. My personal opinion is that a solid faith, regardless of what religion it's based on, gives you a useful foundation. That faith could be based on Taoism, Catholicism, Judaism, Hinduism, or whatever. Getting involved with a religious group tends to make you more multi-dimensional and gives you a set of values to follow.

I don't think anyone would say you've got to worship formally on a regular basis and do 20 hours of religious duty work a month to be a good person. But again, getting involved in religious activities is a good way to meet people with whom you have something in common. If it gives you a foundation that makes your life run a little more smoothly, so much the better.

Activities for Kids

This category certainly gets my personal vote for community involvement. I know I've gone on and on about coaching Little League in this book, but that's only because it's so important to me. I think that getting involved with kids and their activities is one of the best ways to contribute and give something back to your community.

It's the kids who will inherit our communities, and the work we've done with those communities. By nurturing kids and their values, we're really buying insurance for ourselves that our communities and our work will continue. By showing kids what's important to us and getting them to buy into why it's important, we can pretty much ensure that they'll carry on the work we've started.

Plus that, being around kids is so much fun. Whether you coach Little League, lead a Boy Scout or Girl Scout troop, sponsor an Easter egg hunt, direct a community children's play, or help out with the annual festival in the park, you'll get as much out of the time you spend doing it as the kids will.

Working with kids is the route I choose for most of my community work. I get involved in a lot of other ways, too, because I enjoy being in my community and getting to know people and what's going on. Working with the kids is my main commitment, though, and it's something I've thoroughly enjoyed over the years.

Over the Rainbow

A side benefit of working with the kids in your community is that you come in contact with their parents. Working with a big group of kids means you get to know a lot of people you might not meet otherwise.

Preserving Your Reputation Where It Counts the Most

When you own a business, you're accountable to a lot of people. Think about it for a minute. You're accountable to your shareholders, your board of directors, your management team, your customers, your employees, and yourself.

At times, you're accountable to your lawyer, your accountant, and your insurance agent. You're accountable to your customers, your suppliers, and the guy who owns the restaurant where you have standing reservations for Friday evenings at 7.

You answer to a lot of people. You're responsible for a lot of people. You've got to do things right because you've got your reputation to think about. You've worked hard to build up a reputation as a person who's fair, honest, and hard-working, and you're not about to let anything screw it up.

After you've been accountable to and responsible for all those people, however, there's a few more to think about. It's time to go home and be accountable to those who matter the most. Although your character is of the utmost importance on the job, your best example of character and behavior should be set at home.

When you've handled all the transactions, returned all the calls, answered all the e-mails, checked the orders, gone over the financial statements, pacified the shareholders, confided with the board of directors, pumped up the employees, and turned off the lights to your office, there's another life waiting for you.

Your family and friends are the people with whom you should be most watchful of your reputation, for it is these people to whom you're most accountable. No matter what definition you give to family, it's the most important group of people you'll ever have—more important than investors, shareholders, directors, big businesspeople, or high-level politicians. If your family needs you, you should be there.

Being an entrepreneur is an amazing adventure. Starting businesses, dealing with investors, conspiring with your founders team—it's often a wild ride. It's fun, exciting, and easy to get caught up in.

Entrepreneurs are dreamers, and they chase their dreams, determined to make them happen. Everybody needs dreams, and I say the bigger they are, the better. Just remember that dreaming is more fun when there are people around to do it with.

If you're going to be an entrepreneur, be the best damned one you can. Live your dreams to the fullest, and don't be afraid to fail. Falling down is no big deal, as long as you can get up again.

Life is too short to set your dreams aside, planning to get back to them later. Remember that life isn't nearly as serious as we tend to make it, and that when it's all said and done, only a few things are truly important.

Do the best you can, remember who helped you get to where you are, put your family first, stay healthy, and have fun.

The Least You Need to Know

➤ We all have the opportunity to make our reputations what we want them to be.

➤ Once your reputation is damaged or ruined, it's a difficult task to restore it.

➤ Community involvement is a good way to build a reputation and to let others know what you're all about.

➤ There are dozens of opportunities to give back to your community; just don't try to do all of them.

➤ At the end of the day, only a few things are truly important; never forget what they are.

Additional Resources

➤ *101 Media and Marketing Tips for the Sole Proprietor*, by Nanette Miner

➤ *1001 Advertising Tips*, by Luc Dupont

➤ *The 22 Immutable Laws of Marketing; Violate Them at Your Own Risk*, by Al Ries and Jack Trout

➤ *Achieving Planned Innovation: A Proven System for Creating Successful New Products and Services*, by Frank R. Bacon, Jr. and Thomas W. Butler, Jr.

➤ *Advertising on the Internet*, by Robbin Zeff and Brad Aronson

➤ *Advertising on the Internet: How to Get Your Message Across on the World Wide Web*, by Neil Barrett

➤ *Advertising, Promotion, and Supplemental Aspects of Integrated Marketing Communications*, by Terrence A. Shimp

➤ *The Arthur Andersen Guide to Talking With Your Customers: What They Will Tell You About Your Business*, by Michael J. Wing and Arthur Andersen, LLP

➤ *Basic Marketing Research*, by Gilbert A. Churchill

➤ *Basics You Should Know Before Starting Your Own Business*, by Mel Solomon

➤ *The Complete Idiot's Guide to Starting Your Own Business*, by Ed Paulson

➤ *The Entrepreneur's Handbook: A Complete Guide for Starting, Owning & Running Your Own Business*, by Lew Gaiter

➤ *The Harvard Entrepreneurs Club Guide to Starting Your Own Business*, by Ponam Sharma and Michael Bloomberg

➤ *How Teddy Bears are Made: A Visit to The Vermont Teddy Bear Factory*, by Ann Morris

➤ *The Idea Guide: The Step-by-Step Guide for Planning and Starting Your Own Business*, by David Ceolin

- *The Internet Marketing Plan: a Practical Handbook for Creating, Implementing and Assessing Your Online Presence*, by Kim M. Bayne

- *The Legal Guide for Starting and Running a Small Business*, by Fred S. Steingold, Mary Randolph, and Ralph E. Warner

- *Radical Marketing: From Harvard to Harley, Lessons from Ten That Broke the Rules and Made It Big*, by Glenn Rifkin

- *The Small Business Handbook: A Comprehensive Guide to Starting and Running Your Own Business*, by Irving Burstiner

- *Starting Over: How to Change Careers or Start Your Own Business*, by Stephen M. Pollan and Mark Levine

- *Starting Up: Do You Have What It Takes to Make It in Your Own Business*, by David E. Rye and Craig R. Hickman

- *What No One Ever Tells You About Starting Your Own Business: Real Life Start-Up Advice from 101 Successful Entrepreneurs*, by Jan Norman

- *Why People Buy*, by John O'Shaughnessy

Glossary

Backdating   A system that allows you to set short- and long-term goals by starting at the goal and working in reverse to meet those goals at particular times.

Big Five accounting firms   The group of major, well-known, and highly regarded accounting firms that includes PricewaterhouseCoopers, Andersen Worldwide, KPMG International, Ernst & Young International, and Deloitte Touche Tohmatsu International.

Board of directors   The group of people appointed to help run your business and improve the quality of your company's stock. The board sets the overall company policy and makes sure management follows those policies and meets its responsibilities.

Business plan   A detailed description of your business and your plans for running it. A business plan is a guide to you, your founders team, managers, and employees for how you want your company to progress and grow, and it also serves as a sales document when you're trying to attract funding for your business.

Collateral   Something of value you use to guarantee that you'll repay a loan. It's the lender's insurance against you defaulting on the loan.

Commitment   An obligation you accept to do something that will be of benefit. You can make a commitment to yourself, your business, your family, your community, and your fellow man.

Confidence   The second most important quality of a successful entrepreneur, confidence allows you to be comfortable with making decisions.

Conscience   The little voice that tells you about the truth, treating people with respect, and all those other ethical issues.

Corporation   A legal structure that makes a company separate from the person or people who own it and limits their liability. The business is registered in the name of the corporation, and the corporation is responsible for all its business activities. You will be an employee and a stockholder, as opposed to a personal owner. The corporation, which is a legal entity, can enter into contracts, buy and sell, sue, and be sued.

Cost of goods sold   All the expenses associated with producing the product or service you sell, including raw materials, time and labor, supplies, purchases, factory overhead, packaging, shipping, change of inventory, and so forth.

Due diligence   The process of finding out every last thing you can about a company, especially in the areas of finances, location, and marketing.

Energy   The internal force that gives you power and allows you to do what you do in a day. It is continually renewed and replenished by enthusiasm, joy, and fun. Energy works with the brain, but it comes from the soul.

Entrepreneur   A person who organizes and directs a business undertaking, assuming the risk for the sake of the profit. Also a person with extraordinary energy, persistence, and determination, who believes in himself or herself enough to follow through on a dream or an idea.

Executive summary   A shortened version of your business plan that allows someone to get an idea of what you're doing without reading the entire plan. It should summarize the plan, touching on everything that's important.

Experience   All the knowledge and skills accumulated over a lifetime that you apply to do everything as well as you can.

Fail   To not attempt to do what is important, such as start your own business to fulfill your dream.

Financial management plan   The part of your business plan that addresses the financial area of your business. It should include startup and operating budgets, income statement and cash flow projections, an explanation of your accounting and inventory control systems, loan applications, a balance sheet, and anything else that pertains to your business's finances.

Financial statement   A three-part document that supplies information about the day-to-day and long-term financial aspects of your business. The statement includes the balance sheet, the profit and loss statement, and the cash flow statement.

Founders team   A group of people who work closely together as a team to help start a business. The group serves as an extension of you and your talents.

Franchise agreement   A legal agreement that permits a person to sell a trademarked product or service, such as Pizza Hut pizza or Wendy's hamburgers. The person selling the product or service pays a percentage of every sale to the manufacturer.

Franchisee   The person who pays a certain percentage of the sales from a trademarked product or service to be allowed to sell it.

Franchiser   The party that allows its trademarked product or service to be sold by another person.

General and administrative costs   The costs of running a business that don't come under sales and marketing or cost of goods sold. They include items such as bookkeeping, legal and accounting fees, insurance costs, office rent, and so forth.

Growth industry   An industry perceived to have a high potential for growth. Investors are far more likely to invest in a growth industry than a non-growth industry.

Independent investor   A person who chooses companies in which to invest money, with the intention of making back more money than he or she put in.

Initial public offering (IPO)   The action of selling part of your company to the public by filing with the Securities and Exchange Commission (SEC) and listing the stock on one of the stock exchanges. Making an IPO is how you take your company public.

Limited liability company   A legal structure that allows a partnership to enjoy many of the same advantages a corporation does. It limits the liabilities of the partners, allowing them to enjoy the same personal financial protection they would within a corporation.

Limited partnership   A legal structure that allows one or more partners to invest in a business but not be involved with the day-to-day operations.

Mainstream education   The process that trains people to be good workers and provides the skills necessary to perform certain tasks. Mainstream education is not training to be an entrepreneur.

Management plan   The part of your business plan that addresses your business background, your founders team and its background, your employees or prospective employees, salaries, benefits, and so forth. It covers all aspects of managing your business.

Marketing   The process of making people aware of your product or service and making them want to have it.

Marketing plan   One of the main components of a business plan that addresses the areas of competition, pricing and sales, and advertising and public relations.

Networking   The practice of making and maintaining contacts with all kinds of people. Networking allows you to help others and be able to ask others for help.

Nonprofit organization   A business that provides a service to the community and operates under a different legal structure than a for-profit organization. Money earned by a nonprofit organization can't be distributed to members, directors, or officers.

Outsourcing   The practice of hiring someone outside your company to do work or perform services for you.

371

Partnership   A form of business ownership in which two or more people share control, management, and liability of a business.

Passion   The quality that makes doing a job fun—not work. Passion for what you do is a necessary quality for an entrepreneur. Without a degree of passion, your business will be just a job.

Persistence   The most important quality of an entrepreneur, persistence is the determination and strength to keep going, long after you feel like quitting. It's the drive inside you that makes you pick yourself up and try one more time.

Perspective   The quality that allows you to set yourself apart from situations you find yourself in so that you can view them calmly and factually.

Pricing strategy   The process used to set a price for your product or service.

Private placement   The act of identifying qualified people and asking them to invest money in your company by buying its stock.

Private placement firms   Firms that will, for a price, sell the idea of your business to investors to get you funding from them.

Private venture capitalist   A person or company that invests money into private ventures in exchange for a degree of control or ownership of the business.

Profit   The money you have left after you subtract general and administrative costs, cost of goods sold, and sales and marketing costs from the price at which you're selling your product or service.

Prospectus   A detailed plan containing information about your company that must be submitted to the Securities Exchange Commission as part of taking your company public.

Raw materials   The materials that end up as part of the product you make.

Sales   The process of handing over your product or service to somebody else in exchange for money or another commodity.

Shareholders   The people who share ownership in a business by holding stock in the company.

Small Business Administration   One of the U.S. government agencies—probably the best known—that assists entrepreneurs by offering information, funding, and other resources.

Sole proprietorship   A form of business ownership in which one person has full responsibility for all business conducted. A sole proprietor assumes total control of the business and is responsible for all its assets and liabilities.

Statement of purpose   The part of a business plan with your company's mission statement, goals and objectives, value statement, and vision statement.

Venture capitalist   One of the many privately owned firms that invest millions of dollars each year in small businesses that are starting up or expanding, or another name for a private investor.

Wealth   Everything that contributes to your physical comfort, happiness, and spiritual well being. Wealth includes your family, your faith, money, your home, and everything else that's valuable to you.

Work ethic   A code programmed inside of you that motivates you to do your work.

Workaholic   A person who's addicted to work the way gamblers are addicted to playing the ponies, for example.

Index

A

Accountants, 121, 126, 260, 265

Accounting firms, Big Five, 126–27, 265

Administrative costs. *See* general and administrative (G&A) costs

Advertising, 191–96
  costs of, 196–98
  franchising and, 140–41
  in marketing plan, 152

Advocate, being your own, 11

Agriculture, Department of, 167

Albom, Mitch, 33

American Institute of Stress, 47

American Performance Products, 42

Amish, 30

Articles of incorporation, 120

Ash, Mary Kay, 76

Audio, 194

Axelton, Karen, 59

B

Backdating, 294–96

Balance, 41

Balance sheet, 284–87

Banks, loans from, 164–65

Beef industry, 100

Benefits, employee, 240–41

Ben & Jerry's ice cream, 73, 215

Bicycles, 88

Billboards, 192

Biotechnology, 98

Blanchard, Kenneth H., 50

Board of directors, 121, 250–52
  choosing members of, 254
  control of the company and, 253–56
  role of, 252–53

Bomberg's, 278

Books
  on advertising, 194
  on growth industries, 95–96
  on nonprofit organizations, 122–23

Borrowing (loans). *See also* Financing
  collateral for, 161–62
  from credit cards, 160–61
  government loans, 166–67

Boss, being your own, 63–65

Boy Scouts, 90

Budget(s)
marketing, 196–98
operating, 152
salary for yourself in, 175
startup, 152

Business brokers, 138

Business description, 148–50

Business hours, in business plan, 149

Business plan, 95, 145–55, 342
contents of, 148–55
cover sheet, 155
description of your business, 148–50
executive summary, 154
financial management plan, 152–53
financial projections, 155
management plan, 153–55
marketing plan, 150–52
statement of purpose, 155
supporting documents, 154–55
table of contents, 155

goals of, 146–47
as a guide to running your business, 146
hiring others to write your, 147
protecting your, 155
as a sales instrument, 147

Buying an existing business, 131–36
advantages of, 134–35
disadvantages of, 135–36
financing, 139
finding a business to buy, 138
as a growth strategy, 297
negotiating a purchase, 139–40
reason for business being for sale, 134

Buyout entrepreneurs, 138

C

C corporations, 118
taxes and, 125

Carson, Johnny, 57

Cash flow statement, 284–285, 289

Center for Corporate Responsibility, 42

Center for Information Law and Policy, 167

Chain of command, 245

Challenges, 18, 25

Chamber of Commerce, 262

Change, 293–301
in inventory, 208

Chicago Bicycle Company, 88

Chicago Bike Company, 114

Chief executive officers (CEOs), 34

Chief financial person, 254

Children, 82. *See also* Family (family members)
activities for, 363

Classified ads, 194

Clubs and organizations, 362–63

Coaching, 89

Coffee industry, 96

Cohen, Adam Ezra, 76

Collateral, 161–62

Commercial finance companies, 166

Commitment, 72–73

Communications skills, 4, 69–70

Community, responsibility to the, 62–63

Community involvement, 63, 73
reputation and, 361–63

Competition, in marketing plan, 151

Competitive pricing, 216

Compliance payments, 176, 180

Computer graphics, 98

Concerts, sponsoring, 198

Confidence, 10–12, 69

Confidentiality agreement, 235

Consignment sales, 185

Consultants, founders team and, 230–31

Corporations
  choosing a name for, 120
  incorporating, 118–23
  limited liability companies compared to, 115, 118
  registering, 123
  secretary of, 121
  shareholders of, 120–21
  taxes and, 125–26

Cost control, 210–11

Cost of goods sold, 201–11
  controlling production costs, 209–10
  predicting, 208–9
  what's included in, 202–8
    change in inventory, 208
    factory overhead, 206
    miscellaneous, 208

packaging, 206–7
purchases, 206
raw materials, 203–4
shipping costs, 207–8
supplies, 205–6
time and labor, 204–5

Cost-plus pricing, 216

Costs, general and administrative (G&A). *See* General and administrative (G&A) costs

Cost-savings plan, 181–82

Coupons, 194

Courage, 12–13

Credibility, community and, 62

Credit cards, 86
  borrowing from, 160–61

Credit Union National Association, 166

Credit unions, 165–66

Customers, marketing plan and, 150–51

D

Daily routine, 49

Decision making, 70
  community and, 62
  self-confidence and, 10

Delaware, incorporating in, 121

Demand pricing, 216

Depression, 60

Description of your business, 148–50

Difficulties, 73–75

Direct mail advertising, 192

Direct materials, 203

Disability
  partnerships and, 111
  sole proprietorships and, 108

Discipline matters, 245–46

Disney, Walt, 8

Divorce, 43

Door-to-door sales, 184

Downsizing, 30–31

Dreams (of being an entrepreneur), 3–13, 25

Due diligence, 134

E

Economic Development Agency, 167

Edison, Thomas, 36

Education, 8–9, 68

Educational institutions, as funding source, 168

Edwards, Susan, 35

Ego, 70

Employee handbook, 244

Employees, 237–48. *See also* Labor costs; Payroll; Salaries

benefits for, 240–41

buying an existing business and, 135

chain of command and, 245

company personality and, 237–38

cost control and, 210–11

discipline matters and, 245

empowering, 239

federal registration of businesses that have, 123

firing, 64, 65, 245–46

honesty of, 242–43

loyalty of, 242

motivating, 246–47

part-time, 247–48

perks for, 241

responsibilities to your, 23, 61

rules and responsibilities for, 244–46

selling your business and, 310

sharing profits with, 220–21

as source of information, 268

as valuable asset, 238–39

what to expect from, 242–43

working conditions for, 241–42

Employee theft, 243

Empowerment, sense of, 16

Energy, 18

Enjoyment in work, 22

Entrepreneur(s)

deciding to become an, 6–7

definition of, 5

dream of being an, 3–13

evaluating your experience as an, 329–30

feeling good about your experiences as an, 333

growth in number of, 345–47

helping other, 339–47

motivation to become, 6

qualities of, 7–10

Entrepreneur's Manual, The (White), 187–88

Environment, confidence in your, 12

Environmental groups, 362

Ernst & Young International, 127

Excuses, for not starting your own business, 24

Executive summary, 154

Exercise, 75

Expanding, 303–9

internationally, 307–9

locally, 306

nationally, 306–7

regionally, 306

Experience(s), 89–91

evaluating your, 329–33

feeling good about your, 333–34

learning from your, 330–33

F

Failure(s), 17–18, 27, 32–37

famous, 35–36

fear of, 28–30

of new businesses, 137

risk of, 30

telling others about your, 35

Faith, 11, 70–71

Family (family members), 271–79

as employees, 278–79

as funding source, 164

as partners, 113

passing along a business to, 311–12

personal criteria for choosing a business and, 84–86

reactions of, 276–78

responsibilities to your, 60–61

time for, 41–45

Family businesses, 82

Federal identification number, 123

Finance companies, commercial, 166

Financial management plan, 152–53

Financial News Network (FNN), 36

Financial projections, 155

Financial statements, 285

buying an existing business and, 132–33

reacting to the ups and downs in, 290–91

Financing, 157–70

approaching someone for money, 168–69

helping other entrepreneurs raise capital, 343–44

needs assessment, 158

sources other than personal assets, 162–68

angels, 168

educational institutions, 168

factoring houses, 168

family and friends, 164

government loans, 166–67

lending institutions, 164–66

money finders, 164

private placement firms, 163–64

private venture capitalists, 163

your assets as source of, 159–62

Firing employees, 64–65, 245–46

Fixed expenses, 177

Flextime, 42–43

Food industry, 100–1

Ford, Henry, 8, 76

Founders team, 225–35

finding people for, 229–32

interviewing and choosing candidates for, 232–34

paying, 235

qualifications for inclusion in, 231–32

who should be on, 226–29

Franchises, 140–43

top-ranked, 142–43

Franchising, as growth strategy, 298

Free publicity, 197–98

Friends, 271–79

as partners, 113–14

reactions of, 276

time for, 41–42, 45

Fun, 45–46, 48, 83, 88

Future of your business, 303–4

G

G&A costs. *See* General and administrative (G&A) costs

Gates, Bill, 36

General and administrative (G&A) costs, 173–82

controlling, 178–81

fixed expenses, 177

insurance, 177

keeping close tabs on, 181

maintenance and repairs, 176

miscellaneous, 177

payroll, 174–75

predicting, 177

professional services, 176

rent, 175

taxes and licenses, 176

utilities, 176

variable expenses, 177

Generally Accepted Accounting Principles (GAAP), 132

General partnerships, 109–10

Geographical location. *See also* Location of business

living in a particular, 85–86

Giveaways, 194

Global expansion, 307–9

Goal orientation, 70

Going public, 315–25

changes in your company after, 324–25

finding someone to help, 320

process of, 319–24

prospectus and, 322

Good will, 62

Government loans, 166–67

Growth industries, 94–98

finding, 95–97

for the next century, 97–100

Growth of your business, 293. *See also* Expanding

evaluating the rate of, 294–97

need for change and, 301

possibilities for further, 297–98

predicting, 298–99

preparing for, 299

removing limits on, 299–301

too-rapid, 296–97

H

Happiness, money and, 56–57

Hard work, 20–22

Hazardous Substance Labeling Act, 128

Health, 46–49

Health care industry, 98, 99–100

Health care professionals, 99

Health considerations, 83

Home-based businesses, 85

Home-care services and products, 99

Homeworkers, 247–48

Honesty, of employees, 242–43

Hospitals, 99

Hours, 40

Hours of work, 18

I

Image

board of directors and, 251

packaging and, 207

Income statement, 153, 287–89

Income taxes. *See* Taxes

Incorporating, 118–23

in Delaware, 121

as a nonprofit business, 122

Independent investors, 349–56

attraction of being, 351–53

finding investment opportunities, 353–54

Infomercials, 193

Information technology, 98

Initial public offering (IPO), 316–17, 323–24

Insurance

controlling costs of, 181

cost of, 177

for sole proprietorships, 106–7

unnecessary, 176

Insurance agents, 266–67

Interests, choosing a business that matches your, 88–89

Internal Revenue Service (IRS). *See also* Taxes

   tax education seminars of, 124

Internet, 84

   advertising on, 193–94

Interviewing, founders team candidates, 232–34

Introductions, to potential lenders, 168

Inventory, 209

   change in, 208

Investing, 354–56

Investment groups, 355

Investors

   independent. *See* Independent investors

   potential, approaching, 168–69

   what to expect from, 169

J–K

James, William, 31

Jordan, Michael, 9–10

Killinger, Barbara, 51

KPMG International, 127

Kroc, Ray, 8

L

Labor costs, 204

   controlling, 209–10

Lam, Thanh Quoc, 54

Lasers, 98

Lauder, Estée, 8

Lawyers, 121, 260, 263–64

Leases, 179

LEGO MINDSTORMS, 98

Leisure, 45

Lenders, potential

   approaching, 168–69

   what to expect from, 169–70

Lending institutions, 164–66

Licenses, as general and administrative expense, 176

Licensing, as growth strategy, 297

Lifestyle, 82, 86

   geographical area. *See also* Personal criteria

Limitations, self-imposed, 11

Limited liability companies, 105, 115

   taxes and, 124–25

Limited partnerships, 110

Lines of credit, 160–61

Little League, 28, 41, 73, 89

Loans. *See* Borrowing (loans)

Location of business, 149–50

   zoning laws and, 127–28

Losing, 28

Lottery winners, 56

Love of work, 22

Loyalty of employees, 242

Luv Feet shoe inserts, 88–89

M

Mackay, Harvey, 162

Magazines, 96

   advertising in, 192

   for franchise opportunities, 143

Maintenance and repairs, 176

   controlling costs of, 179–80

Management, sole proprietorships and, 108

Management plan, 153–55

Marketing, 183. *See also* Advertising

   definition of, 184

Marketing budget, 196–98

Marketing experts, 198–200

Marketing plan, 150–52, 189–91

Marketing strategy, 188–96

Market research companies, 190

Markup pricing, 216

Merging with another company, 311

Merrill, Charles Edward, 8

Mini-vacations, 46

Minority enterprise companies, 167

Mistakes, 10

Money, 54–59. *See also* Financing

  benefits of making, 55–56

  disadvantages of making, 56–58

  personal criteria for choosing a business and, 86–87

  status, status associated with, 58–59

Money finders, 164

Motivation

  to become an entrepreneur, 6

  of employees, 246

for starting The Vermont Teddy Bear Company, 4

Multiply and subtract concept, 175

N

Name of corporation, 120

National Association of Small Business Investment Companies, 167

National Association of State Development Agencies, 268

National Institute for Occupational Safety and Health, 47

Nerves, 70

Networking, 162

  as growth strategy, 298

Newspapers, advertising in, 192

Non-competition agreement, 235

Nonprofit corporations, taxes and, 125–26

Nonprofit organizations, 122

Nursing homes, 99

O

Occupational Safety and Health Act (OSHA) regulations, 128

Operating budget, 152

Operating cash, 158

Optimism, 11

P–Q

Packaging costs, 206–7, 210

Painting buildings, 90

Partnership agreements, 109

Partnerships, 105, 109–14

  benefits of, 110–11

  choosing a partner or partners, 112–14

  disadvantages of, 112

  general, 109–10

  limited, 110

  taxes and, 124

Part-time employees, 247–48

Passion for what you're doing, 89

Patience, 11, 70

Payroll, 174–75

  keeping down costs of, 178–79

Perception, price and sales and, 217–19

Perks, 241

Perot, Ross, 68

Persistence, 9–10, 69

Personal assets
  corporations and,
  118–19
  in spouse's name, 119

Personal criteria, 82–88, 93
  experience and, 89–91
  family concerns, 84–86
  financial needs, 86–87
  finding a business that
    meets your, 83–88
  identifying, 82–83

Personal guaranty, 165

Personality, 87–88

Personal services, 84

Perspective, 75–76

Persuasion, 70

Pete's Brewing Company,
  17

Pharmaceuticals, 99

Politics, 362

Pork industry, 101

Post, William "Bud," 56

President of the company,
  253

Press releases, 197

Prices (pricing), 210,
  215–20
  in marketing plan, 151

methods for determining,
  216–17
  testing, 219–20

Priorities, 41, 49–50

Private placement, 317–19

Private placement firms,
  163–64

Private venture capitalists,
  163

Production costs, controlling, 209–10

Professional organizations,
  262–63

Professional services, cost
  of, 176, 180

Profitability, in business
  plan, 149

Profit and loss statement,
  284–85, 287–89

Profit(s), 213–21
  projecting, 214–15
  reinvesting into the
    company, 221
  sharing, 220–21

Promotion, 191–96. *See also*
  Advertising
  franchising and, 140–41

Proprietorships. *See* Sole
  proprietorships

Prospectus, 322

Publicity. *See also* Advertising
  free, 197–98

Public relations, in marketing plan, 152

Purchases, 206

R

Radio advertising, 185,
  193–97

Raw materials, 203–4, 210

Referrals, to potential
  lenders, 168

Registering your business,
  123

Regulations, 128

Rehabilitation services, 99

Reich, Robert, 30–31

Relatives. *See* Children;
  Family (family members)

Relaxation, 45

Religious organizations, 363

Rent, 175
  keeping down costs of,
    179

Reputation, 70, 357–64
  building a, 358
  community involvement
    and, 361
  damage to, 359–61
  preserving your, 364

Respect, for entrepreneurs,
  34

Responsibilities, 22–23,
  59–63

to the community, 62–63

to employees, 61

to family, 60–61

Retainers, 264

Retired people, 83

Ripken, Cal, 21

Risks, 30–32

Roberts Rules of Order, 254–55

Robotics, 98

Robotics Invention System, 98

Root, Wayne, 36

Routine, daily, 49

Rules and regulations, 128

Ruth, Babe, 36

S

Sacrifices, 4

Salad dressing, 100

Salaries, 18, 239–40

for yourself, 175

Sales, 183

consignment, 185

definition of, 184

stages of, 187–88

Salespeople, 185–86

kinds of, 188

as source of information, 268

Savings, 159–60

Savings and loans (S&Ls), 166

Schedule, 40

Scheduling

flexible (flextime), 42–43

time away from work, 275

Schultz, Howard, 96–97

Schwartz, Morrie, 33

SCORE (Service Corps of Retired Executives), 268

S corporations, 118

IRS pamphlet on, 125

taxes and, 125–26

Secretary of the company, 256

Secretary of the corporation, 121

Securities and Exchange Commission (SEC), 316, 322

Seeger, Pete, 72

Self-assessment, 71

Self-confidence, 10–11

Self-employed tax, 124

Self-fulfilling prophecy, fear of failure as, 17

Selling your business, 309–11

Seminars, 194

Service franchises, 141

Shareholders, 120–21, 249, 253, 256–57

Shipping costs, 207–8

Signs, advertising, 192

Ski resorts, 101

Sleep, 48

Slosberg, Pete, 17

Small Business Administration (SBA), 124

as advice or information source, 267–68

business plan model, 145, 342

loans from, 167

marketing plan, 190

Small business investment companies, 167

Small Business Investment Companies (SBIC), 355

Small Business Taxpayers Education Program (STEP), 124

Social Security taxes, 124

Sole proprietorships, 105–9

advantages of, 106–7

drawbacks to, 107–8

types of, 108

Starbucks, 96–97

Starting a business, 136–38

advantages of, 137

disadvantages of, 137

franchises, 140–43

helping others, 344–45

time needed for, 40–41

Startup budget, 152

Statement of purpose, 155

Stowe, Harriet Beecher, 74

Strawberry, Darryl, 125

Stress, 46–48

Sub-contractors, 248

Suppliers, 135

   controlling production costs and, 209

   as source of information, 268

Supplies, 205–6

Support system, 259–69

T

Table of contents, 155

Taking your company public, 298

Taxes

   corporations and, 118, 125–26

   as general and administrative expense, 176

   limited liability companies and, 115, 124–25

   nonprofit corporations and, 125–26

   nonprofit organizations and, 122

   partnerships and, 124

paying on time, 180

   sole proprietorships and, 107–8, 124

Telemarketing firms, 190

Television, advertising on, 193

Temps, 247–48

Theft, employee, 243

Thrifts, 166

Time

   for family and friends, 274–75

   family and personal, 41–45

   for starting a business, 40–41

Time and labor costs, 204–5

Time management, 90

Travel, 85

Trends, 100–103

Trust, in others, 11

Tuesdays with Morrie (Albom and Schwartz), 33

U

Underpricing, 215

United Parcel Service (UPS), 90, 207

Universities, as funding source, 168

Utilities

   controlling costs of, 180

   costs of, 176

V

Vacation, 46

Variable expenses, 177

Vendors, selling your business and, 310

Venture capitalists, 354–55

   private, 163

Vermont Teddy Bear Company, The, 7, 23, 41, 54–55, 74, 163

   administrative costs, 178

   advertising by, 194–96, 198

   awards, 243

   community involvement of, 63, 73

   employee perks at, 241

   employees of, 61, 65

   expansion of, 306

   going public, 316, 323

   labor costs, 204–5

   marketing strategies for, 189

   motivation for starting, 4

pricing strategy, 216
rules at, 244
sales methods, 184–85
temporary workers at, 247–48
Videotapes, 194
Vo, Le, 54

W

Wallenda, Karl, 17
Walton, Sam, 8, 358–59
Web sites
federal government information, 167
franchise-related, 143
Wenner, Paul, 54
White, Richard M., Jr., 187–88
Wholesaling, 184–85
Windows, Microsoft, 36
Winning, 27–28
Women, 346
stress and, 48
work ethics of, 21
Workaholics, 22, 50–51
Work ethic, 20–22
Work habits, 87–88

Working conditions, 241–42
Worrying, 18

Y–Z

Yellow Pages, 192–93

Zegarac, Nick, 114
Zoning laws, 127–28